Contents

Editor's Note

Where there are differences in the spelling of Chinese names (for
instance *Peking* and *Beijing*), the variation adopted by individual
contributors has been used. Where necessary, the index uses the old
spellings but gives the new ones, as in Beijing *see* Peking.

Preface

John Pilger

In the late spring of 1980, shortly before I was due to leave for Kampuchea, I received a phone call from Paris. A familiar, husky voice came quickly to the point. 'Can you postpone?' he said. 'I've heard about a Khmer Rouge list and you're on it. I'm worried about you.'

That Wilfred Burchett was worried about the welfare of another human being was not surprising; the quintessence of the man lay in what he did not say. He neglected to mention not only that *he* was on the same 'list', but that a few weeks earlier, at the age of seventy and seriously ill, he had survived a bloody ambush laid for him by Khmer Rouge assassins, who wounded a travelling companion. (Wilfred's intelligence was as reliable as ever; I narrowly escaped a similar ambush at the same place he was attacked.) I have known other brave reporters; I have not known another who, through half a century of risk-taking, demonstrated as much concern for others and such valour on behalf of others. He took risks to smuggle Jews out of Nazi Germany, to drag American wounded to safety during the Pacific war, and to seek out prisoners of war in Japan, in 1945, to tell them help was coming; the list is long. He sustained a variety of bombardment, from Burma to Korea to Indochina, yet he retained a compassion coupled with an innocence bordering at times on naïveté which, it would seem, led him into other troubles.

It is important, I believe, to state this about Wilfred early in these pages, if only because such qualities were shared by *none* of the vociferous few who were his enemies and whose attempts to bring him down are examined in several chapters of this book.

Wilfred was born in Melbourne in the aftermath of the 1890s Depression which had ruined his grandfather, Caleb, a pioneer farmer, just as the Depression of the 1930s ruined his father, George, at a critical time in Wilfred's life.

'The day came,' he wrote in his autobiography, 'when the bank manager and his agent came to seize the house. After a few polite words to my father they began looking over the furnishings . . . there was still a substantial amount owing. "You'll be hearing from us again," said the manager as he left. "I don't want to be too hard. You can stay on for a few days until you find another place." My father's face was ashen as he stumbled inside after seeing him to the gate. "We still have ourselves and the children," murmured my mother.'

Soon afterwards Wilfred went 'on the road with a swag' and in Queensland was adopted by a group of cane-cutters whose spirit of one-for-all-and-all-for-one, in the face of thuggish employers, left a lasting impression upon him. It was against such a background that his radicalism was born; I prefer the word radicalism to socialism, for I believe Wilfred was, above all, a peculiarly *Australian* radical. He himself acknowledged this, and a description he relished was that passed on by Morley Safer, a veteran reporter for America's CBS Television, who said of him: 'Burchett? He's not a communist! He's an *Australian*!' In complete accord with this sentiment, Wilfred wrote, 'When we Australian journalists first appeared on the World War II battlefields, the British Raj types referred to us usually as "bolshies". And bolshies we were!'

Certainly his own politics were both instinctive and shaped by the conditions of his upbringing more than by intellectual fashion. Shortly before he died he told me he had never become a communist. 'How could I be a communist?' he said. 'There were so many parties, each drawing on different circumstances, different conditions. Which one was I to choose? I chose none, because I wanted to remain just *me*. . .'

This, of course, comes close to the romantic and popular notion of the Australian iconoclast, the champion of 'fair go' for 'the little bloke', much of which is mythical. However, as most such myths are probably half true, it can be said that the valid half of this one embraced Wilfred's character. And although his innate decency and affable personality eschewed doctrine (many of Wilfred's friends were non-socialists, even anti-socialists) both qualities were perhaps exploited by the doctrinaire. At times, for instance, he seemed more diplomat than journalist. Wilfred would have explained this as being part of the 'icebreaker', or go-between role he adopted and which was, as he put it, 'a useful and honourable thing to do'. However, there is another aspect to this role, which David G. Marr touches upon in his chapter, 'Burchett on Vietnam'. In discussing Wilfred's reporting of the disastrous land-reform campaigns in North Vietnam in the 1950s, Marr writes about Wilfred's 'readiness . . . to repeat official explanations uncritically'. The instances of Wilfred going against the doctrines of those he supported are numerous; and yet the question remains: was he too close to governments? In my terms, which are to distrust all governments and officialdom, he was much too close. In his terms, he was not. Certainly, he was seldom as close as many Western journalists are to governments and institutions, with whom the association is often insidious and deeply compromising. Like all originals, Wilfred Burchett was also something of an enigma.

What is beyond question is that the abiding strength of Wilfred's character – courage – allowed him to surrender commitment to a 'cause' when that cause no longer deserved his support. Although this withdrawal sometimes suffered from delayed action, as in the case of the Khmer Rouge, he would not hesitate to say that he had been wrong. 'You've got to be able to look your children in the eye and look at yourself and not be ashamed,' he said. 'You have to know when to let go . . . The question journalists, and politicians, have to ask themselves is, "Do you get off in time, or do you follow a line out of blind loyalty?" It takes courage to say, "Look, I'm wrong on this; I'm letting go."'

In China his friendship with Zhou Enlai and other vintage revolutionaries was 'let go' with much heart-searching and sadness when he perceived the Chinese leadership's hostility to the Vietnamese at the very climax of Vietnam's struggle for independence. As Ben Kiernan writes in his chapter, 'Burchett on Kampuchea', Wilfred was forced to abandon his old confrere Prince Sihanouk, whom he had supported for twenty-five years, when Sihanouk allied himself with the forces of Pol Pot: '. . . and the wrench, when it came, must have hurt'. Indeed, it did hurt; I remember well his agonizing over Sihanouk who, he felt, had betrayed him personally, not to mention his own people.

At the end of his life it was the Vietnamese who remained alone in his pantheon. Having shared something of the Vietnamese experience, I can understand that. '*They* have never let me down,' he once said in a mellow mood, allowing a glimpse of his vulnerability.

Paradoxically, Wilfred was vulnerable because he was, in the strictly professional sense, such a fine journalist. Indeed, his two greatest 'scoops' added another precarious dimension to his life. The first was Hiroshima. He was the first Western reporter to reach Hiroshima after the atomic bomb had been dropped on 6 August 1945. He had been warned by an official of the Japanese press agency that 'no one goes to Hiroshima; everyone is dying there'. He ignored this of course. He feigned illness at Allied press headquarters in Yokohama, in order to slip away from the press 'pack', and with his beef ration he bought a train ticket to Hiroshima.

The journey, mostly in darkness, demonstrated the Burchett courage. Here was a European alone in a train filled with soldiers, armed and sullen and almost certainly bitter at the moment of defeat. At two o'clock in the morning he reached Hiroshima and was promptly thrown into prison. 'There was some shouting by the police and the interpreter became pale as she translated my rare interventions,' he wrote. The 'shouting', he later learned, was about whether or not he was to be shot. It was only a senior officer of the 'Thought Police' who decided the foreigner should live. 'Show him,' he said, 'what his people have done to us.'

What Wilfred saw was published all over the front page of the London *Daily Express* beneath the headline, I WRITE THIS AS A WARNING TO THE WORLD. 'In Hiroshima, thirty days after the first atomic bomb destroyed the city and shook the world,' he reported, 'people are still dying mysteriously and horribly – people who were uninjured in the cataclysm – from an unknown something which I can only describe as the atomic plague . . .'

In comprehending and identifying an 'atomic plague', he had rumbled the *experimental* nature of this first use of a nuclear weapon against people. 'It was a considerable ordeal to reach Hiroshima,' wrote the distinguished American journalist and writer T.D. Allman in his eulogy for Wilfred, 'but it was an infinitely greater accomplishment, back then, to *understand* the importance of Hiroshima.'

Wilfred returned to Tokyo in time to attend a press conference especially convened to deny and discredit his story. He later wrote, 'A scientist in brigadier-general's uniform explained that there could be no question of atomic radiation or the symptoms I had described, since the bombs had been exploded at such a height as to avoid any risk of "residual radiation". There was a dramatic moment as I rose to my feet [Wilfred's sense of the 'dramatic moment' was highly tuned], feeling my scruffiness put me at a disadvantage with the elegantly uniformed and bemedalled officers. My first question was whether the briefing officer had been to Hiroshima. He had not . . . He discounted the allegation that any who had not been in the city at the time of the blast were later affected. Eventually the exchanges narrowed down to my asking how he explained the fish still dying when they entered a stream running through the centre of the city . . . The spokesman looked pained. "I'm afraid you've fallen victim to Japanese propaganda," he said, and sat down.'

Wilfred had blown a momentous cover-up. Reporters flown to Hiroshima were kept away from the hospitals he had seen and where there was clear evidence of the 'atomic plague'. Burchett had his accreditation withdrawn and was issued with an expulsion order (from Japan), although it was later rescinded. Strict censorship was introduced. Japanese film of the victims of the 'atomic plague' was confiscated, classified 'top secret' and sent to Washington; it was not released until 1968. Three times as many people died from the effects of radiation in the five-year period after the two atomic bombs fell on Japan than on the days of the explosions; and the victims continue to die from it at a rate of at least a thousand a year. Wilfred Burchett was never forgiven for understanding and telling this truth, and telling it first.

For a brief time, however, he was a universal hero, and deservedly so. This is Jim Vine reporting in the Brisbane *Courier-Mail* on 11 September 1945:

A pocket-handkerchief-sized Australian, Wilfred Burchett, left all other correspondents standing in covering the occupation of Japan.

Armed with a typewriter, seven packets of K rations, a Colt revolver, and incredible hope, he made a one-man penetration of Japan, was the first correspondent into atomic-bomb-blasted Hiroshima, and 'liberated' five prison camps . . .

After Hiroshima, Burchett embarked on his one-man liberation tour of prison camps, visiting two on the West Honshu coast and three on the inland sea, before official rescue parties reached them.

At Tsuruga camp he sprang a masterly piece of bluff which caused hundreds of Japanese to lay down their arms and gave the inmates their first steak dinner in three and a half years.

Here the inmates were alarmed at the increasing concentration of Japanese soldiers, all fully armed. Burchett sent for the camp commandant, known as 'The Pig', refused to answer his salute and bow, and, with delighted American marines for an audience, upbraided him soundly for not seeing that the surrender terms were carried out . . .

Just as he was not forgiven for his revelation of an 'atomic plague', Wilfred paid a similar price for reporting from the 'other side' during the first Cold War. For seventeen years, he and his children were denied passports by the Australian government. No charges were brought against him; no 'crime' was ever stated. In a letter in April 1956 to Brian Fitzpatrick of the Australian Council for Civil Liberties, Harold Holt, then Minister of Immigration, wrote that Wilfred Burchett 'left Australia fifteen years ago. He has not since returned,* his wife is not an Australian . . . in addition his activities since his departure forfeited any claim he might have had to the protection he would receive as the holder of an Australian passport.'

In his chapter, 'Burchett in Korea', Gavan McCormack deals concisely with the accusations of 'interrogating' and 'brainwashing' prisoners of war in North Korea, all of which were untrue. (In writing this I have also referred to the Australian Vietnam veteran David Gourlay's excellent 1980 thesis, 'The Burchett Affair 1955–1972', which provides further evidence of the substantially bogus nature of the smears which dogged Wilfred until his death.)

Of course he was naïve to believe he could visit Allied prisoner-of-war camps and not become a 'target'. Or perhaps he did not calculate the risk at the time, since it was his colleagues in the Australian and American press who requested him to go to the camps. He paid dearly for this error of judgement, not only in the intensity of the attacks he endured, but in the hours he devoted to answering his critics and slanderers. One such attack, which Gavan McCormack has called 'Australia's Dreyfus case', demonstrates for me what a journalist who seriously disturbs the established order is up against when he tries to clear mud from his name.

In the 1960s a Soviet defector called Yuri Krotkov named as 'KGB

*In fact, Wilfred had returned, in 1950

agents', John Kenneth Galbraith, Jean-Paul Sartre, a clutch of Western diplomats and others, including Wilfred Burchett. Krotkov, however, admitted to having been a professional KGB liar, pimp and perjurer. British intelligence, to whom he first offered his services, gave him £100 and made him sign a document to the effect that he would not repeat his 'revelations' in published form, for they were both nonsense and libellous.

Krotkov wanted to go to the United States and his chance came when he was asked to appear before a US Senate sub-committee for internal security, whose 'investigators' included the likes of Mississippi Senator Thomas O. Eastland and Senator Strom Thurmond of South Carolina. Again, to a series of leading questions, Krotkov named his 'KGB agents' – John Kenneth Galbraith, Wilfred Burchett *et al.* The charade, which the American press all but ignored, would have ended there had the Australian Democratic Labour Party, an extreme right-wing group, not taken notice. Senator Vincent Gair, then chairman of the DLP, read the references to Burchett into the Australian Hansard from the US Congressional Record. This was the basis for a slanderous article in the DLP magazine, *Focus*, published beneath the headline, 'Burchett KGB Agent'.

Wilfred sued. And not only did the judge in the Australian case acknowledge that no evidence had been produced to link Wilfred with the KGB or with the Russians in any nefarious capacity, but the jury found the libel case proved. *But . . .* the *Focus* article had quoted from Hansard and so the libel was technically protected by parliamentary privilege. Costs were awarded against Wilfred, even though he had won on the point of defamation. When the truth is complex, a smear is made easy; time and again Wilfred's enemies have written that he 'lost' the libel case, which is quite misleading. It is especially so since the New South Wales Court of Appeal later threw out the DLP's defence of parliamentary privilege, while declining to order a new hearing – even though one of the three appeal judges described the original result as a 'miscarriage of justice' and another said there had been an 'error in law'.

T.D. Allman, in his eulogy, posed the question, 'What is objectivity?' He answered this by saying that objective journalism 'not only gets the facts right, it gets the meaning of events right and is validated not only by "reliable sources" but by the unfolding of history'. He then asked whether or not Wilfred Burchett was being objective 'when he perceived a great threat to civilization in Nazi Germany, when he perceived a great moral test for the whole world in the persecution of the Jews . . . when he saw Hiroshima as the gravest threat to the survival of humanity itself . . . when he refused to see the Cold War as a clear-cut battle between Western good and communist evil . . . when he said the communist Chinese were not the pawns of Moscow . . . when he said that the revolutionary ferment of Asia and Africa after World War Two was not the product of some conspiracy to take over the world, but the product of the legitimate yearnings of the Third World for freedom, dignity and progress . . . We all, I think, know the answers to these questions.'

I quote all that because I believe it to be true and because I am biased; I liked the man and I admired his humanity, a quality beyond the analytical terms of this book. He was, as Gavan McCormack has written, 'almost alone in seeing the [Korean] war from the viewpoint of the suffering Korean people rather than that of great powers or his own or any other government'. And his reporting of Hiroshima, as Phillip Knightley points out, 'went totally against everything else being written from Japan at that time, the "they-had-it-coming-to-them" and "I-saw-the-arrogant-strutting-Japs-humbled" type of story'.

In tandem with such qualities was the absence of any discernible bitterness, although God knows he must have felt it at times. He was almost always broke, yet he laboured at his work, 'pounding on my ancient typewriter', as he used to say, with unflagging cheerfulness and optimism which endeared him to so many people in so many countries – countries where until shortly before he died, he had followed his old-fashioned dictum of being 'on the spot'.

I once asked him about his optimism and the scars that did not show. We were in Vietnam at the time and he was pounding on that ancient typewriter, surrounded by screwed-up balls of paper (I think he was writing his thirtieth book at the time), festoons of washing and cans of beer cooling on equally ancient air-conditioners.

'To be happy,' he said, 'you've got to learn to slay only one bloody dragon at a time.' This was followed by a burst of impish laughter, and a beer, and another, and another . . . Wilfred was kinder to his 'bloody dragons' than he was to himself. Alas.

London, October 1985

Introduction

Ben Kiernan

The first thing to be said about Wilfred Burchett is that for nearly forty years he was a leftist committed in his writings to communist-led movements in Asia and around the world. But it is not the last. A fellow Australian journalist of quite the opposite political convictions but equally well-known in Asia – Richard Hughes – described Burchett as 'one of the best and bravest correspondents I've ever known'.[1] Harrison Salisbury, former Associate Editor of the *New York Times*, has written: 'I just don't know anyone who has been at more fronts, behind and between more wars and revolutions . . . [Burchett's] life has been like an old-fashioned Pathé newsreel, one peril succeeding another . . . In his ceaseless travel he has met most of the diplomats and national leaders of his time . . . Probably no other man . . . was on intimate terms with both Ho Chi Minh and Henry Kissinger.'[2]

Burchett wrote thirty-five books, which were published in thirty-five languages. In terms of output alone he was probably the most prolific of all Australian writer-journalists. (Perhaps the only Australian writer to outdo him is Jack Lindsay, who at last count had published 153 books.) Were it not for his politics, Burchett would undoubtedly be hailed as one of the great Antipodeans. He was evidently the Australian best-known in the rest of the world, and indeed he was the only Western reporter to cover 'the other side' of world events for over forty years.

The ironies of Burchett's career are many. This man who brought the world the first eyewitness account of the impact of the first atomic bomb blast, was ten years later banned from re-entering his own country on the grounds that he was some kind of traitor, by an Australian Prime Minister who was at that very time allowing Britain to carry out a series of atomic test explosions on Australian soil, and who as a result has now

been described as 'a lickspittle of the British' by the Royal Commissioner inquiring into those tests.[3] If Burchett was a traitor, he was not the
only one in Australian history. But he is the only person ever to have
been officially branded as one. Or, as the national daily newspaper put
it in 1968, Burchett was 'Australia's only political refugee'.[4]

Burchett in fact wrote very little about Australia; he published more
about Portugal, and Laos. But his life was profoundly influenced by his
childhood and youth, particularly by his experiences in rural Australia
during the 1930s Depression (when the unemployment rate in Australia
was second only to that in Germany). And by Australia's location on the
fringe of Asia. And of course by his experiences at the hands of
Australian conservative governments.

One of Burchett's first publications was not about politics, but about
'Australia's newest boarding-school', Koornong, outside Melbourne,
where he taught carpentry in 1939. In his praise for this school, which
was founded on the theories of the American educator John Dewey,
Burchett set down what can be seen as some of the guiding principles of
his own life: the 'pioneering spirit' (which he inherited from his
parents), participation in the international world of knowledge, and
rural simplicity and flexibility.

It is symbolical of the school that it is set in pioneer surroundings of
lofty blue-gums, scraggy stringy-barks and wattles, for Koornong is a
pioneer school . . . The founders, Mr and Mrs J.C. Nield, toured the
world to make a study of the latest continental and American
educational developments. *Without being bound to any set system*,
they set out to examine the most recent educational methods, and
where practicable, adapt them to Australian requirements . . . The
aim is 'to train happy and alert *citizens of the modern world'*.

It seems that Burchett, then twenty-eight years old, had developed a
rather remarkable mixture of rural sentimentality and staunch rational-
ism. He lauded Koornong for having its students participate in 'making
a complete natural history survey of Warrandyte and district', in
co-operation with the McCoy Society of natural scientists from
Melbourne University, and for organizing 'frequent excursions to
factories and mines'; at the same time, 'the children slumber with the
murmur of the Yarra to lull them to rest . . . [They] live close to reality
in these surroundings, and *get a truer sense of values*.'

Burchett agreed with Dewey, and Koornong's principals, that 'school
should not be preparation for life, but life itself'. It is common to hear
this from people who left school at fifteen (as Burchett did) or younger,
but it is less common for them to explore the theory implied. This is the
Burchett combination which Beverley Smith describes in Chapter 5,
'White Nomad'; as she puts it, it is the case of the 'farm boy who felt
genuinely liberated by knowledge and reason'.

One particular theme raised by Smith, pioneering innovation, is also
evident in the 'School in the Bush' piece which Burchett wrote in 1939:

I remember watching an art lesson of the primary class when one of the youngsters discovered he had lost his paint-brush. He hoped to get another from the art teacher, but the latter told him he would have to find a substitute. The embryo artist went into the bush and returned with a piece of bark, which he very efficiently adapted to his requirements.[5]

The combination of technical ingenuity and social progressiveness was not something admired by Burchett alone. In fact it was an undercurrent of the development of Australian democracy. An example is the work of the philanthropist Hugh Victor McKay. McKay, one of the inventors of the combine harvester, 'used wooden and iron parts of his own design and parts from broken machines, improvising all the time'. The other side of the same Australian coin was that McKay's court actions on behalf of his employees led to the fixing in 1907 of a minimum standard wage – 'the basic wage' – which became a feature of the Australian industrial scene (although women were long excluded from its provisions). McKay's sociological ideas 'were regarded as extremely advanced, not only in Australia, but worldwide'.[6]

However, largely because of the industrial expansion after World War Two, Australia did not retain all of the characteristics of the country Burchett had grown up in. From then on, it was mainly in the Third World that Burchett would find the themes to which he revealed his attachment in 'School in the Bush'.

Another powerful influence on Burchett's thinking was his first visit to Nazi Germany, in 1938. At the end of that year he wrote to his parents in Poowong, Victoria, from London: 'I am back from the land of darkness. I have seen enough misery and frightfulness to last me until the end of my days . . . To go there and talk with the people who are the victims makes me think that all I read was absolutely nothing. . .' But after describing the Nazi pogroms against the Jews, Burchett quickly passed to what could be done about it all. 'Well, I got a few people out of the camps and others will get out with consular letters, etc.' The Jewish immigration sponsorship scheme in his home town could be extended:

> I am very proud of Poowong, and in the Jewish community in London, the name of Poowong stands very high . . . I don't see why people in Korumburra also shouldn't help. There's no finer work that anyone can do at the moment. If they could see the desperate faces of people, the hunted faces of the men who don't dare to sleep at home for fear of arrest. . .[7]

The records of the Poowong Jewish immigration campaign show that by 1939 Wilfred Burchett had personally sponsored thirty-six German Jews for settlement in Australia. His family helped many more.[8]

Not long after he returned home, and while he was teaching at Koornong, Burchett found that the Soviet Union had signed a non-aggression pact with Hitler. This led the Communist Party of Australia into a mire of confusion. As the former National President of the CPA later put it: 'For a few days after the outbreak of war in 1939, the CPA supported an anti-fascist war against Hitler. Then, along with all other CPs, it condemned the war as imperialist. When Germany invaded the USSR in 1941 the communist parties pronounced the war to be a people's war against fascism.'[9]

The latter was Burchett's view from start to finish. His deep-seated hatred of Nazism made it impossible for him to mimic Stalin's twists and turns on the issue.[10] But when Hitler invaded the USSR Burchett welcomed its participation in the 'Grand Alliance' against fascism. As did many others; these were the days when even General Douglas MacArthur could say: 'The hopes of civilization rest on the banners of the Red Army.' And in late 1944 Winston Churchill claimed that: 'Marshal Stalin and the Soviet leaders wish to live in honourable friendship and equality with the Western democracies . . . I feel also that their word is their bond. I know of no government which stands to its obligations even in its own despite, more solidly than the Russian Soviet government.'[11]

As for the USA, in his first book, published before the Pacific war, Burchett praised its democratic, even pioneering tradition, 'the tradition of the New World . . . of sturdy independence and jealous vigilance where a violation of basic rights is concerned'.[12] (The expression 'New World' again seems to convey the combination of frontiersmanship and socialist millenarianism.) But Burchett retained an independent standpoint when it came to America's post-war policies.

Like many Australians, Burchett probably believed that without US help Australia would have fallen to the advancing Japanese forces during World War Two. He spent much of the war with American forces in the Pacific, and later wrote: 'I formed a very high opinion of the qualities of the US marines and the carrier pilots and crewmen. They were briefed not to defend an Empire, but to defend their own way of life, and they accepted the sacrifices involved.'[13] However, when US forces began their intervention in the affairs of Asian countries immediately after the war, Burchett's instinct was to oppose them. He now saw Washington setting out to 'defend an Empire', and lost faith in the US government just as people in Europe, like Churchill, did in that of the USSR.

A second reason for Burchett's disillusion with the United States was relat-'d to the first. From the outset he had considered that not only the United States but also our Asian allies had played an important role in defending Australia from Japanese imperialism. He wrote in September 1941, for instance: 'For some time past the fate of Australia has been in the slim brown hands of a lean-faced, hollow-cheeked Chinaman, forty-one-year-old General Chen Cheng. With his army of humble but heroic shaven-pated warriors he has carried out an historic task in continuing to bar the road of the Japanese drive on Chungking.'[14] It is probable that few Australians shared this view at the time or later. (Just

as few Westerners accepted that the Soviet Union was largely
responsible for the defeat of Hitler, having lost twenty million dead to
German armies four times the size of those facing the Allies on the
Western front.) But there was some truth in it, at least enough to plunge
Burchett into anti-American outrage as he saw US troops restoring
former collaborators with the Japanese to power in the Philippines,
while in south Vietnam British troops used the surrendered Japanese
garrison to repress Vietnamese patriots demanding independence. As
Dorothy Shineberg points out in Chapter 6, Burchett's wartime message
basically called for 'hands across the sea' to Australia's Pacific
neighbours, not for the re-establishment of European colonialism at
their expense.

In the meantime, Burchett returned to Germany to report on the
outcome of Hitler's defeat, and what he saw there finally provoked his
decision to quit the Western press orbit, as Kelvin Rowley shows in
Chapter 3. He eventually made his way to the New York *Guardian*, a
leftist weekly formed in 1948 by New Deal socialists and supporters of
the late Franklin D. Roosevelt and his former Vice-President Henry
Wallace, then leading the Progressive Party. Burchett's choice of this
newspaper in 1956, after he had been deprived of a passport and his
travels had become largely confined to the socialist bloc, suggests a
political inclination not identical with plans to make his home in
Moscow indefinitely. For instance, his colleague Konni Zilliacus, a
former British Labour Party MP and now the *Guardian*'s London
correspondent, had not only already been twice banned from entering
the USA, but he had also been accused, during the Stalinist trials in
Prague, of being an 'imperialist-Titoist-Zionist'. And as Alex Carey
shows in Chapter 4, Burchett himself did not meekly accept exile to the
socialist camp, but never gave up the fight to have his passport, and
freedom to travel to the West, restored to him.

Apart from that in Greece, no civil wars or mass popular uprisings
opposed the establishment of the new post-war order in divided Europe.
Once the communist bloc became established in the eastern sector, and
the political regimes settled in for the duration, Burchett's value as a
source on events in the region diminished. He was no social analyst; he
could not assess the direction of slow, historical changes. He praised the
achievements of Stalinism, and downplayed its repression. History was
taking place around him, but no longer flashing past in front of his eyes.
He turned to something really revolutionary, and wrote two books
about the Soviet pioneers of space, making use of his considerable
linguistic skills and quenching his appetite for new pastures at least
temporarily. But he reported almost nothing of the real social stresses of
communist society. There were mitigating factors: he was an ardent
supporter of détente. And excuses: without a passport he could hardly
up and leave the Soviet Union, which he had made his home in 1957
after his first visit the previous year – and therefore he could not afford
to be very critical.

But the fact remains that Burchett's writing record in these circumstances of communist consolidation was largely poor. This also goes for his work on China in the 1970s, as much as for that on Eastern Europe in the early fifties, and the USSR in the early sixties.

In each of these three cases he soon left for hotter fronts – to Korea in 1951, to Vietnam in 1962, and to southern Africa in 1975. Always the action reporter, he was at his best when history could be photographed. And he *was* usually there for the snapshot. He did not have the skills of time-delay exposure, the ability slowly and exhaustively to piece together a social process. He was the master of the scoop, telephoned, smuggled through by sympathizers, or bicycled out of the jungle. But when the story itself, and the people making it, emerged from the jungle, Burchett's work deteriorated to the point where he took his typewriter 'home' – usually to another tract of jungle.

Burchett specialized in being the man on the spot. (There were few women journalists in his heyday.) But later, when the spot thickened, he was not to be seen. Either he was not worth reading on the subject, or he had spotted a crisis somewhere else. What Burchett couldn't see, he usually couldn't write about. His writing was 'always descriptive', as one author has noted about his Vietnam War reporting.[15] He would travel halfway around the world to cover a hot spot or fast-moving crisis, but would lose touch when it cooled to slow-motion.

I remember a discussion I had with him, in Paris in 1979. He said that his late friend, Zhou Enlai, 'would never have invaded Vietnam', as his successors just had. 'But,' I replied, 'Deng Xiaoping, their leader, was a protégé of Zhou's.' Burchett threw up his hands. 'Oh, I don't know. You're writing a serious book. You can work that one out.' In that period, it was more important to him to make no less than five visits to Kampuchea, recently 'liberated' for the second time. During one of them he only narrowly escaped assassination. Burchett was serious, all right. But he was aware of his real weaknesses, even as he pushed his strengths to the limit.

He was also aware of his political biases. But I think he saw himself as someone filling gaps in existing Western reportage, rather than as a contemporary historian. The 'scoop' was, of course, something that no one had written before. And to reproduce both sides of the story was, he may well have believed, not a priority in view of the urgency he saw in the events he was personally reporting. Undoubtedly, he could never have assumed that his Western readers would become aware only of his side of the story.

And Burchett's political selectivity in his writing did not mean that he was a hack journalist in the pay of (or subservient to) any government, for instance that of the USSR. As Kathleen Rethlake has pointed out, in the mid-1950s:

[Burchett] made several excursions to Eastern Europe including Poland, where he reported the Poznan riots in June 1956 for the *Berliner Zeitung*, an East Berlin newspaper. This was one of the rare occasions when the citizens of East Berlin were treated to different views in their news media. The official organ of the Socialist Unity Party (communist) blamed the riots on United States agents in Poland, while Burchett's article ascribed the riots to the economic difficulties of the workers and considered the Polish industrial workers to have 'justified complaints'.[16]

Moreover, for someone alleged to be a KGB agent (See Appendix), Burchett had surprisingly warm sentiments for China. As early as 1951 he wrote to his father from Beijing that 'this people and their government . . . represent the fullest flowering of all the finest instincts in humanity'.[17] (Of course, this did not necessarily make him a 'Maoist'; for the book he was writing at the time, he rejected the title *Chairman Mao's China* because, he wrote, 'it is too individualistic'. Burchett was much closer to Zhou Enlai whom he knew as a supporter of contact with the West.)

But Burchett's romance with China really had its impact at the time of the Sino-Soviet split. In March 1963 he wrote to his father from Beijing:

There is no doubt at all in my mind that this side [China] is right and not just 80–90 per cent right but 100 per cent right . . . At the moment, the Chinese are in the process of publishing every attack made against them by forty-four parties . . . although the other side has never published a single word of the Chinese case. 'Publish everything of both sides and let the people judge' is the attitude here . . .

The Chinese now have the intellectual and political honesty to come out and call many things by their right names. The result will be good because it forces everyone to think for themselves and abandon the idea of 'papal infallibility' . . .[18]

As the last sentence implies, Burchett does not appear to have countenanced the possibility that the 'correct line' would henceforth always come from Beijing. In fact, in a later split in the socialist movement, over the question of Kampuchea in 1978, it was *Hanoi*'s practice of publishing the case of its opponents as well as its own side of the story,[19] which helped convince Burchett that Vietnam (and the USSR) was 'right' and China 'wrong'.

Wilfred Burchett was a much more complex character than his militant critics or sullen sympathizers claim. He supported the crushing of the 1956 Hungarian uprising but not what he called the 'Russian tanks in Prague' in 1968.[20] He opposed Hitler but not Stalin; smuggled Jews out of Nazi Germany but (till 1978) showed no sympathy for Kampuchean refugees from Pol Pot; exposed the massacre of Korean War prisoners of the Americans but explained away the trials of the Vietnamese boat people; opposed the US invasion of Vietnam but not the Soviet invasion of Afghanistan.

Much of this record might well suggest no complexity at all, but simply one-sidedness; strong sympathies for the victims of right-wing regimes, but much less for victims of left-wing ones. Burchett can be and has been seen as a hardened leftist, inconsistent and cynically political in his choice of friends in need of aid. But it is equally true that he brought them real aid, at least in terms of publicity for their plight. Whether this reporting was accurate is the subject of this book.

There was indeed complexity in Wilfred Burchett, enough to divide seriously those who were his political opponents. One might even imagine that he had a split personality, judging from the widely divergent accounts by Australian, British and American troops who met him as prisoners of the Korean and Vietnamese communists. In each war, some POWs claimed Burchett had treated them with great kindness, others that he interrogated or threatened them. (As Gavan McCormack shows, these divergences even appear, over time, in the accounts of individuals as well. See Chapter 8.) But it is unlikely that one could find a more favourable record of a person's activities by a member of the 'enemy' side, than that of the Japanese doctor in Hiroshima Hospital in September 1945. He described Wilfred Burchett as 'a saint who did not fear'.[21] Whether or not one accepts this assessment, the fact that such people at the centre of events frequently said similar things about him makes Wilfred Burchett one of the remarkable men of our age, and his writings a part of our post-war history, well worth assessing in their own right.

Notes

1. Norman Macswan, *The Man Who Read the East Wind: A Biography of Richard Hughes*, Kangaroo Press, Sydney, 1982, p.63.
2. Wilfred Burchett, *At the Barricades*, Quartet, London and New York, 1980 and Macmillan, Melbourne, 1981, back cover blurb and Introduction by Harrison Salisbury, p.v.
3. *Age*, Melbourne, 25 March 1985.
4. *Australian*, 21 May 1968.
5. 'School in the Bush', by W.G. Burchett, *The B.P. Magazine*, 1 June 1940, pp. 50ff.
6. *Age*, 3 February 1984, p.11.
7. Wilfred Burchett, letter to 'Dear Mother and Father and Clive', from London, dated 9 December 1938. This letter was intercepted by Australian security personnel; a copy was made available under the Freedom of Information Act to Mr Winston Burchett in 1985.
8. 'Details re Refugees Assisted to Australia'; file in the Wilfred Burchett collection, State Library of Victoria, Melbourne. Some of these refugees are still living in Melbourne in 1985.
9. *Tribune*, Sydney, 22 February 1984.
10. See, for instance, Burchett's articles on refugees from Germany, 'Broken Roots' (1 May 1940), and on the 'imperialist' war against Hitler, 'When Winter Comes' (1 August 1940), in the *Digest of World Reading*.
11. MacArthur quoted in H. Carrère D'Encausse, *Stalin: Order Through Terror*, Longman, 1981, p.125; Churchill quoted in Isaac Deutscher, *Stalin*, 1982, p.503.
12. Wilfred Burchett, *Pacific Treasure Island*, Cheshire, Melbourne, 1941, pp. 12–13. For Burchett's early writings on democracy, see 'Wanted: An Australian Dictator?' and 'Should Soldiers Obey Their Officers?', *Digest of World Reading*, 1 January 1941 and 1 April 1942.
13. *At the Barricades*, p.94.

14. W.G. Burchett, 'The Army Nobody Knows', *Digest of World Reading*, September 1941, pp.23–25.
15. Michael Maclear, *Vietnam: The Ten Thousand Day War*, Thames Methuen, London, 1981, p.242. Maclear added that Burchett's reports were 'perhaps the most overlooked intelligence'.
16. Kathleen C. Rethlake, *Wilfred Burchett – Journalist with a Cause*, University of Southern California, Master of Arts (Journalism) dissertation, 1971, p.42. Rethlake cites *New York Times*, 13 July 1956.
17. Letter to his father from Beijing, 16 April 1951.
18. Letter to his father from Beijing, 28 March 1963. Wilfred Burchett collection, State Library of Victoria, Melbourne.
19. In 1978 Hanoi published, in its *Kampuchea Dossier* (vol.1), the fourteen-page 'Statement of the Government of Democratic Kampuchea to its Friends Far and Near Across the Five Continents and to World Opinion': and in its *Hoa in Vietnam Dossier*, Hanoi published thirty-two pages of official statements on the question by the Chinese government. Also in 1978, in *Kampuchea Dossier* (vol.2), Hanoi published China's ten-page harangue, 'Why did Vietnamese Authorities Provoke Vietnam-Kampuchea Border Conflict?', plus another statement by Pol Pot's 'Democratic Kampuchea' regime.
20. *Sun*, Melbourne, 24 February 1970.
21. Quoted in Wilfred Burchett, *Shadows of Hiroshima*, Verso, London, 1983, p.68.

Part One:
Great Power Crises

1

Cracking the Jap: Burchett on World War Two

Phillip Knightley

A GLANCE AT THE MAP SHOWS THE POSSIBILITIES OF
CRACKING THE JAP AT ANY POINT FROM THE INDO-BURMA
BORDER RIGHT DOWN TO THE COAST OF SUMATRA — AND
THAT'S ONLY FROM THE SEA.
WILFRED BURCHETT, IN A LETTER TO HIS PARENTS FROM
DELHI, 9 SEPTEMBER 1943

The outbreak of the Second World War on 3 September 1939 found
Burchett working as a carpentry instructor in a small country school in
Victoria, Australia. He immediately wrote to the Australian government asking if his experience in Europe and his language qualifications
could be of any use to the war effort. While he waited for a reply he
continued to bombard Melbourne newspapers with letters setting out
his views on Germany, and in November tried his hand at an article on
German *autobahns* and their role in Hitler's military strategy. It was
published in the newly started Sydney *Sunday Telegraph* on 26

November 1939 and launched Burchett on his career in journalism. In 1939, Australian newspaper commentators who knew anything about foreign affairs were rare and one who not only had an informed point of view but who had recently been in Germany was a prize. The *Sunday Telegraph* asked for more and soon he began to write regularly for the literary supplement of the *Age*, in Melbourne, and the *Digest of World Reading* offered him commissions.

It was an article for this magazine that decided Burchett's next move. It was published in November 1940 – 'Japan Can be Stopped' – and argued that the Allies' concessions in the face of Japanese aggression had encouraged its expansionism and that faced with the threat of an economic blockade it would back down. 'The question is what action Japan is likely to take if her supplies are cut off,' Burchett wrote. 'Is she in a position to challenge America and the democracies? She is not.' Burchett was, of course, wrong in this assessment, but the writing of the article served to move his focus away from the war in Europe and turn it directly to the threat from Japan. He put up an idea to his newspapers and to the Australian Associated Press: that he should go to New Caledonia to assess Japanese activity there. Burchett was working on this theme and gathering material for his first book, *Pacific Treasure Island*, when he received a cable in reply to his offer of his services to the war effort made sixteen months earlier. It came from the recently formed Department of Information and offered him a job in the foreign-language-monitoring service. Burchett accepted, returned to Australia and took up duties listening to Axis broadcasts in German, French and Spanish.

He could have sat out the war there, but what he heard and what he read made him increasingly convinced that, contrary to his earlier assessment, Japan *was* about to challenge the United States and the democracies. With agreements to write for the *Digest* and the *Sunday Telegraph*, and some money of his own from the New Caledonia book, he left Australia by ship in August 1941 for Rangoon, intent on travelling along the recently reopened Burma Road into China and there to cover Japan's entry into the war. He saw it as a short, one-off assignment, similar to his New Caledonian adventure. Instead he was to be away nearly two years.

Hitching rides, first in a Chinese Air Force staff car and then in a postal truck, Burchett made the gruelling journey over the Burma Road to Chungking. What he saw on the trip formed his first impression of the Chinese that was soon to harden into a lifelong admiration – 'a discipline and intensity of labour combined with . . . a natural dignity which shone through in the most undignified circumstances, as well as the feeling of generations of continuity exemplified by the old man and his toddler working at the same task with equal intensity'.[1]

In Chungking Burchett delighted in the astonishment that his arrival caused to the star-studded international press corps, which included Leland Stowe, Theodore White and Jack Belden. An unknown Australian freelance had travelled over the legendary Burma Road. My belief is that Burchett, consciously or not, learned an important professional lesson from this. In describing other of his adventures he writes of the 'astonishment' and 'amazement' that they caused, which suggests that he decided probably as early in his reporting career as Chungking that being a member of the international press corps, travelling in the pack, was not for him, and that one factor in assessing which story he would chase would be the astonishment he would evoke if he pulled it off.

An interview with the Chinese Foreign Minister on what China's reaction would be if Japan attacked in south-east Asia gave Burchett his entry to Fleet Street. None of his Australian newspapers or magazines had given him collect cable facilities and he was sceptical of their interest in the interview anyway, so he sent it at his own expense to the *Daily Express*. The *Daily Express* published the story, and also appointed him Chungking correspondent, on a rather vague basis.

Why Burchett chose the *Daily Express* is not clear. It was not a newspaper whose politics he admired – 'It was a right-wing paper with belligerently pro-Empire tendencies'[2] – and Burchett had no way of knowing at that stage what editorial freedom it would give him. We can only speculate that he realized that the wealthy *Express* could afford a representative in China and would allow him to travel, whereas left-wing newspapers like the *Guardian* or the *News Chronicle* could not. As it turned out, the interests of Burchett and the *Express* coincided during the war – the quick defeat of the Axis powers – and no major conflict of editorial views arose.

Japan's entry in the war on 7 December 1941 confirmed Burchett's position. The *Express* asked him to join the staff as a member of its team of war correspondents in Asia. He would have preferred, I think, to have represented an Australian newspaper or newspaper group, because his *Express* stories about life in Chungking and his assessments of China's progress in the war had been syndicated to Sydney and Melbourne newspapers. But when he cabled a story on Chinese reactions to Japan's declaration of war to the Sydney *Daily Telegraph* he included in it long quotations from Chou-En-lai. The newspaper's reaction – 'uninterested in Chinese communist pronouncements' – made him realize that the *Express* would remain the best outlet for his work.

In January 1942, the *Express* sent him to Rangoon to write on the Japanese invasion of Burma. This was an important stage in Burchett's career, not so much for what he was able to report – which, as we shall see, was little – but because it was in Burma that he made his first intervention in an attempt to change the course of the events he was observing. This intervention, later a distinctive mark of Burchett's style of journalism, arose over the activities of a Chinese army which was supposed to be helping to defend Burma. The army had got no further than the border because of the reluctance of the British to let them cross in case they would not later withdraw. The *Express* was clamouring for stories from Burchett on the role of Britain's gallant Chinese allies, but local censorship refused to allow Burchett to reveal that the Chinese *had* no role, and to explain why.

So Burchett went to see the Governor of Burma, Sir Reginald Dorman-Smith, told him what was happening at the border, deplored the fact that Chinese battle-hardened troops were being wasted, and suggested that it was time something was done about it. Dorman-Smith arranged for Burchett to see the British army commander, and soon afterwards the first Chinese troops began to move down to the front.

It was no use. By 15 May 1942, the British had been run out of Burma. They abandoned Rangoon, destroying valuable oil installations – £11 million worth went up in flames in an hour – and ordered all correspondents to leave. Burchett and George Rodger, of *Life* magazine, walked 130 miles over the Naga Hills into India. They made notes on the trip which later enabled 40,000 refugees to escape along the same route.

How much of what he had seen and experienced in Burma was Burchett able to publish? Not much. The *Express*'s star war correspondent, O.D. Gallagher, had gone to Burma after surviving the sinking of the *Prince of Wales* off Singapore. As its senior staff man the *Express* preferred Gallagher's stories about the Burma Rifles and the Royal Air Force to what little news of the Chinese and about British bungling the censors allowed Burchett to send.

So in hospital in Calcutta, suffering from malaria, Burchett underwent something of a crisis about his career. The Burma fiasco had been reported in the *Express* from official communiqués issued either in Delhi or Chungking, and interpreted in London in the best possible light. Burchett's best despatches, criticizing the campaign, had never left the censor's office in Rangoon. Only his anodyne 'human-interest' stories had been published, and these, because of a garbled cable, under the name of *Peter* Burchett. Burchett sent his resignation, but the *Express* refused to accept it, offering him virtually his own terms to stay.

After thinking it over he reluctantly decided to continue. 'This is about as valuable a contribution I can make – at least as long as I retain the right to criticize. I wouldn't make much of a soldier I'm afraid, and as long as papers are prepared to pay me for reporting battles and my opinion thereon, I guess I had better be satisfied.'[3]

Although Burchett would have preferred to return to Australia, the *Express* wanted him back in China. In June 1942 he flew over 'the Hump' and from Chungking set out on a three-month tour of China's frontline provinces, witnessing at first hand Japan's 'destroy-all' operations. It was an interesting but frustrating time for Burchett. He saw the poorly armed but highly motivated communist troops fighting desperate rearguard actions while the Kuomintang army of Chiang Kai-Shek spent a considerable amount of time in public-relations exercises, designed to impress visiting American journalists and politicians. But the *Express* gave his stories little prominence. The war in North Africa, of direct and immediate interest to Britain, had reached a crucial stage. For what little space was available in the greatly reduced wartime paper, Burchett's stories had to compete with fellow

Australian Alan Moorehead's reports on the exploits of General Montgomery and the Eighth Army.

In October Burchett was back in India, seriously ill. He was suffering from recurrent bouts of malaria, he was debilitated and under-nourished, he had vitamin deficiency and liver trouble. It was two months before he had sufficiently recovered to leave for advanced British headquarters on the Burmese border, where he was to cover the much heralded counter-attack against the Japanese. Crossing a river with Gordon Waterfield of Reuters, escorted by a British intelligence officer and a major in public relations, Burchett spotted six Zeros searching for a target. The intelligence officer ignored Burchett's pleas to make for the bank, and instead insisted that the planes were RAF Mohawks and that a trick of the sun left visible only the red disc of the RAF's red, white and blue. By the time the officer realized his mistake it was too late; the Zeros were on them, machine guns and canon firing furiously. One of the oarsmen was killed. Burchett was hit in the back, right arm and right leg.

Back in hospital in India, Burchett spent a month recovering. He then went up to the remote area where the Indian border meets that of China and Burma, to see Major Orde Charles Wingate and his men returning from a highly unorthodox guerrilla operation behind Japanese lines. The main story of this venture had been written from Delhi by a *Daily Express* colleague. Burchett could only follow it up, but he met Wingate, who was impressed that Burchett had taken the trouble to make the trip. There now began a relationship between Wingate and Burchett that in my view clouded Burchett's journalistic judgement.

Burchett says that he was first attracted to Wingate because the (British) Indian Army 'blimps' considered him a crackpot with unsound military ideas. In Delhi in May 1943 Burchett spent each morning for several weeks 'cheering Wingate up and listening to his fantastic account of the obstacles his columns had encountered and how they had been overcome'.[4] Burchett was also gathering material for a book (*Wingate's Phantom Army* – also called *Wingate Adventure*). Wingate, depressed at being studiously ignored by the British Army brass, eagerly grasped at Burchett's interest and friendship. Then suddenly everything changed. Wingate was given a star to his DSO; he was flown to London, invited to dinner with Churchill, promoted to Major General on the spot and asked if he would accompany Churchill to the Quebec Conference to meet President Roosevelt and the American Chiefs of Staff. What had happened?

The War Office had belatedly realized that it had a hero on its hands. A British force had engaged the Japanese on their own ground and had had a measure of success, the *only* success at that stage in the whole of the Far East. Burchett's follow-up stories and those of his colleagues had made an immediate and enormous impression in Britain, especially on Churchill, who was drawn to Wingate as he had been to Lawrence of Arabia.

In these circumstances, when Wingate returned to India to organize a second expedition, the War Office arranged an elaborate plan to exploit Wingate's appeal as a war hero. The idea was to put out colourless reports, followed by more detailed ones as public interest was excited, moving towards a climax of sensational despatches on the lines of 'now it can be revealed'. Whether Burchett would have agreed to play any part in this orchestration of the news we will never know, because before it got into full swing Wingate was killed in an air crash in the Assam hills.

But Burchett was certainly partly responsible for promoting the image of Wingate that originally caught public attention. The outline and early chapters of Burchett's book lauding Wingate's exploits had been sent by local censors to the War Office in London where, as Burchett modestly states, it 'aroused some interest'.[5] Burchett considered Wingate a brilliant military planner, and an unorthodox but effective leader. But of the 3,000 men Wingate led into Burma on his first expedition only 2,187 returned, and of these no more than 600 were *ever* fit for active soldiering again. The mission had no strategic objective, except perhaps to exhibit British activity and to demonstrate that the Japanese were not invincible in the jungle. The official British Army historian decided after the war that the results achieved by Wingate's special group were incommensurate with the forces diverted to it, and Field Marshal Sir William Slim's opinion was that the press excitement over the expedition was its only justification. The blame for over-glamorizing a comparatively minor and very costly operation in the Burma campaign must lie with all the correspondents and especially with Burchett, who allowed his admiration for Wingate (another outsider), his distaste for British Army blimps, and his attraction to guerrilla warfare to distort his assessment of the expedition.

When Wingate was killed, Burchett was back in Australia, reassigned to cover the United States Navy and its island-hopping advance on Japan. Here he found he had exchanged one theatre of censorship for another. He managed to set down some percipient views on the change in naval warfare that aircraft carriers had brought about, but these were not published until his book *Democracy with a Tommygun* appeared after the war was over.

The rest of his time attached to the US Navy was marked by long periods of boredom interspersed with violent action, such as the invasions of the Marianas, Guam and Peleliu, the last of which he reported from the back seat of a Helldiver bomber. It was a frustrating war to cover. First, censorship prevented correspondents from writing most of the major stories of the campaign: the bitter US Army–Navy rivalry, the early successes of the Japanese suicide pilots, the Kamikaze Corps, the poor relations between the Australian and American troops, the inflated official reports of damage caused to the Japanese Navy. Next, the navy operated a 'pool system' for major operations and Burchett had to share his stories with his colleagues. When he occasionally had a story to himself, distances in the Pacific were so great and communications such a problem that the official communiqué from

Washington often released the news first. He took instead to writing 'backgrounders', anticipating developments and producing articles that explained their background, which his newspaper could hold until the appropriate moment. But the very nature of the US Navy's role meant that he was often too long out of touch to know what was going on elsewhere. At one stage Burchett had no communication with the *Express* for five weeks.

Not that in 1945 the *Express* was very interested in what he had to report. With the fighting in Europe over and Britain in the middle of a general election, British newspapers lost interest in the Pacific until the atom bomb was dropped on Hiroshima on 6 August. This momentous event provided Burchett with his most important story of the war, perhaps of his whole career.

The origins of his decision to go to Hiroshima are unclear. Burchett later said categorically that on 6 August 1945 he was in a chow-line at a Marine cookhouse on Okinawa when he heard a radio announcement about the dropping of the A-bomb and 'made a mental note that Hiroshima would be my priority objective should I ever get to Japan'.[6] Yet on 14 August, the day Japan announced its decision to surrender, he wrote to his parents saying, 'I hope to take off immediately for the surrender-signing and then get on my way to San Francisco and London.'[7] By the time he reached Tokyo, after landing with the Marines at the Yokosuka naval base, he had decided to miss the surrender ceremony aboard the battleship *Missouri*, scheduled for 2 September, and head for Hiroshima, in defiance of General MacArthur's order placing it 'off-limits' to the press.

He arrived there after a twenty-one-hour journey on the morning of 3 September, and spent several hours touring the devastation with the Domei agency's local representative, Bin Nakamura, who had sent within hours of the bombing the first eye-witness account, including – fantastic though it must have seemed to him at the time – the sentence 'It might have been an atomic bomb.'[8] Nakamura tapped out Burchett's story by morse to the Tokyo office. It had barely gone out when the first American correspondents arrived in Hiroshima, flown in by the United States Air Force. Burchett, worried that his story might not have got through, asked the air force colonel in charge of the group for a lift back to Tokyo or, if this was not possible, for the colonel to carry back a duplicate of his story. The colonel, annoyed that a navy-accredited correspondent had got to Hiroshima ahead of his own star-studded team, refused both requests. (To their credit two of the American correspondents in the group, Homer Bigart and Bill Lawrence, protested about this.)

Burchett was right to be worried about his story. He had asked his *Daily Express* colleague, Henry Keys, to keep in touch with the Domei office in Tokyo, collect any message from Burchett, and put it straight on the telex to London. But MacArthur had placed Tokyo out of bounds to all Allied personnel. Military police pulled Keys off the train from Yokohama to Tokyo and refused to allow him to continue his journey. So Keys hired a Japanese courier to sit in the Domei office, wait for any message from Burchett, and bring it to Keys in Yokohama. Keys's arrangements worked, but this was only the beginning of his difficulties. At the telex office the American censor insisted on seeing the story and when he read it he ordered it to be stopped. Keys insisted that since the war was over, so was censorship. The censor went to refer the matter higher, while Keys stood over the telex operator to ensure that Burchett's story was sent. (A longer and more detailed story on Nagasaki written about the same time by George Weller of the Chicago *Daily News* and sent via MacArthur's headquarters was stopped by censors in its entirety.)

The *Daily Express* ran Burchett's story on 5 September, well ahead of the shorter, less detailed reports of the correspondents Burchett had met with the US Air Force in Hiroshima. Some of the more horrific description was cut by the editor, Arthur Christiansen, but he himself boosted Burchett's main message – 'I write this as a warning to the world' – into a subsidiary headline underneath the main one – THE ATOMIC PLAGUE. Although Burchett's estimate of the area of devastation at the centre of the explosion, twenty-five to thirty square miles, was too high, the main revelation in his story – that thirty days after the bomb people were still dying from the after-effects – was absolutely accurate and caused a worldwide sensation. There is one other important point to make about Burchett's despatch. Its tone went totally against everything else being written from Japan at that time, the 'they-had-it-coming-to-them' and 'I-saw-the-arrogant-strutting-Japs-humbled' type of story. Burchett recognized that Hiroshima was a major watershed in the history of war, and that a new and perilous period for mankind had begun.

Burchett arrived back in Tokyo in time to attend an army press conference called specially to refute this. There was no such thing as radiation sickness, the spokesman said. Burchett had fallen victim to Japanese propaganda. Hiroshima was put out of bounds to all correspondents. Burchett was served with an expulsion order (later rescinded when the US Navy intervened on his behalf) and in the United States Major General Leslie R. Groves, head of the atomic bomb project, declared flatly 'This talk about radioactivity is so much nonsense.'

Burchett went into hospital in Tokyo for tests which revealed that his white corpuscle count was down. This is, of course, one symptom of radiation exposure, but it was attributed at the time to antibiotics he had taken for an infection. As soon as he was discharged and MacArthur had withdrawn his expulsion order, Burchett left for London, his career as a correspondent in the Second World War at an end.

It had been a long hard road. He had been away from home and family for four years. He had served in China, India, Burma, throughout the Pacific and in Japan. He had been wounded and was often ill from malaria, bacillary dysentery, debility, vitamin deficiency, tropical sores and a liver malfunction. He had slept and travelled rough.

Materially the rewards had been poor. He certainly had not made a lot of money from risking his life, and he complained in one letter home that he was actually 'broke' and anxiously awaiting £400 from the *Express*.[9] Nor, until the Hiroshima scoop, did he win much fame. The *Express*'s mistake in by-lining him as *Peter* Burchett prevented a lot of people from recognizing him and even after his success at Hiroshima, he finished the war less well-known to readers than other Australian correspondents such as Chester Wilmott, Alan Moorhead, Ronald Monson and Noel Monks. Why, then, did he do it?

First, he considered that it was the best contribution he could make to the war against fascism. He had no illusions that the Allied side was perfect, but he hoped that under American influence the war would produce a new post-imperial world, in which the countries that made up the old colonial empires would achieve their freedom. That said, he was unable to contribute as much as he would have liked. He was unfortunate in that censorship in the areas he reported was the harshest – with the exception of the Soviet Union – of the entire world war. His more trenchant criticism of what he saw was, therefore, never published in newspapers and had to wait for his post-war books. He could have protested against this censorship as Douglas Wilkie of the *Evening Standard*, London, and the *Herald*, Melbourne, had done. Wilkie first wrote a letter of complaint – 'If war correspondents are to be allowed to write only what the army wants, then it would be easier if you confined your publicity to official handouts'[10] – and then packed up and went home. But Burchett's natural optimism made him believe that matters would get better, and besides, there was more to what he saw as a journalist's duty than publishing reports.

This is what Burchett achieved in the Second World War: a confirmation and a refining of his philosophy as a reporter. Burchett learned that a correspondent can do more than passively record events; he or she can play a part in those events – not only can but *should*. 'For a journalist to use his unique position to transmit discreetly a bit of information from one side or the other to get clogged machinery moving (without making headlines out of it) is a useful and honourable thing to do.'[11]

Burchett entered the Second World War as a radical. The leaders he met, people like Mao Tse-tung and Chou-En-lai, won his sympathies and led him to conclude that although censorship prevented him from writing as much about them as he would have wished, then his sort of reporting would be to support with his typewriter those causes of which he approved – the classic definition of a journalist *engagé*.

Burchett's initiative and perception at Hiroshima were the high point of his Second World War reporting, perhaps of his whole career. But it has to be said that the rest of his work in this period was not outstanding. It was a time of learning, of gaining at considerable personal cost the experience and attitudes that were to mark so distinctly the remainder of his professional life.

Notes

1. *At the Barricades*, Macmillan, Melbourne, 1981, p.63.
2. Ibid., p.119.
3. Letter to mother and father, 13 May 1942.
4. *At the Barricades*, p.90.
5. Ibid., p.91.
6. Ibid., p.105.
7. Letter to mother and father, 14 August 1945.
8. Domei bulletin, Okayama, 6 August 1945.
9. Letter to mother and father, 13 May 1942.
10. *Newspaper World*, 20 February 1943.
11. *At the Barricades*, p.210.

2

Voice and Silence in the First Nuclear War: Wilfred Burchett and Hiroshima

Richard Tanter

HIROSHIMA HAD A PROFOUND EFFECT UPON ME. STILL DOES.
MY FIRST REACTION WAS PERSONAL RELIEF THAT THE BOMB
HAD ENDED THE WAR. FRANKLY, I NEVER THOUGHT I WOULD
LIVE TO SEE THAT END, THE CASUALTY RATE AMONG WAR
CORRESPONDENTS IN THAT AREA BEING WHAT IT WAS. MY
ANGER WITH THE US WAS NOT AT FIRST, THAT THEY HAD
USED THAT WEAPON — ALTHOUGH THAT ANGER CAME LATER.
ONCE I GOT TO HIROSHIMA, MY FEELING WAS THAT FOR THE
FIRST TIME A WEAPON OF MASS DESTRUCTION OF CIVILIANS
HAD BEEN USED. WAS IT JUSTIFIED? COULD ANYTHING
JUSTIFY THE EXTERMINATION OF CIVILIANS ON SUCH A SCALE?
BUT THE REAL ANGER WAS GENERATED WHEN THE US
MILITARY TRIED TO COVER UP THE EFFECTS OF ATOMIC
RADIATION ON CIVILIANS — AND TRIED TO SHUT ME UP. MY
EMOTIONAL AND INTELLECTUAL RESPONSE TO HIROSHIMA
WAS THAT THE QUESTION OF THE SOCIAL RESPONSIBILITY OF A

JOURNALIST WAS POSED WITH GREATER URGENCY THAN
EVER.

WILFRED BURCHETT, 1980[1]

Wilfred Burchett entered Hiroshima alone in the early hours of 3
September 1945, less than a month after the first nuclear war began with
the bombing of the city. For Burchett, that experience was a turning
point, 'a watershed in my life, decisively influencing my whole
professional career and world outlook'. Burchett was the first Western
journalist – and almost certainly the first Westerner other than prisoners
of war – to reach Hiroshima. The story which he typed out on his
battered Baby Hermes typewriter, sitting among the ruins, remains one
of the most important Western eyewitness accounts, and the first
attempt to come to terms with the full human and moral consequences
of the United States' initiation of nuclear war.

Subsequently Burchett came to understand that his honest and
accurate account of the radiological effects of nuclear weapons not only
initiated an animus against him from the highest quarters of the US
government, but also marked the beginning of the nuclear victor's
determination rigidly to control and censor the picture of Hiroshima and
Nagasaki presented to the world.

The story of Burchett and Hiroshima ended only with his last book,
Shadows of Hiroshima, completed shortly before his death in 1983. In
that book, Burchett not only went back to the history of his own
despatch, but more importantly showed the broad dimensions of the
'coolly planned' and manufactured cover-up which continues today.
With his last book, completed in his final years in the context of
President Reagan's 'Star Wars' speech of March 1983, Burchett felt 'it
has become urgent – virtually a matter of life or death – for people to
understand what really did happen in Hiroshima nearly forty years
ago. . .It is my clear duty, based on my own special experiences, to add
this contribution to our collective knowledge and consciousness. With
apologies that it has been so long delayed . . .'[2]

That one day in Hiroshima in September 1945 affected Burchett as a
person, as a writer, and as a participant in politics for the next forty
years. But Burchett's story of that day, and his subsequent writing about
Hiroshima, have a greater significance still, by giving a clue to the
deliberate suppression of the truth about Hiroshima and Nagasaki, and
to the deeper, missing parts of our cultural comprehension of that
holocaust.

One Day in Hiroshima: 3 September 1945[3]

After covering the end of the bloody Okinawa campaign Burchett's goal was to reach Hiroshima as soon as possible after the Japanese surrender on 15 August. He reached Japan in late August aboard the transport ship USS *Millett* and landed with the advance party of US Marines at Yokosuka in Tokyo Bay. With two journalist friends Burchett reached Tokyo by train, days ahead of MacArthur's occupying forces.

Few among the hundreds of journalists who swarmed to Japan with the occupying forces contemplated the hazardous twenty-one-hour trip south to Hiroshima or Nagasaki. Most accepted the claim that the months of aerial and naval bombardment of Japan prior to the surrender had reduced the railway system to rubble, and that it was impossible to travel beyond Tokyo. Even this official discouragement appears to have been almost unnecessary, at least at that stage. The prevailing (and still hardly changed) news values dictated the choice of the majority: 600 Allied journalists covered the official Japanese surrender aboard the battleship *Missouri*: only one went to Hiroshima.[4]

Burchett spoke only phrasebook Japanese, but received enthusiastic help from the staff of the Japanese Domei news agency in Tokyo, who were greatly concerned for their Hiroshima correspondent, Nakamura. A US Navy press officer, tickled at the idea of 'one of his boys' reaching Hiroshima ahead of correspondents attached to the other services, provided provisions for Nakamura and for Burchett.

At 6 a.m. on the morning of 2 September, Burchett boarded an overcrowded train heading for Hiroshima. In his knapsack he carried an all-important letter of introduction to Nakamura, the navy-supplied provisions, a Baby Hermes portable typewriter and a most unjournalistic Colt .45, thoughtfully thrust into his hands by an Australian friend before Burchett left Yokosuka.

Outside Tokyo, news of the war's end had come after the Emperor's announcement of Japan's unconditional surrender two weeks earlier. There were as yet, however, no occupying forces. Burchett had landed with the vanguard of Marines, but MacArthur had barely enough troops to occupy central Tokyo and the ports, and at every point on his journey to Hiroshima and back, Burchett found himself actually leading the occupation.

Boarding the train, Burchett crammed in among ordinary soldiers, 'very sullen at first, chattering – obviously about me – in a very hostile way'. But a packet of cigarettes, displays of a scar from a wound inflicted by a Japanese plane in Burma, and the Baby Hermes as the sign of a journalist, and 'from then on it was smiles and friendship, more cigarettes against bits of fish – and even a drop of saké'.

After a few hours' travelling, the new friends dropped off the train, and Burchett managed to get into a compartment which turned out to be full of belligerent Imperial Army officers. As Burchett was later to appreciate, one of the main impediments to the desire of the Japanese

Emperor and Prime Minister to surrender in July 1945 was their fear of
mutiny by the most extreme of the militarists in the Imperial Army.
Memories of the assassinations by zealous militarists of wavering Prime
Ministers and cabinet ministers in the early 1930s, understandably
disturbed ministers and the Emperor's chamberlains as they searched
for a form of words acceptable to the Allies after Potsdam. They feared
that a small group of army officers would react to news of an imperial
rescript of surrender by seizing the Emperor himself, and quite possibly
using the sacred hostage as the basis for the all-out resistance to the
death both sides feared.[5]

On his slow twenty-one-hour trip south, Burchett sensed the depth of
enmity towards the victors felt by officers nursing their humiliation.

Here the hostility was total. Among the passengers was an American
priest, accompanied by armed guards. He had been brought to Tokyo
from internment to broadcast to American troops on how they should
behave in Japan to avoid friction with the local population, he
explained, warning me in veiled tones that the situation in the
compartment was very tense and that a false move might cost us our
lives. The officers were furious and humiliated at their defeat. Above
all I was not to smile as this would be taken as gloating over what was
happening aboard the *Missouri*. Watching those glowering officers
toying with the hilts of their swords and the long samurai daggers that
many of them wore, I felt no inclination to smile, especially as the
train was in complete darkness as we passed through what seemed
like endless tunnels.

Eventually, at two the next morning, Burchett's neighbour prodded him
awake with the news of their arrival in Hiroshima. At what was left of
the city station, Burchett was arrested by two sabre-carrying policemen,
and placed in a makeshift cell for the night, where he promptly
collapsed into sleep.

Next morning, Burchett showed the guards his letter of introduction
from the Tokyo Domei office, and they made no attempt to stop him
leaving.

I followed a tramline which seemed to lead fairly directly towards the
standing buildings, branching off at cross streets for a few hundred
yards and then returning to the tramline. Walking those streets I had
the feeling of having been translated to some death-stricken alien
planet. There was devastation and desolation, and nothing else.
Lead-grey clouds hung over the waste that had been a city of more
than a quarter of a million people. Smoky vapours drifted from
fissures in the soil and there was a dank, acrid, sulphurous smell. The
few people in the streets hurried past each other without pausing or
speaking, white masks covering their nostrils. Buildings had been
pounded into grey and reddish dust, solidified into ridges and banks
by the frequent rains . . . No one stopped to look at me. Everyone

hurried, intent on whatever it was that brought them into this city of death.[6]

At the police station where he went for help, Burchett was understandably ill-received. After he explained his purpose, the police found Nakamura, who in turn brought a Canadian-born woman as translator. At the headquarters of the surviving police force Nakamura explained Burchett's purpose and his request for help. 'The police were extremely hostile and the atmosphere was tense . . . The more Nakamura explained the more the tension increased. There was some shouting and the interpreter became pale.'

Nakamura later told Burchett that most of the policemen had wanted to have all three shot. Astonishingly, it was the local head of the Kempeitai, the Thought Control Police, who accepted Burchett's explanation of his task, provided a police car, and set out with Burchett to 'show him what his people have done to us'.

Guided by Nakamura and the police chief, Burchett went to the Hiroshima Communications Hospital, 1.3 kilometres from the hypocentre. One of the city's six hospitals, it was, like the others, very heavily damaged, most of the staff having become nuclear casualties. At that time it held about 2,300 in-patients. Of the 300 doctors in the city, 270 were either killed or seriously injured in the atomic attack, as were 93 per cent of the city's nurses.[7]

Relief medical teams from outside the city had been quickly organized. By the end of September some 2,000 medical workers at makeshift relief stations had treated 105,861 in-patients and another 210,048 had received out-patient treatment.[8] Japanese scientists and doctors had already made considerable progress in developing procedures for aiding the suffering survivors with limited resources and an almost complete lack of prior knowledge of the effects of whole-body radiation. The day that Burchett arrived in Hiroshima, a medical meeting was held on what were to become known as A-bomb diseases, with lectures given on treatment of victims by the Japanese relief medical workers and researchers who had been studying and treating the victims' illnesses for almost a month.

The appalling sights Burchett witnessed in ward after ward were to affect him far more than the physical devastation he had already seen. Patients – and their families – on filthy tatami mats among the rubble were being ravaged by the effects of massive blast and primary and secondary burn trauma combined with advanced stages of radiation illnesses, resulting in fever, nausea, haemorrhagic stools and diathesis (spontaneous bleeding, from mouth, rectum, urethra and lungs), epilation (loss of hair), livid purpura on the skin, and gingivitis and tonsillitis leading to swelling, and eventually haemorrhaging of gums and soft membranes.[9] In many cases, without effective drugs, large burns and the haemorrhaging parts of the body had turned gangrenous. Recovery was inhibited by the effects of widespread malnutrition, resulting from the cumulative effects of long-term wartime shortages and the Allied blockade of the past year.

After the party passed through the wards, the doctor in charge asked Burchett to leave:

'I can no longer guarantee your safety. These people are all marked down to die. I will also die. I was trained in America. I believed in Western civilization. I'm a Christian. But how can you Christians do what you have done here? Send some of your scientists at least. They know what this is – they must know how we can stop this terrible sickness. Do that at least. Send your scientists down quickly!'

Burchett left to write the unique despatch to the *Daily Express*, sitting on a piece of rubble not far from the hypocentre, sometime in the early afternoon. What Burchett felt and saw that day is best conveyed as it appeared in the *Daily Express* three days later.[10]

30th Day in Hiroshima: Those who escaped begin to die, victims of
THE ATOMIC PLAGUE
'I Write this as a Warning to the World'
DOCTORS FALL AS THEY WORK
Poison gas fear: All wear masks
Express Staff Reporter Peter Burchett
was the first Allied Reporter to enter the atom-bomb city. He travelled 400 miles from Tokyo alone and unarmed, carrying rations for seven meals – food is almost unobtainable in Japan – a black umbrella, and a typewriter. Here is his story from –

HIROSHIMA, Tuesday

In Hiroshima, 30 days after the first atomic bomb destroyed the city and shook the world, people are still dying, mysteriously and horribly – people who were uninjured in the cataclysm – from an unknown something which I can only describe as the atomic plague.

Hiroshima does not look like a bombed city. It looks as if a monster steamroller had passed over it and squashed it out of existence. I write these facts as dispassionately as I can in the hope that they will act as a warning to the world.

In this first testing ground of the atomic bomb I have seen the most terrible and frightening desolation in four years of war. It makes a blitzed Pacific island seem like an Eden. The damage is far greater than photographs can show.

When you arrive in Hiroshima you can look around and for 25 and perhaps 30 square miles you can see hardly a building. It gives you an empty feeling in the stomach to see such man-made devastation.

I picked my way to a shack used as a temporary police headquarters in the middle of the vanished city. Looking south from there I could see about three miles of reddish rubble. That is all the atomic bomb left of dozens of blocks of city streets, of buildings, homes, factories, and human beings.

STILL THEY FAIL

There is just nothing standing except about 20 factory chimneys – chimneys with no factories. I looked west. A group of half a dozen gutted buildings. And then again nothing.

The police chief of Hiroshima welcomed me eagerly as the first Allied correspondent to reach the city. With the local manager of Domei, leading Japanese news agency, he drove me through or, perhaps, I should say over, the city. And he took me to hospitals where the victims of the bomb are still being treated.

In these hospitals I found people who when the bomb fell, suffered absolutely no injuries, but now are dying from the uncanny after-effects. . .

THE SULPHUR SMELL

My nose detected a peculiar odour unlike anything I have ever smelled before. It is something like sulphur, but not quite. I could smell it when I passed a fire that was still smouldering, or at a spot where they were still recovering bodies from the wreckage. But I could also smell it where everything was still deserted.

They believe it is given off by the poisonous gas still issuing from earth soaked with radioactivity released by the split uranium atom.

And so the people of Hiroshima today are walking through the forlorn desolation of their once proud city with gauze masks over their mouths and noses. It probably does not help them physically. But it helps them mentally.

From the moment that this devastation was loosed upon Hiroshima the people who survived have hated the white man. It is a hate the intensity of which is almost as frightening as the bomb itself.

'ALL CLEAR' WENT

The counted dead number 53,000. Another 30,000 are missing, which means 'certainly dead'. In the day I have stayed in Hiroshima – and this is nearly a month after the bombing – 100 people have died from its effects.

They were some of the 13,000 seriously injured by the explosion. They have been dying at the rate of 100 a day. And they will probably all die. Another 40,000 were slightly injured.

These casualties might not have been as high except for a tragic mistake. The authorities thought this was just another routine Super-Fort raid. The plane flew over the target and dropped the parachute which carried the bomb to its explosion point.

The American plane passed out of sight. The all-clear was sounded and the people of Hiroshima came out from their shelters. Almost a minute later the bomb reached the 2,000-foot altitude at which it was timed to explode – at the moment when nearly everyone in Hiroshima was in the streets.

Hundreds and hundreds of the dead were so badly burned in the terrific heat generated by the bomb that it was not even possible to tell whether they were men or women, old or young.

Of thousands of others, nearer the centre of the explosion, there was no trace. They vanished. The theory in Hiroshima is that the atomic heat was so great that they burned instantly to ashes – except that there were no ashes.

If you could see what is left of Hiroshima you would think that London had not been touched by bombs.

HEAP OF RUBBLE

The Imperial Palace, once an imposing building, is a heap of rubble three feet high, and there is one piece of wall. Roof, floors and everything else is dust.

Hiroshima has one intact building – the Bank of Japan. This in a city which at the start of the war had a population of 310,000.

Almost every Japanese scientist has visited Hiroshima in the past three weeks to try to find a way of relieving the people's suffering. Now they themselves have become sufferers.

For the first fortnight after the bomb dropped they found they could not stay long in the fallen city. They had dizzy spells and headaches. Then minor insect bites developed into great swellings which would not heal. Their health steadily deteriorated.

Then they found another extraordinary effect of the new terror from the skies.

Many people had suffered only a slight cut from a falling splinter of brick or steel. They should have recovered quickly. But they did not. They developed an acute sickness. Their gums began to bleed and then they vomited blood. And finally they died.

All these phenomena, they told me, were due to the radioactivity released by the atomic bomb's explosion of the uranium atom.

WATER POISONED

They found that the water had been poisoned by chemical reaction. Even today every drop of water consumed in Hiroshima comes from other cities. The people of Hiroshima are still afraid.

The scientists told me they have noted a great difference between the effect of the bombs in Hiroshima and in Nagasaki.

Hiroshima is in perfectly flat delta country. Nagasaki is hilly. When the bomb dropped on Hiroshima the weather was bad, and a big rainstorm developed soon afterwards.

And so they believe that the uranium radiation was driven into the earth and that, because so many are still falling sick and dying, it is still the cause of this man-made plague.

At Nagasaki on the other hand the weather was perfect, and scientists believe that this allowed the radioactivity to dissipate into the atmosphere more rapidly. In addition, the force of the bomb explosion was, to a large extent, expended in the sea, where only fish were killed.

To support this theory, the scientists point to the fact that, in Nagasaki, death came swiftly and suddenly, and that there have been no after-effects such as those that Hiroshima is still suffering.

Return to Tokyo

If reaching Hiroshima had been difficult, transmitting the story to London was even more risky. Nakamura undertook to tap the story out on a hand-set in Morse code to the Tokyo Domei office. But while Burchett was in Hiroshima, MacArthur declared Tokyo off-limits to journalists. This frustrated Burchett's plan for his friend Henry Keys to wait in the Tokyo Domei office for the story to be tapped through from Burchett. Twice turned off the train from Yokohama to Tokyo by American Military Police, Keys hired a Japanese journalist to wait for Burchett's story in Tokyo and bring it to Yokohama immediately. Late on the evening of 3 September the story arrived and Keys bullied the reluctant wartime censors to allow the unprecedented story through unchanged.

Burchett was not the only foreign journalist to arrive in Hiroshima on 3 September. A Pentagon press 'Investigatory Group' arrived by plane from Tokyo just as Burchett was finishing his piece. According to Burchett, having been guaranteed an 'exclusive', the journalists in the official party were surprised to see him there. While the journalists felt piqued and threatened by Burchett's scoop the officials accompanying them as press handlers were hostile and suspicious.

In Burchett's eyes, most of the Pentagon press team were headquarters hacks specially flown in from the US, except for a few who had shared his path on the dangerous island-hopping campaigns. According to Burchett, none seriously attempted to survey the human consequences of the atomic bombing, although he advised one whom he knew that 'the real story is in the hospitals'.[11]

. . . the moment they heard a rival had got to Hiroshima before them they demanded to get back to their plane and on to Tokyo as soon as possible to file their despatches. They had no contact with the local population as they were a solid 'all-American' body with perhaps a Japanese-speaking interpreter attached. They saw physical wreckage only.[12]

The reporters toured the wreckage, and later held a press conference at the Hiroshima Prefectural Office.[13] After the press conference, and with fog threatening to close in, the reporters prepared to get back to Tokyo as soon as possible.

> I asked if I could fly back with them to Tokyo, the train journey being rather risky.
>
> 'Our plane's overloaded as it is,' replied the colonel.
>
> 'You've used up more petrol getting here than I weigh,' I argued.
>
> 'Yes. But this airstrip's a very short one and we can't take on any extra weight.'
>
> 'Will you take a copy of my story back to Tokyo at least, and give it to the *Daily Express* correspondent?'
>
> 'We're not going back to Tokyo,' was the colonel's brusque reply. He called the journalists together and they piled into their minibus and headed back for the airport.[14]

As it happened, Nakamura had slowly but successfully transmitted the long story. But Burchett could not be sure, and he must have been deeply angered, with reason.

That night, as the story was wired through to London, Burchett began an eventful trip back to Tokyo by train. In the middle of the next day, as the train passed through Kyoto, Burchett saw two unmistakable Australians – prisoners of war from a local camp left in less than benign confusion as the war ended, with no effective arrangements to feed the starving POWs. Word had filtered in to the camp about the end of the war, and the soldiers had volunteered to leave to look for food in Kyoto. The emaciated pair begged Burchett to come back to the camp to meet their fellow inmates to convince them (and the confused guards) that the war was indeed over.

In the next two days Burchett visited six POW camps, speaking to the prisoners, telling them of the Allied victory and the coming of the occupation forces.

> It was necessary to bluff the Japanese camp commanders, with whatever authority I could muster, that I had come officially to ensure that the surrender terms were being complied with and that living conditions for the POWs were being immediately improved. I have addressed various types of audiences in my time, but never such eager listeners as these. These men were famished. They bore on their faces and bodies all the evidence of physical hunger, but above all their eyes told that they were famished for news. Hesitating for a moment, at that first encounter, while I tried to formulate the most economic way of telling them what they yearned to hear, I felt the compulsion in scores of pairs of eyes glittering with the intensity of their appeal to begin, to tell them it was all over and they would soon be on their way home again, with a few details of how it came to be over so suddenly.[15]

Confronting the Manhattan Project

Back in Tokyo, 'the American nuclear big-shots were furious'. Burchett's article had raised a storm. Not only had the *Daily Express* headlined the story 'THE ATOMIC PLAGUE – I Write this as a Warning to the World', and put it on the front page, but they had released it gratis to the world's press. On the surface, US officials were mainly angry about Burchett's claim that residual radiation was still hazardous and that a month after the bombing people were still dying from radiation illness – what he had referred to as 'the atomic plague'.

On the morning of 7 September Burchett stumbled off the train in Tokyo to discover that senior US officials had called a press conference at the Imperial Hotel to refute his article. He reached the press conference just in time to hear Brigadier-General Thomas Farrell, the deputy head of the Manhattan atomic bomb project, explain that the bomb had been exploded at a sufficient height over Hiroshima to avoid any risk of 'residual radiation'.

There was a dramatic moment as I rose to my feet, feeling that my scruffiness put me at a disadvantage with the elegantly uniformed and bemedalled officers. My first question was whether the briefing officer had been to Hiroshima. He had not. I then described what I had seen and asked for explanations. He was very polite at first, a scientist explaining things to a layman. Those I had seen in the hospital were victims of blast and burn, normal after any big explosion. Apparently the Japanese doctors were incompetent to handle them, or lacked the right medication. He discounted the allegation that any who had not been in the city at the time of the blast were later affected. Eventually the exchanges narrowed to my asking how he explained the fish still dying when they entered a stream running through the centre of the city.

'Obviously they were killed by the blast or overheated water.'

'Still there a month later?'

'It's a tidal river, so they could be washed back and forth.'

'But I was taken to a spot in the city outskirts and watched live fish turning on their stomachs upwards as they entered a certain patch of the river. After that they were dead within seconds.'

The spokesman looked pained. 'I'm afraid you've fallen victim to Japanese propaganda,' he said, and sat down. The customary 'Thank you' was pronounced and the conference ended. Although my radiation story was denied, Hiroshima was immediately put out of bounds, and I was whisked off to a US Army hospital for tests.[16]

At the hospital, Burchett's white-blood-cell count was found to be lower than normal. At the time Burchett accepted the explanation of the low white-corpuscle count as the work of antibiotics he had been given earlier for a knee infection. Only many years later did Burchett discover that the explanation was quite wrong: the number of white corpuscles in his blood ought to have increased to fight the infection. On the other hand a low white-blood-cell count is characteristic of radiation illness.[17]

By the time Burchett emerged from hospital a few days later, his camera containing unique shots of Hiroshima and its victims had been stolen. MacArthur had withdrawn his press accreditation and announced his intention to expel Burchett from occupied Japan. Although the intervention of friends in the US Navy with whom Burchett had worked for much of the Pacific campaign led to the withdrawal of the expulsion order, Burchett left Japan at the call of the Beaverbrook press shortly afterwards, not to return for over two and a half decades.

Hiroshima: Constructing the Silence

Although Burchett dismissed most of the obstructions placed in his way at the time of the Hiroshima story as the predictable overreactions of bureaucrats, he eventually came to see a more deeply disturbing pattern. Reflecting later on his difficulty in transmitting his story, his hospitalization, the theft of his camera, the extreme hostility of US military officials in Hiroshima and Tokyo, and the efforts to limit access to Hiroshima, Burchett came to see his own story in a broader context of official US policy to conceal the truth of Hiroshima. 'In 1945 I was too overwhelmed by the enormity of what happened at Hiroshima and Nagasaki to appreciate the cool deliberation and advance planning that went into manufacturing the subsequent cover-up.'[18]

Here Burchett quite rightly saw his own scoop story as provoking an official US government response. How much was premeditated and planned before the bombing is unclear, but there is little doubt that with Burchett's announcement to the world of the effects of radiation illness, the true character of the holocausts of Hiroshima and Nagasaki could not easily be contained. Hiroshima and Nagasaki were to take on a meaning different to other, comparable holocausts that had come to be morally accepted where they were not condoned – such as the firebombing of Dresden, Hamburg and Tokyo.

The extent of the suppression of the truth of the first nuclear bombings is probably even greater than Burchett guessed in his last book, and certainly more complex. Beginning with the attack on Burchett, there were three strands to official American policy towards information about Hiroshima and Nagasaki. First, access to Hiroshima was denied to Allied journalists. Second, public discussion of the topic was banned in Japan. Finally, Western perceptions were channelled in such a way as to minimize understanding of the human, as opposed to the physical, destructiveness of the weapon.

The first step in the attempt to suppress the truth about Hiroshima was to attack claims of radiation illness, and to deny authority to Japanese-sourced accounts of Hiroshima and Nagasaki. The dismissal of

Burchett was part of this. In the week after Burchett's claim of continuing radiation illness and residual radiation, Manhattan Project officials publicly attacked such claims several times. Statements by General Farrell and his chief, Major General Leslie Groves, appeared in the *New York Times* describing claims such as Burchett's as 'Japanese propaganda', and categorically denying any residual radiation effects.[19]

According to the Manhattan Project's official publicist and historian, *New York Times* science writer, William L. Laurence,

This historic ground in New Mexico, scene of the first atomic explosion on earth and cradle of a new era in civilization, gave the most effective answer to Japanese propaganda that radiations were responsible for deaths even the day after the explosion, Aug. 6 and that persons entering Hiroshima had contracted mysterious maladies due to persistent radioactivity. The Japanese are continuing their propaganda aimed at creating the impression that we won the war unfairly, and thus attempting to create sympathy for themselves . . . Thus, at the beginning, the Japanese described 'symptoms' that did not ring true. More recently they have sent in a radiologist, and since then the symptoms they describe appear to be more authentic on the surface, according to the radiologists present here today.[20]

In fact, Japanese radiologists and nuclear specialists had arrived in Hiroshima within days of the bombing: the first confirmation that the weapon that struck Hiroshima was an atomic bomb was provided by Japan's leading nuclear physicist, Yoshio Nishina, on 10 August. Systematic radiological soil sampling was commenced the same day by Kyoto Imperial University scientists, and continued around Hiroshima for the next week. Within two weeks of the bombing some twenty-five autopsies had been performed to establish the effects of radiation illness.[21] At that period, United States scientists were in no position to be authoritative: no US scientists entered either of the bombed cities until 9 September, six days after Burchett.

The US rebuttal did not stand up. Burchett, and his Japanese sources in Hiroshima, were quite right to stress the radiation effects of the bombing. Contrary to Groves's and Farrell's claims, many thousands of people became ill and died from exposure to radiation emitted from the bomb, principally gamma rays and neutrons. Burchett's newspaper account of people dying from the after-effects of the bomb without any visible injury is quite accurate:

For no apparent reason their health began to fail. They lost appetite. Their hair fell out. Bluish spots appeared on their bodies. And then bleeding began from the ears, nose and mouth. At first, doctors told me, they thought these were the symptoms of general debility. They gave their patients Vitamin A injections. The results were horrible. The flesh started rotting from the hole caused by the injection of the needle. And in every case the victim died.

Radiation deaths were still occurring in large numbers when Burchett visited the Communications hospital – and still occur today as the long-term effects of exposure to radiation are revealed in the form of a variety of blood diseases, leukaemia and other cancers.[22]

Burchett was also correct on the possibility of residual radiation at dangerous levels. Residual radiation comes mainly from irradiated materials that have turned into radio-isotopes and from particles of uranium from the bomb that escaped fission. As fallout, residual radiation could disperse widely and in an uneven pattern of concentration. Radio-isotopes thought to have been generated in the explosion had half-lives varying from a few minutes or hours (e.g. manganese 56, half-life 2.6 hours) through to several years (e.g. cesium 134, half-life 2.05 years). Japanese studies have concluded that 'the total gamma-ray dose from induced radiation up to 100 hours after the explosion one metre above the ground at the hypocentre in Hiroshima averaged about 100 rads' and fell off sharply away from the hypocentre. Fallout effects would be additional, and unevenly distributed according to weather patterns which prevailed after the bombing.[23]

These are certainly levels that could induce radiation illness either through direct exposure or through the breathing or swallowing of induced-radioactive material. In the days after the bombing many people entered the city to help and to search for relatives. Mortality rates cannot confirm the effects of residual radiation among these early entrants,[24] but morbidity rates among survivors certainly do. Immediate radiation effects were clear among substantial numbers who entered the hypocentre area within two or three days. In the long term, 'the crude mortality rate for leukaemia, according to the 1960 national census, was three times greater for those entering Hiroshima within three days after the bombing than the average crude leukaemia rate in all of Japan.'[25]

There had been great anxiety about the possibility of the atomic weapon rendering both cities biologically sterile in toto. The announcement by Tokyo Radio of the sprouting of the first green shoots in the late summer after the bombing was understandably a matter of great joy and relief.[26] Farrell returned to attack the credibility of Japanese witnesses and scientists on 19 September when he denied newspaper reports of biological sterility.[27]

In fact, temporary sterility among men was quite common, and Farrell's attack wrong. 'Since spermatogonia of the testis and follicular cells of the ovary are radio-sensitive, disturbance of the reproductive function was an inevitable consequence of exposure to the atomic bomb.'[28] The month after Burchett's visit, surveys of sperm of men exposed to the bomb showed that nineteen out of twenty-two men one kilometre or less from the hypocentre were effectively sterile. One third of a larger sample of men were sterile in late 1945. Within five years, the majority returned to normal fertility. Among women up to five kilometres from the hypocentre, some seventy per cent suffered irregular menstruation, and more ovarian disorders were common.[29] At this point growth disorders such as microcephaly (a smaller than normal head, often accompanied by mental retardation) as a result of exposure of children *in utero* to massive radiation had not yet emerged.

Immediately after Burchett's story on the radiation effects of the bomb was published, severe restrictions were applied to journalists, both Allied and Japanese. On 5 September, MacArthur's headquarters banned Allied journalists from Tokyo as MacArthur's troops prepared to enter the city. 'It is not military policy for correspondents to spearhead the occupation,' declared a spokesman for General MacArthur.[30] Hiroshima and Nagasaki were immediately placed out of bounds.

The most serious restriction on both journalistic reporting of Hiroshima and Nagasaki and public Japanese scientific and medical surveys was a series of civil-liberties and press codes issued by MacArthur's headquarters. Sophisticated censorship plans had been drawn up in April 1945 at MacArthur's Philippines headquarters in preparation for the expected Operation Olympic invasion in November 1945.[31]

The first civil-liberties code, issued on 10 September, was aimed at achieving 'an absolute minimum of restrictions upon freedom of speech'. The directive commanded the Japanese government to 'issue the necessary orders to prevent dissemination of news . . . which fails to adhere to the truth or which disturbs the public tranquillity'.[32]

In the following week the tranquillity of MacArthur's headquarters was disturbed on three fronts: public opinion at home, the Japanese media and the Japanese government. Each was to contribute to a tightening of censorship about the nuclear bombing. As wartime news restrictions were lifted, and prisoner-of-war camps liberated, appalling accounts of Japanese atrocities towards Allied soldiers flooded the front pages of Western newspapers. Far outweighing the coverage of the nuclear bombings, these stories whipped up an atmosphere of revenge where any suggestion of sympathy for the defeated was to be scourged. Newspaper reports from Tokyo carried the suggestion that the Allied powers were treating the conquered leniently. MacArthur's actions in Tokyo immediately came under scrutiny for evidence of 'softness towards the Japanese'.

In Japan, newspapers and radio were attempting to deal with Allied revelations of Imperial army war atrocities mainly by denial. *Asahi Shimbun* wrote: 'Virtually all Japanese who have read the report are unanimous in saying that the atrocities are hardly believable.'[33] As was to be the case for decades to come, Japanese anger over the use of the atomic bomb obliterated recognition and guilt of the atrocities of a decade of militarism. In some cases this continued the distortion and false reporting characteristic of the state-controlled media of wartime Japan, as when the Domei press agency defended the Empire, declaring, 'Japan might have won the war but for the atomic bomb, a weapon too terrible to face, and one which only barbarians would use.'[34]

The basic fact that a war crime of massive proportions had been

committed to bring down a ferociously militarist government provided
the ongoing grounds for the flawed moral challenge to the authority of
the Allied powers. On 15 September *Asahi Shimbun* reiterated the
argument of the Japanese cabinet when it described the use of the
atomic bomb as 'a breach of international law', which it most certainly
was. Two days later the paper argued that if it were correct, as the
occupying power argued, that Japanese atrocities in the Philippines had
led to Filipinos abandoning their previous support for the Japanese,
then would that not also apply to the Allied forces in Japan?[35]

MacArthur's headquarters was not only dealing with unrepentant
Japanese media and vengeful victorious American (and Australian)
public opinion, but also with a cynical Japanese government still
attempting to extract maximum political concessions from their con-
querors.

According to recently declassified US military intelligence documents, the US code-breaking system MAGIC intercepted the following
message from Foreign Minister Shigemitsu Mamoru on 13 September to
Japanese missions in Lisbon and Stockholm: 'The newspapers have
given wide publicity to the Government's recent memorandum concerning the atomic bomb damage to Hiroshima and Nagasaki . . . since the
Americans have recently been raising an uproar about the question of
our mistreatment of prisoners, I think we should make every effort to
exploit the atomic bomb question in our propaganda.'[36] This provided
MacArthur's hawks with the evidence they needed to justify the most
stringent censorship. The intercepted reply of the Japanese minister in
Stockholm was even more damaging. Why not, radioed the diplomat,
take a more subtle approach, and organize domestic Japanese reporting
of Hiroshima and Nagasaki to be picked up by overseas news bureaux?
Better still, have 'Anglo-American newspapermen write stories on the
bomb damage and thus create a powerful impression around the world'.

Burchett's article published a week earlier could not have come at a
worse time. All the justification the censors believed they needed was
presented to them. Victors' justice prevailed. The enraged MacArthur
ordered 'one hundred per cent censorship . . . No more false statements, no more misleading statements are to be permitted; no
destructive criticism of the Allied powers.'

The press code issued on 19 September was designed to educate the
Japanese by prescribing journalistic ethics:

1. News must strictly adhere to the truth.
2. Nothing shall be printed which might, directly or by inference,
   disturb the public tranquillity.
3. There shall be no false or destructive criticism of the Allied
   powers . . .
6. News stories must be factually written and completely devoid of
   editorial opinion.
7. News stories shall not be colored to conform with any propaganda
   line . . .

9. No news story shall be distorted by the omission of pertinent details.[37]

Pre-publication censorship was exercised by GHQ with any excisions to be rewritten properly, without black patches of ink or XXXs or any other hints of censorship. The pretence of free speech was vital to obtain the full effectiveness of the censorship.

The atomic bombings were a particular concern of the censors. To begin with the press code severely restricted spoken and written reporting about the bombed cities. No Japanese scientific or medical data could be published. It was not until the end of the occupation period in 1951 that newspaper photographs of the victims of the nuclear bombing, the *hibakusha*, showing the keloids on their bodies, were published by *Asahi Shimbun*. As a result of the censorship, all public discussion of the bomb damage, and all medical treatment reports, disappeared, greatly impeding both public understanding of what had taken place and the urgently needed diffusion of medical research and treatment information.

The press code was not applied simply to suppress unfavourable or critical or merely accurate reporting and discussion of the atomic bombings. Such discussion as was allowed had to be slanted in particular directions. According to Japanese historians, the only acceptable treatment of the bombing had to accept and reflect the view that the bombs shortened the war, and were effectively instruments of peace.[38] In April 1947, during the first mayoral election in Hiroshima which inaugurated the national civic democratization programme, a candidate was cut off in the middle of his radio speech by a US military observer because of his failure to comment on the bombing favourably.[39]

When the novelist Takashi Nagai attempted to publish his book *Nagasaki no Kane (The Bells of Nagasaki)*, he was told that it could appear only if a description of Japanese atrocities were added to the volume. But, as Lifton remarks, 'What the particular American, or groups of Americans, who made this decision did not realize was that the equation of the two was a tacit admission that dropping the bomb was also an atrocity.'[40] Not surprisingly, Lifton suggests that beneath the censorship policy's overt concern to minimize any possible retaliation against the victors, or succouring of resurgent militarism, there lay both American guilt and horror over the effects of the bombing, as well as what Lifton rather coyly refers to as 'wider American political concerns'.

Survivors of the bombing turned to writing as testimony to the holocaust. Many poems and other writings were distributed illegally. The Hiroshima poet, Sadako Kurihara, published her poem 'Let the Child be Born' in 1946 in a Hiroshima magazine edited by her husband. The poem, based on a story she had heard, is an evocation of life and its renewal amid otherwise unending suffering, which tells of a baby born in a cellar amid 'the smell of fresh blood, the stench of death':

'I am a midwife. Let me help the delivery,'
said one of the seriously wounded,
who just now was groaning.
So, in the depths of this gloomy hell,
a new life was born.
But before the light of the dawn the midwife,
still stained with blood, dies.
Let the child be born,
let the child be born,
even if it means throwing away one's own life.

After publishing this poem Kurihara and her husband were taken to
General Headquarters and interrogated about the poem, which was
held to violate the press code, and the unwritten code of suitable
treatments of the atomic bombing.[41]

One event in particular has come to symbolize the US censorship
approach. As part of the joint Japanese scientific and medical survey of
Hiroshima and Nagasaki, the film company Nippon Eiga-sha filmed
material for a comprehensive visual documentation of the effects of the
bombing. The film was immediately prohibited. When the Japanese
scientific survey staff protested, the US GHQ reversed its decision, and
allowed the filming to proceed. Then, in February 1946 when the
filming of the 11,000-foot *Effects of the Atom Bomb* (edited from 55,000
feet) was submitted to the US authorities, it was despatched to
Washington, together with all known prints and negatives. In fact, a
group of the film workers secretly hid ten reels of the film, and kept
their existence secret until the end of the occupation.[42]

Celebrating the Bomb

A still more profound form of distortion, one which was to have a
significant effect on Western understanding of nuclear war, becomes
evident if Burchett's article is compared with other accounts of
Hiroshima and Nagasaki by Allied journalists at the time. In the West,
the common images of the nuclear holocaust have always been
essentially technological, or more precisely, without human content.
The hands of the clock ticking towards midnight refer to the
machine-like and apparently inexorable move to the terminal explosion.
The most general image, the mushroom cloud, is even further removed
from the fate of human beings involved. The associations of the
billowing, Technicolored eruption are with an awesome and perhaps
terrible power but not at all with the human beings consumed within it.
Still less does that image suggest the responsibility of the human agency
involved – the pressing of the button and the decision that it should be
pressed.

Just how potent an effect this removal of the human element has had
on our imaginings of nuclear war is revealed by comparing it to the

common images of other twentieth-century horrors of war. The First World War produced an extraordinary set of visual and written images, but all essentially human in scale and implication – trenches, barbed wire, bodies in mud. The Nazi war on the Jews is remembered in the popular imagination by the concentration camp, the SS master and inmate-slave, guards and the almost unbelievable industrialized killing of the gas chambers. But, however far beyond the experience of the watcher, the images are still on a human scale, a direct signification of human suffering. This is not true of our understanding of Hiroshima and Nagasaki. In part, this is a matter of censorship and suppression. But as a comparison of Burchett's account and that of his contemporaries shows, there was another level of distortion involved.

In contrast to the policy of suppressing critical accounts of the effects of the atomic bombing, 'articles that publicized the power of the atomic bomb were warmly welcomed by GHQ'.[43] What was to become the dominant attitude to the nuclear bombing was clear to the Japanese at the very beginning. As some of them wrote later:

A group of American reporters who visited Hiroshima on 3 September 1945 expressed satisfaction with the complete destruction of the city. At a press conference held at the prefectural office, a *New York Times* reporter [W.H. Lawrence] noted the total devastation of the city and extolled the obvious superiority of the bomb's potential. Some Japanese reporters present at this press conference raised questions from the standpoint of the bomb's victims . . . but [Lawrence] refused to answer such questions. His concern was solely with the power of the bomb: its victims interested him only as proof of that might.[44]

The day Burchett's 'Atomic Plague' article was published in the *Daily Express*, W.H. Lawrence, one of the Pentagon press team, wrote of his visit to Hiroshima in the *New York Times*.[45] A reading of the long article substantiates the Japanese reporters' comments on the press conference. Lawrence and his party landed at Kure Naval Base near Hiroshima, and toured the city with a Japanese naval surgeon, speaking occasionally to witnesses. There is no indication that he visited any hospital or medical relief station.

The dominant concern of this description of Hiroshima is the physical damage which made it 'the world's most damaged city, worse than Warsaw or Stalingrad that held the record for Europe'. The tour of the rubble, amid the decay of the remaining bodies, is interspersed with brief coverage of the medical situation, but without any of Burchett's attempts to portray the situation of the burn and radiation victims in the hospitals. Lawrence wrote vaguely that

Japanese doctors told us they were helpless to deal with burns caused by the bomb's great flash *or with the other physical ailments caused by the bomb* . . . They told us that persons who had been only slightly injured on the day of the blast lost 86 per cent of their white blood corpuscles, their hair began to drop out, they lost appetites, vomited blood and finally died. [Emphasis added.]

Surprisingly for experienced journalists, the party made no apparent attempt to substantiate these dramatic claims, or to expand on them. Astonishingly, the presumably well-briefed journalists of the official party made no explicit reference to the effects of radiation. As we have already seen, Lawrence reported the official refutation of Japanese-sourced claims of widespread radiation illness after his return to Tokyo without referring to his own visit. In his report on a visit to Nagasaki, again largely concerned with physical damage, he said, 'I am convinced that, horrible as the bomb undoubtedly is, the Japanese are exaggerating its effects in an effort to win sympathy for themselves in an attempt to make the American people forget the long record of cold-blooded Japanese bestiality.'[46]

Echoing the emerging official US justification for retaining a monopoly of nuclear-weapons use, Lawrence went on, 'It should be the last evidence needed to convince any doubter of the need to retain and perfect our air offense lest the fate of Hiroshima or Nagasaki be repeated in Indianapolis or Washington or Detroit or New York.'

Lawrence's basic attitude, and the one which was to underpin the dominant 'official' meaning of Hiroshima that came to be constructed, is clear from his comment on his own feelings: 'A visit to Hiroshima is an experience to leave one shaken by the terrible, incredible sights. Here is the final proof of what the mechanical and scientific genius of America has been able to accomplish in war.'

Three themes had by now emerged in officially sanctioned American coverage of the nuclear bombing. The first was that the bombs were a just and necessary contribution to world peace, and that a continued US nuclear monopoly would maintain the peace. The second was that the most important quality of the bombs to be emphasized was their physical power. The human consequences were to be conceded so far as was necessary to establish the claim of technological omnipotence, but were otherwise to be ignored or suppressed. Together these made possible an otherwise difficult result: the elimination of any legitimate perspective other than that of the victors and their power.

The contrast between Burchett's view of the bombings and the duty of the journalist becomes even more clear when Burchett's writing on Hiroshima is compared with that of another *New York Times* writer, William L. Laurence (not to be confused with W.H. Lawrence).[47] Seconded from his newspaper to the Manhattan Project, Laurence became the official publicist and historian of the first nuclear weapons. As a science writer he had written on the possibility of nuclear weapons before the war, and been given the task of explaining the atomic bomb to the world public, including writing the statement with which President Truman announced the first atomic bombing.

Laurence witnessed the Trinity test at Alamogordo on 16 July 1945, and accompanied the USAF 509th Bombing Group to Tinian later that month. Listening to Truman's announcement on the radio, he wrote of his pride as a journalist: 'The world's greatest story was being broadcast, and mine had been the honor, unique in the history of journalism, of preparing the War Department's official press release for worldwide distribution. No greater honor could come to any newspaperman, or anyone else for that matter.'[48]

Two days later Laurence flew in an observer plane in the attack on Nagasaki, about which he wrote a long account published a month later in the *New York Times*.[49] For Laurence the Nagasaki plutonium bomb was 'a thing of beauty to behold, this "gadget" '.

> Being close to it and watching it as it was being fashioned into a living thing, so exquisitely shaped that any sculptor would be proud to have created it, one somehow crossed the borderline between reality and non-reality and felt oneself in the presence of the supernatural. Could it be that this innocent-looking object, so beautifully designed, so safe to handle, could in much less time than it takes to wink an eye annihilate an entire city and its population?

Just as his near-namesake Lawrence had conceived of the bombing as an expression of 'the mechanical and scientific genius of America', Laurence saw the bomb in spiritual and aesthetic terms that rendered the deathly qualities of the weapon somehow invisible. The aesthetic, moral, political and scientific claims were interwoven and mutually reinforcing.

In imagery redolent of alienated power and sexuality, the result – the result of the exquisite technology that Laurence recognizes in his transcendent adoration – is a cloud that lives:

> The mushroom top was even more alive than the pillar, seething and boiling in a white fury of creamy foam, sizzling upward and then descending earthward, a thousand geysers rolled into one. It kept struggling in an elemental fury, like a creature in the act of breaking the bonds that held it down . . . It was as though the decapitated monster was growing a new head.

Death and responsibility were banished. In the air over Nagasaki, Laurence – apparently for the only time – addressed himself to the moral question: 'Does one feel any pity or compassion for the poor devils about to die? Not when one thinks of Pearl Harbor and of the Death March on Bataan.'

This standard American defence of the slaughter of the civilians who made up the target was hypocrisy. One might suppose that the innocents below had participated in these events.

As well as establishing the innocence of the bomb, another important supportive myth was being created here, that of the clean atom: 'I saw the atomic substance [i.e. plutonium] before it was placed inside the

bomb. By itself it is not dangerous to handle.' Laurence returned to
Alamagordo after the Nagasaki bombing, and from there wrote the 12
September attack on Burchett and the Japanese-sourced claims of large
numbers of radiation deaths.[50]

It is very hard to imagine a more complete contrast between two
approaches to journalism than that between Burchett and Laurence.
Laurence provides the archetype for Robert Lifton's study of nuclearism – that late-twentieth-century secular religion 'in which "grace" and
even "salvation" – the mastery of death and evil – are achieved through
the power of a new technological deity . . . capable not only of death
and destruction but also unlimited creation.'[51] For Laurence, the
dropping of the nuclear bomb on Hiroshima was a point in a secular
crusade for the new religion. In this new muscular deism, there was no
place for the victims of the holocaust; only a transcendent fusion of
technology and the power that directed it.

'The Alienation is Temporary, the Humanity Imminent.'

Burchett himself was not innocent of this predominantly masculine
worship of technology. As a war correspondent in the Pacific, Burchett
had not expected to survive the war. While he was more radical than
most and anticipated the emergence of post-colonial Asia with
sympathy, Burchett was in some respects a typical male war correspondent.

In *Democracy with a Tommygun*, apparently written in the last year
of the war (the chapter on Hiroshima is 'A Postscript'), Burchett
describes LeMay's US Air Force firebombing of Japanese cities from
November 1944 in glowing and admiring terms. Writing here of the
long-range bombing campaign Burchett praised the wonder of 'American planning, production and organization'. The aircraft in question,
the B-29, evoked Burchett's greatest admiration, as a specifically
American achievement: 'The Superfortress, apart from being able to
deliver heavier bombloads farther than any other plane, is also the most
beautiful aircraft yet produced. Smoothly tapering like an artist's brush
handle, it rides like a feathered dart.'[52] This worship of American
technology then carries over into a description of the Tokyo fire raid of
10 March 1945: 'The world's greatest incendiary target had been
touched off by the war's greatest incendiary raid. Never since the great
fire of London had there been a conflagration as started early that
Saturday morning in the centre of downtown Tokyo, where in the most
inflammable portion of the city, the population density exceeds 100,000
people per square mile.'[53]

In a description very similar to that of W.H. Lawrence describing
Hiroshima in statistics, Burchett tells the externals of that appalling
night, essentially from the perspective of the pilots and aircrew whose

lives and dangers he shared. That night went beyond even the horrors of
Dresden and Hamburg. The United States Air Force had developed the
napalm bomb especially for the firing of Japanese cities.[54] To test the
new incendiaries developed for the highly inflammable Japanese cities,
the air force built a miniature Japanese city block, complete with rooms
and furniture. A nearby army firefighting team was then equipped with
Japanese fire equipment and pitted against the new products. When the
new jellied petroleum bomb produced a fire that defeated the
firefighters, the researchers knew they had met the air force's
requirements. Several hundred B-29s, carrying six tons of napalm or
oil-filled incendiaries apiece, each blanketed an area 2,500 feet by 500
feet with burning gasoline.[55] A factory worker, Hidezo Tsuchikura,
spoke of the scenes among the 750,000 people trapped in the world's
most crowded urban area when 100,000 died:

> Fire winds with burning particles ran up and down the streets. I
> watched people, adults and children, running for their lives, dashing
> madly about like rats. Flames ran after them like living things,
> striking them down. They died by the hundreds in front of me . . .
> The whole spectacle with its blinding lights and thundering noise
> reminded me of the paintings of purgatory – a real inferno out of the
> depths of hell.[56]

What is striking, and to Burchett's credit, is that as soon as he actually
saw the human results of the work of his comrades of the past year, he
immediately responded: in the plain and decent prose of his Hiroshima
account he described the unprecedented suffering before him which
amounted to what he called 'the watershed in my life'.

Burchett's reversion to a shared humanity paralleled that of many
who had completely supported the war's aims in the Pacific. An
Australian prisoner of war who reached Hiroshima a few days later
wrote of the immediate transformation of his consuming hatred:
'. . . we felt no sense of either history or triumph. Our brother man
went by crippled and burned, and we knew only shame and guilt . . .
Our hatred for the Japanese was swept away by the enormity of what we
had seen.'[57]

At the heart of war is a profound alienation from the enemy, an
alienation experienced as hatred, fear and a sundering of any possibility
of communion or fellow feeling. But, as Michael Walzer has put it, 'The
alienation [of the enemy] is temporary, the humanity imminent.'[58]
Burchett and the POW both experienced what the religious call the
conversion of the heart, which makes possible a reconstitution of a
shared humanity, and that was the position from which Burchett wrote
his warning from the hospitals of Hiroshima.

At the heart of the state is the legitimation of its right to violence and
its right to demand that the citizen take part in organized violence. As a
result, states are always engaged in a contest of legitimation with their
peoples – legitimation, not of this regime rather than that, but

legitimation of the right of war. Such rights are never wholly accepted, wholeheartedly, by the whole population, in societies divided by sex and class, and the humanity of the enemy is always in danger of erupting through the state-managed artifice of hatred and alienation. But in the twentieth century, legitimation of the violence of the state has become at the same time more contingent and more necessary than before.

Hiroshima, while so marked a turning point in some ways, is in other respects simply the culmination (or more pessimistically, the lowest point so far) of a trend towards a loss of restraint over the slaughter of civilians that has marked this century. In each war, the proportion of civilians killed as a proportion of the dead has risen steadily. Most important in this trend has been 'the terrific growth of air warfare, and the sweeping disregard for all humane limitations on bombardment from the air. This has produced an extent of devastation, and in some part a degradation of living conditions, that has not been approached since the end of the Thirty Years' War.'

Writing in 1945 before the atomic bomb was dropped on Hiroshima, Liddell Hart continued: 'It is the combination of an unlimited aim with an unlimited method – the adoption of a demand for total surrender together with a strategy of total blockade and bombing devastation – which, in this war, has inevitably produced a deepening danger to the relatively shallow foundations of civilized life.'[59]

The need for legitimation of this new stage of total warfare grew from the resistance to unthinking – or unfeeling – acquiescence in what was palpably atrocious, justifiable, if at all, only by a calculation of means and ends. The American justification was, in fact, widely challenged, both at a political level and by the immediate revulsion felt by many. At the time Burchett wrote, public opinion was quite mixed about the nuclear bombing, and the American justification was by no means universally accepted. The day after the Hiroshima bombing the Vatican had expressed serious concern.[60] US newspapers reported widespread European concern and dismay: the *New York Times* ran an article three days after the bombing headed 'Britons Revolted by Use of Atom-Bomb'. At home, the *New York Sun* claimed that 'the entire city is pervaded by a sense of oppression. Many feel they would have been happier if the 2,000,000,000-dollar experiment had failed, or the knowledge had been thrown in the river like an unwanted kitten.'[61]

Before long an argument emerged that a principal reason for the haste to use the bomb was as a warning to the Soviet Union, and to end the war before the wartime ally would have to be included in a Pacific settlement of Japan. This was buttressed by the report of the United States Strategic Bombing Survey of Japan which concluded that even without the nuclear bombing, Japan could not have continued the war for more than a few months, and that an invasion costing many Allied lives would not have been necessary. All that was at stake was the speed of victory.[62]

It was a time of historic decision, if only the collective means could be found to make it. Burchett sensed it, and wrote his warning to the world with that aim. In this setting, legitimation of the atomic bombing was not at all certain, and since the United States rapidly decided to build its post-war global dominance around a nuclear monopoly, securing public aquiescence was of paramount importance. The uncensored discoveries of Burchett about the effects of radiation illness needed to be stopped, and an official interpretation rendered secure.

Military and foreign policy is always the least democratic area of state decision, but on nuclear matters the state resolved that it would tolerate no serious public discussion of the option of not using the bomb. US state managers were not sure of the reactions of the American people. As National Security Council Document No. 30 of 1948 put it:

> In this matter, public opinion must be recognized as a factor of considerable importance. Deliberation or decision on a subject of this significance, even if clearly affirmative, might have the effect of placing before the American people a moral question of vital significance at a time when the full security impact of the question had not become apparent. If this decision is to be made by the American people, it should be made in the circumstances of an actual emergency when the principal factors are in the forefront of public consideration.[63]

Popular involvement in decisions of the nuclear state was seen as a risk that could be taken only at a time of war fever, when the possibility of a calm and informed decision could be minimized. The silence of Hiroshima is a crucial part of the nuclear state's strategy of maintaining that perpetual alienation of the enemy. Burchett's small voice from Hiroshima helped to render the imminent shared humanity palpable, helped to make possible a collective decision to refuse acquiescence in the next nuclear war. 'One of evil's principal modes of being,' says John Berger, 'is looking beyond (with indifference) that which is before the eyes.'[64] Evil, in this sense, is organized and orchestrated by state and mass media, but never quite successfully. 'In visiting Hiroshima, I felt that I was seeing in the last hour of WW2 what would be the fate of hundreds of cities in a WW3. If that does not make a journalist want to shape history in the right direction, what does? Or should?'[65]

Notes

I am grateful for the help of friends in formulating the ideas in this chapter, and for reading earlier drafts: my thanks to Ben Kiernan, Gavan McCormack, Alison French, Joel Kovel, John Wiseman, Peter Christoff, Belinda Probert and Joan Clarke.

1. Letter to David Gourlay, 9 July 1980.
2. *Shadows of Hiroshima*, Verso, London, 1983, pp.8–9.
3. Burchett told the story of how he got to Hiroshima a number of times in published form. The first is in 'Hiroshima: A Postscript' in his *Democracy with a Tommygun* (F.W. Cheshire, Melbourne, 1946); again in his autobiographies *Passport* (Nelson,

Melbourne, 1969) and *At the Barricades* (1980); and finally in *Shadows of Hiroshima* (London, Verso, 1983). The story of Burchett's trip to Hiroshima and back as told here is drawn from all three.

4. One other journalist also broke through official restrictions at the time and reached Nagasaki. George Weller of the Chicago *Daily News* avoided military public relations 'hawks' and reached Nagasaki by subterfuge on 6 September. The 25,000-word article he wrote on the basis of interviews with witnesses and medical workers was much more detailed than Burchett's. 'As a loyal, disciplined member of the press corps, I sent the material to MacArthur's press headquarters for clearance and transmission . . . The paper . . . received nothing. MacArthur had "killed" the lot.' (*At the Barricades*, p.116.)

5. For the well-founded fears of the Emperor's circle see Pacific War Research Society, *Japan's Longest Day*, Kodansha International, Tokyo, 1980.

6. *Passport*, p.167. Burchett later quotes one of the remaining doctors as saying that they knew they were not dealing with an infection, but that use of these masks provided some comfort in the face of an otherwise incomprehensible experience.

7. Committee for the Compilation of Materials on Damage Caused by the Atomic Bombs in Hiroshima and Nagasaki; *Hiroshima and Nagasaki: the Physical Medical and Social Effects of the Atomic Bombings* , Hutchinson, London, 1981, p.516.

8. Ibid., p.519.

9. Ibid., pp.130ff.

10. The piece that was published in the *Daily Express* on 6 September 1945 was slightly altered by an editor who thought 'poor Peter [Burchett]' had been overcome by the sights of the inferno, and who inserted some gratuitous paragraphs from the Science Editor. The article is reprinted in *Shadows* and in Harry Gordon (ed.), *The Eyewitness History of Australia*, Currey O'Neill, Melbourne, 1981, pp. 361–2.

11. *Shadows*, p.41.

12. *Passport*, p.173.

13. *Hiroshima and Nagasaki*, op.cit., p.15.

14. *Passport*, p.172. In the various published versions of the story, Burchett repeatedly acknowledged the support he received from several of the veteran war correspondents in the official party who protested at this unprofessional behaviour.

15. *Passport*, pp.174–5. A contemporary account of Burchett's POW-camp exploits by Jim Vine was published in the Brisbane *Courier-Mail*, 11 September 1945, and reprinted in Gordon, op.cit., p.364. Burchett must have been the source. Burchett mentions encounters in the Kyoto-Tsuruga area and Kobe-Osaka. Vine places the liberated camps as two on the west coast of Honshu and three on the Inland Sea.

16. *Shadows*, pp.22–3.

17. Even as late as 1970 Burchett still accepted that initial explanation (*Passport*, p.176). Presumably his reassessment of the probable link between his own low white-blood-cell count and his exposure to residual radiation in Hiroshima began when he returned to Hiroshima for the first time a year later.

18. *Shadows*, p.9.

19. Farrell is reported in an article in the *New York Times*, 13 September 1945, p.4 by W.H. Lawrence and datelined Tokyo; Groves's statement is reported by William L. Laurence in the *NYT*, 12 September 1945, pp. 1,4 in an article, datelined New Mexico, 9 September, delayed.

20. Laurence, ibid.

21. *Hiroshima and Nagasaki*, p.504.

22. Ibid., pp. 73–9.

23. Ibid.

24. Ibid., p.243.

25. Ibid., p.270.

26. *New York Times*, 7 September 1945, p.7.

27. *Hiroshima and Nagasaki*, op.cit., p.616.

28. Ibid., p.151.

29. Ibid., pp.152–3.

30. *New York Times*, 5 September 1945, cited in *Shadows*, op.cit., p.23.

31. Marlene J. Mayo, 'Civil Censorship and Media Control in Early Occupied Japan: From Minimum to Stringent Surveillance', Robert Wolfe (ed.), *Americans as Proconsuls: United States Military Government in Germany and Japan, 1944–1952*, Southern Illinois University Press, Carbondale, 1984, pp.292–3. Mayo's important new study of US censorship policy is based on recently declassified US official documents. However, she devotes no attention to the question of censorship of the effects of the atomic bombing.

32. Toshio Nishi, *Unconditional Democracy: Education and Politics in Occupied Japan, 1945–1952*, Hoover Institution Press, Stanford, 1982, pp.86–7.

33. *New York Times*, 18 September 1945.

34. Nishi, op.cit., p.87.

35. Ibid., p.88.

36. Mayo, op.cit., p.294

37. Nishi, op.cit., pp.88–9.

38. Ibid., p.101.

39. Ibid., p.102. Robert J. Lifton, *Death in Life: the Survivors of Hiroshima*, Weidenfeld and Nicolson, London, 1968, p.329.

40. Lifton, op.cit.

41. For the story of the poem and its full text see Rokuro Hidaka, *The Price of Affluence: Dilemmas of Contemporary Japan*, Penguin Australia, Ringwood, 1985, pp.30–1. See also Lifton, op.cit. p.329. Hidaka also reproduces her more recent, critical, reflections on the meaning of Hiroshima for Japan.

42. *Hiroshima and Nagasaki*, op.cit., p.510; Nishi, op.cit., p.102. The film was eventually returned in 1967 after a Japanese campaign, but even then could not be seen by the Japanese public, or the victims: 'The Ministry of Education, however, did not fully release the film to the public, reasoning that much of it would violate the privacy of those people who had been exposed to the bombs and that it contained too many cruel scenes.' Ibid.

43. *Hiroshima and Nagasaki*, op.cit., p.14.

44. Ibid., p.15.

45. 'Visit to Hiroshima Proves It World's Most Damaged City', *New York Times*, 5 September 1945, pp.1,4.

46. 'Atom Bomb Killed Nagasaki Captives', *New York Times*, 10 September 1945, pp.1,5.

47. Burchett – and the chroniclers of *Hiroshima and Nagasaki* – confuse the two *New York Times* reporters, W.H. Lawrence, the war correspondent in Hiroshima the same day as Burchett, and W.L. Laurence, the Manhattan Project publicist. In one passage Burchett tries to work out how and why Laurence/Lawrence took so long to publish his Hiroshima account after visiting Hiroshima the same day as Burchett (Lawrence's report was in fact published the day before Burchett's), and why he moved backwards and forwards across the Pacific. That Burchett has confused the two is clear from pp. 18–19 of *Shadows*, where the author of the *New York Times* article 'No radioactivity in Hiroshima ruin', datelined 'Tokyo, 13 Sept.' is given as W.H. Laurence (in the original *Times* by-line, W.H. Lawrence). The author of the article 'US Atom Bomb Site Belies Tokyo Tales', datelined 'Atom Bomb Range, New Mexico, Sept. 9' is correctly given as William L. Laurence. The chroniclers of *Hiroshima and Nagasaki* also note the presence at a press conference in Hiroshima on 3 September 1945 of 'W.L. Laurence' rather than W.H. Lawrence, (p.15). To make matters worse, Robert Lifton's discussion of W.L. Laurence and nuclearism refers to 'William L. Lawrence'.

48. William L. Laurence, *Dawn Over Zero*, Alfred Knopf, New York, 1947, p.224.

49. 'Atomic Bombing of Nagasaki Told by Flight Member', *New York Times*, (9 Aug. delayed), 9 September 1945, pp.1,35. The same material was later included in *Dawn Over Zero*.

50. 'US Atom Bomb Site Belies Tokyo Tales', *New York Times*, 12 September 1945, pp.1,4.

51. *The Broken Connection*, Touchstone, New York, 1980, pp.371–6.

52. *Democracy with a Tommygun*, p.238.

53. Ibid., p.242.

40 RICHARD TANTER

54. Gene Gurney, 'The Giant Pays Its Way', in James F. Sunderman (ed.), *World War II in the Air: The Pacific*, Watts, New York, 1962. p.249.
55. Ibid., p.258; see also, Wesley Frank Caven and James Lea Cate (eds.), *The Army Air Forces in World War 2*. Volume 5 – 'The Pacific: Matterhorn to Nagasaki', University of Chicago Press, Chicago and London, 1953.
56. Cited in John Costello, *The Pacific War*, Rawson, New York, 1981, p.551.
57. Kenneth Harrison, *Road to Hiroshima*, Rigby, Adelaide, 1983, pp.15, 267.
58. Michael Walzer, *Just and Unjust Wars: an Argument with Historical Illustrations*, Penguin, Harmondsworth, 1980, p.142.
59. B.H. Liddell Hart, *The Revolution in Warfare*, Faber and Faber, London, 1946, pp.67, 74.
60. *New York Times*, 8 August 1945, p.1.
61. Reported in 'Fears of "Atomic" Wars in US', *Herald*, Melbourne, 9 August 1945, p.2.
62. See, for example, P.M.S. Blackett, *Fear, War and the Bomb*, McGraw-Hill, New York, 1949. In one of Clio's little ironies, the leader of the bombing survey in Japan was Paul Nitze, a leading nuclear advocate for the Committee on the Present Danger forty years later.
63. Cited by Peter Pringle and William Arkin in *SIOP: Nuclear War from the Inside*, Sphere, London, 1983, p.28.
64. John Berger, 'Hiroshima – a portrait of evil', *New Society*, 6 August 1981, p.222.
65. Wilfred Burchett, letter to David Gourlay, 9 July 1980.

3

Burchett and the Cold War in Europe

Kelvin Rowley

During his youthful wanders around an Australia in the grip of the
Great Depression, Wilfred Burchett was deeply impressed by a man he
remembered as 'Greybeard'. This man had organized a camp for the
unemployed on the banks of the Murray River near Mildura, and he was
the first communist Burchett ever met. He had been told that
communists were rat-bags and troublemakers, but 'Greybeard' shattered the image.

He was hard-headed and practical, and had devoted his life to the
cause of the oppressed. 'He was kindly, warm, unselfish and, I was sure,
very brave. He had the qualities I used to learn about in Sunday School
as those everyone should strive to cultivate.' The others in the camp
looked up to him as their 'natural leader'.[1]

By the time he left for Europe in 1936 Burchett had already come to
see communists as steadfast fighters for the rights of the common
people, and the most resolute opponents of fascism. His pre-Europe
experiences did much to sharpen his political attitudes. When he arrived
in England, Burchett intended to fight with the International Brigade in
Spain. But the brigade's recruiting committee turned him down, and he
found work in a travel agency. In 1938 he went to Nazi Germany.

Burchett arrived just after the vicious anti-Semitic pogrom of 10
November 1938 (*kristallnacht*). Many of his contacts were with its

helpless and terrified victims. But he also met some of those responsible
for the terror. In his memoirs, he relates an encounter in Frankfurt:

> . . . soon Ernst Kurt, Rudi, Pauli and Wilfried – as they insisted on
> calling me – were gathered around a bottle of schnapps and many
> bottles of beer. They could have been blood brothers: blond, stocky,
> tanned and blue, blue eyes. I was introduced as a *wunderbarer Kerl*, a
> wonderful chap . . . The previous night Ernst and Pauli had *fertig
> gemacht* ('bumped off') a Jewish tailor who lived on the road into
> Frankfurt by hauling him on to the road, beating him up, and then
> running their car over him as he tried to get to his feet. If I wanted to
> see some real fun, they knew where there was another one we could
> 'get' on the way into town. By this time I was thoroughly alarmed.
> Pleading great fatigue (it was already 2 a.m.) and an early-morning
> engagement, I threw myself on their generosity and hospitality to get
> me to my hotel as soon as possible . . . In front of the airport two cars
> were parked. To mark the end of this notable international
> encounter, they kicked in the headlights of one, and we clambered
> into the other. After a long and scary drive on the snow-covered road,
> they delivered me to my hotel, where they frightened a sleepy night
> clerk into giving a 'friend of the Führer' the best available room.[2]

As Burchett saw it, fascism was little more than outright gangsterism.
Dealing with it was a struggle of moral right against moral wrong, not a
matter of diplomacy.

Burchett returned to Australia in 1939, filled with anti-fascist fervour.
But he found it difficult to get his view across:

> To relate my German experiences of the past few months to anything
> within the comprehension of easygoing, tolerant Australians was very
> difficult. To talk of the Gestapo, concentration camps, and the lower
> depths of human beastliness while the blue smoke curled up and lamb
> chops sizzled in a pan on a weekend picnic – it all seemed too
> fantastic, too remote and unreal. The cultured Germans simply could
> not behave like that . . .[3]

For the British government, anxiously supported by the Australian
government, was trying to deal with Hitler by diplomatic means. The
outcome was, of course, appeasement.

Burchett wrote letters to papers attacking appeasement, but they
were not published. Unknown to him, the Australian press was under
conservative government pressure to avoid 'needless provocation' and
'abusive criticism' that would offend the sensitivities of Hitler and
Mussolini, in the hope of creating an atmosphere that would facilitate
'conversations' with the Germans.[4] The press willingly acquiesced: it
was not only 'free', but 'responsible' as well.

After Hitler invaded Poland and Britain declared war on Germany all
this changed. Burchett's first article appeared in the Sydney *Sunday*

Telegraph in November 1939. Over the next few months he published numerous articles in Melbourne newspapers. His approach was a simple, militant anti-fascist one. Neither British-Australian dithering during the 'Phony War', nor the Nazi-Soviet Non-aggression Pact weakened his fervour. Such diplomatic manoeuvring did not interest him, although the local communists had loyally supported the Soviet position, opposing the 'imperialist war-mongers' in Britain, France and the US as well as in Germany.

Burchett became a journalist because he wanted to arouse the reading public to the dangers of fascism. His early articles were reportage of a highly propagandist nature. During the war, however, he did not stand out because of this; most reporters liberally sprinkled their articles with democratic and anti-fascist exhortations, and downplayed the mistakes and atrocities committed in what they saw as the right cause.

One feature of the wartime political climate needs to be emphasized. In Britain and Australia, the war began under the auspices of the conservative circles whose policies had led to the débâcle of appeasement. Many of them feared a radical social and political upheaval more than they feared Nazi expansion. For Bob Menzies, the Australian Prime Minister when the war broke out, the objective was the preservation of a liberal, British-dominated international order which had become threatened by reckless violence.

A week after Hitler launched his *blitzkrieg* against Poland, Menzies wrote a personal letter to S.M. Bruce, the Australian High Commissioner in London, explaining his views. It was essentially a war for 'law and order' in Europe. He feared that a long war would accelerate the breakdown of order. Fortunately, however, 'Hitler has no desire for a first-class war.' Thus, Menzies hoped, an understanding could be reached with Hitler once he had crushed Poland. 'Nobody,' Menzies added, 'gives a damn about Poland as such.' The idea of fighting for the destruction of the Nazi regime was, he thought, 'indefensible'.[5]

Such attitudes were soon overwhelmed by a wave of anti-Nazi outrage. As the war widened, in Australia, Britain and the US, its objectives were increasingly depicted in radical-democratic rather than conservative terms. It became a war to wipe out fascism and usher in the better world promised by progressive ideals. Burchett was more in step with popular opinion than Menzies, whose government in Canberra soon collapsed and was replaced by a Labor administration.

After Hitler invaded the USSR in 1941, the Soviet Union ceased to be a pariah and became a valued ally of the Western democracies. It was praised by wartime leaders as conservative as Winston Churchill and General Douglas MacArthur, and the theme was widely taken up in the press. In 1943, for example, *Life* magazine informed its readers that the Russians were 'one hell of a people . . . [who] to a remarkable degree . . . look like Americans and think like Americans', and that the NKVD (Stalin's dreaded political police) was a 'national police similar to the FBI'.[6]

Burchett had supported a 'Popular Front' to fight against fascism and defend radical-democratic ideals in the 1930s. With the 'Grand Alliance' between the US, Britain and the USSR, this aspiration had become the basic reality of international politics. It is not surprising that Burchett passionately supported the alliance and hoped that great things would flow from it once the fascist enemy had been destroyed.

'A Negation of Our Hopes'

Burchett covered the war in the Pacific, and by 1945 was a seasoned war correspondent. He came back to Germany on New Year's Eve, 1945 – hoping to see the birth of a 'New World'. He later wrote:

> Was it impossibly naïve to think in terms of a 'new world' arising out of the ashes of World War II? It did not seem so at the time. The prospect of some more equitable social order at home and some new deal in international relations was at least partly what enabled the leaders of the anti-fascist countries to mobilize the energies and enthusiasms of their people and have them accept the hardships and sacrifices imposed by the costliest war in history . . . For me, a 'new world' would be one in which, at the least, the old colonial system would have no place, and wartime's friendly relations between the West and Soviet Union would be continued and developed in the post-war years.[7]

Burchett had been appalled by Germany in 1938, and he did not like it much more in 1946. The German people were distressingly unreconstructed.

> My first visit to a German family – a few days after I arrived – was to a mother and grown-up daughter, Helga, in the fashionable west end of Berlin.
> After a few words of general conversation there came a furious tirade against the Russians which was new to me then – at least from German lips.
> 'Why did you British and Americans wait so long on the Elbe?' questioned Helga. 'We were waiting to welcome you with open arms. Instead of that you let the Russians come. Those savages. Those barbarians . . . You let those Mongol apes loose on a cultivated people like us, to rob, rape and destroy us.' . . . At one point the mother paused between mouthfuls of gruel and bread to interrupt.
> 'You know, Helga, our soldiers didn't always behave as they ought to have done at the front,' she said in a mild understatement.
> Helga straightened up and flushed. 'Mutti,' she screamed, 'I won't have you saying things like that about our troops. German soldiers and German troops are always correct. They couldn't have behaved like these . . . these . . .', and she sought for a term sufficiently vile,

'these Slavic gutter pigs. They should be our slaves and would have been but for that awful winter at Stalingrad.' I thought at the time that Helga was an exception, a candidate for a lunatic asylum, but I soon realized she was the normal spokesman for the Berlin upper middle class.[8]

Burchett also found that many British officers and officials in Berlin sympathized with the German 'enemy' rather than their Soviet 'allies'. 'The bars and clubs resounded with anti-Russian stories and it was particularly noticeable that it was just those officers who had no combat experience who were the most vocal about the necessity for, and ease with which, the Russians had to be "pushed back into their own country".'

In this atmosphere, Burchett spent much of his time in Germany checking out Western allegations against the Soviets, and Soviet accusations against the Western powers. Which side was undermining the wartime alliance? Burchett came to believe it was the US.

In a letter he wrote to his brother in 1947, he describes a fairly typical venture:

I spent most of last week checking a story put out in an official US army report that large bands of the Ukrainian Independence Army were crossing from Czechoslovakia into the American zone of Germany having engaged Soviet and Polish divisions in Poland during June and July, and since having fought their way through the whole of Czechoslovakia. Units between 15,000 and 20,000 strong had been engaged in the fighting. The report said another 1,500 to 2,500 were expected across the border by Sunday, 21 September. I drove altogether 1,350 miles to check the story. Right down to Passan, the lovely Bavarian town bordering the frontiers of Czechoslovakia and Austria through which the army was supposed to be passing. None of the locals had seen or heard of any Ukrainian soldiers. After most pressing enquiries the chief of US Intelligence on the spot said, actually they had rounded up a total of fifty-four rag-and-tag men who said they had fought with the Ukrainian Independence Army. On the basis of reports from these fifty-four, the whole story had been cooked up. And that's the way it works brother.[9]

Burchett decided that most of the accusations against the Soviets were baseless, and that they played into the hands of the real enemy – the Nazis.

On the other hand, he decided that there was much truth in Soviet charges that American and British policy was motivated more by anti-communism than by anti-fascism. In *Cold War in Germany*, he documented the conservative, business-orientated background of many of the American and British officials responsible for Western policy in Germany. He noted that key British officials in Germany had been actively involved in the débâcle of appeasement. To Burchett, these were essentially men of the shabby pre-war era, not of the 'New World' he was looking for.

Burchett charged that the Western powers were protecting former Nazis. By 1949, he said, West Germany had been made 'safe for the Nazis'.[10] Outrage bred exaggeration, but Western efforts at de-Nazification were indeed tardy, despite the publicity given to the Nuremberg trials. The Americans and the British thought of de-Nazification in narrowly political terms – as no more than the destruction of the Nazi party élite. This accomplished, and with no alternative élite of their own to install, they looked to the professional and business classes to run the new Germany. Yet these were the very groups that had been most deeply implicated in the whole Nazi venture. The result was that more than eighty per cent of those involved in Nazi war crimes got off scot-free, and the Western powers were responsible for only about one in five of the prosecutions that did take place.[11]

Furthermore, the Americans especially were anxious to build up an anti-communist intelligence network, and naturally took an interest in the work of their Nazi predecessors. In Eastern Europe in the years after 1945, much American intelligence came from the 'Gehlen organization' – a network of spies left behind by the retreating German army. The career of Klaus Barbie, the Gestapo 'Butcher of Lyons' recruited by the CIA in its anti-communist crusade, vindicates much of what Burchett was saying.

Initial American enthusiasm for breaking up the great industrial combines that had provided Hitler's regime with the sinews of war also evaporated. De-Nazification of big business would mean destroying much of Germany's private managerial expertise, either by de-industrializing Germany or socializing its industry. The Americans found both courses abhorrent, and by 1947 they had settled for ensuring that a 'competitive' private-enterprise economy was restored. Plans for socializing the Ruhr Valley and placing it under international control were scrapped.

It was also true that ex-Nazis played an important role in the West Germany that was built up under Konrad Adenauer. Under him the public service, the foreign ministry, the judiciary, and the universities were run by the men who ran them for the Nazis. In his foreign policy, Adenauer was a fervent anti-communist, advocate of German rearmament, and sought to regain the territories which Germany had lost to the Soviet Union and Poland in 1945. Burchett was not the only one who found all this alarmingly reminiscent of the post-1918 German revanchism which had spawned Hitler.

Burchett's reaction was to accept the communist charge that Adenauer and his Germany were 'neo-Nazi'. But this was too simplistic. Adenauer was basically a politician of the Weimar era of the 1920s, rather than a Nazi; and the West Germany he built was essentially a return to Weimar rather than to the Nazi state of the 1930s. The Americans were not displeased with the result, but it was deeply disappointing to a man like Burchett who had taken the radical rhetoric of wartime anti-fascism seriously. In the western zones Germany would not get the clean sweep that he believed was essential.

In the east, however, it was a different story. Burchett visited the Soviet zone of Germany frequently from January 1946 (when he was the first Western reporter to do so). He filed a number of important stories, including an account of the German rocket base at Peenemunde, which it had been claimed was being rebuilt by the Russians. He derided the claims of American officials that it was inaccessible, sealed off by an 'iron curtain'.

In the Soviet zone of Germany, Burchett found that the discredited old rulers were being swept aside, and that far-reaching social reforms were being implemented. The Soviets carried out a thorough-going de-Nazification of the administration, and of the managerial staff of industry in their zone of Germany. Many were arrested as war criminals. A German 'People's Democracy' began to emerge in the eastern zone as 'reborn Weimar' emerged in the west. Burchett praised the anti-fascism of the communist-dominated government, and the vigour with which it set about the job of remoulding German society. He emphasized the democratic participation of workers and peasants in the process of reform and de-Nazification, and seems to have been oblivious to the consolidation of top-down control and the gradual emergence of a one-party state.

By 1949 two fiercely antagonistic German states had been established, after the bitter Russo–American confrontation of the Berlin blockade. Yet in 1945 the Allies had agreed to maintain a unified German state. How had this about-turn taken place? Who was responsible?

By 1949, at least in the West, most blamed the aggressive stance of the Soviets. Burchett wrote a book, *Cold War in Germany*, arguing that it was the right-wing turn in *American* policy which was primarily responsible for the division of Germany, and that in fact the Soviets had consistently adhered to the policies agreed upon at Potsdam in July 1945.

In early 1947 Burchett had been the first to report that the British and Americans were contemplating the establishment of a West German state, permanently dividing Germany in a blatant violation of the Potsdam Agreement.[12] Although it was immediately denied, Burchett's information was accurate. But the final decision was not made until August of that year, after the Marshall Aid Plan had been adopted (this provided the funding essential for the rehabilitation of a West German economy closely integrated with that of western Europe and America).

The prelude to the division of Germany was bitter Soviet–American quarrels over the issue of currency reform in 1948, a technical issue which involved their conflicting ideas for the reorganization of Germany. The Americans pushed through a unilateral currency reform in the western zones which they saw as the prelude to setting up a separate West German government which would exclude Soviet influence. The Soviets responded by blocking all western ground access to Berlin, deep inside the Soviet zone. Thus began the Berlin Blockade.

Burchett had come to Germany nurturing an idealistic vision of the 'New Society' for which the war had been fought. He found in Berlin a ruined and divided city, where teenagers lived by the black market, women prostituted themselves for a cigarette, and 'allies' slandered each other incessantly. His conclusion was that it was the conservative leaders of the US who had betrayed his dream.

'A Liberty Undreamed Of'

By this time, the *Daily Express* was refusing to publish Burchett's pro-Soviet despatches from Berlin. For his part, he decided it had become impossible to work in Germany 'unless one was prepared to become a propaganda hack for cold-war handouts'.[13] By this stage, Burchett's hopes for the 'New World' were increasingly focused on the countries in the Soviet sphere of influence.

He did not have an extensive background knowledge of the eastern European countries, although he had made several trips there while based in Berlin. Nor did he study the theories guiding the Soviet experiment, or know the political history of Stalin's rule in any detail. But in the late 1940s he was one of the few Western reporters with access to the eastern European countries. Doubtless, the sympathetic view he had taken of Soviet policy in Germany facilitated this. He moved to Hungary in April 1949, and then to Bulgaria in 1950, working as a stringer for *The Times*.

The book he wrote about his experiences in eastern Europe, *People's Democracies* (1951), bubbles over with his enthusiasm for what he found in eastern Europe – villages set in rich, intensively cultivated farmlands, peasants with exotic national costumes and a vigorous folk culture, cities rising anew out of the rubble of war, workers with tales of struggle, heroism and sacrifice. Material poverty there was, even worse than in post-war western Europe. But Burchett thought that he had found a 'new spirit' among the people, entirely lacking in the drabness and demoralization of Berlin.

He was convinced that the general picture painted by Western anti-communists, of peoples enslaved in misery by communism, was wrong. He believed that Western officials paid undue attention to the views of the minority who had lost out under communist rule. He painted a scathing portrait of these people:

> They fill the cafes in fashionable Vaci Utca, recline in chintz-covered armchairs in tiny bars and cafes in the Var, the aristocratic quarter of Buda, and have coffee with whipped cream or a glass of *barack* brought to them by some countess turned waitress or barmaid. They exchange rumours, pass on the latest news they have gleaned from the 'Voice of America', and believe themselves to be the best-informed people in Budapest.

And often enough the rumours they have invented will be broadcast as news next day over the American radio.

They bitterly complain about their poverty, do not work and in general live by selling off bits of jewellery or dealing in black-market currency. They provide a disgusting example of what happens to a privileged class when it is robbed of its privileges.[14]

In general, he found the stream of sturdy workmen, resistance-heroes and enthusiastic, reformer-administrators provided by the government more admirable and more reliable.

In September 1948 Burchett interviewed Cardinal Jozsef Mindszenty, the Prince Primate of Hungary. Mindszenty told Burchett that Hungary should remain a bulwark of Catholicism against 'Jewish Bolshevism', and he looked to the Western powers to save his country from the Slavic hordes. Burchett saw him as a leftover from the Middle Ages. Five months later Burchett saw Mindszenty again – in a 'People's Court', charged with conspiring against the state, in collusion with foreign espionage services, and corrupt black-market deals. Although he made no overall confession, Mindszenty admitted to many of the specific accusations made against him.

The trial caused a worldwide sensation. Burchett was incensed that Mindszenty was widely depicted as a Christian martyr in the struggle against communist tyranny. Many insisted that the admissions made by Mindszenty and his co-defendants must have been extracted by torture or the use of drugs. Burchett sat in the courtroom, able to observe the defendants at close range, and was convinced that they had not been maltreated. Mindszenty 'looked just as he did when I interviewed him four months previously, but there was a change. Some of the arrogance was missing.'[15]

But Burchett noted that the case for the prosecution rested heavily on the uncollaborated admissions of the accused. He wrote: 'People's Court procedure . . . is disquieting to anyone accustomed to British justice . . . The state prosecutes only those it has already decided are guilty . . . . There must always be a suspicion that the evidence was extracted by third-degree methods.'[16] Yet by the time he wrote *People's Democracies* his worries on this point had subsided. Soviet-bloc police procedures were not very different from those of western Europe, he now suggested.

Since the Mindszenty trial he had interviewed a cleric charged in an earlier trial. He told Burchett that he had not been beaten or tortured, but simply questioned 'for long hours on end'. In the end, he had agreed to confess in the hope of leniency, and had been given a suspended sentence.[17] That was enough to satisfy Burchett.

He was of course terribly mistaken. It is true that, by and large, the security forces did not use the 'third-degree methods' Burchett had in mind. Physical torture was a primitive, unreliable method used mainly only where confessions were needed in a hurry. But the memoirs of Eugen Loebel and Artur London, both communist casualties of the purges in Czechoslovakia, give a vivid picture of what the bland phrase 'questioned for hours on end' could cover. Loebel, for example, was interrogated for sixteen hours a day, always in a standing position. While resting between interrogation sessions, he had to jump to attention every ten minutes and repeat his prison number. Loebel withstood this for more than a year (and wore out a whole team of interrogators) before he finally agreed to make the required confession. He was tougher than most.

Burchett also did little investigation into the background of the trial. Mindszenty, it is true, was a leader of the clerical right wing, implacably opposed to the post-1945 government in Hungary (his attitudes were so extreme that, after fêting him as a martyr until his release from prison, the Vatican felt compelled to disown his views). But politically, he and his allies were a spent force at this time.

Of much greater importance than the highly publicized Mindszenty trial was the destruction of the Smallholders' Party and the absorption of the Social Democratic Party by the communists in 1947–48. Between them, these two parties had commanded the support of the overwhelming majority of the Hungarian electorate. Burchett, apparently, simply did not notice their disappearance.

The intensification of the Cold War in 1948–49 produced a crisis in eastern Europe, as communist leaders who had been advocating a 'national road to socialism' found themselves faced with Stalin's demands for strict subservience to the wishes of Moscow. Few were in any position to defy Stalin, for their governments had been put in power by Soviet occupation authorities. But in Yugoslavia Tito had come to power without the support of the Red Army, and resisted Soviet pressures. Stalin was furious.

Burchett could not comprehend how comrades-in-arms could fall out among themselves. He flew to Yugoslavia – wisely, perhaps, not to Stalin's Moscow – and began asking about it. But, he found: 'Nobody knew what had actually happened except Tito and a few other leaders. There had been no discussions about it in party circles, although as became apparent a few weeks later, the quarrel had been looming for months past.'[18] He read the main documents of both sides, and gave a fair summary in *People's Democracies*.

But, overall, Burchett decided, Tito was a narrow-minded nationalist, unable (in contrast to Stalin) to take the wider view. He had also departed from the monastic standards which Burchett expected of an authentic leader of the people. He wrote: 'One had the impression that Tito had lost touch with reality, had isolated himself from his people . . . His very mode of life with his palaces and villas, gaudy uniforms and white duck suits, his bejewelled fingers and bemedalled breast, seemed out of place for the leader of a People's Democracy.'[19]

Burchett was also distressed to find that, unlike an authentic leader of a People's Democracy, Tito relied on police-state methods to silence critics. He built a 'Tito Party' rather than a worker's party; and, revealed a distressed Burchett, something like ten per cent of its membership had been arrested without trial when the conflict with Stalin erupted.

Innocent Wilfred – no doubt he was unaware of the full extent of the purges of the 1930s, but had he really failed to notice that the 'Stalin cult' in the USSR far exceeded the most immodest of Tito's efforts? In Belgrade, he actually met one of Stalin's closest henchmen, Vishinsky, and produced an effusive portrait: 'Pink and affable, in splendid form . . . tireless in debate and just as energetic when listening to others as when speaking himself . . . He never missed a point; good-humoured and witty, he answered with apt quotations the sallies of Sir Charles Peake . . .'[20] Vishinsky had been the Public Prosecutor in the Moscow Trials, and for those who cared to read the transcript, his viciousness was a matter of public record. Burchett gives not the slightest hint of awareness of this.

Embarrassed by his failure to put Tito in his place, Stalin moved quickly to stop the rot elsewhere in eastern Europe. In Hungary, Laszlo Rajk, the Foreign Minister and former Communist Party secretary, along with a string of other leading figures in the government, was arrested in May 1949. Burchett had just arrived from Berlin, and he covered the ensuing trial in October.

Rajk and his colleagues confessed that they had been working for Yugoslav, British and American intelligence, and plotting a coup. They were found guilty, and executed. The Hungarian Communist Party was swept by a wave of arrests of 'Titoist' agents. The police terror became so intense that the secret police arrested people for spitting on the sidewalk. But by this stage, Burchett had moved on.

Within three months, he was in Bulgaria reporting on the trial of Traicho Kostov, Bulgarian Communist Party secretary and Deputy Prime Minister, and his colleagues. Kostov created a sensation by repudiating his confession in the courtroom. None the less, he too was found guilty and swiftly executed. This was followed by a purge of 'Kostovites', to which about a quarter of party members fell victim. The Bulgarian party leadership cabled Stalin: 'Only your deeply penetrating eye could see in time the criminal gang of Kostov.'

The significance of this statement, of course, completely escaped Burchett. Burchett had accepted Stalin's version of the Soviet–Yugoslav quarrel, and he now accepted the official version of the trials as well. He was shocked by disclosures of political intrigue in the People's Democracies. But only in the case of heretical Yugoslavia could he bring himself to acknowledge that they were police-state dictatorships. Given this, a naïve and profoundly misleading interpretation of the trials was inevitable.

Burchett described Rajk's confession as 'incredible'. Yet he devoted a whole chapter to summarizing it. He concluded:

> In the Western press, even in the so-called liberal sections, an attempt was made to present Rajk, Palffy and Co as a small group of nationalist-minded communists, people who wanted communism but

independent of the Soviet Union. This is nonsense. There was not one convinced socialist among the whole band. They were mostly cheap police spies . . . They were a miserable collection of plotters without a human ideal between the lot of them . . . Before the court and before the Hungarian public, as all proceedings were broadcast from the court, Rajk and his gang were disclosed as miserable, bloodthirsty adventurers who would not hesitate to plunge the country into a ferocious civil war, to destroy everything of the new life which had been so painfully built up, to hand the country over, lock, stock and barrel to a foreign power . . . There were no regrets except from a few of the dispossessed and Horthy hangers-on, when the chief culprits were condemned to death and speedily executed.[21]

In the case of Kostov, Burchett's endorsement of the official verdict was not so ringing, but it was still definite: 'By Kostov's bearing, the knowable parts of his background and the testimony of the others accused in the case, I believe the truth of the conspiracy was that outlined by Kostov in his written statement.'[22]

Years later Burchett said he had been 'considerably shaken' by Kostov's refusal to endorse his confession. If so, it is a pity he did not say so at the time. Nevertheless, he continues, it was 'still possible' to believe the official verdict: 'If Kostov's whole confession was false, what of those of Rajk and the others? On the other hand what madness had seized those who destroyed cadres of the level of those in the Rajk and Kostov trials unless they really represented a threat to the socialist regimes?'[23]

What madness indeed? For Burchett, this was just a rhetorical question, and he did not attempt to answer it. Burchett had witnessed the consolidation of Stalinist control over eastern Europe. And he didn't even notice it. While it was 'possible' to take an optimistic view of eastern European developments, he would do so.

In 1951 he argued that while a privileged minority had been stripped of liberties it had enjoyed before the war, the mass of the population had 'been granted an extension of basic liberties on a generous and ever-expanding scale'. He concluded in *People's Democracies*:

If the same advance is made in the next twenty years as has been made in the past five years in bringing real liberties to the workers and peasants of the People's Democracies, and if the Western powers give up their morbid plans to destroy the People's Democracies by force of arms and the hydrogen bomb, the whole population will be enjoying liberties of a quality not yet dreamed of in the Western world.[24]

Burchett left eastern Europe in 1950, and did not return until 1956. He thus missed the high tide of Stalinist repression, but in Hungary he saw something of its bitter aftermath. Incidentally, in both Hungary and Bulgaria, it was now officially admitted that the 1949 trials had been frame-ups. For many communist and communist-sympathizing intellectuals, all this caused much disillusion, anguish and rethinking. It was now no longer 'possible' optimistically to ignore the 'madness'.

But Burchett did not embark on any thoroughgoing reconsideration of the recent history of eastern Europe, or what he had written about it. Even his autobiography, published in the early 1980s, had little to add. That, he probably would have said, was a task for historians rather than journalists. As a journalist, he threw himself into the search for new stories rather than raking over 'old' ones.

The Khrushchev years in Russia were a time of dramatic change. There were major economic and political reforms, a thaw in the Cold War, and growing Sino–Soviet tensions. Burchett reported on all of this, but there was nothing here that really captured his imagination.

And so he turned his attention to the Soviet space effort, on which he co-authored two books with Anthony Purdy: *Gargarin: First Man in Space* and *Gherman Titov's Flight into Outer Space* (London, 1961). (The latter was published in the US under Titov's name rather than Burchett's as *I am Eagle!*) Their tone is one of gushing wonderment and promethean exhilaration, common in much popular-science literature of the period, and also in much Soviet literature from the years of the First Five-Year Plan – a spirit we might call 'the romance of the machine'.

Two decades later, they are of very little interest. They tell us much about the derring-do of the early astronauts, but little about how the Soviets organized their space venture. We do not even learn that the man in charge was the (recently deceased) Dimitri Ustinov, who later became the head of the Soviet armed forces.

His main venture into more terrestrial matters in these years showed consistently bad judgement. Amid the historic struggles over de-Stalinization, involving vital issues such as how to democratize the political system and rationalize the economy of the Soviet Union, Burchett penned a euphoric account of Khrushchev's campaign to open up the virgin lands, *Come East Young Man* (Berlin, 1962). He does provide an account of a picturesque and little-known part of the Soviet Union, and for this some may still find parts of his book useful. But once again he was seduced by utopian strivings, overlooking all the practical 'detail' that proved to be of such vital importance. This badly planned, wasteful venture played a substantial role in Khrushchev's downfall, but one would never realize it from Burchett's book.

Thereafter, Burchett was increasingly preoccupied with the unfolding drama of the Vietnam war. Justifiably, much of his autobiography is devoted to the years he reported this conflict from the 'other side'. Yet shortly before his death he wrote a book about an eastern European country which he had visited frequently over the years, and where he was to die – *Bulgaria: Past, Present and Future*. In a sense, this was a return to one of his earliest passions – for his love of Bulgaria had grown out of his admiration for Georgei Dimitrov, anti-fascist hero and communist leader of the 1930s.

This work remains unpublished. It is a gushing review of Bulgaria's transformation from a backward agrarian society into a modern industrial one. It is based on interviews with communist officials and prominent citizens in 1981–82. All are sturdy, cheerful and frank, concerned to combine the fullest possible democracy with the most rapid improvement in living standards. As an incorrigible 'optimist', he does not dwell on the darker side of modern Bulgarian history – the trial of Kostov, the purges – all this might never have happened; official explanations of how the government, the police and security forces work today are quoted at length, and apparently taken at face value.

Now this approach would be perfectly acceptable to the Western press if it were adopted by a conservative journalist dealing with, say, the US government. Burchett must have known that the same sort of uncritical reportage on a communist government is unacceptable. But he had no real way of surmounting this problem. For, *Bulgaria – Past, Present and Future*, despite the details it presents of life in that country, offers not so much analysis as the expression of an attitude, an outlook, which had remained essentially unchanged since Burchett's youth.

'Communist or Fellow Traveller'

Burchett has often been accused of being a communist. 'What motivates Burchett?' asked Denis Warner, a fellow journalist and friend from the war years who became one of his bitterest critics during the Cold War. 'Despite the occasional inconsistency of word and action, the answer is not hard to discern . . . Far from being muddle-headed, he is a clever, calculating communist.'[25]

Those who were convinced of this found Burchett's shifting sympathies within an increasingly fragmented communist bloc difficult to explain. But Stephen Morris has put forth an original if unconvincing explanation. He castigates those who view Burchett as in any sense an 'independent radical', and then reveals a previously unsuspected puppet-master dictating Burchett's political dance across three continents. 'What these observers do not realize,' he announced, 'is that the twists and turns in Burchett's communist sympathies, and his current firm attachments to the regimes in Hanoi, Havana and Pyongyang, have correlated exactly with the foreign-policy line of the Communist Party of Australia.'[26] It is the CPA's strategy for world domination – rather than Moscow's or Peking's – which, in Morris's view, 'motivates Burchett'.

But the CPA has in fact followed a 'Eurocommunist' path quite different to Burchett's. It is sympathetic to Hanoi, but regards North Korea with abhorrence and rarely comments on Cuba. Burchett did have friends in the CPA, such as fellow journalists Alec Robertson and Malcolm Salmon. But his closest contacts in Australia seem to have been drawn from radical Christians, notably the Unitarian Church, and peace groups such as the Congress for International Co-operation and Disarmament.

In his autobiography, Burchett relates that before he left Australia he had seriously considered joining the CPA. But he was put off by the esoteric language of Marxist-Leninist doctrine, and by a dislike for the exacting discipline which the party demanded.[27] There seems no reason to doubt the accuracy of this statement.

For better or worse, Burchett did not view the Soviet bloc countries from a Marxist standpoint. He saw them as 'progressive' states, embodying the hopes of Western democratic ideals rather than as revolutionary dictatorships. His hopes for the Western world appear to have been for a vaguely defined 'more equitable social order' and for a pacific foreign policy, rather than their communist transformation. Burchett's basic commitment was to a broad unity of 'progressive' forces against the evils of fascism and reaction. He was a supporter of the Popular Front and the Grand Alliance (with all the illusions about the Soviet Union these embodied), rather than a hard-line Stalinist. He simply did not see a contradiction between democracy and communism.

But the Grand Alliance, and the hopes for international co-operation pinned on it, collapsed in the wake of the Nazi defeat. Western and Soviet zones of occupation froze into rigid political and military blocs confronting each other. In the West, the idea that Soviet 'expansionism' was solely responsible for this alarming development was soon widely held. The radical rhetoric of wartime mobilization gave way to conservative panic at the spread of communism. Stalin's image underwent a drastic transformation – the smiling 'Uncle Joe' of the war years became a bloodthirsty despot, usually bracketed with Hitler. By 1950 McCarthyist anti-communism was riding high in the US; and in Australia, Bob Menzies had come back to office bewailing the 'Red Menace'.

This great about-face was too much for Burchett to swallow. In *Cold War in Germany*, he wrote:

I can see the word 'traitor' forming on some people's lips as the book is read. It may be charged that some material should not be published, some secrets not revealed 'in the public interest'. As I interpret the role of a journalist or writer, his duties far transcend those contracted with his editor or publisher, or those wished on him by Foreign Office or State Department. His wider duties are to the general public, and in terms of peace, the world public. This needs restating today when there is an increased tendency to turn correspondents into political warfare agents.

Those who cry 'traitor' because certain information revealed does not suit the Foreign Office or State Department might well ponder whether the latter always follow policies which are in the best interests of their own peoples . . .

History will one day decide who were the traitors in Germany from 1945 onwards. Traitors were those who betrayed the hopes of the whole progressive world for peace and continued co-operation with the Soviet Union. Traitors were those who betrayed the policies on which they were elected by the general public in Britain and America. Traitors were those who sabotaged the policies of their own government while acting as administrators in Germany. Traitors were those who evaded orders given by their own military governors in Germany when those orders conflicted with the interests of Anglo-American and German capitalism. These are the traitors, not those who expose their intrigues.[28]

Of course Burchett did not succeed in living up to these admirable words when he turned his eyes on the communist bloc. But they are not the words of a servile party hack (this was the era of Zdhanovist sterility, when 'orthodox' communists denied even the theoretical possibility of independent individual judgement).

For all his admiration for the supposed virtues of the People's Democracies, then, Burchett was not a communist but a fellow traveller.[29] But he was not a fellow traveller in the spirit of, say, Sidney and Beatrice Webb, who saw Stalin's dictatorship as an interesting exercise in Fabian social engineering. He was interested in moral awakening and redemption rather than social statistics.

Wilfred Burchett's father was a lay preacher, and his upbringing pious and conservative. His basic outlook arose from his Protestant background, with its strong tradition of evangelist moralism, its faith in progress, its vision of redemption through suffering. Like many of his generation, Burchett became disillusioned with Western capitalism through the experience of the Great Depression, the rise of fascism, and the policy of appeasement adopted by the political establishment.

He viewed communists sympathetically, as important allies in the struggle against fascism, but he was not himself a communist. During World War II, his views were part of the political mainstream. It was not until he witnessed the great reversal of alliances by the Western powers that marked the onset of the Cold War, that he transposed his hopes to the Eastern bloc. In so doing, he isolated himself from the political-professional journalistic mainstream in which he could, without doubt, have achieved great acclaim.

Burchett did this because he had always been a principled, left-wing journalist, not just a hack. But he was essentially a reporter, not a political analyst. He had a set of attitudes rather than an elaborate political philosophy. He sympathized instinctively with those he saw as the underdogs, but this was poor preparation for what happened when yesterday's underdogs became today's masters. He was not prepared for the reversal of alliances by the Western powers after the defeat of the Axis powers, and never came to terms with the harsh realities of a Stalinist police state. He believed passionately in progressive ideals, and never came to terms with the fact that the war and post-war politics were essentially about power – not ideals.

The interest of Burchett's work lies in the places he went, the news stories he broke, and the anecdotal details he provided, not in his own interpretations of events. He was often wrong, but he told the truth as he saw it. He wrote first-hand accounts of events in places that were often inaccessible to more conventional reporters, and often dangerous. It was his unfailing ability to go out and get a good story that earned him the respect of many fellow journalists who did not share his political views.

Notes

1. *Passport: An Autobiography*, Nelson, Melbourne, 1969, pp.20–1. This contains more details of Burchett's early life in Australia than *At the Barricades*, Macmillan, Melbourne, 1981, which is concerned mainly with his career as an international reporter.
2. *At the Barricades*, pp.54–5.
3. Ibid., p.60.
4. *Documents on Australian Foreign Policy 1937–49*, Vol.1: 1937–38, ed. R.G. Neale, Australian Government Publishing Service, Canberra, 1975, pp.272–3, 276.
5. Ibid., Vol.2: 1939, pp.256–7.
6. Quoted in John L. Gaddis, *The United States and the Cold War 1941–1947*, Columbia University Press, New York, 1972, p.38.
7. *Passport*, p.177.
8. *Cold War in Germany*, World Unity Publications, Melbourne, 1950, pp.75–6.
9. Letter to Winston and Mary Burchett, 28 September 1947. Burchett file, State Library of Victoria, Melbourne.
10. *Cold War in Germany*, p.160.
11. Tom Bowers, *Blind Eye to Murder: Britain, America and the Purging of Nazi Germany – A Pledge Betrayed*, André Deutsch, London, 1981, p.385.
12. *Daily Express*, 6 February 1947.
13. *At the Barricades*, p.130.
14. *People's Democracies*, World Unity Publications, Melbourne, 1951, pp.162–3.
15. Ibid., p.102. Mindszenty's own account of these events is given in his *Memoirs*, Weidenfeld and Nicolson, London, 1974.
16. *Daily Express*, 9 February 1949.
17. *People's Democracies*, pp.130–1.
18. Ibid., p.43.
19. Ibid., p.73.
20. Ibid., p.57.
21. Ibid., pp.252–3.
22. Ibid., p.260.
23. *At the Barricades*, p.146.
24. *People's Democracies*, p.287.
25. 'Who is Wilfred Burchett?', *Quadrant*, July–August 1967, p.75.
26. 'A Scandalous Journalistic Career', *Commentary*, November 1981, p.73.
27. *At the Barricades*, pp.47–8.
28. *Cold War in Germany*, pp.11–12.
29. He is treated as such in David Caute, *The Fellow-Travellers: A Postscript to the Enlightenment*, Weidenfeld and Nicolson, London, 1973, pp.276–7, 301–2.

Part Two:
Crisis at Home

4

The Bureaucratic Passport War: Wilfred Burchett and the Australian Government

Alex Carey

From 1952 to 1972 conservative Australian governments sought to obstruct and discredit Wilfred Burchett by every means available to them, from quite lawless denial of his rights as an Australian citizen to pressure on Australian newspapers not to publish his material.[1] Throughout this period government spokesmen sought relentlessly to portray Burchett as a communist and a subservient mouthpiece of every communist regime. For Burchett's especial benefit a whole new theory of citizenship was developed under which Australian citizenship became not a right of birth but a privilege which governments might confer or withdraw at will, according to whether they approved or disapproved of a citizen's values and conduct.

Throughout this period Australian governments encouraged the belief, at home and abroad, that Burchett was guilty of disloyalty and indeed of treason of a particularly odious and inhumane kind: brainwashing and even torture of Australian prisoners of war. [See Chapter 8, page 181.] Yet they were never prepared to make these charges specific. It was simply asserted that his behaviour abroad had been such as to warrant withdrawal of his rights to an Australian passport. So far from *requiring* Burchett to return to Australia to face whatever charges his conduct was believed to warrant, Australian governments refused to provide him with a passport or otherwise facilitate his return on the grotesque ground that to facilitate his travel anywhere would imply approval of his alleged disloyal and discreditable conduct. At no time was an Australian government willing to provide Burchett with details of the offences he was supposed to have committed, to charge him formally with the offences or to give him opportunity to answer popularly credited charges which the government, at the very least, did nothing to discourage.

This attitude to Burchett was maintained for twenty years. It was maintained in the face of a worldwide appeal supported by a pantheon of internationally renowned artists, writers, scholars and scientists, including eight Nobel Prize-winners. Burchett's supporters ranged from members of the House of Lords to civil-rights and professional organizations at home and abroad, distinguished friends and relatives and at least two Australian ambassadors.

Outside the communist countries there can have been few occasions in this century when infringement of the rights of a citizen by that citizen's government has attracted such widespread attention and protest. Yet Australian governments remained totally unresponsive, neither modifying their behaviour nor making any serious attempt to justify it. Such intransigence suggests that the motives for their behaviour went far beyond the moral and patriotic indignation which was their proclaimed basis.

No doubt the solution to this puzzle lies deeply hidden within federal cabinet papers, Lord Casey's diaries and other such sources, most of which will remain concealed for thirty years and will then be made available only in so far as conforms to the Security Service's fine judgement about the national interest. However, using the limited resources of the Freedom of Information (FOI) Act, Mr Winston Burchett, Wilfred's brother, has already obtained material of considerable value. So far, this material comprises only fifty-four documents out of a total of such documents in government files that certainly runs into thousands. Yet even this minuscule, much bowdlerized sample provides confirmation of the extraordinary character of Australian governments' preoccupation with Burchett, and of the intransigence of their hostility towards him.

I shall first review evidence from the FOI material and elsewhere about such preoccupation and intransigence on the part of Australian governments. Then I shall attempt to establish some perspective on the foreign-policy objectives and tactics of Australian governments between 1950 and 1970. This perspective will be necessary for a discussion of clues, from the FOI material and elsewhere, which suggest an at least plausible explanation for the governments' attitude to Burchett. An explanation, that is, of how the discrediting, exile and restriction of movement of a single Australian journalist and writer – though an exceptional one – could come to be regarded by Australian governments as so important in relation to the goals and tactics of their foreign policy. I may observe in advance, for I believe evidence on the point to be persuasive, that the foreign policy in question did not at all match common perceptions of it as based on subservience to American policy and trust in American protection. By contrast it was, in fact, characterized by a hard-headedness, at least in aspiration, and by a scale of deception that might make Machiavelli quail. The deception was applied, moreover, without prejudice or favour, both to the domestic electorate and to our great and powerful friend. These conditions of Australian foreign policy contributed largely, I shall argue, to attitudes to Burchett that otherwise appear extravagant to the point of irrationality.

Scale and Detail of Australian Governments' Preoccupation with Burchett

A spokesman for the Department of Foreign Affairs has advised that, while that Department holds 'ten major files of papers relating to [Burchett]', Foreign Affairs in general was involved only 'on the fringes', so that 'other departments would hold the great bulk of the primary documents'.[2] So far as can be discerned from the FOI sample of documents, the other departments principally involved include Immigration, Prime Minister and Cabinet, and ASIO (the Australian Security and Intelligence Organization).

From the material available it is clear that files on Burchett are likely to contain anything and everything about his life and activities during the relevant decades. They contain details about his most innocuous conversations, about his movements, about when his British passport would expire, about his travel arrangements – with photocopies of completed departure and arrival forms, certified as such by two witnesses; comments about exactly how he described his occupation, nationality and citizenship when arranging travel with his Vietnamese or Cuban substitutes for an Australian passport; reports of and comments about any views or changes in views he expressed to anyone about almost anything but especially about the USSR, China, Vietnam and eastern Europe; reports about the disenchantment he experienced with various communist regimes and about the strain or unhappiness he felt in consequence of his isolation from the West; about his domestic affairs and living arrangements, his social contacts and his drinking habits; whom he talked to (and whom he *did not* talk to) at international conferences; copies of newspaper and magazine articles by and about him and of interviews involving him.

The extraordinary interest maintained by Canberra in the journalist it so consistently exiled and disowned is illustrated by a letter headed 'W.G. Burchett' which, in 1963, the Australian Ambassador in Moscow

(Stewart Jamieson) sent to the Secretary, External Affairs, in order to keep Canberra apprised of the latest lunchtime talk about Burchett (spaces indicate censorship deletions): 'Further to earlier correspondence on this subject,   were among guests at a luncheon here on   .Both, at different times during the meal, told me that they saw Burchett from time to time and that he was becoming disillusioned and was in a fairly bitter mood about communism in general and the Russians in particular.'[3]

Since Burchett moved about a lot, and talked a great deal and very openly to many people, the result of this remorseless Burchett-watching is a seemingly incessant flow of letters, memos and cables from Australian embassies, consulates and trade commissions around the world, giving details of the latest Burchett sighting or Burchett comment or activity. Cables and memos to the Department of External Affairs about Burchett often required copies to be sent to around twenty different people and departments or agencies. One's eventual impression is of a worldwide network which constituted a virtual Burchett-watching industry, rivalling the China-watching industry of the period. It would be fascinating to have some measure of how many million dollars' worth of time and attention was devoted to this remarkable industry by Australian bureaucrats and agencies around the world, over a period of twenty or more years.

Intransigence of Government Attitudes to Burchett

The extravagance and rigidity of Australian government attitudes is already evident in 1956 with the first response (by Immigration Minister Harold Holt) to Burchett's many requests for renewal of his passport. It reaches something of a highlight in a sustained battle in 1961–63 by a senior diplomat to persuade Canberra to behave sensibly about Burchett. It achieves a level of high farce when, in 1970, the government intimidates international airlines into refusing to carry Burchett to Australia, only to have him arrive in a small privately hired plane; and it culminates in a sort of poetic justice when, with the election of the Whitlam Labor government in 1972, the aforementioned senior diplomat – by now Secretary of the Department of External Affairs – asks Whitlam for, and is granted, the privilege of writing to Burchett to tell him his passport has been restored.

Mr Holt's Logic

On losing his passport in North Vietnam in May 1955 (it was probably stolen, since it is unlikely that a traveller of Burchett's experience would 'lose' his passport under the circumstances in which Burchett's disappeared), Burchett at once applied for a replacement, first to the British and then to the Australian government. Replacement was refused and the Australian Council for Civil Liberties intervened. After two letters and a six months' delay, Immigration Minister Holt replied in April 1956, refusing both a passport and registration of Burchett's children as Australian citizens. Reasons for refusal were contained in two short paragraphs.

> Mr Burchett left Australia fifteen years ago. He has not since returned, his wife is not Australian (she is a Bulgarian national) and generally he has apparently severed all connection with Australia. In addition his activities since his departure have been such that he is considered to have forfeited any claim he might have had . . . as the holder of an Australian passport.[4]

In fact Burchett had never been away from Australia for longer than five years. Moreover he had spent four of Mr Holt's fifteen years as an accredited war correspondent with the Allied forces and had spent four months in Australia in 1950–51 campaigning against the Menzies referendum to ban the Communist Party. So far from severing all connections he had published six books in Australia, maintained wide family and other connections and had arranged visits by his family while overseas. His marriage to a Bulgarian was transparently irrelevant to his right to a passport. (It is worth noting that, in the following fifteen years, Holt's reference to 'activities since his departure' was as far as any Australian government was willing to go in publicly defining this ground for Burchett's banishment.)

The Council for Civil Liberties responded pointing out the errors 'of fact and of law' in Holt's letter. Mr Holt replied, 'I do not think there is any doubt that Mr Burchett has spent the greater part of the last fifteen years outside Australia' (a point never in dispute). In consequence, Holt concluded, 'The main point which I made in my previous letter remains true that he has severed connections with Australia to all intents and purposes.'

'I adhere to the view,' Mr Holt summed up, with a dogmatism which precluded all challenge, 'that an Australian passport may and should be withheld from him irrespective of his nationality because of the factors mentioned in my letter.'[5]

An Ambassador Takes up the Fight for Burchett

Keith Waller (later Sir Keith) joined the Department of External Affairs in 1936 and was its Assistant Secretary from 1953 to 1957. Thereafter until 1970 he was, successively, Australian Ambassador to Thailand, Moscow and Washington. (From 1970 to 1974 he was Secretary of the Department of Foreign Affairs, Canberra.) During Waller's period as Ambassador to Moscow, Burchett, who was then Moscow correspondent for the *Financial Times*, pursued with the embassy the matter of his passport. Waller, in this context, renewed an acquaintance with Burchett that went back twenty years, and became interested in his case. A considerable correspondence ensued between Waller and the Department of External Affairs. Only Waller's side of the correspondence has been made available under FOI. Even so, it is revealing on several counts: Waller's judgement of Burchett and sense of outrage at the injustice of the treatment accorded him; the seemingly irrational intransigence of official attitudes about Burchett's case; and the quality of the evidence (as judged by Waller) produced in support of the official view of that case, when eventually it was produced.

On 3 August 1959, some time before Waller took up his appointment in Moscow, the embassy's Second Secretary (R.A. Woolcott) wrote to External Affairs, Canberra, advising that Burchett had called on 15 July. Woolcott observes that Burchett is expecting to publish material in the Melbourne *Herald* despite the fact that a Mr Hamilton[6] (presumably in Foreign Affairs) has received an assurance from the Editor in Chief of the Melbourne Herald Group of newspapers that they would use Burchett's material sparingly, if at all. Woolcott continues that Burchett wants, and believes he is entitled to, an Australian passport; and wants his three children registered as Australian citizens. He wishes to return to Australia for a visit but 'as he earned his living as a travelling journalist he would want to be able to depart again if and when he so desired'. Woolcott concludes with a request for advice about 'the type of proceedings or action which might be taken against [Burchett] should he return to Australia'.[7]

On 20 September 1960 the Department of External Affairs (EA) sought from Waller, now Ambassador in Moscow, full details of a conversation, restricted to personal matters, which he had mentioned as occurring on first meeting Burchett again after an interval of eighteen years. Waller made clear his astonishment at the request but obliged.[8] On 23 November 1960, Waller forwarded to EA an application from Burchett for an Australian passport and the registration of the birth of his children. In a supporting statement Burchett observes, 'It has been suggested to me that I have been accused, by whom I am not entirely clear, of conduct during the Korean War which has militated against my request for a passport. If this is so, I believe I should be given an opportunity to answer these charges.' In his covering letter Waller notes:

> Burchett has discussed at length with the embassy his conduct during the Korean War. I have known him personally for twenty years and I am sure he is convinced his position has been misrepresented. Since I do not know precisely what the view of the department is, nor do I know what he is believed to have done, I cannot express any very helpful view as to the adequacy of his defence. However, I think it should be kept in mind that he has a defence.[9]

On 7 March 1961, replying to a telegram from External Affairs, Waller notes that the telegram 'presupposes that Burchett is in fact a

Soviet agent and I should have doubted whether we had yet established this'. Waller continues:

> If you are convinced that his conduct is such as to disqualify him from any moral (as distinct from legal) claim to protection which an Australian document of identity or passport confers, then I agree the logical step is to deny him a passport. My own impression, from hearing admittedly only his side of the story, is that this may not in fact be so and that since he is an Australian citizen by birth, no harm would be done by hearing his version of events in Korea.

This is particularly the case since 'In Moscow . . . he is regarded as a journalist in good standing, representing an important and conservative newspaper.' To continue to deny him a passport may 'cause us some embarrassment here'. Waller concludes:

> Without having all the evidence at my disposal my own recommendation would be to give him a passport. If however you feel this is not possible, then perhaps we could issue him with a document of identity for a limited period – say twelve months and see what he does with it. In the meantime, I suggest that I might be authorized to say that his conduct during the Korean War has come under scrutiny and ask him to state his case. This could then be examined in concert with the appropriate United States authorities . . . It seems to me that a firm decision on whether or not he is to get a passport might then be more readily taken.[10]

Some weeks later, having received an account (not made available under FOI) of the official view of Burchett's case from the Department of External Affairs, Waller replied by letter dated 24 April 1961:

> It seems clear that little more can be done. I must however say that I think a grave injustice is being perpetrated and that the whole case is permeated with illogicalities. For instance . . . you say, 'It was assumed from his record in Korea and in Indochina, from the book he wrote in Hanoi and from his continued residence in bloc countries, that he is a communist sympathizer and will continue to work for communism.'

Waller then details, point by point, the insecurity of the assumptions from which these conclusions are reached. He stresses Burchett's entitlement at least to have his defence heard, and notes in passing the absurdity of the argument by which the government, having 'refused to give him any sort of travel document which would enable him to leave the Communist bloc', makes his failure to do so a part of the grounds for continuing to deny him a passport.

Waller comments, also, on a further paper provided by External Affairs in support of the government's position. The paper, Waller observes, 'suggests either that you have much more positive information about Burchett than has been vouchsafed to me or that someone is making assumptions without evidence'. The paper begins, Waller notes, 'The communist journalist Wilfred Burchett . . .' and continues to observe that while 'he might not be acting, overtly at any rate, as a straight-out communist', his children 'are likely to grow up as fully indoctrinated communists'. Waller comments:

> The picture you draw of Burchett . . . is certainly not a recognizable one so far as we are concerned. I see him about once a month. Other members of the embassy see him more frequently. We have mutual friends, communist, non-communist and anti-communist, and he does not sound in the least like the person described in your minute. This may not be evidence or at any rate inferior to the hard facts on which your assessment is based. In this case may I please have the hard facts?

Waller refers to the departmental view that 'our treatment of Burchett is unlikely to have adverse effects on our credit overseas' and responds:

> [Burchett] is now recognized by the British Embassy (only the Americans abstain) and has a good reputation among the foreign press in Moscow . . . He is in short a highly respected journalist in a capital where the general level of journalistic attainment is above average. To pillory such a journalist as a communist without reasonably firm evidence . . . would in my view be very likely to damage our standing. If you have evidence, well and good . . . I am sick and tired of this argument. This is the third lengthy piece I have written about a man whom I like well enough but is far from being a particular friend. My only anxiety is to be sure that Canberra knows what it is doing and is not mistaking clichés for arguments.[11]

On 31 May 1961, Waller wrote to External Affairs acknowledging receipt of a memorandum 'containing the [source deleted] assessment of Burchett'. Waller observes:

> Clearly, in the light of this, a favourable answer on Burchett's application is unlikely. It is perhaps relevant to say that members of this embassy have on several occasions heard Burchett vigorously deny the allegation that he had participated in the interrogation of prisoners . . . I still therefore wish that, since he is an Australian citizen by birth, it were possible to give him a hearing.

In a filed, hand-written note on Burchett's case Waller observes, 'I should feel much happier about this case if we could disentangle it from the tissue of lies and half-truths which have grown up around it.'[12]

Almost two years later Waller wrote to the Australian Ambassador in

Cairo about a memo from Cairo which 'contained all the old misjudgements of Burchett by which he has been bedevilled for years'. Waller continues:

> The position is that Burchett has been refused an Australian passport after consideration of his dossier . . . [source censored]. In effect he has been deprived of Australian citizenship without trial and without a hearing . . . To anyone who has known [Burchett] as I have for nearly twenty years [the dossier] is an appalling piece of special pleading. However, I see no means of undoing this short of Burchett returning to Australia . . . leaving his wife and children behind in Bulgaria or Russia and forcing the government to attempt to prosecute him . . . I don't believe he is a communist and doubt whether he ever was one. I do not believe that he was guilty of treason, especially since I have heard his own version of what happened in Korea. He is a silly fellow with ideals and strong left-wing sympathies who is always fighting lost causes . . . He was until last year the Moscow correspondent of the *Financial Times* of London and did odd jobs for the *Express* as well. He threw this up because of what he saw in Laos and Vietnam last year. This was a silly and emotional act . . . Such widely diverse people as Malcolm Morris and myself hold identical views about him. I suggest you ask him to lunch and see for yourself. If you do, give him my best regards.[13]

Support and Opposition in Government and Bureaucracy

Between 1964 and 1975, Arthur Malcolm Morris, CBE, was successively: Ambassador to Laos; Assistant Secretary Defence Liaison, Department of External Affairs (1964–66); Ambassador to Austria, Switzerland, Vietnam, Pakistan and Afghanistan. The FOI material reveals that in 1965, two years after Waller's reference to Morris cited above, External Affairs received 'a query from the Department of Immigration as to whether the time might not have come to reopen the question of the grant of an Australian passport to Mr W.G. Burchett'. This query, together with a letter on the same subject from the Australian Journalists Association (AJA) to External Affairs Minister Paul Hasluck, was referred to Morris. The AJA had written to Hasluck, *inter alia*:

> No doubt your government has been influenced by the fact that Mr Burchett has done his writing in Asian countries – he reported the North Korean side of the Korean War and the South Vietnam side of the war in that area. But he is a writer of worldwide reputation and an Australian. He is among the best known and most widely read journalists this country has produced and has some famous stories to

his credit. Apart from holding the view that as an Australian he should be given an Australian passport, my association believes there should be free movement throughout the world of journalists.

On the personal side Mr Burchett's father is ninety-two, and he is hoping to see his son again before he dies.

Burchett senior had already travelled to Moscow for this purpose at the ages of eighty-six and eighty-nine. However, Burchett's principal complaint to the AJA was that 'Over the past ten years, my professional activities have been gravely hampered by the refusal of the Australian government to issue me with the Australian passport to which I am entitled.' He provided recent illustrations of ways in which he had 'suffered a great deal' professionally on this account.[14]

On 24 March 1965, Morris responded to the query from the Department of Immigration (and the related letter from the AJA) that had been passed to him:

I have known Burchett on and off for nearly twenty years, and have never been able to reconcile the official picture of him as a communist agent with my own personal experience of him as an idealist and convinced left-wing socialist. He knows of the accusations that have been made against him, though perhaps not the full detail, and must be aware that he might run a real risk of prosecution were he to return to Australia. If, nevertheless, he did return, it would probably be in Australia's interests for the matter to be put to the test and the charges either substantiated or withdrawn. This however cannot be done unless he is given facilities to travel to Australia . . . In my view the matter should be reopened and it might be suggested to the minister that this be done by reconvening the interdepartmental committee meeting which on   [deleted] recommended [deleted] policy towards Burchett.[15]

The day before Morris's proposal that Burchett's case be reopened and that the government's policy towards him be relaxed, at least in some degree, External Affairs Minister Hasluck received a letter from an old journalist acquaintance, E.W. Irwin. Mr Irwin's letter, written to support the AJA's appeal, comprised a long and carefully argued description and defence of Burchett's career. Hasluck passed the letter to the Secretary of his Department with an annotation which is an epitome of the closed-minded, almost McCarthyist inflexibility on which all appeals by or on behalf of Burchett eventually foundered: 'The Secretary; I do not know Mr Irwin's present political affiliations but at one time in his career he himself had the same sort of associates as Burchett had. He is an emotional person, full of sympathies of all kinds. P.H.'[16]

(Four years later Sir Ronald East, Past President of the Institute of Engineers of Australia and a cousin of Burchett, wrote to Prime Minister Gorton setting out in detail the case for Burchett and the grounds for rejecting the calumnies against him, principally by Denis Warner and one or two others. It is perhaps not surprising that East concluded his long letter with the observation, 'It is no use referring this letter to Mr Hasluck. He is determined to keep Burchett out and, anyhow, it is now too late for Hasluck's reputation to be saved from the taint of McCarthyism.'[17])

On 31 March 1965, a week after Morris's memo (and Hasluck's annotation to Irwin's letter), the Department of External Affairs made the following proposals to the Department of Immigration. When Burchett 'next expresses a wish to return to Australia', he should be issued with a travel document of some kind 'even if valid for a single journey only', and the 'question of the issue of an unrestricted passport' should be discussed at a reconvened interdepartmental meeting (as proposed by Morris). EA's file copy of the letter to Immigration is annotated: 'Held by Immigration: no action is being taken.'[18]

In 1968 the focus of Burchett's efforts shifted from attempts to obtain an Australian passport to attempts to return to Australia (preferably with official sanction) and thereby oblige the government either to prosecute him or acknowledge it had no grounds to deny him a passport. The shift may have been influenced by the fact that in 1968 he was able, without relinquishing Australian citizenship, to obtain a Cuban passport. This development greatly reduced the severe handicaps long imposed on his professional work in consequence of withdrawal of his Australian passport thirteen years before.[19]

During 1968 Burchett was granted an entry certificate to visit Britain and attended a conference on peace and disarmament in Canada. But his request for an entry permit to attend a similar conference in Sydney was refused. 'The government has decided,' he was flatly informed, 'that you will not be granted an Australian passport or the alternative document which you have requested.'[20] Meanwhile Burchett had publicly challenged the Australian government to put up or shut up. As reported by the Melbourne *Age*, 'If they have charges against me, let them make the charges, I will go back and fight them on it.'[21] Late in 1968 the 'Burchett Passport Committee' was formed under the chairmanship of Arthur Calwell, lately leader of the Federal Opposition, and soon spread far beyond Australia to attract support from a veritable galaxy of international figures and eight Nobel Prize-winners.[22]

Also late in 1968 Minister for Immigration Snedden was induced to acknowledge that the government had never made specific charges against Burchett. None the less Prime Minister Gorton refused a request from Burchett for an official inquiry at which he would have opportunity to confront 'charges made against me in certain newspapers' with, in Burchett's view, 'strong hints that they were based on leaks from official quarters'.[23]

On 17 February 1969 Frank Galbally, a well-known Melbourne barrister acting for Burchett, wrote to Prime Minister Gorton 'to respectfully ask [him] to open a judicial inquiry into the truth of the allegations made against [Burchett] and to afford him the opportunity of answering these allegations'.[24] A fortnight later Galbally wrote again asking that Gorton either 'institute proceedings which will allow our client to defend himself' or 'grant . . . a passport enabling him to return to his country in an honourable way'.[25] In April 1969, the AJA reported that the Minister for Immigration (Snedden) had refused to meet a delegation from the association or to 'set out the government's reasons for denying Burchett a passport'.[26] Nothing came of these requests or of a further appeal from Galbally to both Snedden and Gorton.[27]

In September 1969, Burchett's father died at the age of ninety-six and Snedden publicly affirmed that Burchett would not be allowed to return for the funeral.[28] In February 1970, Burchett's elder brother Clive died and Galbally sent a telegram to Prime Minister Gorton requesting that Burchett be allowed temporary entry to Australia to attend a memorial service. Gorton replied publicly that the government would 'do nothing either to grant Mr Burchett an Australian passport or to facilitate his travel in any other way'.[29] Burchett had already decided to 'force the government's hand' by returning to Australia without a passport, and Clive's death led him to act at once.[30] (There had been considerable newspaper speculation that Burchett could, if he wished, return to Australia by using his birth certificate in place of a passport.)

Burchett reached Noumea with the French airline UTA on 18 February 1970. However, pressure from the Australian government led UTA to refuse to carry him on to Sydney. Qantas was similarly leant on. Burchett was in consequence stranded in Noumea where his attempt to return home became a dramatic focus of largely sympathetic media attention. A TV team and newspaper reporters flew to Noumea. Cartoonists had a field day. Shortly, Gordon Barton, a wealthy industrialist and newspaper proprietor, made arrangements to fly Burchett to Brisbane in a small chartered plane.[31]

Burchett reached Brisbane in a six-seater Piper Navajo on 1 March to a largely hostile airport reception. However, in Sydney, Melbourne and Canberra the response was different. Burchett was virtually lionized, and the following days were occupied with an endless round of TV, radio and press engagements, including a conference at the Canberra Press Club and an address to a packed Melbourne Town Hall.[32]

Seven years earlier Ambassador Waller, outraged by the government's treatment of Burchett and appalled by the secret 'dossier' offered as 'evidence' in support of the government's actions, had written: 'In effect [Burchett] has been deprived of Australian citizenship without trial and without a hearing . . . I see no means of undoing this short of Burchett returning to Australia (as he is entitled to do as an Australian by birth) leaving his wife and children behind . . . and forcing the government to attempt to prosecute him.'[33]

Now Burchett had taken the course that Waller had judged to be the only remedy open to him. In Federal Parliament, three days after Burchett's arrival, Prime Minister Gorton was asked, 'Has counsel for journalist Wilfred Burchett asked for a court of inquiry to hear charges against Mr Burchett? Will the Prime Minister meet this request, or does he prefer to establish guilt without trial?' In his reply the Prime Minister gave the only specific description ever officially provided of the government's attitude to Burchett:

> Mr Burchett has asked for a court of inquiry . . . There is no need whatever for a court of inquiry . . . Mr Burchett was living behind enemy lines in the course of two wars. There is no need for a court of inquiry for that whatever . . . [or] to establish the published documents which he has put out – the published reports which he has sent to the communist *Guardian* here, which were progaganda designed to assist the enemy, and there is no need for a court of inquiry to establish whether or not he went through prison-of-war camps in which Australian troops were incarcerated . . . [T]hese matters are sufficient in the government's view to refuse him a passport . . . If there are other charges against him . . . they do not affect the government's decision which is made on the basis I have put before the House and which requires no court of inquiry to substantiate it.

The Leader of the Opposition, E.G. Whitlam, then asked Attorney General Hughes whether 'now that [Mr Burchett] is in Australia' any investigation or prosecution would be undertaken. Hughes replied that he had no intention 'to bring any charges against him'.[34]

It should be remarked that after all Burchett's efforts to obtain justice by 'forcing the government to prosecute him', the government's response was effectively (i) to deny that it had ever made charges against him that were sufficiently serious to require that their truth should be tested by a formal inquiry; yet (ii) to continue to insist that the same charges were both so serious and so self-evidently true as to warrant withdrawal of his passport and refusal of any right of appeal – a bizarre combination of *Nineteen Eighty-four* and *Catch-22*.

It should be noticed just how far Gorton's charges against Burchett, when at last given some specification, are from the calumnies which Australian governments allowed (perhaps encouraged) to circulate. Reports in the American press, for example, suggested that Burchett had 'brainwashed' and 'tortured' prisoners of war. These reports had long been brought to the attention of the Department of External Affairs by Australian officials overseas without eliciting any sign that they were regarded as in any way unsatisfactory.[35] Yet all Gorton was prepared to say was that Burchett 'went through prisoner-of-war camps'.

Burchett's return to Australia, dramatized through the extravagant, almost farcical attempts by the government to prevent it, attracted worldwide attention. It is not, after all, every day that a plausibly reputable government adopts such extraordinary measures to obstruct the attempts of a miscreant (whose misdeeds are supposedly so black as to warrant withdrawal of rights of citizenship from him and all his heirs) to put himself voluntarily within the reach of judicial and legal prosecution. An editorial in *The Times* of London, entitled 'An Australian Asks for Justice', commented that 'Mr Gorton has compounded the Australian government's earlier mistakes over Mr Wilfred Burchett in announcing that he will be refused a passport now he is back in his native land,' and continued

> If Mr Burchett has committed an offence . . . he ought to be charged, as indeed he has asked. The government's spleen should not be vented by withholding a passport . . .
>   Few Western journalists . . . would think [Mr Burchett] anything but misguided in his enthusiasms . . . but his writings show him to be an advocate of détente rather than a tough committed enemy of the West. He indeed asked the communist authorities to allow Western reporters in to make their own assessments. His disapproval of Australian support for the United States in Vietnam was shared by a considerable minority of Australians at home, if less articulately.[36]

Fifteen days after his arrival Burchett left Australia to return to Paris and the Vietnam peace talks. He departed, as he had arrived, without a passport. But no one made any difficulty about that. There is little doubt an embarrassed government was relieved to see him go. None the less Liberal Country Party governments, except for subsequently granting citizenship to Burchett's children, remained obdurate.

In the election of December 1972 the Labor Party under Gough Whitlam won office for the first time in twenty-three years. As one of its first acts it restored Burchett's passport. Keith Waller, who had become Secretary of the Department of External Affairs some two years earlier, requested the privilege of advising Burchett of this happy development and Whitlam agreed.[37]

On 6 December 1972 Waller cabled to Burchett in Paris: 'I am personally glad to be able to inform you that the Prime Minister has decided that you may be issued with an Australian passport if you apply to the Australian Embassy.'[38] The long saga of Burchett's battle for his passport was over.

Why Such Persecution?

I believe the explanation of the animosity of Australian non-Labor governments towards Wilfred Burchett from 1952 to 1972 lies in a number of relationships to which his unique ability to move and speak across propaganda barriers presented unending threat and embarrassment. Most important in this regard were relationships between Australian and US governments and between each of these and public opinion.

In my view the animosity Burchett attracted was related to the extraordinary deception and misrepresentation in which both Australian and US governments engaged with respect to their own electorates. It was probably related also to the even more remarkable ruthlessness and deception towards their great and powerful friend that Australian governments practised behind their masks of subservient devotion to American purposes. I shall first elaborate this broad argument in more concrete terms. I shall then fill it out with such documentation as space permits.

Both US and Australian governments found it necessary to support the losing side in three Asian civil wars (Korea, China/Taiwan, and Vietnam). These interventions were undertaken for reasons primarily unrelated to actual events and circumstances in the countries affected. US interventions were primarily determined by public opinion. US public opinion had been abused and misled for domestic political purposes successively by Truman, the Republicans and McCarthy, until it reached a level of anti-communist extravagance that was, by mid-1950, quite beyond anybody's control. It remained more or less in that condition for the next fifteen years.

Australia's interventions were decided upon for reasons having solely to do with its relationship to the US. It was assumed that Australian support (diplomatic in respect of China, military in respect of Korea and Vietnam) for these interventions would help to influence broader US policies in ways advantageous to Australia's long-term security. More specifically, for a decade Australian governments hoped to trade unfailing 'loyalty' to American rhetoric and policies for a wholly reliable formal guarantee of American protection. By the late 1950s Australian leaders were losing confidence that any such guarantee by the US would prove attainable. Consequently, foreign-policy objectives shifted, first to obtaining American bases on Australian soil; then, after the 1963 West Irian débâcle,* to promoting the long-term engagement of American troops on the ground, anywhere, anyhow, between Australia and 'the yellow hordes'.

It is important to notice that while the motives for American and Australian interventions differed, they had one thing in common – regard for the interests of the peoples whose lives and homelands were most directly affected played virtually no part in them. (It is significant that both sides of the civil wars in which Australia intervened insisted passionately that they, that is the two sides, were part of a single country. Only the interveners arbitrarily insisted, as a justification for intervention, that they were not.)[39] In consequence the interventions had two fairly predictable results: (i) they led more or less rapidly to violence and suffering out of all proportion to any benefits they conferred; (ii) the intervening governments found it necessary, in order to justify their behaviour before world and domestic opinion, to invest their interventions with moral purposes: protection of freedom and

---

* When Indonesia, with US acquiescence, took over the former Dutch colony of West Irian.

democracy; defence against 'aggression'; containment of evil tentacles
reaching out from Moscow.

These moral justifications were as little supported by the real
consequences of American/Australian interventions as by the real
motives for those interventions. It therefore required propaganda and
misrepresentation on a quite massive scale, both at home and abroad, to
keep such moral justifications at all plausible to the relevant publics.
Even then the plausibility achieved was permanently vulnerable to
exposure by an observer moving freely about Asia who had the talent,
courage, mobility and access to Asian leaders and to Western
newspapers that Burchett possessed. This combination of circumstances
was sufficient to make Burchett anathema to American governments.

Since it was the policy of Australian governments to endorse (for their
own purposes) virtually all American rhetoric and action in the Asian
sphere, they had all the same reasons for hostility to Burchett that
Americans had. But Australian leaders had, in addition, several reasons
for hostility to him that Americans *didn't* have.

Ever since 1948 until popular disenchantment with the Vietnam War
set in in the late 1960s, the principal problem of public opinion for
American governments was that the intensity of popular anti-
communist fears and anti-communist belligerence required those
governments to adopt irrationally belligerent foreign policies or face
electoral judgement as 'soft on communism'. Thus American popular
opinion was not seriously open to influence by reporters of Burchett's
viewpoint, however good their work.

By contrast Australian public opinion was always *less* belligerently
anti-communist than Australian leaders wished it to be (witness their
failed attempt to ban the Communist Party in 1950–51), and it had to be
continually stiffened by fantastic accounts of threats from an expansionist, aggressive Communist China. For this reason Burchett was capable,
from the Australian government's point of view, of a much more serious
impact on domestic public opinion – unless he was exiled and
discredited.

Australian governments were intensely concerned to establish a high
degree of American confidence in their 'mateship' solidarity with
American purposes. From 1950 to 1960 it was hoped a relentless surface
display of loyalty would yield solid guarantees of American protection;
later, and especially after 1963, the same display was judged necessary
in order to induce Americans to trust sufficiently in Australian good will
that they would be responsive to Australian attempts to push them
deeper and deeper into Vietnam. It was therefore always a matter of top
priority to dissociate the Australian government in some very public
way from Burchett the Australian journalist, and the offence his work
gave to Americans.

It is noteworthy in this connection that as early as October 1953 (well
before Burchett 'lost' his passport) Alan Watt, Secretary of the
Department of External Affairs, was greatly perturbed by an article in
an American newspaper which reported that although Burchett had

done much 'to hurt the United States in the eyes of the world', had committed treason, and was associated with torture of Americans, he retained his 'Australian citizenship and passport' and was 'in good standing at home'. The article complained that Burchett's reports were still published in countries allied to the US despite the fact that: ' "Lord Haw Haw" was tried and hanged for less.' Watt sent the article to the Attorney General with a covering letter which concludes 'You will appreciate the harm that could be done to Australia's standing in the United States and its relations with the American government by an article of this nature.' One thing, at least, is manifestly clear from Watt's letter. He was not remotely interested in whether the charges against Burchett were true. What matters was that Americans believed them.[40]

By contrast with the situation in the US, Australian government leaders were always in command of, never victims of, the far milder McCarthyism that was aroused and exploited here. In consequence the minds of Australian leaders remained quite clear about what they were doing, however fraudulent or deceptive, and why they were doing it. (Hasluck, who possessed an apparent capacity to believe anything whatever touching on the Red threat, should perhaps be excepted.)

Thus while American leaders, their minds unsettled by McCarthyism, could more or less genuinely believe (until they need his advice and assistance) that Burchett was merely a communist propagandist, Australian leaders always knew that he was not – and feared and detested him the more for that.

According to the thesis I have argued so far, the architects of Australian foreign policy during the whole period of Burchett's banishment were enmeshed in lying and deception in furtherance of policies they believed vital to Australia's long-term security, and were simply reckless of the consequences of these policies for the lives and suffering of many millions of Asians. If this thesis is correct, it is little wonder that Australian leaders should have wished to use every power they possessed to exile, calumniate and immobilize someone with the first-hand knowledge Burchett possessed of the gulf between their high-minded rhetoric and the appalling human consequences it concealed.

The argument I have developed rests on several key claims about the period from 1948 to 1972. These claims concern: (i) Truman's use of anti-communism for domestic political purposes; (ii) the consequences of McCarthyism for American minds and American foreign policy; (iii) changing strategies and unchanging deception in Australian foreign policy; and (iv) invention, ignorance and indifference in Australian foreign policy. I shall briefly review evidence for each of these claims.

TRUMAN'S USE OF ANTI-COMMUNISM

In 1947 American leaders believed the creation of markets for American products by the provision of billions of dollars in reconstruction aid to Europe was the only way to avoid recession and massive unemployment in the US. Senator Arthur Vandenburg warned Truman that if he was to get bills for such aid through a Congress which was in an isolationist mood he would have to 'scare hell out of the country', and Truman believed it.[41] In March 1947 he proclaimed the Truman Doctrine, which pictured a world menaced by a global communist conspiracy directed from Moscow, and pledged the US to defend 'freedom' against external and internal communist threats everywhere. Thereafter Truman, by means of a national, year-long campaign to arouse anti-communist fears, achieved the goal Vandenburg set him and got the bills through Congress, but was left with his foreign and domestic policies helplessly captive to the false picture of the world he had created and the extravagant fears he had aroused.[42]

In 1950–51, while the Republicans and McCarthy rode the tiger Truman had loosed, Hans Morgenthau, Professor of Political Science and Director of the Center for the Study of American Foreign Policy at the University of Chicago, wrote a book to deplore the folly of the Truman Doctrine and point prophetically to disasters in prospect. The insistence on treating all communist revolutions alike, which derived from the rhetoric of the Truman Doctrine, entailed, Morgenthau warned, a profoundly confused view of the world. For while 'the revolutions in Europe are phoney revolutions, the revolutions in Asia are genuine . . . [In consequence] opposition to revolution in Asia is counter-revolution . . . resistance to change on behalf of an obsolescent status quo, doomed to failure from the outset.'[43]

The administration's use of 'synthetic scare' and 'spurious promise', Morgenthau observed, had made 'illusory hope, fear and hysteria the prime movers of popular support'. Truman's policies must now, regardless of national interest, be 'fashioned in the image' of the prejudices of 'a deceived populace'. In his anger and dismay Morgenthau addresses Truman directly. Having deceived once, he warns Truman, 'you must deceive again', or the Republicans, citing the Truman Doctrine rhetoric, 'will convict you out of your own mouth as appeaser and traitor'. 'You have falsified the real issue between the United States and the Soviet Union into a holy crusade to stamp out Bolshevism everywhere on earth, for this seemed to be a good way of arousing the public: now you must act as though you meant it.' Having 'presented the Chinese communists as the enemies of mankind, in order to appease the China lobby, you must now act as though you meant it'.

'In a word,' Morgenthau concludes, 'the administration has become the prisoner of its own propaganda,' and, 'Only future historians will be able to determine the extent to which the administration has . . . subordinated foreign policy to considerations of domestic politics.'[44]

McCARTHY, AMERICAN MINDS AND AMERICAN FOREIGN POLICY

The extent to which the Truman campaign, the Republicans and

McCarthy drove American minds towards protective adherence to the fantastic view of the world required by the Truman Doctrine, may be briefly illustrated with respect to China, Korea and Vietnam. On 18 May 1951, Dean Rusk, Assistant Secretary of State, announced: 'The Peiping regime [of Mao Tse-tung] may be a colonial Russian government . . . It is not the government of China. It does not pass the first test. It is not Chinese.'[45] In late 1950 a Department of State team combed the archives of occupied North Korea for evidence of Russian complicity in the Korean War, and found none. They concluded that the Russians had achieved the creation of 'a new kind of person', and labelled their discovery a 'quasi-Russian Korean'. This new species was Korean on the outside, Russian on the inside. It knew and carried out Russian wishes without needing to be told. Hence no evidence of control from Moscow.[46] In 1955, the *Reporter*, a highly regarded liberal-intellectual journal, used the same argument with respect to Ho Chi Minh. 'That [Ho Chi Minh] is our enemy is obvious,' the *Reporter* announced. 'He belongs to that particularly dangerous species of men whose nervous system has been rewired to make it obedient to remote control from Moscow.'[47]

McCarthy, and the view of the world he imposed, completely dominated American foreign policy. 'He held two Presidents captive,' Richard Rovere wrote in 1959, 'in their conduct of the nation's affairs . . . from early 1950 through late 1954 . . . He had enormous impact on American policy when that policy bore heavily on the course of world history, and American diplomacy might bear a different aspect today if McCarthy had never lived.' McCarthy drove leading Democrats to 'ridiculous' demonstrations of anti-communist zeal. For example,

In 1951, in the course of the Senate hearings on Far Eastern policy, [Secretary of State] Dean Acheson and his immediate predecessor General . . . Marshall – both . . . under savage attack by McCarthy – testified that they would never so much as *consider* the recognition of Communist China or . . . its admission to the United Nations. They assured the Senate that the very idea of recognition was so abhorrent to them . . . that it was never even *discussed* in the Department of State, which simply was not the truth. Pressed further they made a pledge . . . that the United States would never offer recognition. Deception, stupidity, stubbornness and a commitment in perpetuity – these were the lengths to which McCarthy and McCarthyism drove these intelligent men.

Even so, Rovere concludes, 'The paralysis . . . Truman suffered . . . was as nothing to that which . . . overcame President Eisenhower . . . at least through his first two years in office.'[48] For example, when in 1953 a senior official sought the support of the Secretary of State, John Foster Dulles, against McCarthy's depredations, all Dulles could manage was a plaintive, 'Why have they got my cousin on that list?'[49]

For domestic political reasons, as Morgenthau and Freeland describe,

Truman reversed earlier policy in the twelve months following
McCarthy's attack on the State Department in February 1950 to become
involved in Korea, China and Vietnam.[50] Even then Truman could not
end the Korean War at the 38th parallel, where in all reason he should
have ended it some twelve weeks after it began. 'I would have been
crucified for that armistice,' Truman observed when Eisenhower ended
the war on the same line two years and millions of casualties later.[51]
(Truman thereby effectively confirmed Burchett's reports, which two
years earlier had exposed American stalling on the peace negotiations at
Panmunjom.)[52]

Moreover, Australian diplomats and political leaders, as Casey and
Renouf have made clear, were perfectly well aware of the extent to
which domestic politics rather than Asian realities determined American involvement in Korea and Vietnam and American policies toward
China.[53] Casey even goes so far as to mock (privately) the emotional
irrationality underlying American attitudes. He reports raising, in 1954,
the question of recognition of China with Cabot Lodge, 'who did not
have a fit as I thought he might'.[54]

CHANGING STRATEGIES AND UNCHANGING DECEPTION

Sir Walter Crocker, long-serving Australian ambassador, has claimed
that from 1950 to 1971 Australian foreign policy followed every aspect
of American foreign policy with an abject subservience: 'We made
speeches at the UN and we made diplomatic representation in various
capitals, at American behests, and at times in the very phrases
concerted in Washington. Our assiduity and docility have been
paralleled only by Russian's tamest and most cowed satellites.'[55] This
judgement is accurate only so far as rhetoric is concerned, and then not
wholly accurate. Australian rhetoric often outdid American rhetoric
(especially after 1963) in its exaggeration of communist threats to the
'Free World' and in its insistent optimism about the character of our
Asian allies and prospects for success in the long Vietnam venture.[56]
This rhetorical excess could have given warning that Australian foreign
policy was not simply based, as was commonly held, on a sentimental
assumption that if Australia behaved like a fifty-first American state it
would be protected like one. Both the single major change in Australian
foreign policy during the post-war decades, and its ruthlessly unsenti-
mental character throughout, are most easily seen by contrasting the
ways in which Australia became involved in the Korean and Vietnam
wars.

Although the Korean War was sanctioned by the UN, with the
consequence that Australian participation had bipartisan support
at home,[57] the initial response of Australia's leaders was wholly
unenthusiastic. The Joint Chiefs of Staff and the Defence Committee
opposed Australia's involvement beyond token air and naval contribu-

tions, as did Prime Minister Menzies and his cabinet. For a full month after the outbreak of war, intensive effort was given to *preventing* the Americans from asking for a contribution of ground troops.[58] Strong support for ground troops came only from Spender, Minister for External Affairs. Anxious about the possibility of a resurgent Japan, Spender's first concern was to obtain a treaty with the US covering the Pacific region. With this objective in mind Spender argued that prompt commitment of token ground forces while other countries held back, would so favourably influence American attitudes as to pave the way for a 'one hundred fold' return on a small investment. By the time Spender's views prevailed on 25 July 1950, a Pacific pact had become an assumed *quid pro quo* for Australia's commitment of ground troops;[59] and was indeed obtained (in agreed draft form) within six months of that commitment.[60]

Meantime Menzies was overseas, out of reach on the *Queen Mary*, when the British government inconsiderately advised Canberra that (entirely for political reasons relating to the American alliance) it would announce troop commitment within twenty-four hours. There followed an unseemly scramble, led by Spender, to win maximum Brownie points with the US by announcing Australian troop commitment before Britain announced *its* commitment. Australia won by sixty minutes.[61]

It is entirely clear that Australia's substantial involvement in Korea had nothing to do with freedom, democracy or communist threats; and nothing whatever to do with knowledge about the history, politics or aspirations of the people whose country it invaded. Thus the official rhetoric by which the commitment of troops was justified in Australia was deceptive – a point acknowledged by the official history of the war.[62]

In brief, where the US entered the war and continued in it for domestic reasons unrelated to the justifying rhetoric or the realities of Korea, Australia did so for foreign-policy reasons of a similarly extraneous character. In these circumstances it was not to be expected that American or Australian governments would have any (unless hostile) interest in accurate reporting or independent scholarship relating to the war or its human consequences.

As early as 1952 External Affairs Minister Casey acknowledged (to his diary) that he felt 'more and more' that Australia was 'living in a fool's paradise of ignorance' about Asia. He found it 'extremely difficult to get a realistic discussion in Australia about affairs in the East, in matters that vitally affect Australia's future'. Evidence that this lack of interest in Asia (except as a locus for display of 'loyalty' to British and American military involvement) continued throughout the 1950s is provided by the fact that from 1949 to 1958 'not a single Australian diplomat was trained to proficiency in any Asian language'. Moreover, once Hasluck became Minister for External Affairs in 1964 the dogmatic conviction he had already held for a decade that developments in Asia could be adequately understood in terms of a global power struggle, resulted in systematic discouragement of any attempt to alleviate the

82 ALEX CAREY

'fools' paradise' of wilful ignorance that thereafter guided Australian foreign policy.[63]

Ignorance aside, there was a certain unreality about the Australians' expectation that their Korean exercise in *real politik* would secure a reliable guarantee of protection against all comers in exchange for just one battalion of troops (and one more when the fighting was largely over). The expectation was doubly ill-founded given the expressed view of John Foster Dulles, who had opposed the treaty as unnecessary and with whom it was negotiated. One month before the treaty was ratified by the Australian parliament, Dulles went out of his way to warn, with direct reference to 'security in the Pacific', that 'treaty words in themselves have little power to compel action. Treaties of alliance and mutual aid mean little except as they spell out what the people concerned would do anyway.'[64]

Richard Casey, Minister for External Affairs from 1951 to 1960, was soon to discover the truth of Dulles's warning. 'Consistently over a period of years Casey sought contingency military planning in conjunction with the US, in the reasonable belief that it was helpful to know what your powerful ally might be prepared to do in given circumstances.' His requests were persistently rebuffed. By late 1956 Casey decided it would be 'unwise' to rely on American aid under SEATO or ANZUS,* since there could be situations where America's 'vital interests' would lie elsewhere and Australia's would be 'marginal'. He proposed therefore to do 'everything possible' to 'attract American interest down to the South West Pacific and Australia', including an offer of bases and facilities – which was shortly made.[65]

Casey, like Menzies, employed Truman Doctrine rhetoric about the threat and illegitimacy of Communist China as domestic politics and the American alliance required. But, also like Menzies and the cabinet, he did not believe it (as his diaries make clear). Casey was well aware of the stultifying influence on American policy of McCarthyism and domestic public opinion. Throughout the fifties he sought, behind the scenes, to soften American policy on the recognition of China and its acceptance in the UN. He regarded lack of progress in that connection as a matter 'greatly to regret'. At the time of his departure from External Affairs in 1960 he had more grounds for disquiet about the attitude of the US, in particular towards Indonesia. None the less Australian policy was still 'based on the belief' that forcible acquisition of Dutch New Guinea 'would be resisted by . . . the Americans and the British'. Mr B.A. Santamaria, on whose Democratic Labor Party the coalition parties depended for re-election, did not share this expectation and in 1959 already predicted that West New Guinea (West Irian) would demonstrate the unreliability of the American alliance, as in fact it did.[66]

By the end of 1961 it was clear the US would be effectively on Indonesia's side, not Australia's. T.B. Millar has described the impact

* SEATO – South East Asia Treaty Organization
ANZUS – Australia, New Zealand and the United States pact

of this development: 'the meaning of ANZUS was challenged by West Irian', which became 'a permanent reminder that there are political boundaries to ANZUS . . . [I]t was a chastening if salutary lesson that the US did not see the world as Australia saw it, did not wholly share our concept of vital, or even important national interests.'[67]

Garfield Barwick was Minister for External Affairs from 1961 to 1964. His biographer, David Marr, sums up the impact of West Irian on Australian foreign policy. By Christmas 1961, Marr observes, 'Australia's great and powerful friend was on the other side', and continues:

> West Irian marked the end of the Australian assumption, which had operated since the war, that United States support for Australia was somehow automatic. Despite years of friendship, despite the ANZUS treaty, despite the ties of language and blood, the United States had refused to help and had sided with Indonesia.
>
> In Canberra it was believed that American support could only now be guaranteed if the United States was encouraged to be directly involved in the region; they gave West Irian away (so the argument ran) because they didn't want to be involved. Australia now had to see that the United States was drawn into the affairs of South East Asia . . . It was a policy of entanglement. Only then would ANZUS work, for the treaty was little guarantee of security on its own, despite its great symbolic importance in Australian politics.[68]

It was the end of the road for Australian confidence in the American alliance.

In July 1964, in an address to the National Press Club, Mr Santamaria prescribed the two features that would shape Australian foreign policy during the next five years: wild and unsupported claims about a Chinese threat; pursuit, by any means, of American military involvement in South East Asia. Mr Santamaria dramatically outlined the scope of Japan's imperial ambitions in World War II, including 'the occupation of Australia and New Zealand, which were', he says, 'to become Governor-Generalships'. Then, referring to unrevealed (but supposedly supportive) 'evidence from the documents of the Chinese Communist Government', he asserts, '*it is obvious* that all that has happened in the past twenty-five years is that the Chinese communists have substituted themselves for the Japanese militarists in the achievement of exactly the same enterprise' (emphasis added).

The magnitude of the Chinese threat thus established, Mr Santamaria instructs the government in the course it would in fact follow thereafter: 'It should be an incontrovertible end of Australian foreign policy to do everything practical to keep the Americans actually engaged in South East Asia. *Operations in hand are a better alternative than promises for the future*' (emphasis added). If Bruce Grant is correct the instruction was superfluous for, long before Vietnam, the Australian government's primary objective 'was to get the United States engaged in South East Asia in precisely the way' she became involved. 'Obviously,' therefore, 'we would do whatever was necessary by our diplomacy and our commitment of forces, to achieve this end.'[69]

After West Irian Australian policy towards China shifted categorically from Casey's attempts to ameliorate American hostility to Hasluck's efforts, as relentless as they were ill-informed, in the opposite direction. With formal alliances devalued, with Britain moving into Europe, the basic strategy changed. From now on Australia would be satisfied with nothing less than American troops on the ground in South East Asia (the more deeply entangled there the better) and American bases on Australian soil. In consequence both the positive and negative rhetoric aimed at 'attracting American interest' to the region was greatly intensified – both the 'all the way to the stars with the USA' rhetoric, and the 'Chinese threat to the Free World' rhetoric. Thus Australia added a strenuous, supposedly local and informed, voice to the domestic pressures pushing the US into Vietnam. Between 1962 and 1965 Australian foreign-policy attitudes, Gregory Clark reports, became 'frozen into a rigid orthodoxy that ruled out any study or suggestion that questioned the official line. Peking was the enemy; Hanoi was its puppet; the NLF was the creature of Hanoi; and that was that.' This foreign policy was only *apparently* subservient to American policy: 'There were large areas of independence in the Canberra/ Washington relationship. On China/Vietnam Australia actually stood to the right of the US. We skilfully lobbied the US right wing to encourage the greatest and firmest possible commitment in Vietnam.'[70]

Whether by luck or by design, Hasluck's combination of 'almost theological' anti-communist bigotry and remarkable ignorance of Asia[71] fitted well with the anti-Chinese rhetoric required by the new policy. No matter that the coincident widening of the Sino–Soviet split gave less grounds than ever for fear of China. Hasluck's double talent and the needs of the new policy would triumph over all mere matters of fact.

After the assassination of President Ngo Dinh Diem in November 1963 an American decision between escalation of the war and a negotiated withdrawal from Vietnam became unavoidable. The Australian Ambassador in Saigon, David Anderson, had reservations about escalation, the alternative adamantly preferred by Hasluck. In September 1964, to prevent any diplomatic weakening, Hasluck sent a cable to Australian embassies worldwide setting out the three 'major' Australian interests to which they should conform their views on Vietnam. In essence these interests were (i) a government in Saigon which would 'enable the US to keep a foothold in South East Asia'; (ii) to 'retain an active US presence in South Vietnam'; and (iii) to prevent 'any failure' there that would weaken the 'will to resist' communism elsewhere. No sign, it should be noted, of any interest in what all this might mean for the people of Indochina; for, as Sexton observes, South Vietnam, including its 'governmental structure', 'had no real significance for Australia's policy-makers except as a battlefield'. In January 1965 the Department of External Affairs, at Hasluck's direction, explicitly instructed Anderson that they wished to hear no more of his doubts about escalation.[72]

Hasluck divided his efforts between urging expansion of the war and pressing the US to ask for Australian ground troops in Vietnam. His manoeuvring in the latter regard began *three months before* the US itself committed ground troops. After four months of sustained effort Hasluck at last obtained 'requests' for one battalion. Again there was a frantic, last-minute exchange of cables, this time to secure reluctant South Vietnamese agreement before a deadline set by Menzies for announcement of Australian troop commitment on 29 April 1965. Again the deadline was met with only hours to spare.[73]

The hugely portentous American decision to commit ground troops to Vietnam was surrounded by confusion and vacillation. It was substantially a product of the McCarthy inheritance. For as Alan Renouf, who was deputy to the ambassador in Washington from 1964 to 1966, has observed, 'In terms of domestic politics there never was a year from 1951 onwards which a President,' and especially a Democratic President, 'could consider a good year to "lose" Vietnam.' Even so, just how and why the US got involved so deeply was sufficiently obscure that in 1967 Robert Macnamara commissioned dozens of historians to try to find out.[74]

By contrast the Australian decision to commit troops in Vietnam, which was determined by the crude and simple objective of deepening the involvement of American military power in South East Asia, was unhesitating and untroubled by doubts. Again, as for Korea, the commitment of ground troops was unrelated to knowledge of, or even interest in, the social and political circumstances of the country invaded; a fact which would, as later acknowledged by Denis Warner, bedevil the operations of the Australian Task Force in Vietnam. Again, informed scholarship or reporting – especially first-hand reporting from the other side of the war – could only be regarded with hostility as a hazard to the credibility of recklessly ignorant official rhetoric about freedom, democracy and threats from China; rhetoric which was the instrument of wholly extraneous purposes. For, as Professor Hedley Bull later observed, 'The principal objectives of Australia's participation in the war had been to encourage the US to remain present in the area and to sustain America's will to assist her ally.'[75]

While the strategy of Australian foreign policy changed over time, deception remained a major part of it. Until about 1960 the strategy of relying for protection on the American alliance, as defined in formal treaties, was assumed to require only an unrelenting demonstration of loyalty to the official American world-view and policies (that is to the Truman Doctrine), regardless of whether, as in the case of China, this was known to be foolish and unwarranted. Australian leaders found little difficulty with such a requirement, since a judicious exaggeration of the threat of international communism (and of domestic communism) was invaluable in keeping the Labor Party out of office. After 1960, when the new strategy called for American troops to be permanently involved in the region, the amount of deception required increased greatly. Most notably it became the objective of Australian governments to persuade both US leaders and domestic opinion that China represented the pre-eminent threat to the world and to Australia.

Thus, when announcing troop commitment to Vietnam in April 1965, Prime Minister Menzies claimed that 'The takeover of South Vietnam would be a direct military threat to Australia . . . It must be seen as part of a thrust by Communist China between the Indian and Pacific Oceans.'[76] Since China lacked any sort of navy, sceptics may have wondered how this 'thrust' would stay afloat. Menzies met that problem by sheer metaphorical fantasy. 'I can see this murky shadow,' he said in Washington a month later, 'coming down over the whole of the South East Asian peninsula . . . and then across a strip of water to my own land.'[77] Transformed into 'murky shadows', Chinese battalions cease to require surface transport.

Hasluck, a global-power buff, was disposed to give a wider context to creative fantasies devised to attract American troops to SE Asia. In Washington late in 1964 he claimed that China was 'the major threat to peace today'. China's 'aggressive intent', Hasluck continued, 'is a threat to the world. This is not just a regional or an Asian question. It is part of a world conflict. It is the most significant factor in the long-term problem of world peace.'[78] In Australia a year later the problem is no less ominous, but more local: 'the dread of domination by the new imperialism of China and the throttling grip of communist aggressors' is threatening 'freedom and independence' throughout Asia – and in South Vietnam in particular.[79] Back in the US in late 1966 it's all global again: 'We are fighting' in Vietnam 'for the . . . right of every nation to maintain its independence against aggression . . . The future of every one of us is at stake;'[80] and later, at the UN, Asia is 'the front line of both the power struggle and the ideological struggle'.[81] To all of this the Minister for Defence, Mr Fairhall, on 15 March 1966, added the assurance that 'there is not the slightest doubt that the North Vietnamese are puppets of the Chinese . . . What is happening in South Vietnam today is perhaps only the first round of an attack by the Chinese communists in an effort to dominate the world.'[82]

Among Australia's most reputable – and commonly most pusillanimous – academics only Professor Hedley Bull has come anywhere near treating this reckless nonsense with the scepticism it deserves:

> The containment of North Vietnam was not an objective which by itself could make Australia's sacrifices in the war seem worthwhile. Still less could it be made to justify the sacrifices which the US was making, and which the Australian government hoped it would go on making. Only the containment of China could provide an end to which the means could seem proportionate. We do not have to doubt that men such as Mr Holt, Mr Hasluck and Mr Fairhall believed what they said; but we do have to note that what they believed was what

the course to which they had committed Australia required them to believe.[83]

This circumstance of required belief had two major consequences: the apotheosis, from 1964 onwards, of ignorance about Asia which supported a policy objective to which Australia was irrevocably committed anyway – American troops in SE Asia; and the firm discouragement of any advice or research not supportive of this objective. To these consequences I shall return shortly.

I observed earlier that after West Irian both the 'Chinese threat to the Free World' rhetoric and the 'undying mateship with the USA' rhetoric, were stepped up as means of encouraging American military commitment to the Australian region. It remains to consider the inflated 'mateship' rhetoric and its outcome.

The effectiveness of Australian mateship rhetoric in deceiving its great and powerful ally provides one of the more remarkable, if minor, ironies of the war. In 1968 the Australian American Association published a book about Australian–American relations which enjoyed the imprimatur of forewords by both President Johnson and Prime Minister Gorton. A chapter by Frank Hopkins, former American Consul in Australia, discusses the mateship theme. Hopkins apparently takes at face value the rhetoric about 'all the way with LBJ' and eternal, fraternal commitment to the American alliance. In consequence he goes to some pains to offer friendly warning to America's supposedly ingenuous ally that international relations are not really conducted on so personal and sentimental a basis.

Hopkins observes that the disposition to 'carry over into international relations' the 'Australian concept of mateship' and so 'the expectation that mates will always put their loyalty to one another ahead of other relationships' was the cause of 'a certain embarrassment' to Americans. It led Australians to expect 'to be given a priority position in American affections, to be expressed in military terms [and otherwise]'. However 'as a world power [Americans] tend to think in world terms' and Washington's policies 'are not oriented towards special relationships with other nations, even when they share our language and ancestral descent . . . [but] are conducted with a certain cosmic impartiality'.[84]

Before the book containing Hopkins's well-intentioned warning reached publication the American government had been given compelling reason to divest itself of any last illusion about the role of sentiment in Australian–American mateship. In October 1967, after sustained pressure from President Johnson, Prime Minister Holt reluctantly agreed to provide one more battalion of troops but warned that 'Australia could do no more'. (So much for Holt's 'All the way with LBJ' of the previous year.) The Johnson administration was 'disillusioned' by this response, Renouf observes, and it 'had considerable impact on future American policy'. For the Australian troops, together with a few New Zealanders, were the only military forces in Vietnam that the Americans were not paying for.

Renouf sums up the infinitely cynical objective behind the sentimental and idealistic Australian rhetoric about mateship and common purpose. Australian governments urged the US deeper and deeper into Vietnam and 'opposed any real US attempt at negotiations'. While Australia's leaders 'continually *talked* of the tremendous historical world-wide significance of Vietnam, her governments never *acted* as if they believed their own statements. This inconsistency was obvious to Clark Clifford when he visited Canberra in 1967 . . . [It] played a considerable part in convincing him that the US had to get out of the Vietnam War and he subsequently convinced Johnson.'

This episode, Renouf concludes, 'reveals an important fact'. Throughout the Vietnam War Australia had

> a rare opportunity of significantly influencing US policy [towards a wiser and more humane course]. Australia was the only material US ally of any importance. Other troop-contributing countries were lavishly rewarded although their troops were national mercenaries. Australia's role was therefore crucial to the US. Just as South Vietnam would have collapsed at any time from 1954 had the US ceased her assistance, so Australia could have markedly affected US policy at any time she chose. All that Australian governments did was to urge the US along the road to disaster.[85]

This view, of squandered Australian influence, cannot be lightly dismissed, coming from someone as well placed as Renouf.

It deserves notice that before the war ended Denis Warner, Burchett's most intemperate critic, acknowledged in terms similar to Renouf's the fraudulence and folly of the Australian government's involvement in Vietnam – thereby providing implicit vindication of his fellow journalist who had said it all so much earlier. In December 1969 Warner wrote:

> Australia became involved in the war for political and diplomatic reasons . . . Australian policy was to ensure the maintenance of an American presence in South East Asia . . . [But] the Australian tactic of maximum applause with minimum participation was bound eventually to excite unfavourable comment, if not to be self-defeating . . .
>
> [T]he Americans slipped by inadvertence into an ever-increasing commitment, and with them, always lending encouragement, but only . . . limited material support . . . went the Australians . . . [I]t is not easy to believe that [Canberra] regarded the war itself as a serious threat to the security of Australia.[86]

ARROGANCE, IGNORANCE AND INDIFFERENCE

The circumstance noted by Bull, that the strategy of military involvement in Vietnam *required* extravagant beliefs about China, had ramifying consequences. It produced an inflexible opposition between the government and informed students of China such as Professor C.P. FitzGerald, Gregory Clark and Stephen FitzGerald – and Wilfred Burchett. It led the government to adopt extreme measures to discourage independent research or judgement throughout the foreign-affairs bureaucracy. Renouf and Clark have provided devastating accounts of the intimidation of dissent and rejection of all arguments and evidence that challenged the official view.[87] (Renouf's account is also a confession.) Pressure to conform was evident from 1962. When Keith Waller, whose efforts from Moscow on Burchett's behalf were so admirable and courageous, returned to Canberra to take over the Asian division of External Affairs in 1962 he resolved to adopt an open-minded approach to China. 'His resolution,' Clark observes, 'lasted all of one week.'[88]

Later, during 1964–66, Waller was Australian Ambassador in Washington, with Renouf as his deputy. Neither questioned Hasluck's definition of the world and both co-operated fully in his strategy of urging the US towards deeper involvement in Vietnam.[89] 'I regarded it as a period,' Renouf observes, 'when advice critical of the government's policy was not welcome in Canberra at all . . . It believed its policy to be absolutely correct, and anybody who thought the government was wrong was a fool. People shut up. That's all there was to it.' Renouf further explains his and others' silence and conformity by embarrassing references to career and pension prospects; and to David Anderson who, as ambassador in Saigon in 1964, was 'severely reprimanded' for 'sending telegrams saying the United States could not win'. (According to Gough Whitlam, Anderson 'was told by the permanent head [of External Affairs], on the minister's instructions, that his interpretation of events was defeatist, that it was not for him to advise on policy, and that he was not to question it again'. This message to Anderson was also 'distributed . . . widely through the department to encourage the others'.)[90]

According to Renouf, Waller believed in 1964 that 'the Americans would never win the war', and adopted the same attitude that Renouf did: 'this is the government's policy, it should not be questioned. We are public servants, we carry out our instructions.' Hasluck, Renouf observes, 'never had any doubts' about Vietnam 'so far as I knew'; for Renouf that was determinate.[91]

Gregory Clark, almost alone it appears, made sustained efforts to induce his superiors in External Affairs and the government to pay attention to relevant evidence.[92] He was discouraged and rebuked until he resigned in disgust in 1965. One of Clark's minor efforts involved Burchett. Late in 1964 Burchett returned to Moscow from a long visit to NLF-controlled areas in South Vietnam with a mass of photographs of NLF units and jungle factories. These established that the NLF was a more independent and substantial force than Canberra allowed. Clark sent much of this material to Canberra for evaluation. The only reaction he got was 'a sharp rebuke for seeming to endorse a pro-communist like

Burchett'.[93] Clark had questioned a 'required belief' – with predictable consequences.

Hasluck, whose 'influence on Australian foreign policy' is acknowledged to have been 'so great',[94] was, in the Canberra political context, a more or less solitary intellectual.[95] These characteristics may have contributed to an arrogant confidence in his own superior understanding of world affairs and a consequently extravagant self-perception as a world statesman. Clark describes an occurrence which illustrates both Hasluck's domination of Australian foreign policy and the apparent influence of these personal characteristics.

In November 1964 Hasluck journeyed all the way to Moscow, without prior arrangement with Soviet leaders, to convey an important message which, he hinted to Australian diplomats there, 'could change the course of world affairs'. After a wait of some days the Soviet Premier and Foreign Minister, Kosygin and Gromyko, agreed to see him. Hasluck opened with 'a complex discourse on the nature of world affairs'. Kosygin shortly 'suggested that it would be simpler for all if the discussion could move from philosophy to practical details'. Hasluck then outlined his view of contemporary world affairs in which nothing was of much significance except the power of the US, the Soviet Union and China. He represented China as a bandit nation threatening the whole world and urged the overriding need, in the interests of world stability, for the Soviet Union to assist the US in constraining China's expansionist designs, especially in Vietnam. To underscore the universality of the Chinese threat Hasluck observed that 'Australia had noted how Peking was laying claim to the Soviet territory of Sinkiang.'

Gromyko eventually intervened. 'Sinkiang', he noted dryly, had 'belonged to the Chinese for a long time'. Soviet relations with China, Gromyko continued, did not involve Australia; and the Soviet Union wholly rejected Hasluck's view of Vietnam. Hasluck's olympian enterprise collapsed on the spot, though he and External Affairs persisted in it, if a lot more obliquely, for years thereafter.[96]

Hasluck constitutes something of an enigma for the assessment of Australian foreign policy I have developed. There is much ground for believing that other leading members of Australian governments throughout the 1950s and 1960s wittingly inflated the China threat for political purposes and had, especially after 1960, little or no interest in the human realities of Asia because they regarded these as irrelevant to the overriding purpose of involving the US militarily in the region – a purpose Menzies described in 1965 as 'vital' to Australia's long-term security.[97] However there is much evidence that Hasluck not only believed, but believed dogmatically in the world-view he promoted, and especially in a Chinese threat to the world. This must be accepted if only because it is inconceivable otherwise that he would have undertaken such an ill-prepared and humiliating mission to Moscow, or have persisted thereafter in his aspirations to recruit Russia as an ally in containing China.

It is clear, I think, that Hasluck's world-view was not based on any considerable study of evidence about Asia. Moreover, his dogmatic attachment to it (he 'never had any doubts', so far as Renouf knew) suggests that it was derived from an intellectual realm of assumptions and theory in which Hasluck regarded himself as among the cognoscenti. It has been widely observed that Hasluck conceived international affairs primarily in terms of power politics at a sufficiently elevated level to allow little importance to local causes and conditions in any Asian development. Indeed Hasluck's insistence on understanding (or misunderstanding) local political developments as mere by-products of a global power struggle was of long standing. In 1953 he insisted that 'the French are defending liberty in Indochina' in a war that 'is part of a world struggle'. He persisted in this view of Indochina, with total dogmatism, for the next fifteen years.[98]

It happens that Professor Hans Morgenthau was a leading student of power-centred approaches to international relations. From the late 1930s his views 'were known and respected in academic and government circles'; and he 'became one of [America's] most respected foreign-policy analysts in the 1960s and 1970s'.[99] It is therefore perhaps not surprising (if grotesquely ironical in the outcome) that for Australian conservative governments 'since 1949 the basic . . . analysis of international relations [was] in Morgenthau terms of balance of power'. Moreover for Hasluck, in particular, 'his basic assumption' – at least as he understood it – was 'that of Hans Morgenthau'.[100] If only he had read Morgenthau on Asia's revolutions.

It is clear that Hasluck's role as Minister for External Affairs combined ignorance of Asia, dogmatic commitment to the aggressive, expansionist China thesis and a tyranny over External Affairs that first punished and then silenced all attempts to correct his ignorance and illusions. On the face of it this combination appears sufficiently remarkable for its explanation to lie in personality dynamics outside the scope of this essay.[101] I shall therefore not pursue the enigma of Hasluck's role in Australian foreign policy except to consider briefly the possibility of understanding that policy as a superficial and ill-informed attempt to apply Morgenthau's ideas.

Two ideas are central to Morgenthau's work. These are a *real politik* concern with 'balance of power' and an emphasis on 'the national interest' as the *sole* criterion that should guide foreign policy. The emphasis on national interest carries the explicit corollary – to which Morgenthau attaches great importance – that moral principles, as such, or indeed moral considerations of any kind, should have no place in foreign policy (this rule need not, of course, inhibit either the employment of moral rhetoric or conformity to moral principle whenever these are judged to serve the national interest). Morgenthau maintained, in a fashion reminiscent of Adam Smith, that if every country bases its foreign policy solely on an informed judgement about what is in its own self-interest, the best possible (or anyway, least bad) overall results will be obtained.[102] (He did not, of course, resolve the problem of the subjectivity of any definition of 'national interest'.)

It is evident, I think, that foreign policy under Hasluck was, in its intention at least, guided by the principles advocated by Morgenthau. The overriding objective of Australian policy was to involve American military power so deeply (and so permanently) in the region that it would offset what Hasluck saw as a threatening imbalance of Chinese power. Moreover it is beyond dispute that Australian foreign policy unhesitatingly subordinated every consideration of truth, loyalty and humanity to the realization of this supposed 'national interest', even when it became clear that the cost of so doing would include at least a million lives and the virtual destruction of three Asian societies. As Bruce Grant has observed, the objective of keeping the Americans 'militarily committed to South East Asia . . . was what shaped Australian policy'; the 'way in which this was done was incidental'.[103]

Morgenthau's Australian disciples showed, then, no want of commitment to his principles; but they differed drastically in the way they understood the world to which they applied those principles. In Morgenthau's view the Truman Doctrine set American policy on a disastrous course, and did so for two principal reasons. One, it rested on a false representation of all communist revolutions as part of a monolithic movement and hence as a unitary, worldwide threat; two, by proclaiming a (moral and ideological) commitment to oppose communism everywhere it precluded rational discrimination about where communist movements did and did not constitute a threat to American national interests.[104] If we are to believe Hasluck's rhetoric, his foreign policy applied the Truman Doctrine to Asia with an ignorant rigidity that insisted on perceiving a united, communist Vietnam as an extension of Chinese power, rather than as a likely barrier to it.

Hasluck has a reputation for scholarship and breadth of reading. Perhaps it was earned outside foreign policy. In any case there is an appalling irony in his application in 1964 and after of Morgenthau's principles. He applied them on exactly the basis of ignorance and miscomprehension of the world that Morgenthau had thirteen years earlier written a whole book expressly to warn Truman against. Worse still, Hasluck's supposition that the rationale for his policy derived from a renowned and sophisticated foreign-policy analyst may have supported the arrogance with which he silenced criticism within External Affairs and the tenacity with which he persisted until he had proved, in 'the greatest foreign-policy defeat' ever suffered by Australia,[105] the truth of his mentor's neglected warning that 'the revolutions in Asia are genuine . . . opposition to revolution in Asia is counter-revolution . . . resistance to change on behalf of an obsolescent status quo, [is] doomed to failure from the outset'.

Leaving Hasluck aside, there is I think a great deal of evidence that suggests that Australian foreign policy was conducted on a basis of lies and deception. It is, of course, a common occurrence for such governments to invent threats to national security for electoral or other benefit. But this practice is liable to complication by the fact that when politicians engage in sustained and profitable threat-mongering – as the

Liberal–Country Party coalition certainly did from 1949 to 1969 – it becomes difficult to know to what extent they are consciously lying and to what extent they have come to believe their own propaganda. For all of the 1950s the question is pretty much settled by Casey's diaries, which make clear that members of cabinets generally (including Casey) did not believe Australia was externally threatened from anywhere, hence did not believe their own rhetoric.[106] For the 1960s we have seen that the extravagant China-threat thesis was imposed on External Affairs by Hasluck; moreover, as Renouf observes, our political leaders 'never *acted* as if they believed their own statements'. A review of some of the more significant discrepancies between claimed beliefs and behaviour provides strong circumstantial evidence of monumental lying and deception.

Why, during the 1960s, while the rhetoric about China's threat to the world climbed towards hysteria, did defence expenditure remain at such 'low levels' that it 'made the government exceedingly vulnerable to Labor attack'?[107] Why was a task force of 8,000 soldiers the absolute limit that Australian leaders were willing to provide to meet an alleged 'direct threat' to Australia from the downward thrust of China in Vietnam? Why, during the decade in which Australia sent its token military force to confront this direct threat from China, and its fear of China escalated (at least in its leaders' rhetoric), did its trade with China also escalate, until Australia had sent, between 1961 and 1971, more than a billion dollars' worth of wheat and wool to nourish and comfort the alleged source of the threat?[108] If Australia's leaders believed their claims about the origins and record of the movement which they were fighting in Vietnam, why did their handouts on the war (which drew heavily and selectively on International Control Commission Reports for 1962 and later, to show breaches of the Geneva Agreements by North Vietnam), omit ever to mention ICC Reports for the previous eight years which revealed that by 1956 'our' side had first comprehensively breached and then officially abandoned those same Geneva Agreements?[109] If Australia's leaders believed what they said about the circumstances of the war in Vietnam why was so much effort given to shielding Australian soldiers there from direct contact with reporters? Why were returning officers and men forbidden to speak to the press? Why from 1961 to 1965 did the executive maintain such 'excessive and unwarranted secrecy' as to allow a 'negligible role' to parliament in foreign policy? And why were government members of parliament instructed not to participate in any forum on Vietnam which they did not control?[110] Finally, if the government believed a single word of its rhetoric about dominoes and the downward thrust of China, how could Prime Minister John Gorton, when in 1969 it became clear that the war was lost, blandly announce that Australia was under no threat from anywhere for at least ten years?[111]

Much has been written about the ignorance of Asia and especially about the remarkable 'mistakes' that supposedly explain Australia's foreign policy. Indeed there appears to be an almost universal, if tacit, understanding among the most reputable scholars that the innumerable false statements by Australian leaders about the Vietnam War and the China threat must be attributed to ignorance, however extraordinary, and mistakes, however incredible ('puzzling' is the usual word). These scholars live in a world which is saturated as never before by professionally composed, calculatedly deceptive propaganda; where, as Neil Sheehan observes of the Pentagon Papers, the language of description creates a 'looking-glass . . . world'. Yet one simple and obvious hypothesis would at once remove the need for a hundred special explanations in terms of improbable ignorance and puzzling mistakes – the hypothesis that Australia's political leaders engaged in sustained lying and deception on the ever-available excuse that they believed it served the 'national interest' (i.e. the objective of American military involvement in the region).[112]

Real ignorance there was, of course, though much of it was preferred ignorance, even cherished ignorance, serviceable to the propaganda and the beliefs required by the foreign-policy course to which the government had committed Australia. Real mistakes were few; probably only two of consequence. In the 1950s, the mistake of expecting, despite Dulles's express warning to the contrary, that Australia could buy a great power's blanket commitment to its defence by any means at all, let alone with 5,000 troops and unfailing endorsement of US rhetoric. In the 1960s there was only one mistake, but it was a momentous one. 'Australian leaders', as Renouf puts it, 'could not accept that the US', the greatest military power on earth, 'could be beaten by a mob of Asian peasants', and 'they persisted in this belief until the bitter end'. All the rest was lies and indifference. Lies about a threat from China; lies about the reasons for Australian involvement in Korea; uncounted lies about the origin and character of the war in Vietnam and about the reasons for Australian involvement. Indifference, total and enduring indifference, to the horrendous human consequences for Asian societies of the tactics by which Australia pursued, for almost a quarter of a century, the holy grail of Big Brother's assured protection.[113] Most of this was understood, and unhappily, by the officers of the Australian Task Force in Vietnam, as I discovered during a visit to Nui Dat in 1970. 'Words fail me,' Captain David Brown of the Task Force's public relations section told me, 'when I try to express my disgust with the political use the government has made of this war.'[114]

In late 1969, in the context of the Gorton government's abandonment of the idea of the communist threat to Australia, Dr Frank Knopfelmacher described some part of the lying found expedient during the past two decades. Knopfelmacher observed that while 'many, perhaps most of the leading Liberal politicians' did not seriously believe in 'the red menace', it had provided '*a sustaining myth* which keeps them in power'. By abandoning their myth the Liberals had, Dr Knopfelmacher complained, 'deauthorized the anti-communist stand . . . on which they depend for re-election', and had 'left themselves open to the charge that their past anti-communist crusades were cynical stunts to get votes'.[115]

Amen to that.

On the indifference of Australian foreign-policy architects to the human realities of Asia, Graham Freudenberg, press secretary and speech writer to Opposition leaders Calwell and Whitlam, has said all that is necessary (and, one can only hope, more than is true). During the Vietnam War Australian governments became, Freudenberg observes, 'locked into a process of lies' aimed at sustaining the

> myth . . . that our involvement was undertaken on behalf of the people of Vietnam, at their request to serve their interests and needs . . . The truth is that the fate of the people of Vietnam never weighed a feather in the scale as far as Australia was concerned. That applied essentially as much to the Labor Party as to the Menzies Government or any of its successors down to this day. For the Labor leadership the essential dilemma of the war was how to oppose it without opposing the United States [i.e. without prejudicing the search for US protection]; and how to denounce the war without denouncing the United States . . . Much of the moral indignation was rhetorical (I suppose I am entitled to say that as I provided a great deal of the rhetoric myself).[116]

Conclusion

It is probable that the relentless persecution of Burchett can be largely explained in two observations. First, if those of his persecutors whose leadership extended into the 1960s had been tried by the standards applied to Japanese and German war criminals after World War II, they could have been hanged for the contribution of their foreign policy to the monstrous war crime that engulfed Indochina (certainly the Japanese general Yamashita was hanged for incomparably less);[117] second, Burchett opposed and exposed this criminality with all the journalistic skill and moral and physical courage he possessed. But if one looks for more prosaic reasons for his persecution they, too, are abundant, both in the domestic and international contexts.

As Renouf has observed, 'Coalition governments from 1950 to 1972 . . . exaggerated the communist "threat" . . . [and] constantly hawked upon the menace of "international communism" . . . [T]o win domestic political favour they flogged the theme to death and when this worked so well they became its unthinking prisoner.' This tactic required, if only for credibility and consistency, that governments do everything possible to discredit and disown Burchett – quite apart from the political inconvenience that would result from leaving him free to tour the country at will (as he had done at the time of the anti-communist referendum), and offer a first-hand account of the world wholly contradictory to the government's profitable myth-making.[118]

Coalition governments would also have been under pressure from the Democratic Labor Party (DLP), on whose support they commonly depended for election, to keep Burchett out. Indeed, the recklessness with which the DLP worked the anti-communist pitch made the coalition conservative parties look almost scrupulous.[119] In 1964, as we have seen, the DLP's founder and moral standard-bearer, Mr B.A. Santamaria, claimed to be acquainted with internal documents of Mao Tse-tung's government which provided details of Chinese communist plans for the conquest of Australia and New Zealand. In 1966 he strenuously advocated that Australia 'should subordinate every aspect of foreign policy' – hence, the human consequences of that policy for Indochina – 'to the aim of keeping the United States in South East Asia'.[120] This is precisely the policy the government had adopted two years earlier. Moreover if Dr Knopfelmacher's estimate of the DLP's relations with coalition governments is correct the policy probably originated with the DLP.[121]

Despite these considerable domestic influences, it is likely that the most important cause of Australian governments' intransigence towards Burchett was their concern for American opinion. Even the relatively sober *Sydney Morning Herald* argued that 'our supreme interest must be to preserve the alliance with the United States which alone could protect us in a Great War . . . Any Australian government in its senses will be ready to go a long way to keep American trust, to meet American needs and win American respect.'[122] Given that the governments' long-continuing attempts to talk the US deeper into South East Asia while they themselves held back required all the American trust they could cultivate, Burchett's passport would hardly be regarded as a serious sacrifice. Certainly Burchett's allegedly 'anti-American' reports and activities during the Korean War were the reasons commonly given in American newspapers for the Australian governments' denying him a passport,[123] which suggests that Australian governments were at least content that Americans should have that impression. Moreover, the *US News and World Report* published as late as 1967 an article about Burchett[124] that referred to his activities in much the same vein as its 1953 article which had so disturbed the then head of External Affairs, Alan Watt. If one supposes American opinion to be the key, some incidental and ironic light is thrown on the ineffectiveness of Waller's plea on Burchett's behalf that, 'He is now recognized by the British Embassy (only the Americans abstain) and has a good reputation among the foreign press in Moscow.'

Finally, there is scant reason to take seriously the justification for their behaviour that Australian governments were happy to gain popular currency: that Burchett was a committed communist who had harassed Australian prisoners of war and otherwise behaved treasonably in Korea. In 1953 Peter Robinson, currently associate editor of the Sydney *Sun Herald*, then working for Reuters, interviewed most of the Australian POWs when they were exchanged for North Korean POWs. While Robinson found the Australians resentful and suspicious of Burchett on account of his sympathy with their enemy, none claimed to have been brainwashed or interrogated by him. Some two years later

Robinson was interviewed by ASIO, still searching for evidence against Burchett.[125] It is reasonable therefore to suppose that by 1956 at the latest the Australian government had good reason to believe there was no basis for the charges about POWs. We have seen that in 1961 the Department of External Affairs was unable to provide Ambassador Waller with remotely plausible evidence for these charges; and that Malcolm Morris, who shared Waller's views about Burchett, was later blocked from reopening his case, probably by Hasluck. Moreover when Burchett returned to Australia in 1970 especially for the purpose of compelling the government either to lay charges against him or clear his name, nobody in the government was willing, in or out of parliament, to accuse him of any improper behaviour with respect to POWs. Even the 'communist' label so assiduously attached to Burchett was false. Bill Gollan, a prominent member of the Australian Communist Party, has revealed that in 1964 he was deputized to invite Burchett to join the party. Burchett politely declined.[126] One thing is certain, whatever the reasons for the long exile imposed on Burchett, they were not the reasons Australian governments gave or allowed to be believed.

The two decades that earned Burchett most enmity and obliquy were dominated by Cold War anti-communism which found its principal origin in American domestic politics, and its principal outlet in the physical devastation of four Asian societies. This period has been likened by historian Hugh Trevor-Roper to the witch crazes of the sixteenth and seventeenth centuries. Dissidents from orthodoxy were then pilloried as 'patrons of witches'.[127] More recently those who denied the diabolism of Ho Chi Minh and Mao Tse-tung and the mass movements they led were pilloried as 'communist sympathizers'. During these oppressive decades the vast majority of Australian politicians, diplomats and scholars followed the career-safe paths of anti-communist orthodoxy and accommodation to official claims that 'national interest' required aiding and abetting 'some of the most barbarous killing the world has seen'.[128] Burchett followed a different path.

One other pervasive circumstance obstructed Burchett's efforts. The Cold War decades saw the establishment of propaganda and opinion-management in the West on a scale unknown since World War I, and quite without peacetime precedent.[129] Carried worldwide by modern media the American anti-communist crusade that escaped Truman's control fuelled fear and intemperance. A tiny index of the scale of the 'information' war that resulted is provided by the US Information Agency, which claims that by 1962 its films alone, distributed worldwide in forty languages, were reaching audiences of 750 million annually.[130]

It is within this context that Burchett's one-man worldwide campaign for truth, justice and decency, so far as he was able to discover or discern these, must be seen. To set so small a means to so epic a task appears, on the face of it, absurdly quixotic. Indeed, some element of the quixotic, an impulsive generosity of feeling that carried over into action, marked Burchett's life throughout – as Waller observed in connection with his resignation in 1962 from his positions with the

Financial Times and *Express* in protest against what he had seen in Laos and Vietnam. However, quixotic or not, 'in an over-eventful time . . . Burchett covered the ground at fabulous speed'.[131] His energy and persistence created in time an epic of human endeavour and achievement: countless despatches and some thirty books published worldwide; almost ceaseless travel to places, however remote or dangerous, where history was being made; unique access to Asian leaders of half the world's population and close friendships with many of them; remarkable friendships even in the countries officially most hostile to him (Harrison Salisbury and US Army General Dean; Prime Minister Whitlam and Australian ambassadors); and the active respect of hundreds of world-famous figures in almost every walk of life, as the petition of 1968 made clear. This is a remarkable odyssey for a self-educated youth from the Victorian bush.

Burchett's achievements are the more surprising when measured against the essential simplicity of the qualities by which they were attained. Even his American critics allowed that 'Burchett never lied so far as anyone could discover',[132] and his openness and good-natured sociability won him friends everywhere. But perhaps his most distinctive characteristic was an abiding faith in ordinary people which seemed to reach back to his rural childhood. In this connection a reviewer for the *Economist* remarked, in 1981, that all Burchett's writing was done 'in the conviction, which has come touchingly unscathed through so many demonstrations to the contrary, that if people are told the "true" facts they will do the right thing'.[133]

In 1980, three years before his death, Burchett published his autobiography, *At the Barricades*. With few exceptions reviews were highly appreciative of both the work and the man. Even the conservative *Economist* noted that

> Mr Burchett's professional colleagues have . . . never shared the distaste of those in authority for his maverick attitudes and behaviour. He has always been a good colleague. Quite often . . . Mr Burchett was the only one who knew what the other side had to say and could be relied upon. By the way he handled [this circumstance] . . . he earned as much professional good will as he did official disapproval.

When all limitations are allowed for, the *Economist* concludes, Burchett's work is a 'source for the world history of the age'.[134]

Burchett was 'enormously pleased' by the reception of *At the Barricades* and 'was especially cheered by the enthusiastic reaction of colleagues'. 'Burchett,' Margaret Jones wrote from London, 'denied an Australian passport for seventeen years, labelled a traitor and a KGB agent, has become, at seventy, eminently respectable;' and, indeed, something of a celebrity.[135]

In reporting and interpreting post-war history as it happened, Burchett was in a sense the first revisionist historian.[136] And as American scholarship escapes the long McCarthyist legacy, the influence of this school will surely increase. One thing is clear. Time will be kinder to Burchett than to his persecutors. Two final citations show this process already well under way.

The devotion of Professor Hans Morgenthau to America, and the ideals he believed its history to enshrine, is beyond dispute.[137] But, unlike some of his Australian disciples, Morgenthau cared also about truth and evidence.

In 1974, at the time of American involvement in the overthrow of the Allende government and before the end of the Vietnam War, Morgenthau wrote:

> The moral storm that has broken over our intervention in Chile has obscured what seems to me to be the crucial issue transcending this particular intervention: with unfailing consistency we have since the end of the Second World War, intervened on behalf of conservative and fascist repression against revolution and radical reform. In an age when societies are in a revolutionary or pre-revolutionary stage, we have become the foremost counter-revolutionary status quo power on earth.
>
> Such a policy can only lead to moral and political disaster. While we wax indignant or apologetic over our most recent anti-revolutionary intervention, we might do well not to lose sight of the political root of the problem.[138]

Burchett never wrote more harshly of American policy.

The Australian Army Training Team, Vietnam, was the first Australian unit to go into Vietnam and the last to leave. The official history of the team's ten years of war was published in 1984. It concludes with a graphic summary of the circumstances of the team's work. In South Vietnam its members found they had to try 'to develop in the Vietnamese the will to fight'.

> Several factors may have led to this. One was the lack of widespread appeal of the South Vietnamese government's policies when compared with the revolutionary fervour of communism and nationalism . . . Another was the self-defeating influence and presence of the allied forces which appeared simply to be replacing the French . . . [Moreover] North Vietnam could demonstrate a greater legitimacy to be heir to the future of a united Vietnam. By its efforts French colonial rule had been terminated and independence reached; the spirit of nationalism seemed now to be frustrated by the Americans. Under the venerated Ho Chi Minh the claim by the North Vietnamese to represent the abiding aspirations of all the Vietnamese was more convincing than the counterclaim by the shifting junta in Saigon. The South Vietnamese army seemed to reflect this position . . . [It] had no traditions on which to draw. In its infancy it had represented the French colonial power; in 1966 it appeared to be fighting for the Americans.[139]

This entire judgement, by an official army historian, could have been taken almost verbatim from first-hand reports twenty years earlier by the man whom Australia's leaders insisted on reviling and exiling as a communist propagandist. Had Burchett's accurate reporting been given attention more than a million lives, including some hundreds of Australian lives, could have been saved.[140] In the longer perspective of history it will not be Wilfred Burchett who will want for honour, but his Australian persecutors and critics who applied so much effort and deception to tip the balance towards barbarism in Indochina when another course might have been possible.

Notes

1. R.A. Woolcott, Second Secretary, Moscow, to Secretary, Department of External Affairs, Canberra. Memo No. 378, 3 August 1959.
2. Rod Irwin, Assistant Secretary, Executive Secretariat, Department of Foreign Affairs, Canberra, to Mr Winston Burchett, 8 March 1984.
3. S. Jamieson, Australian Ambassador, Moscow, to Secretary, Department of External Affairs, Canberra, 12 July 1963. Memo No. 408, File No. 62/1/2/1.
4. H.E. Holt, Minister for Immigration, to B. Fitzpatrick, General Secretary, Australian Council for Civil Liberties, Melbourne (undated); see also W. Burchett, *Passport: An Autobiography*, Nelson, Melbourne, 1969, pp.281–2.
5. *Passport*, pp.283, 285–6.
6. The reference is presumably to Mr Ian Charles Hamilton. Hamilton, following an extended journalistic career, was Public Relations Officer with the Australian Commission in Singapore from 1953 to 1957. From 1957 to 1962 he was a member of the Department of External Affairs. From 1962 to 1964 he edited the *Australian News and Information Bulletin*. (*Who's Who in Australia*, 1983, p.379.)
7. See reference 1 above.
8. J.K. Waller, Ambassador, Moscow, to Secretary, Department of External Affairs, Canberra, 10 October 1960. Memo No. 412, File No. 500/62/1/2/1.
9. J.K. Waller, Ambassador, Moscow, to Secretary, Department of External Affairs, Canberra, 23 November 1960. Memo No. 457, File No. 500/62/1/2/1.
10. J.K. Waller, Ambassador, Moscow, to Secretary, Department of External Affairs, Canberra, 7 March 1961. Memo No. 190, File No. 500/62/1/2/1.
11. Keith Waller, Australian Embassy, Moscow, to D.J. Anderson, Department of External Affairs, Canberra, 24 April 1961. No File No. recorded. Refers to 'Your File 131/6 – W. Burchett'.
12. J.K. Waller, Ambassador, Moscow, to Secretary, Department of External Affairs, Canberra, 31 May 1961. Memo No. 414, File No. 500/62/1/2/1. The filed note is undated but from its location in the FOI material was written in 1962 or early 1963.
13. J.K. Waller, Ambassador, Moscow, to F.H. Stuart, Australian Ambassador, Cairo, 5 March 1963. Marked 'Personal'. File 131/6.
14. S.P. Crosland, General Secretary, The Australian Journalists Association Federal Executive, Sydney, to Hon P.M.C. Hasluck, Minister for External Affairs, Parliament Ho., Canberra, 16 March 1965.
15. A.M. Morris, Assistant Secretary, Defence Liaison Branch, Department of External Affairs, 24 March 1965. (Internal Memo, destination not clear.) File 131/6.
16. E.W. Irwin, Melbourne, to Hon Paul Hasluck, Minister for External Affairs, Canberra, 22 March 1965.
17. Sir Ronald East to Hon J.G. Gorton, Prime Minister, Canberra, 2 February 1969.
18. G. Hartley for Acting Secretary, Department of External Affairs, to Secretary, Department of Immigration, 31 March 1965.
19. *Passport*, pp.292–3.

20. H.J. Grant, Deputy Chief Migration Officer, Canberra Ho., London, to W.G. Burchett, Paris, 9 October 1968.
21. *Age*, 20 July 1968. See also *Passport*, p.289.
22. W. Burchett, *At the Barricades*, Melbourne, Macmillan, 1981, p.260; and *Passport*, pp.291–2, 295–8.
23. *Passport*, p.291.
24. F. Galbally to Rt Hon J.G. Gorton, Prime Minister, Canberra, 17 February 1969.
25. F. Galbally to Rt Hon J.G. Gorton, Prime Minister, Canberra, 4 March 1969.
26. Letter, *Sydney Morning Herald*, 18 April 1969.
27. F. Galbally to Hon B.M. Snedden, 11 April 1969, with copy and cover letter to Rt Hon J.G. Gorton, Prime Minister, Canberra.
28. *Passport*, p.292.
29. Press release, 'Mr Wilfred Burchett'. PM No. 27/1970, Canberra, 12 February 1970.
30. *At the Barricades*, p.262.
31. Ibid., pp.262–5.
32. Ibid., pp.266–70.
33. See reference 12 above.
34. *Hansard*, 4 March 1970, pp.30–1.
35. See e.g. Cable No. I.104425, dated 5 December 1968 from the Australian Mission to the United Nations, New York, to Department of External Affairs, Canberra, and article 'Burchett, Kissinger Conferred' by S. Karnow, marked *Washington Post*, 25 December 1971 and included in material released by the Department of External Affairs.
36. 'An Australian Asks for Justice', *The Times*, 5 March 1970.
37. G. Freudenberg, *A Certain Grandeur*, Macmillan, Melbourne, 1977, p.246.
38. J.K. Waller, Secretary, Department of External Affairs, Canberra, to Wilfred Burchett, via Australian Embassy, Paris. Cable No. 0.109967 12 December 1972.
39. G. Clark, *In Fear of China*, Lansdowne, Melbourne, 1967, pp.195–200.
40. Memorandum from A.S. Watt, Secretary, Department of External Affairs, to the Solicitor General, Attorney General's Department, 16 October 1953. Article to which Watt refers is 'Strange Case of Two Traitors: Aided Reds . . . Faked Germ-War "Confessions" . . . Needled Prisoners', *U.S. News and World Report*, 2 October 1953, pp.22–4.
41. R.M. Freeland, *The Truman Doctrine and the Origin of McCarthyism*, Knopf, New York, pp.64–5, 89.
42. Ibid., H.J. Morgenthau, *In Defense of the National Interest: A Critical Examination of American Foreign Policy*, Knopf, New York, 1951.
43. Ibid., pp.78–81.
44. Ibid., pp.234–40.
45. R. Porter, 'Rusk Hints US Aid to Revolt in China', *New York Times*, 19 May 1951, pp.1, 3 at p.3.
46. US Department of State, *North Korea: A Case Study in the Techniques of Takeover*, Department of State Publication 7118 Far Eastern Series 103 (released January 1961), pp.3–5, 104, 118–20.
47. 'Who-What-Why', *Reporter*, 27 January 1955, p.8.
48. R. Rovere, *Senator Joe McCarthy*, Methuen, London, 1959, pp.10–11, 17–19. See also pp.29–32.
49. M. Merson, 'My Education in Government', *Reporter*, 27 January 1955, p.8.
50. B. Fall, 'Containing China', *Commentary*, May 1966, p. 34; D. Horowitz, *The Free World Colossus*, MacGibbon and Kee, London, 1965, pp. 118–19; A. Renouf, *The Frightened Country*, Macmillan, Melbourne, 1979, p.68. Renouf observes that 'President Truman decided to intervene [in Korea] more because of the need to show the incorrectness of Republican charges of Democratic softness towards communism (the "loss" of China accusation) than because of the announced rationale of defending freedom and resisting aggression.' Op.cit., p.69.
51. Rovere, op. cit., p. 18. Truman told Attlee that it was not possible to end the Korean War at the 38th parallel 'because the American people would not stand for it'. Freeland, op. cit., p. 356.

On the illegality of carrying the war into North Korea and the consequent scale of casualties and destruction see Horowitz, op. cit., pp. 126–9.

On 27 September 1950 Prime Minister Menzies observed, 'The point everyone has in mind is that nobody is going in for a war of invasion of North Korea – a war of conquest.' 'UN initiative in Korea', *Sydney Morning Herald*, 28 September 1950, p. 4.

52. *Passport*, pp. 187–96; I.F. Stone, *The Hidden History of the Korean War*, Monthly Review, New York, 1952, pp. 316–17.
53. T.B. Millar (ed.), *Australian Foreign Minister: The Diaries of R.G. Casey 1951–1960*. London, Collins, 1972, pp. 65–6, 94, 132, 145, 164, 189, 194, 203, 302; Renouf, pp. 16, 69, 119, 242, 276, 301.
54. Millar, op. cit., p. 164.
55. W. Crocker, 'Foreign Policy for Australia', *Institute of Public Affairs Review* 25(4), 1971, p. 92.
56. Gregory Clark reports that 'in any assessments of developments in South Vietnam the usual EA approach seemed to be to take the most optimistic of the various US assessments available and to put that forward as the official view'. G. Clark 'Vietnam China and the Foreign Affairs Debate in Australia: A Personal Account' in P. King (ed.), *Australia's Vietnam*, Allen and Unwin, Sydney, 1983, p. 21. See also ibid., pp. 26–7; Clark, *In Fear Of China*, pp. 169–71, and Renouf, op. cit., pp. 276–7. pp. 276–7.
57. R. O'Neill, *Australia in the Korean War, 1950–53*, Australian War Memorial and Australian Government Publishing Service, 1980, pp. 58–61, 69.
58. Ibid., pp. 48–56, 61, 66–7, 71–2.
59. ibid., pp. 53, 58–61, 65, 70, 75; see also A. Watt, *Australian Diplomat*, Angus and Robertson, Sydney, 1972, p. 173: 'When the Korean War broke out on 25 June 1950 the United States decided to intervene . . .[T]he UN Security Council asked members of the UN to assist American Forces. Spender was anxious to comply and with speed. His main policy objective was to secure a Pacific Pact including the United States.' See also O'Neill's comment that Spender's successful conclusion of the ANZUS Treaty 'depended upon the particularly favourable climate of opinion created in Washington, and above all with President Truman, by Australia's assistance in the Korean War'. Op.cit., p. 200.
60. A. Watt, *Australian Diplomat*, p. 181.
61. O'Neill, op. cit., pp. 68–71, 75–6.
62. O'Neill observes, 'In early 1951, Spender was much more concerned about the Japanese peace treaty and the Pacific pact than about the baffling complexities of the Korean conflict.' Op.cit., p. 198.

On the gap between actual motives and the rhetoric by which Australian participation in the war was justified see O'Neill, op. cit., pp. 61, 76; also Renouf, op. cit., pp. 77–9.
63. Millar, op. cit., p. 82; Clark, op. cit., p. 192. For Hasluck's views in 1953 see text at Note 98.
64. Renouf, op. cit., pp. 77–9; J.F. Dulles, 'Security in the Pacific', *Foreign Affairs*, 30 January 1952, p. 183.
65. Millar (ed.), *Australian Foreign Minister*, editorial footnote, p. 179; for rebuffed appeals to the US see pp. 178–9, 195, 198–9, 207, 210, 214–15, 216–18. For Casey's subsequent decisions see ibid., pp. 248, 253.
66. Ibid., pp. 337, 311; B.A. Santamaria, 'New Guinea: The Price of Weakness', 1959, cited in *The Defence of Australia*, Hawthorne, Melbourne, 1970, pp. 11, 82–3; see also p. 98 on the lessons provided by West New Guinea.
67. T.B. Millar, 'Australian Defence, 1945–1965' in G. Greenwood and N. Harper (eds.), *Australia in World Affairs 1961–1965*, Cheshire, Melbourne, 1968, p. 283. See also Clark, op.cit., pp. 171–2.
68. D. Marr, *Barwick*, Allen and Unwin, Sydney, 1980. See also Clark, op.cit., pp. 171–2 and Renouf, op.cit., p. 530: 'The US did not help in Australia's trials with Indonesia over West New Guinea and Timor and gave only some equivocal solace over Indonesia's confrontation of Malaysia. Hence the almost slavish adherence to the US did not oblige the US to help Australia in time of national need.' In

consequence 'Australia has tended . . . to fall into the role of "urger" in the belief
that if American forces were actually engaged in South East Asia, so much more
certain were American guarantees to Australia.' B. Grant, *The Crisis of Loyalty: A
Study of Australian Foreign Policy*, Angus and Robertson, Sydney, 1972, p. 25.
69. B.A. Santamaria, *The Price of Freedom*, Campion Press, Melbourne, 1964, pp. 4–6;
Grant, op. cit., pp. 45, 43. See also Sexton: the 'central proposition' of Australia's
foreign policy was that 'locking the Americans into the Vietnam conflict could keep
them in South East Asia and maximize their role as Australia's protector'. Michael
Sexton, *War For the Asking*, Penguin, Melbourne, 1981, p.120.
70. Clark, 'Vietnam, China . . .', pp. 25–6. See also Clark, *In Fear of China*, pp. 168–70;
Sexton, op. cit., pp. 96–9 especially, 'The plan was therefore that the Canberra
hawks should combine with their Washington counterparts to overcome the doubters
in the American administration;' and Renouf, op. cit., p. 273: 'The policy was
Australia's own work . . . it was not the policy of a satellite.'
71. Clark 'Vietnam, China . . .', p. 18.
72. Sexton, op.cit., pp. 94–5, 98, 122.
73. Ibid., pp. 51–69 and 89–107.
74. Renouf, op.cit., p. 242; N. Sheehan, H. Smith, E.W. Kenworthy and H. Butterfield,
The Pentagon Papers as Published by the New York Times, Bantam Books, New
York, 1971, pp. ix–x.
75. D. Warner, 'Blunder and Achievement', *Sydney Morning Herald*, 31 December
1969, p. 6 and 'Vietnam's Lessons for Australia', *Sydney Morning Herald*, 1 January
1970, p. 6; H. Bull, 'Australia and the Great Powers in Asia' in Greenwood and
Harper (eds.), *Australia in World Affairs 1966–1970*, Cheshire, Melbourne, 1974, p.
348.
76. R.G. Menzies: statement in House of Representatives 29 April 1965. *Current Notes
on International Affairs 36*, 1965, p. 179.
77. R.G. Menzies, 'Address . . . to the American/Australian Association in Washington
on 11th June 1965'. *Current Notes on International Affairs 36*, 1965, p. 342.
78. P. Hasluck, 25 November 1964, *Current Notes on International Affairs 35*, No. xi,
p. 33.
79. P. Hasluck, *Commonwealth Parliamentary Debates*, 10 March 1966, p. 173.
80. P. Hasluck, *Current Notes on International Affairs 37*, 1966, p. 230.
81. Ibid., p. 531.
82. A. Fairhall, *Commonwealth Parliamentary Debates 62*, 15 March 1966, p. 247.
83. H. Bull, op.cit., p. 334. See also B. Grant, op.cit., p. 15. 'The government parties
fell victim to the Frankenstein monster they had created to justify the war – that
China would march south, . . . the dominoes would begin falling . . .'
84. F.S. Hopkins, 'The American Image of Australia', in N. Harper (ed.), *Pacific Orbit*,
Cheshire, Melbourne, 1968, pp. 234–5.
85. Renouf, op.cit., pp. 261–2, 277–8. See also Sexton, op.cit., p.94: 'during this month
[January, 1965] the Americans were not locked into any firm decisions . . . If . . .
Australia had, like New Zealand, discouraged the escalation of the war . . . a
different result might have followed . . . What is clear . . . is that Australia
encouraged escalation . . . in the clear realization that its view *could* have some
significance in the confused conditions that prevailed inside the administration.'
86. D. Warner, 'The Australians in Vietnam', *Sydney Morning Herald*, 30 December
1969, p.6.
87. G. Clark, *In Fear of China*, esp. Chapter 10; 'Between Two Worlds: the
Radicalization of a Conservative', *Meanjin Quarterly 2*, 1974, pp. 177–27. J.
Edwards, 'Career Diplomat Alan Renouf Speaks Out', *National Times*, 25 August
1979, p. 33. Renouf finds 'a baffling irrational constancy about Australia's policy'
and concludes that 'the explanation . . . lies at least partly in the way it was
formulated. Successive prime ministers and ministers considered they knew
everything about Vietnam and did not welcome objective advice. A public servant
unable to provide confirmation got out of the way or lay low. Those remaining active
were by character and experience as conservative as their political masters. An
Australian ambassador in Saigon once had the temerity to tell the government of his

doubts about US policy. He was severely and publicly rebuked; to criticize US, and hence Australian, policy became unthinkable.' Renouf, op.cit., pp. 276–7.
88. Clark, 'Between Two Worlds . . .', p. 120.
89. Sexton, op.cit., pp. 44–107.
90. Edwards, op.cit., p. 33; E.G. Whitlam, 'Whitlam on Renouf', *Australian Financial Review* 24 August 1979, p. 40. Renouf elsewhere reports that Anderson was 'severely and publicly rebuked', op.cit., p. 277. See note 87 above.
91. Edwards, op.cit., p. 33.
92. Clark, 'Between Two Worlds . . .', pp. 117–27 and 'Vietnam, China . . .', pp. 19–35.
93. Clark, 'Vietnam, China . . .', pp. 21–2.
94. Bull, op.cit., p. 336.
95. Edwards, op.cit., p. 33; Sexton, op.cit., p. 48.
96. Clark, 'Vietnam, China . . .', pp. 18–20.
97. D.E. Kennedy, 'Australian Policy Towards China' in G. Greenwood and N. Harper (eds.) 1968, p. 404.
98. G. Greenwood 'Australian Foreign Policy in Action' in Greenwood and Harper, op.cit., pp. 33–6, 49–50; G. Greenwood, 'The Political Debate in Australia' in Greenwood and Harper, 1974, pp. 37–8; N. Harper, 'Australia and the United States' in Greenwood and Harper, 1968, pp. 316–17 and 1974, p. 271; Bull, op.cit., p. 349; Renouf, op.cit., pp. 268–9; Sexton, op.cit., p. 35.
99. 'Hans J. Morgenthau, Author and Teacher Dead at 76', *New York Times*, 21 July 1980, p.A14.
100. N. Harper, 'Australia and the United States', in Greenwood and Harper, 1974, p. 271 and 1968, p. 316.
101. For consideration of the psychology and possible pathology of Australian attitudes to China under Hasluck's regime see Clark, *In Fear of China*, pp. 172–91; on Hasluck in particular see p. 181.
102. Morgenthau, *In Defense of the National Interest*, pp. 3–39. Morgenthau claims specifically that 'A foreign policy derived from the national interest is in fact morally superior to a foreign policy inspired by universal moral principles' (p. 39).
103. B. Grant, op.cit., p. 3.
104. Morgenthau, op.cit.
105. Renouf, op.cit., p. 273.
106. Throughout the 1950s Casey made what he called 'my annual plea' for increased defence expenditure; 'repeatedly . . . he was met with the query: "And who is about to attack us?"' Australian defence expediture continued at a rate between one third and one tenth of the US, Canada and the UK. Casey's immediate concern seems to have been more that the US would regard Australia as not pulling its weight than with foreseeable threats from anywhere. Millar, *Australian Foreign Minister*, pp. 172–3, 237, 259, 262, 295.
    So far from emphasizing any threat from China Casey endlessly expressed dissatisfaction (to his diary) with the unreasonableness of American attitudes to China – which he correctly attributed to the McCarthyist influence on American public opinion. Throughout the 1950s he favoured recognition of China and sought to soften US attitudes towards China. (None of this was reflected of course in his public rhetoric.) Ibid., pp. 63, 65, 108, 131, 134–5, 137–8, 145, 164, 189, 194, 213–14, 294, 302, 309, 326.
107. Greenwood, 'Australian Foreign Policy . . .' 1968, p. 46. See also p. 119.
108. Bull, op.cit., p. 335; Greenwood, 'The Political Debate . . .' 1974, pp. 82–3. See also H. Gerber, *The Australian American Alliance*, Penguin, 1968,pp. 94–5 and A. Watt, *The Evolution of Australian Foreign Policy*, C.U.P. 1967, pp. 244–5: 'Despite strong American objections to such trade, Australia has sold to Communist China not only wool but large quantities of wheat;' and while the Menzies government rarely acknowledges differences with the US on foreign policy, it made a 'notable and remarkable exception of differences over . . . trade policy!'
109. A. Carey, 'Clockwork Vietnam: Gaining Physical Control', *Meanjin Quarterly*, March 1973, p. 45; 'Australian Atrocities in Vietnam', Sydney Vietnam Action Campaign, 1969, p. 19.

110. Warner, op.cit., p. 6; Carey, 'Australian Atrocities . . .', p. 19, 'Australia in Vietnam', *New Statesman*, 6 November 1970, p. 599; Greenwood, 'Australian Foreign Policy . . .', pp. 16–18.
111. B. A. Santamaria, *The Defence of Australia*, Hawthorne, Melbourne, 1970, pp. 4, 9; Grant, op.cit., p. 58.
112. N. Sheehan et al., op.cit., p. xii. Renouf implicitly acknowledges the calculated deception – which is progress of a sort – but still opts for ignorance, 'mistakes' and 'puzzling' misjudgements to explain everything. Thus, 'Australia's Vietnam policy as an exercise in foreign relations was technically well handled. The policy was repeatedly and clearly explained *but the public were told only what the government wanted it to know*. Australia's support of the US had a hand in getting the US increasingly involved, as the Australian governments planned. Australia's policy was energetically explained abroad, particularly when Hasluck was at the helm. The only defect was that the policy was wrong,' (Renouf, op.cit., p. 274 emphasis added).

 Yet the possibility that lies and deception played a significant part in Australian foreign policy is not entertained even while acknowledging the great political benefits that flowed from 'mistakes' and misjudgements: 'Successive Australian governments from 1954–72 shared the *mistakes* made by their counterparts in Washington . . .They were obsessed with Communism and with China *and found that obsession served them well electorally*. Between 1950–72 Australia was the world's most strongly anti-communist country and the domino theory flourished with conservative politicians as it did nowhere else . . . The North Vietnamese were firstly nationalists and secondly communists. Australian governments *could not understand* this; it was a fundamental *mistake* making them believe that the Vietnam War was a southward push of "international communism" led by China and the USSR' (ibid., pp. 274–5 emphasis added).

 For Renouf it remains simply 'puzzling' that 'the defeat of "international communism" has been a stronger and more enduring element of foreign policy in Australia than in any other country, including the US', although this clearly should not have happened because 'Australia did not have the same emotional "hang-ups" as the US to the loss of China and Cuba . . . had not experienced McCarthyism to anywhere near the same extent and her interests were not so directly involved in the Cold War' (ibid., pp. 2–3, 276, 277).

 The possibility – even likelihood – of lies and deception is often recognized hypothetically, e.g: 'A threat analysis which erred on the side of alarmist would have twin benefits. It might, especially if it came from a close and reliable ally, attract additional American support. And the domestic fears which the analysis aroused could be used to consolidate support for the alliance and discredit opposition' (H. Gelber, *The Australian American Alliance: Costs and Benefits*, Penguin, 1967, p. 28). But, in general, that is as far as scepticism is allowed to go. No attempt is made by professional students of politics to explore the extent or consequences of such deception. The two principal exceptions to this rule are Evan Whitton, a journalist who happens to combine scholarly skill with uncommon courage, and Michael Sexton whose academic discipline is law. (See Whitton's series of articles in the *National Times*, 28 April 1975 et seq., which constituted the first significant attempt to document the extent of government lying and deception over Vietnam, and Sexton's later development of Whitton's thesis in *War for the Asking*, Penguin 1981).
113. Renouf, op.cit., p. 276; Bull, op.cit., pp. 346–7: 'Australian support for the US in Vietnam . . . derived primarily not from convictions about the merits of the issue, but from the belief that Australia needed to support whatever policies the US pursued in Vietnam – partly so as to demonstrate Australia's willingness to contribute to the alliance, and partly so as to encourage the US to remain militarily present in the area.'

 Australian governments remained simply indifferent to criticism about the Vietnam War, however well founded, because 'the judgement that underlay the Holt government's policies – like those of the Menzies government before it – was that however numerous the critics and sceptics might be, the United States, having embarked upon its great enterprise in Vietnam, and having made the enormous

commitment in money and in blood that it had made, could not fail'.
114. Carey, *Australia in Vietnam*, p. 599.
115. F. Knopfelmacher, 'The Myths In Australian Politics', *Australian*, (Letters), 31 October 1969.
116. G. Freudenberg, 'How the Vietnam War Was Made', *Sydney Morning Herald,*23 May 1981, p. 45; see also Sexton, op.cit., pp. 1–2, 40, 147.
117. Telford Taylor, *Nuremberg and Vietnam*, Quadrangle, New York, 1970, pp. 83–8, 91–2, 176–82, 205–7.

Taylor was chief US counsel at the Nuremberg trials with the rank of Brigadier General. He makes the following observations which, with appropriate substitutions, apply to Australian civilian leaders of the 1960s: 'At Nuremberg . . . nearly all the defendants stood at or near the top of the military or civilian hierarchy. Their punishment gave real meaning to the injunction . . . that the primary responsibility for war crimes . . . rests on those in authority who gave the orders . . . Cabinet ministers and other civilian officials were a majority of those put to trial' (p.83).

'The [Vietnam] War, in the massive lethal dimensions it acquired after 1964, was the work of highly educated academics and administrators . . . It [is] . . . the Rusks, Macnamaras, Bundys and Rostows . . . who must bear major responsibility . . . How could it ever have been thought that air strikes, free-fire zones and a mass uprooting and removal of the rural population were the way to "win the allegiance of the South Vietnamese"? . . . [How] could a ratio of 28 to 1 between our investments in bombing, and in relief for those we had wounded and made homeless, have ever been contemplated, let alone adopted as the operational patern? . . . [W]e have smashed the country to bits and will not even take the trouble to clean up the blood and rubble . . . Somehow we failed ourselves to learn the lessons we undertook to teach at Nuremberg' (pp. 205–7).

Menzies, Holt, Gorton, Hasluck and Fraser were all leading accomplices to this outcome.
118. Renouf, op.cit., p. 19; op. cit., *Passport,* pp. 181–3.
119. E.g. 'If Formosa goes then Australia's days as a European democracy are numbered', *Newsweekly* (editorial), 9 February 1955, p. 10; see also Santamaria, *The Price of Freedom*, op. cit., pp. 3–5.
120. B.A. Santamaria, *The Politics of 1966*, Hawthorne, Melbourne, 1966, p. 3.
121. Knopfelmacher, op.cit; see also J.A. Camelleri, *An Introduction to Australian Foreign Policy*, Jackaranda, Milton, 1979, p. 55: The 'militantly anti-Communist' DLP controlled sufficient votes to 'give it a determining influence over the outcome of most elections from 1955 to 1969'.
122. Editorial, *Sydney Morning Herald*, 1 January 1969.
123. 'Wilfred Burchett Finds He Can Go Home Again', *New York Times*, 1 March 1970, p. 2; S. Karnow 'Burchett, Kissinger Conferred', *Washington Post,*25 December 1971.
124. 'Mouthpiece for Reds: the Strange Role of Wilfred Burchett', *US News and World Report*, 27 February 1967, pp. 19–20.
125. Personal communicatioh from Mr Robinson, 26 June 1984.
126. Personal communication from Mr Gollan, 18 May 1984. See his letter to *Sydney Morning Herald*, 20 August 1985.
127. H.R. Trevor-Roper, *The European Witch–Craze of the 16th and 17th Centuries*, Pelican, 1967, pp. 48, 53, 93.
128. Clark, 'Between Two Worlds . . .' 1974, p. 118.
129. A. Carey, 'Reshaping the Truth: Pragmatists and Propagandists in America', *Meanjin Quarterly*, December 1976, pp. 370–8.
130. W.P. Davison, *International Political Communication*, Praeger, New York, 1965, pp. 253–4.
131. 'Militant Maverick', *The Economist*, 17 October 1981, p. 122.
132. 'Mouthpiece for Reds . . .', p. 20.
133. 'Militant Maverick', p. 122. For an appreciation of Burchett's humanist commitments and values see Harrison Salisbury's introduction to *At the Barricades*.
134. 'Militant Maverick', p. 122.

135. M. Jones, 'After Russia, China, Burchett's Cause is Now Vietnam', *Sydney Morning Herald*, 3 November 1981, p. 7.

136. 'As early as 1945–6 Burchett embraced what became known as the revisionist interpretation of the cold war'. P. Hollander, 'His Master's Voice', *New Republic*, 18 July 1981, p. 35.

137. H.J. Morgenthau, *The Purpose of American Policies,* Knopf, New York, 1960.

138. H.J. Morgenthau, 'Regression's Friend', *New York Times* (Letters), 10 October, 1974.

139. I. McNeill, *The Team: Australian Army Advisers in Vietnam 1962–1972*, University of Queensland Press in Association with the Australian War Memorial, 1984, p. 482.

140. It deserves notice that this official summary of the difficulties our 'side' encountered in its endeavours to maintain the governments it preferred in Saigon makes no reference to China. Indeed the 500-page history of ten years of Australian military involvement in Vietnam contains *one* inconsequential reference to China. Compare the lying or culpably ignorant description of the war provided by Sir Robert Menzies as late as 1970: The US 'intervened in Vietnam because, more clearly than any of the European powers, it saw the defence of South Vietnam as a defence against the aggression of Communist China, an aggression which . . . if unrestrained, could threaten the peace and security of the whole world'. R.G. Menzies, *The Measure of the Years*, Cassell, Melbourne, 1970, p. 219.

5

White Nomad: Burchett's Approach to Asia in the Australian Context

Beverley Smith

Until December 1960, the masthead of Australia's leading weekly, the Sydney *Bulletin*, carried the words 'Australia for the White Man'.[1] The British settlers acknowledged the proximity of Asia and the validity of the term 'Australasia'[2] in the early years of the colony, but the foundations for racism and contempt for alien cultures were daily being laid by the ruthless dispossession of the aborigines.[3] From the outset there were individuals whose attitude to the aborigines was enlightened, but these were minority voices.[4] Over time, occupation of the vast Australian inland dominated the imagination of the European. On the discovery of gold in the 1850s, and with the emergence of a sense of national identity, new factors reinforced isolationism and racial prejudice. Violent anti-Chinese riots broke out on the gold diggings.[5] In mines, on ships, in factories and on the canefields, workers perceived a threat to hard-won improvements in wages and working conditions. They opposed Asian (and Pacific Islander) immigration and the use of 'coloured' indentured labour, often under conditions of virtual slavery.

Wilfred Burchett was a direct product of the Australian labour tradition, yet he spent most of his life writing sympathetically about Asians. And when he was finally about to return home in 1974 to take on the Australian establishment in his libel suit, he wrote to his brother: 'To keep my newspapers happy, I should do some stories, perhaps on the Aborigine question. I notice that Whitlam has made some new moves on land rights recently.'[6] This topic would not have occurred first to many Australians under such circumstances. Yet it was an idea traceable to Burchett's pre-journalistic background all the same.

One of the prominent nineteenth-century Australian writers was William Lane, author of *The Workingman's Paradise* (1892). Lane's first novel, serialized in *The Boomerang* in 1888, was entitled *White or Yellow? A Story of the Race War of A.D. 1908*. According to the historian Michael Wilding, this book 'predicted an alliance of pastoralists of the Queensland establishment and Asian capital. The alliance is destroyed by white, working-class unionists taking up arms and fighting. The Chinese are driven up to the northern tip of Queensland and then deported. The economic predictions may yet come true, but over and above that there is a racism.'[7]

From its beginnings in 1880, the *Bulletin* articulated the emotional response to Asian immigration of those who aspired to egalitarian independence in the New World – free from the class oppression of the Old – and who saw these millenarian hopes threatened by the deliberate introduction of 'cheap labour'. In the debates on immigration during the first federal parliament in 1901, speakers referred to the need to protect Australia from 'racial contamination'.[8] The White Australia policy was given legal force by the Immigration Restriction Act in that year, and was not phased out until the mid-1960s. Australian attitudes to foreign relations and defence have been deeply affected by all this. Literature, rhetoric and cartoons bear sad witness to the haunting images of the Yellow Peril, Mongol hordes and, after World War II, the Red Peril and falling dominoes.

In reality it was the peoples of Asia who had much to fear. Most of the region came under Western or Japanese imperialist domination. China was carved up into European 'spheres of influence'. The British took control in India, Burma, Malaya and Hong Kong; the French occupied Vietnam, Kampuchea and Laos; the Dutch ruled in the Indies; the Portuguese held East Timor and Macau; after the Spanish, the United States conquered the Philippines. The expansion of Japanese power began in the late nineteenth century when the ruling oligarchy, apprehensive about Western intrusion, set out to match European and American military strength by adopting their economic and military strategies. Having occupied Taiwan and Korea, Japan in 1931 began a steady advance on the Chinese mainland. The first real threat to Australia arose out of conflict between the Western powers and Japan in Asia.

Australian attitudes still did not take into account the many ways in which Australia and colonial Asia shared similar historical experience. From the outset, the Asian response to Western power included both co-operation and resistance, and it was foreign domination which eventually brought about the rise of nationalism and new forms of

political organization. In China, Vietnam and Korea, this took the form
of revolutionary movements against the imposed social order resulting
from the rise of industrial capitalism and imperialist expansion.
Similarly, the Caucasian victims of industrialization who arrived in
Australia, not always by choice, perceived it as a refuge from the evils of
the Old World, a place to establish a new nation with a new philosphy.[9]
Wilfred Burchett was reared in this radical and nationalist tradition. But
he rejected quite early those of its attitudes which gave rise to racism,
and adopted a new perspective on Australia's relationship with the
peoples of Asia, based on what he saw as shared aspirations for social
justice and national independence.

Until the advent of press oligopoly, Australia had a thriving
independent journalism, recognized at home and abroad as an
important aspect of Australia's culture.[10] For instance, on the Western
Australian goldfields (where Burchett's parents met and were married),
no less than sixty newspapers were published between 1892 and 1909,
many of them containing political comment as well as stories and
verse.[11] And Australia's great World War II Prime Minister, John
Curtin, was a former journalist. Wilfred Burchett maintained this
tradition in a period when opportunities were few for an independent
journalist to work as an accredited newspaperman. He published
thirty-five books, many of which were translated into a wide range of
languages, including twenty-three in Japanese and four in Arabic. His
second book went through three Indian editions in a year; [12] later books
were published for the first time in Beijing, Hanoi and New Delhi.
Twenty-four of his books were about Asia. Their content would have
astonished the readers of the popular press in the bush and towns of
Australia in the 1890s; yet among the unfamiliar ideas and sentiments
were many which they would have claimed as their own.

Burchett did not publish his first autobiographical work until 1969.[13]
When his books on Korea and Vietnam appeared in the fifties and
sixties, few Australians knew much about his background. This made it
easier for his critics to deflect attention from what he wrote, to his
alleged motives, and to hypotheses about his relationship with foreign
powers and adoption of an alien ideology. Even in *Passport*, Burchett
mostly left it to the reader to draw conclusions about the general
framework of his ideas. His approach to knowledge was practical, not
philosophical. He was more drawn to action than to speculation, a
quality perhaps characteristic of the background from which he came.
This is suggested in a letter to his father in 1962, on completion of *The
Furtive War*, his first book about United States intervention in Vietnam.
He described it as 'the most important book I have ever written'. 'It is a
pioneer book in keeping with the family's pioneer traditions. The news
will grow into the book . . . to elucidate what will be a world story for
several years – I'm afraid.'[14]

Living and working together in the town and the bush with their many
children, the Burchett family itself was a rich repository of historical
insight. As farmers and carpenters they were hard-working, enterprising

and innovative, but this was not enough. Debts, mortgages and the vagaries of the market during the Great Depression took a grim toll on their independent efforts. Young Wilfred's despair at the repossession of the family home in Ballarat perhaps contributed to the compassion, the sense of outrage, he expressed later whenever he encountered uprooted peasants in Asia.[15]

The family returned to the small country town of Poowong where Wilfred had been born. His father, a Methodist lay preacher for forty years, and for long conservative in politics, began to look for new ideas.[16] The Burchetts and their local friends, including the Irish blacksmith, a schoolteacher, and the manager of the local butter factory, as well as many of the poorer farmers, formed the Poowong Discussion Club.[17] Speakers from Melbourne and elsewhere were invited to address audiences of up to fifty local people on matters of public interest. When some members of the Poowong community – in particular the local branch of the Returned Soldiers' League – heard that talks had been given on the Soviet Union, the club was denounced as harbouring 'subversives'. Burchett recalls this controversy as his first encounter with 'the world of heresies and witch-hunters'.[18] It cannot have been totally unexpected. In the perspective of Australian history, the experience of the Poowong Discussion Club had its antecedents in the harassment of free-thinking working men who, in the nineteenth century, made use of Mechanics' Institutes to discuss the problems of the day and the reasons for conflict between classes and nations. (Topics discussed at the Swan River Mechanics' Institute in Perth in the 1850s and 1860s ranged from 'Is the Alleged Essential Intellectual Inferiority of the Coloured Races Correct?', to 'What Form of Government Does Man Live Under with the Greatest Happiness?')[19]

The history of the Burchett family suggests that radical ideas associated in the nineteenth century with life in the bush or the towns did not fade away with the rise of large cities at the turn of the century. Many Australian families were at any rate still 'pioneering' when the Depression hit, and up to the outbreak of World War Two. Their outlook was no doubt very similar to that of Henry Lawson when he wrote in May 1891:

> They struggled hard to make a home
> Hard grubbing 'twas, and clearing,
> They weren't troubled much with toffs,
> When they were pioneering.
> But now that we have made the land
> A garden full of promise,
> Old Greed must crook his dirty hand
> And come to take it from us?[20]

It did not escape Burchett's attention, while cane-cutting in Queensland in the thirties, that his fellow workers shared such values: 'Several of them knew poems by Henry Lawson, "Banjo" Paterson and other inspired by the "outback", and these were recited around the camp fire, which is their proper setting.'[21]

Wilfred Burchett's early experiences were vastly enriched by his efforts at self-education – he left school at fifteen. In this he had much in common with a long line of Australian radicals and rebels, including, for example, bullock-driver novelist Joseph Furphy and his literary contemporaries. (Burchett himself regarded the 1890s as the 'Golden Age of progressiveness' in Australian history.)[22] Presented by his brother with six volumes of Hamerton's *New Popular Educator*, Burchett at a young age began to absorb a wide range of knowledge and took an interest in foreign languages. 'Morning and evening milking sessions were excellent for what I had read the previous night on philosophical and kindred subjects,' he recalled. 'If I swung my fern hook or wielded the axe with extra vigour it was because I was muttering the declensions of a German verb.'[23] Other languages he learnt from Hamerton were French, Italian and Spanish. In this way was Burchett equipped to discuss dairy cattle with Fidel Castro;[24] and his knowledge of French and interest in French history were to serve him well in his later travels in Indochina and in Africa. Thus he broke out of the confines of Anglo-Saxon thought to which most Australians are limited through their exclusive dependence on the English language. This showed up later in England itself, when Burchett wrote home to his father from London in 1937: 'Last night to my surprise the landlady brought me out some of Voltaire's works. I think she had hopes of converting me to free thinking and was quite delighted to know that there was no longer any need.'[25] Here one can sense a reason for one of the characteristics that Burchett demonstrated throughout his life: a prodigious energy – that of a farm boy who felt genuinely liberated by knowledge and reason.

Since the nature of Australian formal education, with its British emphasis, often estranged the Australian child from his or her immediate environment, the informality and flexibility of Burchett's education may well have been an asset. He put down deep roots in Australia, yet at the same time acquired a keen interest in the world at large and confidence in his own judgement. He moved easily in 1939 from teaching carpentry to journalism, and from an early age saw no contradiction between farming and intellectual pursuits: '. . . although like cabbages we had sunk our roots deep into the soil, drawing our livelihood from it, we did not entirely live the life of cabbages.'[26] As late as 1974 he still drew an analogy between the two lifestyles when he complained that he was owed money by publishers: 'I'm like a farmer who has invested heavily in seed, fertilizer and labour, and goes broke before he can get the harvest in.'[27] He considered it important to 'keep the balance between physical and intellectual work right'.[28]

Burchett's most radicalizing early experience was taking to the track after he left school. Through seasonal work on farms and among the sugar-cane cutters, he came into contact with organized labour and its assault on exploitation. Ignorance was another target:

Like the cow cocky and his wife, the Boss and his whole family had a deep mistrust of books. As there was never a word spoken at mealtime I always brought a book with me to read while waiting for the meal to be served. This used to infuriate the whole family. There were constant mutterings and snide remarks such as: 'What'll book-learning ever do for you?' from one of the brothers, or 'Think you'll be making yourself better than others?' from the girl. 'Words, words, trash and nonsense', the Boss would roar while his wife glared at me balefully with her puffy eyes, usually incapable of saying anything. Once the Boss stalked in in an especially bad mood. I was reading at the table waiting for him to come so the meal could be served. He snatched the book – it was *Men and Machines* by the American economist Stuart Chase – and hurled it to the other end of the room. 'At that trash again?' he roared. 'I'll burn the whole dang lot of it.' I flew after the book and turned on him: 'Books like that cost money. What I do in my own time doesn't concern you.' . . . I knew he was cornered because the cutters would soon be back . . .[29]

Back in the city Burchett sold vacuum cleaners from door to door, and spent Sunday afternoon listening to speakers in the Sydney Domain.[30] He was among the large crowd who gathered there on 18 November 1934, to listen to the anti-Nazi Czech author Egon Kisch. Kisch had come to Australia to attend the second All-Australia Congress against War as a delegate of the Paris-based World Committee against War, and was sponsored by its Victorian affiliate.[31] Robert Menzies, then federal Attorney-General (later Prime Minister), tried to deny Kisch entry to Australia, a ban he was unable to sustain in the face of a vigorous public campaign and a court decision. The attempt to keep Kisch out on the contrived ground that he had failed a dictation test in the Gaelic language, did not add lustre to Menzies' cause. The dictation test, it should be noted, was a device introduced by the federal government in 1901 (and several years before in some of the colonies) for the purpose of excluding unwelcome immigrants from Asia.

Egon Kisch and the controversy surrounding his visit made a lasting impression on Burchett, as it did on others who became associated with the anti-Nazi movement.[32] Discussion of fascism was a leading preoccupation in the intellectual circles in which Burchett mixed before the war, including the radical New Theatre in Sydney and the weekly meetings in Melbourne of the Australian Writers' League. Among the latter's members were writers associated with the Australian radical tradition, such as Vance Palmer, author of *The Legend of the Nineties* (1954).[33] Here one can discern a continuity between certain conceptions of the Australian past and approaches to the major issues of the day, both national and international. The Writers' League, in its 1935 Statement of Principles, deplored the way in which the media and the arts had been trivialized. As they saw it, many people were reading and thinking seriously. They were 'hungry for honesty': 'They look to the writer to make articulate the growing spirit of the age: that virile fearlessness and thoughtful realism without which existing wrongs cannot be righted nor a just order be built.'[34]

According to his own account, Burchett had an interest in joining the Communist Party at this point, and did not. It is not known what his attitude to Asia was during this period, but if he had kept his ear to the ground he would have heard rumblings of change. From the early 1920s there had been discussion in the labour movement about the likelihood of an imperialist war in the Pacific, and the need to make contact with unions overseas. Between 1927 and 1930 the Australian Council of Trade Unions (ACTU) was actually affiliated with the Secretariat of the Pan-Pacific Trade Union Movement, which in spite of repression had attracted support from labour groups in Japan, Java, Korea and the Philippines. The objectives of the PPTUM referred to the need 'to help all the oppressed people of the Pacific to liberate themselves from the yoke of imperialism', and 'to fight against and remove all racial and national barriers which still divide the exploited classes and oppressed peoples to the advantage of the exploiters and oppressors'.[35] This ACTU policy initiative, however, could not be sustained in the face of criticism – notably from the right-wing Australian Workers' Union – that the communists were trying to overturn the White Australia Policy. Much of this ferment continued in the 1930s when Burchett was attending his first political meetings. If he was close to the Communist Party, he would also have known of the 1928 novel *Coonardoo* by one of its founding members, Katharine Susannah Prichard, the first novel to make an aboriginal woman the central character; and of the party's drawing up in 1931 of the first Aboriginal Rights policy to be adopted by a major Australian political party.

In 1936, Burchett and his brother Winston set off for Europe via the Panama Canal, farewelled by members of the Poowong Discussion Club, 'who felt they were sending off two emissaries to report back on the state of the world'.[36] In London Burchett continued his study of languages; and in Nazi Germany what he had formerly encountered only in books, speeches and discussions became a grim personal experience. It was in this context, while on his way home again by ship in 1939, that he first wrote about non-European peoples:

> The enlightened coloured elements in both Guadelope and Martinique know very well what would be their fate if the islands should fall as spoil to the Nazis. The racial theories of the Nazis with their complete contempt for coloured peoples would mean a return to an even more debased form of slavery than existed in the West Indies a hundred years ago.[37]

Back in Australia he found an overwhelming gap between local perceptions of world affairs and the ominous reality. It was only after the Nazi invasion of Poland that any of his articles were accepted by the press. Almost immediately he began writing about Asia as well. His first article on Asia was published in *Adam and Eve* ('a monthly journal for men and women incorporating *Australian Farmer*') in July 1940. It was entitled 'Are We Still Asleep?' At the time, Attorney-General Menzies was contributing to Japan's war effort in China by the export to Japan of Australian scrap iron and minerals.[38] It was on these issues that Burchett took the first of his many stands against national policy and public complacency.

Burchett wrote that Japan's 'share in the dividend of the Fascintern World Exploitation Co.' was intended to be 'Indo-China, the Dutch East Indies, the Pacific Islands and Australia'. All were now threatened. 'What are we doing in Australia to meet this danger? This country is in deadly peril, and we must be prepared to face it on our own . . . How many tanks have we got? How many armoured cars? How many first-line aeroplanes? Is every possible means exhausted for supplying our army with mechanized equipment?'[39] In a second article, in the *Digest of World Reading* in November 1940, he elaborated on this:

> The pact with Germany and Italy clearly reveals on which side Japan stands . . .
>
> In Australia we have our part to play. Japan declares that she entertains the most friendly feelings for us. We welcome that declaration, but we remind Japan that the Chinese have at least as ancient claims on our friendship. Our friendship for Japan does not mean that we acquiesce in the murder of thousands of Chinese citizens . . . Japan can be stopped and must be stopped. A fight must be declared sooner or later.[40]

These articles are notable for their global perspective, with their stress on the link between Berlin and Tokyo, as well as the clear distinction between the Asian powers, Japan and China, on the basis of their regimes.

As the second article appeared, Richard Hughes, the other famous Australian 'old Asia hand', was about to return from several months in Japan and China. Hughes was the first Australian journalist representing a newspaper to visit Japan since 1934. His forecasts of Japanese expansion into the Pacific were published in early 1941, while a third Burchett piece, 'Nippon's Undeclared Pacific War', appeared in February 1941.[41]

It is interesting to compare these two men. Hughes, who was five years older, came from a lower-middle-class, urban background; his father had been a travelling ventriloquist, journalist and writer. Hughes went to a Catholic college in Melbourne. His first job was as a poster artist, from which he soon moved into journalism. He was not out of work in the Depression, nor does he appear to have spent much time at all in rural Australia. But in 1934, a mentor, the Chief Commissioner for Railways, advised him to go to Asia, saying: 'Australia belongs to Asia, you know, and the future of this country will be as part of Asia.' Hughes remembered the advice and acted on it in 1940; only later did he go to Europe.[42]

For Burchett it was the other way around. He came to Asia via his political experiences in 1930s Europe, and by 1940 he had seen much of the Pacific region as well; but he had no job. (Already in 1939, Hughes had become chief-of-staff of the Sydney *Sunday Telegraph*.)[43] Whereas Hughes was a product of Anglo-Irish culture and took to Asia largely because of its proximity to Australia, Burchett had imbibed much of European thought as well, and he saw Asia as part of a worldwide picture which he was slowly piecing together in his mind.

One does not have to rely on what Burchett wrote in his fifties for insight into his reaction to the events of his youth. His first book, *Pacific Treasure Island*, which arose out of his visit to New Caledonia and was published in 1941, expounds a viewpoint derived from Australian experience and prompted by concern for national interest.[44] Burchett had gone to New Caledonia to investigate Japanese activities there. As his book reached the bookstalls, Japan attacked Pearl Harbor. But Burchett had come back with another idea as well, which he made the central theme of his book.

In *Pacific Treasure Island*, Burchett set out a bold, new manifesto on Australia's place in the world. 'The Pacific,' he wrote, 'is the world of the future. There are signs aplenty that it is now coming into its own; that as the old Mediterranean world gave way in importance to the wider world of the Atlantic through the development of the Americas, so the centre of Weltpolitik is being shifted to the Pacific.'[45] More striking is the fact that Burchett set out clearly on what social terms Australians should construct a new relationship with Asia.[46] Apart from the economic and strategic significance of the Pacific, it was the opportunity to create in the region a new kind of society which was the focus of his attention. In his view the nations of the Pacific held in common a popular tradition of resistance to social injustice and to religious and political intolerance. He developed an idea of the way in which Australian culture and mores, as they had emerged from the pioneers' experience, could develop in harmony with those of the liberated peoples of neighbouring Asia.

Unlike many Western travellers in Asia, he did not regard the social scene as a panorama of exotic cultures, but as the outcome of historic forces which embraced both the old world and the new. In New Caledonia, French colonial rule had brought among the local Melanesians, Frenchmen deported for their revolutionary ideals, Arabs who had rebelled against the French in Algeria, Vietnamese uprooted from Indochina, and even Javanese from the Dutch East Indies.[47] Political persecution and capitalist exploitation had left their imprint. In addition, the contemporary conflicts within French society were revealed in September 1940 when supporters of the Free French movement rose up and overthrew the pro-Pétain French authorities.[48] It seemed to him obvious that the problem of fascism was not confined to Germany.

Before going to New Caledonia Burchett had learnt that some of the settlers who supported the Free French movement were descendants of radical Communards deported there in 1871.[49] In this community he found the same kind of earnest discussion he had known in Poowong. 'As is often the case with communities out in the backblocks, these people were used to doing hard thinking, and had original and well-thought-out reasons for the opinions they expressed.'[50] To these French settlers, the pro-Nazi Pétain and his supporters were 'the same class of people that always fought against the 1789 revolution; that never accepted any change . . .'[51] Burchett was pleased to be able to indentify the progressive groups in France, Australia and in the French colonies, and the way in which these movements impinged on one another. From French sources he recounted the lives of Henri Rochefort and Louise Michel, who were transported to New Caledonia for their activities in the 1870 Paris uprising; they '. . . could have lived sheltered and peaceful lives if they had cared to remain blind to the injustices rampant in the age in which they lived'.[52] With some justification, he described the life of Louise Michel as 'one of the most exciting careers of any woman in history'.[53] Her book on Melanesian culture, published in 1885, was one indication of the bridge being constructed between progressive thought in Europe and the societies of Asia. It is clear Burchett hoped to emulate her in this, and that New Caledonia with its rich mixture of races was his own gateway to Asia.

He also noted the fact that Rochefort had spent a short period in Australia and had praised it as 'a land of true liberty and equality where master and man met on equal terms'.[54] There were other links between Australia and the Communards, including one which involved Egon Kisch. In *Australian Landfall*, Kisch described how in Perth he had met an old man whose father had been transported to New Caledonia; he himself still possessed and treasured a flag of the Commune which he had brought from Paris as a child.[55] Burchett reached the following conclusion:

When France expelled its Communards and sent them bound in chains to languish in the convict prisons of New Caledonia, when England's Irish Nationalists and Chartists despaired of reforming the Old World and set out to build something new in the dominions and the United States, where no preconceived ideas of privilege and tradition existed, when the Pilgrim Fathers set out in the *Mayflower* for America, a movement was started which was to lay the foundation of the New World.

Those who fought at the barricades in the American War of Independence, those who fought at the barricades at Eureka Stockade to defend the rights of Australian citizens, those who armed themselves with guns and iron railings, and stormed into the Noumean streets in September 1940, to chase out of office – and out of the colony – those who had betrayed their interests and their honour, all belong to the same tradition of the New World. It is a tradition of sturdy independence and jealous vigilance where a violation of basic rights is concerned.[56]

Burchett's 1941 journey to New Caledonia was his first overseas assignment as a correspondent. Briefly, before the escalation of the war in the Pacific, he was able to enjoy the region in peace. As a war correspondent in Burma, China and the Pacific he had an exceptional opportunity to become familiar with the region. More directly and explicitly than in *Pacific Treasure Island* he commented on the White Australia policy, the structure of the Australian economy and the prospects for national independence and social change in Asia. All the issues of power, the conflicts of interest and political objectives, came to the surface during the Western and Asian resistance to the Japanese. The idealism of his manifesto concerning the future of the Pacific gave way to a more realistic understanding of the social conflicts within Asia and the basis on which America would become involved in world affairs at the end of the war.

Along with other Western observers in wartime China, Burchett was critical of the ruling Guomindang for its corruption, and impressed by the quality of leadership and village politics of the communists.[57] Following the attack on Pearl Harbor, the Sydney *Daily Telegraph* cabled Burchett to get China's reaction to 'Japan's entry into the war'. For the *Telegraph*, the ten-year-old anti-Japanese war in China did not exist; nor was the newspaper interested in the subtleties of Chinese politics. Burchett attended a meeting with Zhou Enlai and sent home a report; but the *Daily Telegraph* cabled back: 'Uninterested in Chinese Communist pronouncements.'[58] This lack of Establishment interest persisted for another thirty years. Only in 1972 did Australia (under a new Labor government) recognize the Chinese Communist government, of which Zhou Enlai had been Premier since 1949.

Before the Pacific War was over, Burchett began to consider Australia's future too. He could see, in the burgeoning of the machine-tool industries for wartime purposes, the foundation for post-war industrialization. In the past, he argued, Great Britain had placed restraints on Australian industry in the interest of British exporters.[59] With Britain in a state of collapse, and the corporations of Japan constrained by the consequences of defeat, Australia need no longer be 'a market gardener for empire', but could become an industrial centre in Asia.[60] New economic policies would call for new social attitudes, and to this end Burchett argued in 1946 for 'scrapping the whole conception of White Australia':

Today . . . (w)e have established our living standards, and our unions are strong enough to enforce acceptance of union conditions by both employers and workers from whatever country the latter originate. Economically, there is no longer justification to make any distinction between Asiatics and Europeans in the administration of the Immigration Act. Politically, it is suicidal for Australia to persist in carrying such a dangerously poised chip on her shoulder.[61]

Burchett was confident that Australians would readily abandon the racist attitudes still trumpeted by the *Bulletin*. He had observed during the war that Australians got on well with Asians whom they treated as 'normal human beings'.[62]

Burchett's comments on the Australian economy are reminiscent of the writings of Brian Fitzpatrick, whose histories of Australia took a critical view of the effect of British imperialism on the Australian economy.[63] A central aspect of Burchett's radicalism was abhorrence of colonialism. This he had in common with many Asian radicals. He also took a global view of history which helped him to put particular Asian events into appropriate historical context. In summing up his views towards the end of the war, he wrote:

> Liberation of the coloured peoples, both mentally and physically, is just as important for the welfare and progress of humanity as that of the white races. The quality of freedom everywhere is depreciated by its denial to the coloured man. Today the gravest charge that can be levelled against all imperialisms is that their subject peoples have been compelled to live in a backwash of civilization bypassed by the creative forces which only freedom and education can release . . .
>
> As fellow citizens of one world it should be a matter for congratulation not for alarm that the Spirit of Democracy is stirring throughout the East, and that these people are determined to use such weapons as are available, from tommyguns to automatic bows and arrows, to gain for themselves what has been denied for centuries by their masters.[64]

The spectacular ending of World War Two, with the dropping of the atomic bomb on Japan, provided a test of Burchett's sincerity on this issue of race. He was very gung-ho about the war against Japan, even to the extent of favouring the use of poison gas against Japanese troops to get the war over quickly.[65] But the atomic destruction of cities was another thing. Rather than gloat at the Japanese surrender ceremony, he took off for Hiroshima – and wrote his 'warning to the world'.[66] The resulting scoop was very much a product of his background and the sympathies he had developed.

After the war, as a correspondent for British newspapers in Germany, Burchett came to the conclusion that the United States was the new imperial power. Ever uneasy about fascism, he discerned that the Allies in their antagonism towards the Soviet Union were prepared to co-operate with former Nazis and their sympathizers.[67] A similar trend was even more widespread in Asia. In Japan itself, the American administration, while introducing a measure of democratic reform, such as the new Constitution, at the same time began to restore conservative political rule and the power of the corporations, not simply as a bulwark against a perceived external threat of communism but also against popular movements of the left seeking social change in Japan.[68]

In the case of Korea, the Americans co-operated with the defeated Japanese, in their former colony, in suppressing popular movements of the left.[69] In 1946, Burchett drew attention to the fact that the British and the surrendered Japanese had collaborated in the suppression of nationalists in both the Dutch East Indies and Indochina.[70] The situation in the Philippines he had seen for himself.[71] During the war he had sought out and interviewed the leaders of the leftist Hukbalahap movement and was impressed with what they had to say about social relationships and the need for land reform. The Huks, who had borne the brunt of the guerrilla war against the Japanese, believed that after the war they would enjoy independence and political freedom. But the returning United States forces moved to support wealthy Filipinos who had collaborated with the Japanese. They regarded these people as 'safe men who will protect American investment in the Philippines whether America retains political control or not . . . In spite of their ugly background of collaboration and fascism they receive special dispensations with expanded authority.'[72] Later on Burchett was to report a similar situation in Korea.[73]

Burchett was deeply disturbed at the motivation behind such policies and their probable outcome. He was not alone in his analysis. In a prescient essay on the Cold War published in 1947, American journalist Walter Lippmann warned that if the United States applied its containment-of-communism policy to Asia, it would find itself compelled to rely on

> satellites, puppets, clients, agents, about whom we know very little. Frequently they will act . . . on their own judgments, presenting us with accomplished facts that we did not intend and with crises for which we are unready . . . We shall have either to disown our puppets, which would be tantamount to appeasement and defeat and the loss of face, or support them at an incalculable cost on an unintended, unforeseen and perhaps undesirable issue.[74]

Lippmann's political stance was not Burchett's, but his analysis on this issue was much the same.

When Burchett revisited China in 1951 and crossed the Yalu River into North Korea he acted on the basis of past experience and knowledge of world affairs. He had spent many years in wrecked cities and burned-out villages; he had been in Hiroshima and understood the meaning of atomic war. He was convinced by his observations as a correspondent in Germany that it was the United States that was prepared to run the risk of war to secure its economic and political objectives. His experience in Asia had given him an understanding of liberation movements and their political objectives and popular support. He gravitated towards communism because of his experience of capitalism and fascism, and his knowledge of the origins, objectives and achievements of communism in Asia. By 1951, then, a wide gap existed between Burchett's knowledge and influential opinion in Australia. He had experienced the same situation prior to the outbreak of World War Two when his judgement was vindicated; it is not surprising that he should act again with confidence in 1951.

In Australia, in the early post-war years, an attempt was made to take an independent stance in world affairs. Public opinion now tended to view favourably the emergence of independent nations in Asia. Indicative of this was the boycott imposed on Dutch shipping by Australian trade unions, with widespread public support, during the Indonesian struggle for independence.[75] (Robert Menzies, by contrast, supported the Dutch effort.)[76] This was a period of open, lively public debate on political issues, when the intellectual climate was conducive to a review of old assumptions in the light of global change.

At the United Nations, Dr Evatt, Minister for External Affairs in the then Labor government, became a conspicuous advocate of the rights of small nations. In a speech to the House of Representatives on 13 March 1946, he stated that Australia was 'setting out to make her own assessment of the problems of the Pacific'.[77] Australia sent a large delegation to the United Nations and took on major diplomatic commitments in Korea and Japan. In both situations the Australian representatives involved took a critical view of American policies and their implications for peace in Asia.[78]

The Australians in Korea, in their reports to Canberra, were highly critical of the relationship between the American government and Syngman Rhee, and of the systematic repression of Korean political organizations.[79] They considered that the Australian government should not endorse the creation of a separate government in the south. Nevertheless, in spite of initial opposition, the Australian government supported at the United Nations the holding of separate elections in the south.[80]

Again, during the Allied Occupation of Japan, Australians involved in an official capacity had had serious reservations about American policies.[81] Not only Australia, but other nations also, were critical of the American decision to restore the power of the corporations.[82] On the Far Eastern Commission, the Australian representatives were critical of the administration's crackdown on the activities of Japanese trade unions.[83] The most serious issues, from the viewpoint of the Australian government, were the signing of the separate peace treaty, and partial rearmament.[84] During the debate on the subject in the House of Representatives, volatile Labor member Eddie Ward described the treaty as 'the greatest leg-pull in history . . . the old elements are still in control'.[85] Yet by 1950 the Australian government was determined to seek an alliance with the United States. Australia's willingness to participate in the Korean War was seen as an inducement to this end.[86] This commitment was made not on the basis of what happened in Korea but on assumptions about Japan and Australian security. The ANZUS treaty came into force in 1951.

The implications of this military alliance with the United States were all the more serious because on the outbreak of war in Korea in mid-1950 the United States committed military aid to Taiwan, to the French in Indochina, and to the Philippines (self-governing since

1948).[87] When China entered the Korean War in support of North Korea in October 1950, following warnings to the Allies about approaching its border, China was declared an aggressor nation. On these grounds China was denied a seat in the United Nations.[88] This was certain to increase difficulties in resolving any problems which should arise in the Asian region.

It was in these circumstances that Australia abandoned its tentative first steps towards a more independent stance in foreign relations. Among the critics of this reversal was Dr John Burton, Secretary of the Department of External Affairs from 1947 to 1950. In *The Alternative* (1954), Burton discussed the conflicts of opinion over foreign policy in Canberra. Burton believed that powerful groups in the military and bureaucracy had opposed the foreign policy of Dr Evatt.[89] In his view,

> . . . the judgement which has been made by both parliamentary political parties, namely that Australian interests are better served by an alliance with the United States rather than by independent policy directed towards Asia is a judgement made through fear and because of the pressure of certain minorities. It is not a judgement based on a critical analysis of political conditions in Asia or on Australian long-term economic and social interests.[90]

Burton was deeply disturbed at the constraints imposed on public debate during this critical period of the early 1950s.[91] They seem to have resulted, at least in part, from pressure on the Australian government by American and British intelligence sources.[92] Though connected with Cold War politics emanating from the United States, the atmosphere was reminiscent of the early 1920s, when left-wing trends in Australian domestic politics were checked by invoking 'the Red Peril'.[93]

Seen in this context, Burchett was by no means an isolated extremist. As Joseph Waters recalled in the seventies, 'It is as well to remember that Wilfred Burchett and his approach to world affairs did have support here. Substantial sections of the labor movement were not in entire agreement with the policies of either Eisenhower or Menzies.'[94] In Asia, too, Australians working in an official capacity had expressed criticism similar to Burchett's. In their view the Korean situation had nothing to do with global communist expansion but was a Korean political crisis brought about since 1945 by American policies in the South. Burchett's writings were particularly dangerous in the eyes of Australian power elites precisely because of existing opinion in favour of an independent foreign policy, and susceptible to the information he was in a position to supply. Harassment of an informed opinion at home ran parallel to the denunciation of Burchett abroad. But the appeal to historically deep-seated attitudes about potential threats in Asia so soon after war in the Pacific was bound to make an impact. Public opinion was swept along by Cold War propaganda. At a time when Australians most needed to make an independent study of the region, a climate of fear, suspicion and inhibited debate quickly set in and prevailed for many years. Burchett was its best-known victim, but not the only one.

When Australian troops were committed to fight in Vietnam in 1965 most Australians had only a distorted or dim memory of the Korean War. But Burchett had gone directly from the wreckage of Korea to the guerrilla war in Vietnam. On his many journeys with the NLF he came to realize that the Front was a grassroots organization which survived because of popular support.

> The self-defence units in the villages are actually the base of the pyramid on which the whole structure of the National Liberation Front armed forces rest. They are the most concrete expression of people's war. They are the people, for the people, appointed by the people. It would be difficult to imagine a more democratic form of armed forces or a more perfect form for the tasks imposed by the resistance struggle.[95]

In spite of differences of culture, society and economic context, the intellectual self-reliance which Burchett developed in his youth and which became an important part of his personality included the same qualities which sustained the strategy of people's war. In an article published in *Digest of World Reading* in 1942, he had described the Australian soldier as a person who lacked respect for military hierarchy as such and was unwilling to give unquestioning loyalty to a superior officer.[96] He would fight on the basis of personal conviction, and he expected democratic leaders who would share the hardship and undergo the same dangers. Burchett himself admired Major-General Orde Charles Wingate as an officer who was prepared to run the same risks as his men, and whose strategies, akin to guerrilla warfare, he had praised in *Wingate Adventure*, published in 1944. In Vietnam it was the guerrilla forces which fought with conviction in contrast to the demoralization of the American foot soldier.

As the conflict dragged on, the United States made increasing use of bombing and automated war. In these circumstances, war was sustained on the basis of an elite technical professionalism. Considerations such as these prompted American journalist I. F. Stone, a critic of American involvement, to speak of the guerrilla victories as the triumph of 'the primacy of man in an age of technology'.[97] Similarly, Burchett admired the improvised tactics and weapons used in the North and by the NLF as an expression of grassroots ingenuity and determination.

As the war escalated, Hanoi and the National Liberation Front had access to war materiel from Russia and China; but at all stages much depended on the improvisation which Burchett described on many occasions, such as booby traps, floating bamboo bridges, improvised hospital equipment and the maze of tunnels which in some places had been in use for ten years and more.[98] In the Australian bush, the pioneers had also survived because of ingenuity and improvisation, epitomized in the many popular sayings which refer to the use of 'stringy bark and greenhide'.[99] New Zealander Rewi Alley, who collaborated

with Burchett in a book on China, and who had been involved in
small-scale manufacturing in inland China from the 1920s, came from a
similar rural background and had similar attitudes.[100]

Burchett's account of the ethnic minorities in Vietnam is also
noteworthy.[101] In the passages which relate to his meetings with these
people one can detect his intrinsic interest in their customs and
viewpoint. It is significant that he compares the position of the
aborigines in Australia with discrimination against tribal minorities in
Vietnam.[102]

When Australian troops were sent to Vietnam the Australian public
was told they would be defending Australia from Chinese aggression. A
typical statement is that of Australia's Minister for External Affairs,
Paul Hasluck, in the House of Representatives, June 1964: 'There is no
doubt that . . . part of this [insurgency in South Vietnam] is the
determination of Communist China to establish hegemony through
South East Asia, working in the first place through the agency of her
North Vietnamese puppets.'[103] As Alex Carey has shown, Prime
Minister Menzies made a similar claim in April 1965.[104]

Australian policy-makers sought United States military intervention
in keeping with the obsessive belief that Australian security depended
on the American presence in Asia.[105] To some degree these misguided
policies were the outcome of ignorance and closed minds. Very little
attempt was made to study the situation in Asia, whether the languages,
history or any other aspect. The Establishment had done little since the
war to encourage Australian scholarship on Asia or the study of Asia in
schools. In view of the continuous misrepresentation of the many issues
in which Australia was involved there was much to be gained by public
ignorance. Yet it was not only lack of knowledge which determined the
public response to Asian politics. The difference between Burchett's
perception of Asia and views at home was partly due to social change in
Australia.

With the onset of the long boom, people had more cash, leisure,
possessions and greater social mobility. But increasing access to formal
education did not necessarily mean a gain in social knowledge and
insight. There was urgent need for a restructuring of disciplines in
response to global change and Australia's changing position in world
affairs. Commensurate changes in educational institutions just did not
take place. Furthermore, the social content of science and technology
for the most part was, and still is, confined to the requirements of
advanced industrial society, and has made little adjustment to third-
world realities and Australia's proximity to Asia. Adult education began
to expand in the sixties, but without much increase in the area of current
affairs which had been popular in the early post-war period.

Perhaps most serious of all in the face of such deficiencies, was the
decline in self-education, which had been an important part of social
mores in the past. Australian radicalism had been concerned in the past
not only with demands for higher wages but also with aspirations
towards independence: to have a mind of one's own in solving the

practical problems of life. This was part of the contempt for 'wage slavery' which led many Australians to 'take to the track'. After World War Two, improvements in working conditions and relationships gave the worker a somewhat greater sense of self-respect; but over time, access to goods was traded for independence in applying skills and making social and technological choices. Although Burchett did not discuss his own politics in a general way, he was clearly attracted to the grassroots self-reliance of the liberation movements of the third world, on the basis of his own experience in a 'pioneering' community.

In the late seventies and early eighties, with the deepening of the economic recession, one can detect a more critical awareness of third-world issues in Australia than was evident in the sixties, notwithstanding involvement in the Vietnam War and the anti-war movement. American intervention had been presented as the defence of democracy against communism, but most of Asia has known only repressive, authoritarian rule. In the past, it was not unusual for Australians to justify this reality, when it could no longer be denied, as a necessary evil in the face of intractable economic problems. Strong government, it was said, is best able to find solutions. This lapse of faith in democracy is not shared by many people in Asia. Attempts to secure constitutional rule, the right to a free press, to organize trade unions and peasant federations, and to have civil liberties in general, have been frustrated by regimes which in many cases have been aided and abetted by the United States.

Today in Australia there is increasing awareness of this situation. As I write, fifty delegates from all states of Australia except Tasmania have met in Melbourne for a National Conference of Timor activists.[106] Many small groups are studying world affairs and taking action on specific issues in an organized way. The focus of their interest includes race relations at home and abroad, foreign aid, the study of Central America, East Timor, and the Philippines, nuclear issues and the arms race. As in the past some trade unions (for example, the Amalgamated Metalworkers' Union), maintain contact with the labour movement in Asia.

Recent developments in the Philippines have direct bearing on Burchett's views on Asia. After World War Two, the United States, on granting independence, secured special privileges for American investors, as Burchett during the war had predicted that they would.[107] By the late sixties there was growing anti-American feeling in all sections of Filipino society.[108] The revolutionary movement, which had been contained in the fifties, re-emerged with new vigour, and an attempt was made by a section of the Filipino elite to regain control of the national economy from American domination.

In 1972, on declaring martial law, President Marcos reversed steps already taken to curb foreign investment in the economy. Since then the economic crisis has become much worse.[109] In the countryside, Filipino villagers must defend themselves from the military in situations reminiscent of South Vietnam under Diem, as described by Burchett. In some districts, the people have been relocated in new settlements to disrupt contact with the New People's Army. This is the same policy of strategic hamlets which was used by the Japanese in Manchuria, the British in Kenya and Malaya, and the Americans in Vietnam. In the slums of Manila, grassroots political organizations have flourished in spite of the strains of unemployment, poverty and official harassment. In the Cordillera mountains, the Bontoc and Kalinga tribespeople have responded to repression in a manner similar to the ethnic minorities in Vietnam. The writings of Burchett have in this respect a continuing relevance to developments in Asia. Recent public reaction in Australia has been to look closely at Australian involvement in the Philippines and to ask, who benefits from official aid programmes? Who gains from the provision of military aid?[110] The situation poses the important question raised by Burchett when he went to New Caledonia as a young man: on what social terms should Australians relate to Asia?

The same question arises in connection with the independence movement in East Timor, and the invasion by Indonesia. The generalized notion of being on good terms with Asia, which Gough Whitlam, then Prime Minister, had come to support in the seventies, cuts across the more important questions: whose Asia? In whose interests? It is worth recalling Burchett in 1940: 'Our friendship for Japan does not mean that we acquiesce in the murder of thousands of Chinese citizens.'

Whitlam's position, although an advance on the racist and imperialist strands in Australian perceptions of Asia, was not far off the commonly expressed view that 'If we criticize Indonesia for its takeover of East Timor, they could have a lot to say about our treatment of the aborigines.'[111] (The comparison is apt: in the nineteenth century white men formed a human chain to hunt the aboriginals across Tasmania, while in 1983, Indonesian armies drew a cordon across the island of Timor and attempted to close in on nationalist resistance.)[112] But fear of moral blackmail is scarcely a basis for foreign policy. Nor is a conspiracy of silence between two established orders.

Because of its proximity, East Timor was one of the most important foreign-policy issues for Australia in the 1970s. Partly because of his exile, and partly because of his global perspective, Burchett came to the issue from a different angle. In 1974 he went to Lisbon when the fascist government was overthrown, and subsequently visited Angola and Mozambique, which, like East Timor, were colonies of Portugal. In Mozambique in 1976 he interviewed another exile, the East Timorese Foreign Minister, Mari Alkatiri.

In considering Burchett's work as a whole and its place in Australian culture, his departure for Africa is significant. Not only did he learn that his writings on the people's war in Vietnam had reached African liberation leaders;[113] he also encountered there a number of Australians who had gone to Africa for reasons similar to his own: to support the liberation and advancement of the peoples of the third world.[114]

Burchett's interests had always ranged more widely than the question of Australia's relationship with Asia. Indeed the very concept of Asia as a discrete region has come about mainly because of an externally imposed order created by colonialism; it was perpetuated after the war in keeping with American and Japanese interests using the region as a co-prosperity sphere. For this reason Burchett's departure for Africa was as significant as his journey to New Caledonia. It was an affirmation of a global view of history and of Australia's relationship not only with Asia but in world affairs generally. It was a view that more Australians were beginning to share.

In East Timor the Australian government had the opportunity to assist in the process of decolonization.[115] As it transpired, successive Labor and Liberal governments have condoned aggression and forcible annexation, at the cost of thousands of lives.

Also relevant to an understanding of the life of Wilfred Burchett is the fate of the five newsmen killed in Balibo.[116] In October 1974, three months before the major landing at Dili, Indonesian forces infiltrated across the border from West Timor. Five newsmen from Australian television networks had gone to Balibo near the border in the hope that eyewitness reports would alert international opinion, and that action would be taken at the United Nations to deter aggression.[117] They stayed at a small white house in the village, where Greg Shackleton chalked an Australian flag on the outside wall as some form of identification and protection. But to no avail. Indonesian forces entered the village and murdered the five unarmed men.

The crude chalked flag had no significance for the Australian government either. No official action was taken on the circumstances of their death; it even seems that the Australian government was aware before the attack that the men were in danger. James Dunn in his well-informed study described the response as 'probably the most disturbing cover-up in Australia's diplomatic history'.[118]

Since the sixties there has been a tendency in Australian thought to debunk or denigrate the Australian radical tradition on the grounds that it had no basis in reality or little use as political thought.[119] Burchett, for his part, took the old egalitarian ideas seriously. He did not attach these ideas to his life as an afterthought or as a badge of national loyalty. Their foundation was personal experience. He held to these ideas and acted upon them, and in many ways they proved relevant to his study of Asia and contributed to his insight. The boy who rode a cow to school in Poowong could relate to the Asian village, just as the culture which produced a book called *Make-shift Home-made Furniture from Kerosene Cases* was not altogether alien to that of Asian shanty-towns.[120]

Some of the critics who reject the radicalism of the past do so on the grounds of its association with the White Australia policy and discrimination against the aborigines. Burchett was equally critical of these aspects of Australian history but his attitude was to consider the past and present, to accept and to reject, and to create a new synthesis.

He would have expected readers to take the same attitude of discrimination towards his own ideas. There is much that should be rejected. He was poorly prepared intellectually for the power struggles within and among communist states, and often enough lapsed into rationalization as a matter of political expediency. This does not make for the writing of durable historical narrative or sound political analysis. Yet he had a fine sense of history in the making, and was at his best in writing from life about the experiences of national liberation movements. He saw through the murk of Cold War propaganda and understood well the imperatives of peaceful coexistence.[121]

After World War Two, social changes throughout the world presented a challenge to Australian culture. It was a matter of urgent necessity to rethink historical knowledge and to develop a more rigorous theoretical approach to politics. Advance in theory, however, depended upon advance in historical knowledge and insight. It was in this area that Burchett made a positive contribution to Australian thought. His writings on Korea and Vietnam provided the general reader in Australia with the opportunity to consider and to re-evaluate information highly relevant to current Australian policy-making. To the extent that the Establishment denunciation of Burchett set up a barrier between Burchett and Australian readers, so much the poorer was Australian experience.

In Australia, as in other former colonies, there are formidable difficulties in achieving cultural independence. In the arts, in science and technology, much remains to be done to develop ideas which are a realistic response to geographical location and physical environment; to reflect upon the kind of society Australians want, to consider how it can be reconciled to the well-being of the majority of people in neighbouring countries as well as the world at large. Burchett's writtings, when viewed in an open-minded and critical way, are relevant to this kind of cultural regeneration.

Notes

1. The slogan first appeared on 7 May 1908 and was abandoned by Donald Horne who became editor in November 1960.
2. This name was given to the continent in the seventeenth century by the French geographer de Brosses. See Jack Shepherd, *Australia's Interests and Policies in the Far East*, New York, 1940, pp. 2–5.
3. A.T.Yarwood and M.J.Knowling, *Race Relations in Australia*, Sydney, 1982, pp. 173–4.
4. Bernard Smith, *The Spectre of Truganini*, 1980 Boyer lectures, Australian Broadcasting Commission publication, p. 16. See, for example, R.M.Lyon, 'A Glance at the Manners and Language of the Aboriginal Inhabitant of Western Australia', *Perth Gazette*, 30 March, 6, 13, 20 April 1833, and the views he expressed at a public meeting in Perth 1832. B.J.Smith, 'Early Western Australian Literature, A Guide to Colonial and Goldfields Life', M.A. thesis, University of Western Australia, 1961, p.17.
5. Yarwood, op. cit., pp. 168–73. There was, however, some disquiet about what was seen as a conflict between racialism and 'a spirit of fairness and justice consistent with our national character'. See Andrew Marcus, 'The Chinese in Australian

History', *Meanjin Quarterly*, Vol. 42, No. 1, March 1983, p. 91. Also Kathryn Cronin, *Colonial Casualties, Chinese in Early Victoria*, Melbourne 1982.

6. Letter to Winston Burchett from Paris, 28 September 1974. Wilfred Burchett Papers, State Library of Victoria, Latrobe Collection.

7. *The Workingman's Paradise*: *An Australian Novel* by 'John Miller' (William Lane), with an introduction by Michael Wilding, Sydney, 1980, p. 32.

8. Yarwood, op. cit., p. 235. Douglas Cole, 'The Crimson Thread of Kinship; Ethnic Ideas in Australia 1870–1914', *Historical Studies*, April 1971.

9. Ian Turner, *Room for Manoeuvre*, Victoria, 1982, pp. 3–17.

10. Francis Adams, *The Australians*, London, 1983, pp. 47–8, 95–6, 104.

11. This was a legacy of earlier developments in journalism in the eastern colonies as well as local conditions. Most of the prospectors came from the east, which was hit by the economic depression of the 1890s. Smith, op. cit.

12. This was *Wingate Adventure*. Wilfred Burchett, letter to his parents, 28 March 1945. Wilfred Burchett Papers.

13. *Passport*, Nelson, Melbourne, 1969.

14. Letter to his father from Moscow, 29 June 1962. Wilfred Burchett Papers.

15. *Passport*, op. cit., p. 45

16. Ibid., p. 51. Burchett's father George had stood as an endorsed conservative candidate in the Ballarat area in parliamentary elections in the 1920s.

17. Ibid., pp. 51–2. The club was not unique. C.E.W.Bean, in *War Aims of a Plain Australian*, Sydney, 1943, p. 115, refers to the existence of 'Farmers' clubs' in this period as useful centres of debate on public issues. Bean was official World War One historian; his work is often associated with the 1890s tradition.

18. *At the Barricades*, Macmilliam, Melbourne, 1981, p. 26.

19. Concerted efforts were made by the colonial elite to break up the discussion group at the Swan River Mechanics' Institute, where a leading figure was the radical carpenter Joseph Chester. Among other contentious issues discussed there were 'A love of life is the most fundamental principle of man: how can one understand the soldier's contempt for death?' 'Was the French Revolution of 1789 productive of human progress?'; 'What effect did the Magna Carta have on English liberty?'; 'Knowledge and how it is acquired'; 'Has the introduction of machinery benefited the working man?'; 'For the peace and security of nations is war at any time necessary?' Detailed minutes of some of these discussions have survived. Smith, op. cit., pp. 49–55.

20. Henry Lawson, 'Freedom on the Wallaby', in *Henry Lawson Poems*, ed. Colin Roderick, Sydney, 1979, p. 50.

21. *Passport*, p. 70.

22. *Pacific Treasure Island*, Cheshire, Melbourne, 1941, p. 222.

23. *At the Barricades*, p. 23.

24. Letter to his father from Phnom Penh, 31 August 1967. Wilfred Burchett Papers.

25. Letter to his parents from London, 28 August 1937. Wilfred Burchett Papers.

26. *Passport*, p. 52.

27. Letter to his brother Winston from Cairo, 17 February 1974. Wilfred Burchett Papers.

28. Letter to his brother Winston from Paris, 30 November 1974. He considered the combination of cooking, carpentering and writing 'just about perfect'. Letter to his brother from Peking, 19 June 1973. Wilfred Burchett Papers.

29. *Passport*, pp. 68–9.

30. Ibid., pp. 56–89.

31. Ken Slater, 'Egon Kisch, A Biographical Outline', *Labour History*, No. 36, May 1979.

32. See, for instance, Don Watson, *Brian Fitzpatrick*, Sydney, 1979, pp. 64–5; Robin Gollan, *Revolutionaries and Reformists: Communism and the Australian Labour Movement, 1920–1955*, Canberra, 1975, p. 44–8; A.F.Howells, *Against the Stream*, Melbourne, 1983, Chapters 7, 8.

33. *Passport*, pp. 20–1, 51, 80, 87; *At the Barricades*, p. 38. Palmer himself had undertaken enterprising journeys in his youth, notably his pilgrimage to Russia in

1907 in search of Tolstoy (he wrote that Russian peasants were closer to him than Hardy's villagers), and his return via Siberia and Japan. Harry Heseltine, *Vance Palmer*, University of Queensland Press, 1970, p. 9.

34. *Documentary History of the Australian Labour Movement 1850–1975*, ed. Brian McKinlay, Victoria, 1979, p. 669.
35. Frank Farrell, *International Socialism and Australian Labour*, Sydney, 1981, pp. 134, 138.
36. *Passport*, p. 96.
37. *Age*, Melbourne, 29 June 1940, 'Outposts of France. Their Uncertain Fate', by W.G. Burchett.
38. Farrell, op. cit., p. 220. The labour movement and the Australian government came into open conflict over this issue, when in 1939 wharf labourers in Port Kembla refused to load pig iron bound for Japan. Attorney-General Menzies became popularly known as 'Pig Iron Bob'.
39. *Adam and Eve*, 10 July 1940, 'Are We Still Asleep?', by W.G. Burchett.
40. 'Japan Can Be Stopped,' by W.G. Burchett. *Digest of World Reading*, November 1940, pp. 1–4. An Australian who did foresee this threat was adventurer journalist Dr George Morrison (1860–1920). Morrison became involved in Chinese politics as adviser to Yuan Shikai. He directed his warnings about the intentions of Japan to the British Foreign Office and British newspapers, as well as to Australian Prime Minister W.M. Hughes in 1917. (Cyril Pearl, *Morrison of Peking*, Angus and Robertson, Sydney, 1967, pp. 290, 331, 351–2, 387.) Similarly, W.H. Donald (1874–1946) an Australian journalist who lived in China for thirty-seven years and was a confidant of Jiang Jie-shi took a stand against appeasement. Donald was war correspondent in Tokyo for the Hong Kong *China Mail* during the Russo-Japanese War. (E.A.Selle, *Donald of China*, Harper Bros., New York, 1948.)
41. *Digest of World Reading*, February 1941, pp. 37–40.
42. Norman Macswan, *The Man Who Read the East Wind: A Biography of Richard Hughes*, Kangaroo Press, Sydney, 1982, p. 21 and Chapters 1–3, passim. Concerning other journalists from Australia and New Zealand who worked in Asia just before, during and after the war, Robert J. Gilmore and Denis Warner, *Near North*, Angus and Robertson, Sydney, 1948. Biographical notes, pp. 346–8.
43. Macswan, op. cit., p. 30
44. It was the late Andrew Fabinyi at Cheshire who chose to publish *Pacific Treasure Island*. His discernment led to the publication of some of the best Australian progressive writing in the 1960s. Fabinyi emigrated from Hungary in 1939. He made an important contribution to Australian intellectual life. See John McLaren (ed.), *A Nation Apart, Essays in Honour of Andrew Fabinyi*, Melbourne, 1983.
45. *Pacific Treasure Island*, Cheshire, Melbourne, 1942, 2nd ed. pp. 11–12.
46. Ibid., pp. 11–12, 122.
47. Ibid., Chapter 6; passim.
48. Apart from *Pacific Treasure Island*, see also the feature supplement, 'Revolution in New Caledonia', *Digest of World Reading*, 1 May 1941.
49. *Passport*, p. 142.
50. *Pacific Treasure Island*, p. 67.
51. Ibid., p. 122.
52. Ibid.
53. Ibid., p. 121.
54. Ibid., p. 118.
55. Ibid.
56. Ibid., pp. 12–13.
57. *Democracy with a Tommygun*, Cheshire, Melbourne, 1946.
58. *At the Barricades*, p. 67.
59. *Democracy with a Tommygun*, p. 198.
60. Ibid., p. 198.
61. Ibid., p.192. Cf. *Pacific Treasure Island* pp. 141–2.
62. Ibid., p. 193.
63. Among Fitzpatrick's early publications were *British Imperialism and Australia*,

1788–1833, London, 1939; *A Short History of the Australian Labor Movement*, Melbourne, 1940; and *The British Empire in Australia*, Melbourne, 1941. Fitzpatrick's biographer, Don Watson, op. cit., describes his life as a 'continuous private war with the Establishment', p. 1.

64. *Democracy with a Tommygun*, pp. 286–7.
65. *At the Barricades*, p. 103.
66. Ibid., p. 113.
67. Ibid., p. 123.
68. Howard Schonberger, 'Zaibatsu Dissolution and the American Restoration of Japan', *Bulletin of Concerned Asian Scholars*, September 1973, pp. 21–31; J. G. Roberts, *Mitsui*, New York, 1973, pp. 391–5; Joe Moore, *Japanese Workers and the Struggle for Power, 1945–47*, University of Wisconsin Press, 1983.
69. Bruce Cumings, *The Origins of the Korean War, Liberation and the Emergence of Separate Regimes, 1945–1947*, Princeton University Press, 1981, pp. 127, 135–78.
70. *Democracy with a Tommygun*, op. cit., p. 286. Cf. Harold Isaacs, *No Peace for Asia*, United States, 1947 (1967 edition), pp. 131–2, 158, 209. Isaacs also took a very critical view: 'The United States never took a step to check the cynical use of Japanese troops to fight both the Annamites and the Indonesians' (p. 238).
71. *Democracy with a Tommygun*, pp. 244–60.
72. Ibid., p. 260.
73. *This Monstrous War*, 1953; *Koje Unscreened*, 1953.
74. Walter Lippmann, *The Cold War*, Harper and Bros., New York, 1947, p. 23. (From articles originally published in *New York Herald Tribune*.)
75. Rupert Lockwood, *Black Armada*, Sydney, 1975, pp. 8, 11.
76. Ibid., pp. 6–7.
77. Gordon Greenwood, *Approaches to Asia*, Sydney, 1974, p. 15.
78. William Macmahon Ball, *Japan, Enemy or Ally?*, Melbourne, 1948, Chapter 7. Trevor Reece, *Australia, New Zealand and the United States*, Oxford University Press, 1969. Gavan McCormack, *Cold War, Hot War*, Sydney, 1983.
79. McCormack, op.cit., p. 41.
80. Ibid., p. 42.
81. William Macmahon Ball, 'Australian Policy Towards Japan Since 1945', in Greenwood and Harper, *Australia in World Affairs, 1956–60*, Cheshire, Sydney, 1963; John Dower, 'Occupied Japan and the American Lake, 1945–50', in Mark Selden and Edward Friedman, *America's Asia, Dissenting Essays on Asian-American Relations*, New York, 1971.
82. Dower, op.cit., p. 183.
83. Ibid., p. 185. The Australian viewpoint is of interest in the light of later research. Moore, op.cit.; Chalmers Johnson, *Conspiracy at Matsukawa*, University of California Press, 1972.
84. Macmahon Ball, loc.cit.
85. W. F. Mandle, *Going It Alone*, Penguin, 1980, p. 135.
86. McCormack, op.cit., p. 104.
87. *American Foreign Policy 1950–1955, Basic Documents*, Vol. II, Washington, 1957, p. 2539.
88. Alan Whiting, *China Crosses the Yalu, The Decision to Enter the Korean War*, New York, 1960.
89. McCormack, op.cit., pp. 46–7.
90. John Burton, *The Alternative, A Dynamic Approach to Our Relations with Asia*, Morgans Publication, Sydney, 1954, p. 87.
91. Ibid., p. 92.
92. McCormack, op.cit., pp. 47–9.
93. Farrell, op.cit., pp. 144–7.
94. Joseph Waters, *Nation Review*, 8-14 November, 1974, pp. 104–5. Waters was responsible for the publication of *Cold War in Germany*, *This Monstrous War*, 1953, and *The Peoples' Democracies*, 1951.
95. *Vietnam Will Win!*, New York, 1968, p. 146.
96. *Digest of World Reading*, 1 April 1942.

97. Stone in an interview, documentary *I. F. Stone's Weekly*. Burchett discusses the military organization of the NLF in *Vietnam Will Win!*.
98. *North of the Seventeenth Parallel*, Delhi, 1956, pp. 140, 141, 125; *Vietnam North*, New York, 1966, p. 9, 11, 80, 88; *Vietnam Will Win!*, op. cit., pp. 140–42; *My Visit to the Liberated Zone of South Vietnam*, Hanoi, 1966, pp. 17, 84; *Vietnam, Inside Story of a Guerrilla War*, p. 137.
99. Russel Ward, *The Australian Legend*, Melbourne, 1958, p. 82. Bush makeshift and ingenuity in the use of materials had varying implications depending on social circumstances, as can be seen from the career of Australian inventor, H.V.McKay, whose social outlook was both conservative and philanthropic. See Francis Wheelhouse, *Digging Stick to Rotary Hoe*, Sydney, 1966.
100. *China, The Quality of Life*, Penguin, 1976. Edgar Snow, *Scorched Earth*, London, 1941, Vol. I, pp. 92–100; Vol. II, pp. 309–16.
101. *North of the Seventeenth Parallel*, Chapter 10; *My Visit to the Liberated Zone of South Vietnam*, Hanoi, 1966, pp. 23, 31, 49, 62; *Vietnam, Inside Story of a Guerrilla War*, p. 128; *The Furtive War*, Chapter 6; *Vietnam Will Win!*, Chapters, 10, 11.
102. *Vietnam, Inside Story of a Guerilla War*, p. 128; on Aborigines, see also *Pacific Treasure Island*, p. 134.
103. Gregory Clark, *In Fear of China*, Melbourne, 1967, p. 170.
104. Ibid., p. 171.
105. Michael Sexton, *War For the Asking, Australia's Vietnam Secrets*, Penguin, Melbourne, 1981, pp. 1–3.
106. *Age*, 28 January 1984.
107. *Democracy with a Tommygun*, p. 260.
108. Alejandro Lichauco, *The Lichauco Paper*, Monthly Review, July/August 1973; Stephen Rosskamm, Shalom, *The United States and the Philippines, a Study of Neocolonialism*, Philadelphia, 1981, pp. 161–9.
109. An American scholar endorses the Filipino assessment of the effect of American business operations: '. . . by aiding in the preservation of this favourable business environment under martial law the United States government shares responsibility for the consequences – the poverty, the malnutrition, and the absence of freedom'. p. 187, Shalom, op.cit. See also Walden Bello, David Kinley and Claire Elinson, *Development Debacle, The World Bank in the Philippines*, San Francisco, 1982.
110. See recent publications of Community Aid Abroad (Discussion Sheets) and the Philippines Action Support Group (Philippines Briefs) also *Asian Bureau Newsletter*. Australian Broadcasting Commission television documentaries have been informative on this subject.
111. Dr Peter McCawley of the Australian National University argued very much along these lines on the ABC Radio programme, 'The World Today', 20 June 1984.
112. Yarwood and Knowling, op. cit., p. 78. Clive Turnbull, *Black War*, Cheshire, Melbourne, 1948, Chapter V. 'On Timor', *Age*, 28 January 1984.
113. *Southern Africa Stands Up*, Melbourne, 1978, p. 49.
114. For description of one such encounter, Jim Gale, 'Wilfred Burchett', *Labour Herald*, Adelaide, October 1983.
115. James Dunn, *A People Betrayed*, Brisbane, 1983, pp. viii–x, 281. Dunn, who served as Australian consul in East Timor from 1962 to 1964, is one of a number of Australians very active on this issue.
116. The following account is based on Dunn, op.cit.
117. Statement by Greg Shackleton in film footage taken near Balibo and sent back to Dili; a sequence of great historic significance in the documentary *Island of Hope, Island of Fear*, concerning Fretilin's situation just prior to the invasion.
118. Dunn, op.cit., p. 250. See also Jill Joliffe, *East Timor, Nationalism and Colonialism*, Queensland, 1978; Walsh and Munster, *Secrets of State, A Detailed Assessment of the Book They Banned*, Angus and Robertson, 1982, Chapter VI.
119. For one view of this debate from a viewpoint similar to Burchett's, Turner, op.cit., pp. 3–17, 26–40, 157–66.
120. This handbook, published in Melbourne 1925, drew on longstanding bush practice for the benefit of new settlers.

The Burchett family outside their house in Poowong, Victoria, displaying a Giant Gippsland earthworm

The Burchett family bids farewell to sons Winston (left) and Wilfred (right) on their departure for Europe, December 1936

George Burchett, Wilfred's father

Wilfred Burchett as war correspondent in the Pacific

Wilfred Burchett, from inside cover of *Wingate Adventure*

Burchett's first wife, Erna Hammer, with their son Rainer, in Australia during World War Two

Burchett and his second wife Vessa, from Bulgaria, with Burchett's father in the late 1940s

Burchett's son George in a Russian forest

The Burchetts in Hanoi, 1966, with Ho Chi Minh

With Ho Chi Minh and Vietnam's Prime Minister Pham Van Dong

Burchett with Prince Norodom Sihanouk of Kampuchea

With friends like this photographer, who
needs enemies?

Wilfred Burchett, undated

"Take cover, he's armed with a typewriter!"

Cartoon appearing in the Melbourne *Herald* at the time of Burchett's unauthorized entry into Australia (1970) (Courtesy the *Herald*)

"I'd rather fight him over there than have to do it in my own backyard."

Cartoon appearing in the Melbourne *Age*, 1970, depicting Prime Minister John Gorton and his deputy Phillip Lynch on Burchett's departure (Courtesy the *Age*)

Burchett in the Vietnamese jungle

Burchett in Paris, 1970s

Wilfred Burchett, undated (Courtesy André Degon)

121. Don Watson's biography of another Australian radical, Brian Fitzpatrick, contains many insights relevant to an understanding of Burchett. In both men one can see a lack of systematic thought, 'romantic and utopian elements', blind spots concerning communism which might seem to be irredeemable flaws, qualities he attributed to Fitzpatrick; yet his conclusion about Fitzpatrick would apply also to Burchett: 'an individual alive in – and to – his time. And measured against both his contemporaries and comtemporary society, it is difficult to judge against Fitzpatrick on the scores either of "openness" or "humanity".' Watson, op.cit., p. xx.

Part Three: Crises in the Third World

6

Wilfred Burchett's New Caledonia

Dorothy Shineberg

A young man's passionate concern for the struggle against fascism, as well as a young journalist's keenness to get a story of world interest, sent Wilfred Burchett to New Caledonia on the last day of 1940 on his first assignment as a foreign correspondent. The event he covered for a number of newspapers and magazines had occurred in the previous September: a popular demonstration had forced the resignation of the pro-Vichy French governor, and with Australian and Allied help the French resident-commissioner for the New Hebrides (now Vanuatu), Henri Sautot, who had already rallied to the Free French cause of General de Gaulle, was installed as the new Governor of New Caledonia. The pro-Vichy elements were despatched to Indochina and New Caledonia was to become an important Allied military base for the rest of the war.

In his first autobiography, Burchett recalls the assignment thus:

> After the Nazis overran France and set up the puppet Vichy government, there was little news as to what was happening in New Caledonia. There were rumours that French settlers – some of them descendants of the Communards, deported there in chains after the Paris Commune was crushed in 1871 – had revolted, rounded up the pro-Vichy officials and packed them off in a boat to Indochina. I

decided to find out and, after negotiating with several newspapers, was in a position to do so.[1]

The news of New Caledonian happenings was not as sparse as he records. There were reporters in Noumea at the time, and the event was in fact well covered in the four months before Burchett arrived on the scene. The *Sydney Morning Herald* had even reported popular demonstrations before the 19 September *ralliement* from stories (with pictures) brought to Sydney by a group of American travellers.[2] Burchett was taking a little journalistic licence; an official pronouncement on the demise of the Vichy regime in Noumea by the Prime Minister, Mr Menzies, the day after the event,[3] plus a number of follow-up stories, scarcely qualify as 'rumours', nor is it likely that many descendants of Communards had in fact been associated with the popular demonstration since few political deportees settled in the territory. All the same, the event did deserve more prominence than it had been given at the time. In spite of the dangerous implications for Australia in having a pro-Vichy regime so close to its most populated shore, the news of the government's overthrow made only page nine of the *Sydney Morning Herald*. The 'real' news was still news of Europe, an extraordinary mentality in the Australia of the period and one which Burchett set out to remedy. Moreover, the articles he did for the *Digest of World Reading*[4] certainly brought a detailed account of the important episode in New Caledonia before the eyes of a world public for the first time.

As well as articles for this magazine and for the local press, Burchett's New Caledonian visit of 1941 resulted in his first book, *Pacific Treasure Island*, which appeared in December of that year on the eve of Pearl Harbor. The book drew as well on two previous short trips to the island. Exactly four years before, Burchett had paid a brief visit to Noumea, as well as a much longer one to Tahiti, when on his first overseas trip to Europe via the Pacific. On his return home in 1939 with his first wife Erna Hammer, he had another stay of two weeks in the French colony thanks to a dockers' strike in Noumea. By 1941 his European travels and his experience in the French Pacific had sharpened up his self-taught French to the point where he was able to travel about New Caledonia and talk freely to the local people.

The overthrow of the Vichy regime in Noumea touched two chords in Burchett's heart. First it appealed in general to the romantic revolutionary in him, as well as to his particular campaign against fascism at the time. He saw the spontaneous uprising in Noumea in the same heroic light and in the same tradition as the popular revolutions in Paris in 1789, 1848 and 1871 (as, of course, did the *ralliement* participants themselves). Secondly, the event appealed to his nationalism, which with him had a strong populist and anti-colonial flavour. What if New Caledonia, only 800 miles from Brisbane, had remained in the hands of the Axis? The thought is a springboard for his perennial theme: the necessity for Australia to have an independent and regional foreign policy, for Australia and its neighbours to free themselves from the Old World of Europe and together to follow their true destiny in the Pacific.

Although *Pacific Treasure Island* was written around the *ralliement* to de Gaulle, a spirited account of which forms the dramatic climax, it also succeeds in presenting a lively picture of New Caledonia in 1941 with not a little historical background. The book had an instant success. It has to be said that this was partly due to the sins of omission of others. It is one of the few books in English on New Caledonia to this day, and the first attempting any broad picture since the book of another journalist – Julian Thomas, alias Stanley James, alias the Vagabond – published in 1886. This neglect appears to arise from the shameful fact that few Australian writers were sufficiently able to penetrate the language barrier to report on Australia's nearest eastern neighbour. As was to happen so often in his life, Burchett's early self-training in foreign languages put him a mark ahead of other journalists. While for the purpose of this book Burchett clearly delved into the territory's past mainly for 'background', he and Erna Burchett[5] did their historical research well enough to be quoted on historical matters to the present day.[6] His own keen observations, conversations and collection of reminiscences (which nowadays might be classed as 'oral history') are in turn now of interest to modern scholars.

Since Burchett saw New Caledonia in wartime and through the spectacles of his current prime concern – the defeat of the monstrous fascist regimes – it is perhaps not remarkable that the real heroes of his story are the white settlers who helped to rout the Vichy government. The story of the 1940 'revolution' is told with panache. In the light of a modern scholarly account[7] it appears to exaggerate and idealize the role played by the citizenry. Certainly, the impression given that the Melanesians were morally right behind the settlers is misleading: the whole episode was carried on over their heads. Nevertheless, it is a good journalistic account of the incident, based on a variety of conversations with participants and augmented by quotations from official despatches.

In 1941, the term 'New Caledonians' meant to him, by and large, the *colons* or white settlers. In view of his international socialist sympathies and his later interest in the struggle of the Asian peoples against colonialism it is perhaps surprising that he did not see the indigenous peoples – at that time the large majority – as the true heirs of any emerging New Caledonian nation.

He does indeed devote a chapter to the history of Melanesian revolts against the colonial power. Burchett is interested in this theme of insurrection, and as mentioned above had gone to considerable trouble in researching the New Caledonian past. He talked to people (all whites, alas) who were alive at the time of the uprisings; most valuably he recorded the reminiscences of the then old Miss Paddon (with a photograph as well), daughter of the famous English trader, who was a young woman of twenty at the time of the 1878 revolution. In addition he (and/or Erna Burchett) had read the account of Commandant Rivière, who participated in the repression of this revolt, as well as contemporary and later material inquiring into the cause of the uprising. Burchett had to do his history rapidly and on the basis of published material, mostly old French books and periodicals. The quantity of these, properly set out in a formal bibliography at the end, does him great credit, but even if he had had the training he would not have had the means to check their credibility. In his account, therefore, everything in print tends to be accepted at face value. Popular historical legends – like the story of the English narrowly being beaten to the annexation by France, and the resultant suicide of the English commander[8] – became through his book perpetuated in English as well as French accounts.

With hindsight, however, Burchett's preoccupations of 1941 can be seen to have distorted his perception of the position of the Melanesians, a perception reinforced by contemporary thinking about 'primitive peoples'. While he described the oppressions of the past, he saw these as part of ancient history, now superseded by humane 'treatment'. Basically he believed that the exploitation of the Melanesians was 'a thing of the past'. He was 'impressed by the position of the natives today'.[9] He even used the supposed simple idyllic life of the 'ignorant natives'[10] to preach the evils of the capitalist system. It would take a learned economist, he said, to explain to these 'simple uneducated savages' that their self-sufficiency was backward.

> They would feel that they were not a civilized people at all until they had about 10% of their tribesmen unemployed, with the balance working much harder because of the shortage of labour, destroying portion of their crop because of lack of markets, and then giving part of their profit back to the 10% of unemployed, who would not be able to buy much of the original production because of the increased prices the local tribesmen must pay, due to the lack of markets. Either they would feel like that, or they would solve the problem by hitting the economist over the head with a '*casse-tête*', and turn back to their taro beds again.[11]

In this account the 'simple uneducated savages' were once again serving their historic function in European literature of providing an idealized contrast to the vices of Western society. These vices were indeed real, but the contrasting idyll was imaginary.

While Burchett rejoiced in the lack of 'outside interference' enjoyed by the Melanesians, his observation that they tended to 'stick to their own reserves'[12] neglected the fact that they had no choice in the matter. In fact the land he saw being worked by the *kanaks* was not their own, and was often far away from their ancestral heritage. It was generally the poorest land in the country on the slopes of hills and on the floors of deep valleys where the sun appears for only a few hours a day. It was owned by the state, as it still is. The *kanaks* were forced to live on these reserves, many having been uprooted from their own lands with which they had spiritual connections. Although conditions had improved in some ways for the Melanesians since the mid-1920s, at the time Burchett was writing they were still an oppressed and subject people. It was still an offence for 'natives' to leave their reservations without an official pass: like the Australian aborigines they were not even free to travel in their own land and were liable to administrative arrest and imprisonment.

As a good observer, Burchett noted 'exceptions' to his general remark that the *kanaks* remained on their reserves: for example, those he saw engaged in road-work and coffee-picking. He was not there long enough to discover that *corvée* labour on the roads still existed and that the coffee-pickers would have been forced by the obligatory head-tax (imposed for the purpose) to work as very cheap labour on the settlers' plantations. The bitterness of the *kanaks* about the theft of their land was great, and remains so. No happy peasants they.

Burchett was too good a journalist not to pick up some of this discontent. He talked with enough Melanesians to find out that they resented the whites' seizure of the best land, and quotes a Melanesian coffee-planter's complaint by way of illustration.

> I well remember the disgust with which one native coffee-planter waved his arm in a comprehensive gesture to show me many acres of a beautifully laid-out flourishing coffee plantation just in front of his house. 'See all that? It belongs to missions. Natives work it, help pick it, and Fathers get all the money. Oughta be our land,' waving this time towards the native village. 'We gotta go 12 kms from here, to little bit of dry land by the sea, to grow our coffee. Gotta work here on other people's plantations to make enough money.'[13]

But Burchett quickly leaves this subject, using it only as a bridge passage to his favourite topic of revolution, this time the Melanesian revolt of 1917. The fact that all was not perfect led to this event, which Burchett describes with some lurid detail of doubtful accuracy from the account of a white official who had participated in quelling it. Characteristically, Burchett concludes the historical section by attributing the 'comparatively good conditions' of the *kanaks* to their frequent revolts, implying that they improved their status by standing up for their rights. The truth is rather that the administration used the insurrections as an excuse to dispossess the Melanesians of yet more land. The insurrections did in fact discourage white settlement, as Burchett recognized, but to the Burchett of 1941 this was a minus rather than a plus for the colony. 'Actually the revolts had the opposite of a beneficial effect on the colony, and are one of the chief reasons for the present low white population.'[14] He was right, of course, in comparing the *kanaks'* conditions favourably with those of the Australian aborigines, and though such a base-line could hardly be lower, it seemed enough to reassure him. 'Even today, the natives aren't completely satisfied with their treatment – although one must admit that in comparison with our own Australian aboriginals the New Caledonian natives are well-off.'[15]

It appears that he mentally equated the New Caledonian *colons* with the pioneer white settlers of Australia: it was to them that the future belonged. The comparison was, to begin with, a false one in terms of their ratio to the total population, even more so then than now. In 1941, the whites represented at most (with *assimilés*) about thirty per cent of the population of New Caledonia. Although much less visible than the whites (Noumea was even more of a white town than it is today) the *kanaks* formed the overwhelming majority of the population at the time, and are still the largest single ethnic group at forty-three per cent. Burchett made plain his belief that the original inhabitants should be 'well treated', as they had not been in the past, but in his perspective of the period, they played the part of extras on the stage of history, like the aborigines in Australia. Most references to them in this book, like the chapter on 'Emile, the High Commissioner', serve the purpose of providing contrast or light relief. In this respect Burchett was in step with the paternalistic liberal thought of the period, but not in advance of it. He noted with approval, however, that physical segregation was not practised in the French colony: seats in the bus, for example, were allotted in order of booking regardless of race. He knew that that would never have happened in an Anglo-Saxon-dominated country in 1941.[16]

The fact that New Caledonia had a convict past reinforced in his mind the parallel with Australian history. There was no way that Burchett's readers would be allowed to overlook this romantic episode in the colony's history, especially since among the deportees were the exiled revolutionaries of the 1871 Paris Commune. Burchett tried – this time with scant success – to set up interviews with time-expired convicts of the ordinary kind, but to fill out this section he described some of the horrors of transportation largely by way of quotation from an old book by George Griffiths, *In an Unknown Prison Land* (1901), taking the opportunity of upbraiding the author for his view that the treatment meted out to condemned criminals was too lenient.

Most space, however, was reserved for the story of the unlikely appearance of the Paris Communards in this far-off colony of the Antipodes. It would have been irresistible to any journalist, but it was utterly entrancing to one with Burchett's predilections, especially as among the political prisoners were the remarkable woman revolutionary Louise Michel and the radical journalist and famous escapee Henri Rochefort. Their stories are good for a chapter. Burchett (and/or Erna Burchett) had read the works of both. The chapter gave him the excuse to recount the story of the ill-fated Commune, the extraordinary career of Louise Michel, and the exciting episode of Rochefort's escape. This is acceptable journalism: all the stories are worth the retelling, especially to an anglophone audience. The assumption he makes, however, that Communard ancestry is 'directly responsible for [the settlers'] independence and lack of subservience to privilege'[17] is disquieting. The number of descendants of Communards in 1940 would have been negligible. The political deportees who survived to 1880 were pardoned and allowed to return to France: most of them did return within a few years. In this case, *colon* informants can hardly be blamed for the error, since the return of the survivors was well-known to all. It may have been the case, that, in the heady days of the *ralliement* to Free France, the settlers chose to remember the Communard presence in their colony's past, but it seems more likely that Burchett himself gave way to the temptation of indulging his own view of the role of political dissidents in history. 'The Communards of New Caledonia, the Chartists and Irish Nationalists in Australia, the Pilgrim Fathers and the long line of political refugees who for centuries past have sought sanctuary in America, have helped to establish a new tradition of liberty and tolerance.'[18]

Through Burchett's book readers were also introduced to the fact that the New Caledonian population was a patchwork of ethnic groups, most of them brought in as indentured labourers. This led the author to include a thumb-nail sketch of the labour history of the colony which went far beyond the perceptions of most short-term visitors. It probably represents the rough knowledge of his *colon* hosts who showed him around 'the bush', which term included anything outside Noumea, and still does.

In this view, the Melanesians were supposed to be too well-off to be coerced into becoming a docile work force, so other labour resources had to be found. The earliest were the convict labourers and later, when mining began to flourish, were added Japanese, Javanese and Indo-chinese immigrant labour.

In fact the convicts contributed very little to the work force developing the country. They were responsible for some public work in the vicinity of Noumea, but most of their labour was used in penitentiary works, such as building walls to enclose themselves or future convict arrivals and in working prison farms. For a brief period of the governorship of Pallu de la Barriere (1882–84), convicts had been more freely assigned as labourers for settlers and were put to making public roads but this was soon halted by the recall of the governor. There was a nefarious 'deal' in convict labour between the penal administration and selected large firms, but this also was exceptional.

In general, by far the major supply of the colony's labourers had been New Hebrideans (ni Vanuatu) until the 1890s when the Asians began to trickle in and when, as well, the supply of indigenous labour began to be tapped. Solomon Islanders were also indentured, mainly in the period from 1890 to the First World War. After the 1920s the number of imported Pacific Island indentured labourers dwindled to insignificance. It is interesting to be able to infer from Burchett's account that these 'Oceanian' labourers (as the French called them) had apparently disappeared from the memory of the *colons* by 1941, although in 1900 imported islanders had made up thirty-four per cent of the indentured work force and still exceeded by far the combined total of Asian immigrant labourers. By the twentieth century, too, the colonial government had overcome difficulties in forcing the local *kanak* to work, through the imposition of the head-tax, which increased as the years went by. At the end of 1900 indigenous labourers made up forty per cent of the indentured work force, then exceeding the number of imported Oceanians as well as the Asians under indenture.

The Indochinese and Javanese workers do appear in Burchett's book, but for the most part, once again, as 'colourful' characters. The author briefly visited the Tiebaghi chrome mines in 1941, essentially as a tourist who spent only a few hours there as the guest of a white *colon*. He did not go down the mines (heeding the advice of his host) but gives an account of the observable features of the surface-works. The advice concerning the unpleasant dampness underground did not pass unnoticed in relation to the health hazards of the workers. 'I begin to understand then why the Dutch government had forbidden the employment of Javanese labourers underground, because of the risk of tuberculosis.'[19] The remark is a good example of Burchett's eagerness and ability to put together little scraps of information to form a broader picture; this sometimes led him astray but more often led him to most useful perceptions. In this case the conditions of his visit had not entirely blinded him to the risks and hardships of the working population. In retrospect he described the conditions of these mineworkers as 'bordering on slavery',[20] but there is no general condemnation of the indenture system in *Pacific Treasure Island*.

His nearest approach to discovering its brutalities comes characteristically from a story he heard in a pub, which began to raise questions in his mind. No one who knows anything about the labour history of the period can seriously doubt the story's theme, at least: the vulnerability to sexual exploitation and physical abuse of an indentured Indochinese woman. Burchett tells the tale graphically and in the callous language of the (non-French) mine-owner. 'I told him [his rival] I was boss, and I'd bought the girl for five years, and I'd do what I liked with her.' Burchett typically checks around, having been shocked out of complacency. 'From investigations made after hearing this lurid story, it really seems that among many of the employers, it is taken for granted that they buy their labourers body and soul for the period of indenture.'[21] It remained for the novelist, Jean Vanmai, a descendant of an Indochinese worker, to give a full account of the hardships and cruelties of the indenture system in his prize-winning novel *Chan Dang*, yet to be translated into English.[22] Ironically, Vanmai's scene is set at precisely the time and place of Burchett's somewhat innocent visit to the mines. Fundamentally Burchett's only opposition to the 'coolie system' represented the orthodox Australian leftist view of the period: that it tended to put at risk the conditions of white workers[23] and impede the development of a 'white-man's colony'.[24] On the other hand his humanity insisted that if coolie labour *were* to be imported it should be accorded just treatment.

Burchett's intellectual position at the time seems to have been roughly that of a progressive of the thirties, including an anti-colonial nationalism typical of the old *Bulletin* school. It is not in any way original, but of course so far at variance with the establishment that his views (especially his anti-fascist ones) would have got into print only with great difficulty in the 1930s. By 1941, however, Australia was at war with the fascists and apparently abandoned by Britain: under these conditions his message, although still bold, was acceptable.

The positive side of his nationalism was his view of Australia's place in its own region rather than as an outpost of Empire. He was vitally interested in the future of the small South Pacific archipelagos – unusually forward-looking for his time – but his interest related almost exclusively to his perception of them as part of the defence system of Australia. New Caledonia was the 'Malta of the South Seas'.[25] 'Possession of New Caledonia is essential to any Power thinking of attacking Australia.'[26] The politics of this school of nationalism could be considered radical for the time, but did not yet fully include people of non-European race. Nor was it aware of its sexist bias. The women who appear in the book are the Javanese maids who get breakfast ready and the *'popinées'* (the New Caledonian equivalent of *'gins'*) in their 'monstrous Mother Hubbards' who were 'out for conquests'.[27] 'Groups of them wandered about hand in hand, barefooted, and when they saw their man they didn't easily let him escape.' His male heroes are the hard-drinking, hard-swearing men of action who can be relied upon to develop the country, like his Mick Griffiths who discovered the 'biggest . . . iron-field in the world'.

The book, then, is that of a young freelance journalist with progressive ideas who is making his name. He is forward-looking, afflicted by what Salman Rushdie calls the 'optimism disease'. He indentifies with the tough bushman image of the white Australian pioneers and New Caledonian *colons*. He is *against* missionaries, colonialism and the big brass. He is *for* the shirt-sleeved worker (white) who bows to no man. He is humane in his attitude to non-Europeans when they come into his view. He shared the current belief that New Caledonia was a rich country (hence his title), which had only to throw off the shackles of colonialism and bureaucracy to attain its full potential.

His forte is that of a good journalist. The best part of the book comes from pub stories – that classic primary source for journalists – chance encounters and set-up meetings. He had a lively curiosity and a keen sense of observation. In a few months he was able to see most of the west coast, half of the east coast and the southern plains of New Caledonia. He was prepared to travel uncomfortably in wartime conditions to go to Noumea for his story, and to venture out to see the rest of the country whenever the occasion presented itself. To an unusual degree he researched available documentary sources, past as well as present. His style was racy – if a little corny by modern standards – and he was not above the odd titillating reference to sex and cannibalism to stimulate 'human interest'.

A most readable book resulted and was reprinted within a year. Two further reprints appeared in 1944, this time in America. The text was unchanged, despite his intention early in 1944 of writing a new introductory chapter.[28] One would like to record that Australia's interest in New Caledonia was thereafter sustained, but that, alas, was not the case. Under the impetus of wartime interest in the Pacific, his book was followed by H.E. Lewis Priday's *Cannibal Island*,[29] an attempt at the history of New Caledonia in the nineteenth century, and in the following year by *The War from Coconut Square*, [30] Priday's account of Allied bases in the south-west Pacific, which has a chapter on New Caledonia. However, Australian interest died as quickly as it arose. The anglophone world had to wait nearly thirty years for another book on the French Pacific territories, a hastily researched effort by a pair of American academics.[31]

It appears then, that the basic thrust of Burchett's book was as unsuccessful in practical effect as it now appears outmoded in politics. His was essentially a sort of 'hands-across-the-seas' message – the brotherhood of anglophone and gallic settlers against the old colonial regimes.

> New Caledonia and Australia are both younger sons of old Empires, and a shirt-sleeve and hand-shake diplomacy is much more apt than that of the silk hat and formal bow of the old days. New Caledonians, like Americans, look to Australia to provide something more virile and realistic and approachable in the way of their official representatives than those that come from the Old World.

One wonders whether, during his last (enforced) stay in New Caledonia in 1970 when his return to Australia had been forbidden, he mused on the irony of his earlier prediction arising from the 1940 revolt against the Vichy regime: 'Personally, I feel sure there are enough hard-headed citizens in the colony to ensure that New Caledonia will never again occupy the obscure position in the French Empire that she occupied before September 1940.'[32] At the time of writing (1985) New Caledonia remains an anachronistic relic of that empire.

Notes

1. Wilfred Burchett, *Passport*, Nelson, Melbourne, 1969, pp. 142–3.
2. See *Sydney Morning Herald* from mid-August to the end of December 1940, including a special article on New Caledonia, 8 November 1940. For coverage of prior events, see *SMH*, 5 September 1940 (story with pictures of pro-de-Gaulle demonstration) and 'Revolution forecast', 18 September 1940. *Pacific Islands Monthly* reported at length on the September take-over in its October issue, and kept its readers well informed thereafter.
3. *SMH*, 20 September 1940.
4. April and May 1941.
5. In the acknowledgement Burchett thanks his wife for her 'painstaking research', so we don't know how much of it was her work.
6. E.g. Virginia Thompson and Richard Adloff, *The French Pacific Islands*, University of California Press, 1971. The second half of this book is devoted to New Caledonia, and the historical chapters make good use of *Pacific Treasure Island* referring its readers to Burchett's 'detailed account' of the 1878 insurrection. Thompson and Adloff has now become a source for others. Many other modern works of scholarship include *Pacific Treasure Island* in their bibliographies, such as Cyril Belshaw's *Changing Melanesia*, Oxford University Press, 1954; John Lawrey, *The Cross of*

Lorraine, Canberra, 1982; Myriam Dornoy, *The Politics of New Caledonia*, Sydney University Press, 1984.

7. John Lawrey, *The Cross of Lorraine*, Canberra, 1982.
8. Captain Denham, who in fact was eventually promoted to Admiral and died in his bed over thirty years later.
9. *Pacific Treasure Island* (hereafter *PTI*), p. 135. The edition used is the 1942 one but except for preface and dedication the other editions are exact reprints.
10. *PTI*, p. 139.
11. Ibid., p. 140.
12. Ibid., p. 135.
13. Ibid., p. 134.
14. Ibid., p. 35.
15. Ibid., p. 134.
16. Ibid., p. 185.
17. Ibid., p. 122.
18. Ibid.
19. Ibid., p. 57.
20. *At the Barricades*, Macmillan, Melbourne, 1981, p. 43.
21. *PTI*, pp. 86–7.
22. J. Vanmai, *Chan Dang: Les Tonkinois de Calédonie au temps colonial*, (Prix de l'Asie 1981), Nouméa, 1980.
23. *PTI*, p. 84.
24. Ibid., p. 85.
25. Ibid., p. 216.
26. Ibid.
27. Ibid., p. 191.
28. Burchett to his parents, 31 March 1944, Burchett Papers, State library of Victoria.
29. Wellington, 1944. In his 1981 autobiography, *At the Barricades*, Burchett overlooks Priday's work, referring to *PTI* as 'the only contemporary book in English on New Caledonia'.
30. Wellington, 1944. In this book Priday refers to the *ralliement* in Noumea, at which he was actually present, but does not cover the story again. As Burchett had long talks with him in Noumea in 1941, Priday is presumably one of the first-hand sources for Burchett's account.
31. Virginia Thompson and Richard Adloff, *The French Pacific Islands*, University of California Press, 1971.
32. *PTI*, p. 215.

7

When the East Wind Prevailed in China

Michael R. Godley

THERE IS A CHINESE SAYING: 'EITHER THE EAST WIND PREVAILS OVER THE
WEST WIND OR THE WEST WIND PREVAILS OVER THE EAST WIND'

MAO ZE-DONG

From the days of Marco Polo China has been a mirror attracting
foreigners with distant glimmer. Up close they have often seen little
more than their own reflections. This was certainly true of the cold
warriors, who had icy stares returned. For Wilfred Burchett, the lure of
Mao's revolution was irresistible.[1] As he wrote to his father not long
after arriving in Peking in February 1951: 'There is such humanity and
beauty here, such tolerance and understanding that I feel very small and
conscious of my inability to express just what is going on. I would do
anything at all for this people and their government because they
represent the fullest flowering of all the finest instincts of humanity.'[2]
Just what he *did* is controversial.

Burchett will always remain an enigma. Although he wrote two
autobiographies, he left little for an objective scholar to work with.

However, it is possible to reconstruct the Peking he knew from other sources. If some of the mystery is removed, it may be easier to evaluate his place in history.

Like many other reporters, he first visited China during the Sino-Japanese War. He was still trying to establish himself in Chungking when the Pacific phase began. After a trip back to Burma, he returned in June 1942. He travelled overland along a sporadic front to Fukien and back and managed, early on, to catch the battle for Changsha. The arrival of Wendell Willkie in September allowed him to latch on to an officially escorted tour to Chengtu and then northward 500 kilometres to Lanchow where the Japanese advance had been stopped. Shortly thereafter he left China for India.[3]

The consummate name-dropper, he later tooks pains to mention his famous friends: Leland Stowe, Theodore White, Harrison Forman, Jack Belden and Betty Graham. They do not seem to have returned the favour. With little knowledge of the complex political manoeuvres in the disguised civil war, he was quite out of his league and does not appear to have established very close connections with the international press corps. He did admit that his coups came when everyone was asleep or out of town. As he parenthetically noted: 'There is no shortcut as effective as being on the right spot at the right time and, if possible, without competitors.'[4] I could think of no better epitaph.

A problem with Burchett – in no sense unique – is the self-serving nature of his autobiographies. His 1981 comment that 'my first weeks in China [in 1951] only reaffirmed my earlier impressions of the moral and intellectual qualities of Chinese communists' is not evident in what he wrote in the early 1940s. I doubt that he reached this decision before he followed their successes from his abode in eastern Europe. Although he may have had an inkling of the extent of KMT corruption and the ability of communists to mobilize the peasantry by the time he published *Democracy with a Tommygun* (1946), he had never been an accomplished political reporter. He recalled in 1981 how uncomplimentary the Chungking journalists had been toward Chiang Kai-shek and Hollington Tong, the press secretary, but earlier works made much too much of his close contacts with 'Holly' and persistent efforts to interview the Generalissimo. In later years when boasting that he interviewed Zhou Enlai the day after Pearl Harbor, he neglected to add that the entire press corps was in attendance. The excuse that his Sydney editor was not interested in communists fails to explain why Burchett neglected to pursue the story. The truth, I think, is that he felt more secure reporting the visible war. Moreover, the young reporter was very proud of 'a magical pass with an enormous red seal' given him by the KMT's Military Affairs Commission.[5]

When he went off to find the south-eastern front, he had the good fortune to meet Yang Gang, a leading journalist. After she joined the *People's Daily*, he would list her as one of his important Peking friends. In 1942, she was not identifiably communist. Historian John King Fairbank arranged her a post-war scholarship to Radcliffe College.

Helen Foster Snow described her as 'forceful and masculine': 'She was one of the few Chinese I have ever known who was not either naturally charming or artificially so.' Once married to a banker, fluent in English and on all accounts brilliant, she had changed her name to Gang (meaning steel) just before Burchett met her. He later admitted that she became famous for her own coverage of the war but earlier, when he was trying to make a name for himself, he left the impression that she had come along to serve as his interpreter. While she did interpret, it was surely Burchett who tagged along. The very next year, at the age of thirty-eight, Yang Gang was the literary editor of the *Ta Kung Pao* which, as Fairbank noted, was 'like being editor of *The Times Literary Supplement*'.[6]

The Australian gave away the nature of the relationship: 'At times, in her eagerness for her own story, she would take an interview right out of my hands, then tell me what she thought I ought to know afterwards.' He also said that Yang Gang's 'job' was a 'difficult one': 'to interpret as accurately as her intellectual honesty urged her, and at the same time as a patriotic Chinese to prevent me from seeing and hearing those things which would give me a bad impression of China'. Burchett also observed how the scenes in Chungking had been 'staged by the efficient Information Ministry' for Willkie. Had he recognized the same thing when he returned to China in 1951, his own reputation might have been saved. He could be more reflective about another 'one world' idealist: 'Willkie's naïveté, his sentimentality and lack of real political knowledge were assets in his favour.'[7]

He did predict that 'Yang Gang is a great woman, and a good example of the type that will help build China's future', but he had good things to say about Jiang Jingguo who now rules Taiwan.[8] To be fair, Burchett made up for what he lacked in sophistication about political matters with concern for the human suffering he encountered. Some of his last cables to the London *Daily Express* describing the famine in Honan province are packed with emotion. But he had not been an eyewitness.[9] His readiness to believe tales of woe, like his later belief in Maoist redemption, was characteristic. As he identified with the heroic Chinese struggle against the Japanese, he came to admire 'the goodness, honesty and dignity of China'. It was David versus Goliath.[10]

Burchett was best at what, in the age of television, we call the 'live eye'. He was good at describing what he saw. He was the cameraman not the investigative reporter, and seldom the polished journalist who could treat event as metaphor in some greater drama. It is easy for an academic to call his writing simplistic. His wartime books pale by comparison with Belden or Stowe. The few words he devoted to the 'Burma Road' in *Democracy with a Tommygun* lead me to think that he had kept his eyes shut. He was always in a hurry to move his lens to another story.

The style he developed, while reflecting some of the obvious limitations of covering a war, would easily fit the canons of 'socialist realism'. A self-made man who believed that he was delivering truth to the working class, Burchett quite naturally adopted an approach easily confused with propaganda. Cinema verité, the reporter as camera, was popular in leftist circles when he first visited China. By 1951, 'reportage literature' had become unabashedly didactic: to record the misery and oppression which had existed before the revolution and the great progress thereafter. As co-author Rewi Alley explained when asked why he wrote 'only about the good things in China', criticism might have obscured 'the total picture of the emergence of a great nation'. Biographer Willis Airey put this perspective honestly: 'Rewi Alley strove for objectivity but denied that it meant detachment that feared all enthusiasm, that must qualify any positive judgement by insisting that there was "another side" that more or less balanced it.'[11]

Having caught the 'East Wind' in Budapest, Burchett decided to try to get back to China. He probably wrote to a number of people including the first eastern European reporters in Peking. Betty Graham's alleged reply that 'old friends – by then in high places – had not forgotten' him is typical of his autobiography but I would suggest that his Budapest address was more important. China closely followed Russian advice in those days and even acceped Stalin's paranoid belief that Anna Louise Strong was an American agent.[12] Burchett's claim that he made arrangements through the China Travel Service in Hong Kong tells us no more than where he picked up his visa. The real questions concern who gave authorization and why. The answers do not have to be sinister.

My guess for a contact is Chen Jiakang who had worked with Graham and served as Zhou Enlai's private secretary in Chungking. He made it his business to keep tabs on foreigners. He is known to have been at the World Peace Congress in Prague in the spring of 1949 and to have travelled widely in eastern Europe.[13] The first piece Burchett wrote for *People's China* identified him as 'representative of the Australian Peace Council' and 'now the China correspondent of *Liberty* and *Labour News* of Australia and *Ce Soir* of France'.[14]

Although I am sceptical of how 'friendly' they had been with him before, it is not difficult to guess who his sponsors were. Yang Gang was in Peking. Gong Peng, Zhou Enlai's press secretary, was known to every foreign correspondent in Chungking. As Fairbank noted, she was 'the official appointee for contact with barbarians'. She subsequently became head of the Foreign Ministry's Information Department and accompanied Zhou to Geneva and Bandung. Until her death in 1970, she remained the person ultimately 'responsible' for visiting journalists. Burchett would have been one of the first.[15] His dramatic account in 1981 of that post-Pearl Harbor meeting with Zhou relates that Gong Peng warned him that 'from the moment I entered the compound I would be a marked man. . .' This is vintage stuff but pure vinegar. Most reporters had some contact with the left in those days.[16]

Gong Peng and her sister Gong Pusheng who held an MA in religion from Columbia University had spent a number of years working with the YWCA. Pusheng had, in fact, worked with the UN Commission on

Human Rights from 1946 to 1948. Helen Foster Snow believed that the sisters combined 'the best of East and West'.[17] The same could be said of their husbands. Qiao Guanhua married Gong Peng with the blessings of many of the foreigners in Chungking. Fluent in French, German and English, he held a PhD from the University of Tübingen in Germany. After the revolution he became editor of *People's China*. Qiao was also involved in the Korean negotiations, served as an 'observer' at the UN during the peace talks and was ambassador when Peking was admitted.[18] Pusheng's husband, Zhang Hanfu, was an American-trained journalist who edited the communist *Xinhua ribao* in Chungking and became a vice minister for foreign affairs and part of Zhou Enlai's entourage.[19] Students of Chinese politics will know that these people composed a 'conservative' faction that consistently pressed for peaceful coexistence with the West. They received the highest marks from all those who had dealings with them abroad or in China. Burchett's boast in 1981 that Gong Peng and Qiao Guanhua 'became among my closest friends in China' is, like many of his claims, subject to corroboration. Since Gong was responsible for his accreditation and Qiao was his editor, some working relationship was certain.[20]

His 'very best friends from China', he wrote to his father, died in a plane crash off Sarawak which also killed the director of the New China News Agency. 'Shen', as he named his 'very best friend' who had worked with him 'shoulder to shoulder, one could say, throughout the whole Korean period and again at Geneva', was another well-known English-speaking journalist. 'Shen' and also 'Li Ping', another of his friends, escorted James Cameron of the *News Chronicle* (London) when he toured China in late 1954.[21]

Trying to sort out the 'expatriate' community in Burchett's time is like reading a LeCarré novel. Humphrey Trevelyan, the British chargé d'affaires from 1953 to 1955, recalled that there were 'British and Australians in Peking, whom we only saw when they came to have the births of their babies registered or in the vain hope of having their passports renewed'. 'They were Communists, mostly old journalists, employed by the Chinese on minor literary tasks.'[22] One birth was possibly that of Burchett's son George. One passport almost certainly belonged to Alan Winnington of the *Daily Worker*.[23] Perhaps under-standably in those days, Lord Trevelyan was hard on 'the twilight brigade':

> They were pathetic. Who knows what private disturbances or maladjustments had caused them to tear up their roots and plunge into the Chinese communist world where they could never assimilate themselves to Chinese life and would always be suspect as renegades. There would be the initial excitement, the welcome, the flattery accorded the recruit from the other side. Then would come the inevitable change to neglect and indifference. They could hardly expect a welcome if they returned home. One [Winnington?] at least might have to face prosecution.[24]

There is no doubt some truth to what Trevelyan said but the foreigners who stayed on in China after the revolution are more complex. As the Canadian John Fraser observed in 1980 after he got to know several of them quite well: 'Instead of intolerant hacks, I found a small world of intensely committed people about whom few generalities could be made.'[25] Sidney Rittenberg who first arrived with the US Army worked for NCNA* in the late 1940s but ended up in prison because of his association with Anna Louise Strong. When it was decided that neither was in the pay of the CIA, he joined Radio Peking and may have broadcast Burchett's despatches.[26] Strong, the most vilified by anti-communists in the West, was settled into Count Galeazzo Ciano's former quarters which happened to be next to the Chinese People's Association for Friendship with Foreign Countries. Rewi Alley lived downstairs until Strong died and then took the top position.[27]

The list of 'the old retainers', to use Marcuse's term[28] is fairly long. Sidney Shapiro helped launch *Chinese Literature* in the Bureau for Cultural Relations with Foreign Countries but moved to the Foreign Language Press in 1953. His book about his experiences recently sold well in an American edition.[29] Gladys Yang, an English woman with a Chinese husband, is well known for her superb translations. Gerald Tannebaum worked for the China Welfare Institute and *China Reconstructs* but found time to play the 'foreign devil' in films. I am not certain of the fate of Talitha Gerlach, once of the YWCA, or Shirley Barton who assisted Alley until 1952. Dr Hans Van Müller discovered that he was legally dead when he went home to Germany in 1980. Israel Epstein reported the civil war for the *New York Times* but returned permanently to the PRC in the second half of 1952 to write for *People's China*. His wife (née Fairfax-Cholmeley) may have kept her British passport.[30] Joan Hinton got into trouble with Joseph McCarthy for things she wrote. But the most famous case (Burchett makes a passing reference to it in *Passport*) was that of John W. Powell and his wife Sylvia, who kept their *China Monthly Review* (originally a famous weekly) going in Shanghai throughout the 1949 revolution. After the couple and an assistant, Julian Schuman, got home four years later they were charged with 'un-American' activities and indicted for sedition. One of the sins was writing enemy propaganda; another was publishing Winnington and Burchett. The matter was eventually dropped.[31]

It is something of a pity that Burchett told close to nothing about the world he inhabited. When K.M. Panikkar, the Indian ambassador, met him he was with Alley and the Lebanese-American doctor, George Hatem.[32] Shapiro remembered that those two had been regulars at 'a bar and grill called "the dump" which still had beer on tap, steak and french fries'. The foreign community was so small, 'a handful of left-wing journalists and people working in government organizations or teaching school', that 'everyone knew everyone else'. He also remembered hearing all about the Panmunjom peace talks from a 'foreign

* New China News Agency

correspondent' who sounds very much like the Australian.[33]

I assume that Burchett worked out of the NCNA since the Press Club was not finished until late 1954.[34] Although he did not want his father to 'spread this news outside our own circle', he was being 'treated on the same basis as a local writer' and did 'not have to worry about finances'. 'I am experiencing for the first time in my life the practical application of "from each according to his abilities; to each according to his needs". What I need for example, comes to me, from food to writing paper and typewriter ribbons. I sign for it and it's a book entry somewhere. That's how all artists and writers operate here and I am treated as an honoured foreign guest writer.'[35]

When Burchett arrived in China native speakers of English were in short supply. Jack Chen, a Jamaican-Chinese who returned from London in 1950 to work at *People's China* had to fill jobs ranging from artist to copy editor as well as writer. Everyone, he remembered, was in 'a state of elation'. 'I was asked what salary I wanted and I named a modest figure based on a rough calculation of my expenses, rent, food, clothing, transport, laundry. It was fairly high compared to most salaries of Chinese cadres (official and office personnel), but less than half that paid to foreign advisers.'[36] Although Burchett may not have received a salary, if his expenses were covered he was certainly being paid in kind. Since Jack Chen and Gerald Tannebaum now live in the United States and both Shapiro and Rittenberg have visited the land that invented McCarthyism, the point is not very important. Panikkar and Sartre also contributed articles to *People's China* in those early years and I have no way of knowing whether they asked for a fee.

Alan Winnington is the dark figure in Burchett's China. Co-author of two works on Korea, a member of the British Communist Party, he was the conspicuous companion of Burchett at Kaesong where he was widely regarded as an official spokesman for the Chinese side. Burchett's own activities will never be fully understood until light is cast on their relationship. *Plain Perfidy* and *Koje Unscreened* were advertised in *People's China*. Nothing was being 'privately' published in Peking. Journalist Richard Hughes described Winnington as a 'dignified, lonely figure who would sometimes talk with pathetic casualness' about 'going back home sometime'.[37] George Gale found him living alone in the Peace Hotel in 1954.[38] Burchett added only that the two had been dubbed 'Caucasian Communists'.[39]

Esther Cheo Ying, in her book *Black Country Girl in Red China*, says not only that she worked at NCNA but married Winnington after becoming pregnant with his child. She described him as a 'flirt' who 'skimmed round the edges of the foreign community. His position as a journalist working for a left-wing paper gave him the independence which they did not have.' No real names are given to others. 'Stanley' plays the part of the 'communist from Australia' with a 'Bulgarian wife' who claimed to have known Chinese leaders in his youth. The book could be a clever hoax but it is accurate in many details. We know that Winnington, like Anna Louise Strong, was addicted to detective novels.

Sam Russell of the *Daily Worker* had problems with Customs when he tried to import Alan's paperback 'entertainment'. The author was certainly correct when she noted: 'Foreigners were kept under control by being rewarded with special favours if they had done something well and ignored if they had not.'[40]

The question of Burchett's own independence is a testy one. There is no reason to believe that he made anything up but as an enthusiast, like Alley, he had no qualms about leaving the negative out. When George Gale was in China he had long arguments about the freedom of the press with reporters who were probably alongside Burchett in Korea. 'Can you conceive of the possibility of your having to criticize the government?' 'Surely you can imagine it. You are a journalist. You must have some imagination?' Invariably the Chinese said: 'My job is to deal with facts. I report what happens.'[41] Jacques Marcuse, who had similar debates with Israel Epstein, was convinced that his friend would never tell a conscious lie. Nevertheless he knew that Epstein had 'accepted a certain discipline and become converted to a certain faith'.[42] Fraser felt the same about Rittenberg who never quite managed to tell two people the same story.[43]

No one who ever studied history would deny that there are always, at the very least, two 'sides'; 'truth', if it is to be uncovered, comes from comparison. The line between fact and propaganda, truth and exaggeration, is a thin one. Raja Hutheesing, an Indian visitor to the 'Germ Warfare' display in 1952, was willing to accept that the United States had experimented but felt that continuous Chinese exaggeration destroyed the case. He was most sceptical when Gong Peng produced evidence from 'the correspondent of the *Daily Worker*'.[44] But the *New York Times* found Burchett's report of his interview with General Dean which made the front page 'in the main . . . convincing as well as fascinating'.[45]

With customary ego, Burchett told his father how, when American reporters begged for handouts: 'We were in the lovely position of ignoring all those who had tried to injure us and handed priceless information to the few who had written honestly about the talks.' Later he wrote that his Korean book was 'too long and perhaps wearying in part, but I did have the feeling that I was writing history and that the full details should be there'.[46] A strange confession for a propagandist!

China's Feet Unbound, which he rushed to his Melbourne publisher[47] after less than six months in the country, truthfully conveyed the enthusiasm with which many people greeted the new regime and caught the spirit of change. But it was written mostly from an historical perspective, hardly analytical and not at all critical. The book revealed more about its author than what was actually going on behind the 'bamboo curtain'. China-watchers in Hong Kong painted a better picture.[48]

There is some question as to how much he personally witnessed. Most of what he wrote was obviously adapted from secondary sources. This was a time of great paranoia when the movements of foreigners were restricted. Russians were gathered together in a compound on the outskirts of town and even Chinese needed a pass to leave Peking.[49] He informed his father in mid April that he was already 'half way through the book'. He worked from 5.30 to noon, went out for interviews, then returned to his desk from 5.30 to dusk. Although he claimed 'to see what I want to see, travel where I want to travel, interview who I want to interview',[50] he could not have got far from the capital. Burchett did cross part of the countryside by train but barely recorded the journey. I believe that he visited the Huai River flood control project. In any case he saw enough of China to conclude that the Chinese were conquering nature: physical and human. 'You know,' he wrote to his father, 'I have lived in many lands and my emotions have been correspondingly toughened but I never experienced anything as moving as here where a new life designed to eliminate every tiniest injustice is being built.'[51] Burchett was right in thinking that the Huai River scheme was important; he might not have known that much of it was being constructed with forced labour.[52]

Supplementary chapters completed some time later and added to a second edition are more interesting. By then he had seen self-criticism sessions at a local re-education centre. Although idealized, the process of thought reform is described. Thirty pages on 'spies, saboteurs and bandits' provide an idea of the extent of the counter-revolutionary terror and document the growing siege mentality. Allegations of KMT or CIA intrigue could be true but Burchett always took too much on faith. A claim that there was no corruption was disproven by mass campaigns against it which had begun by the time the words were printed. The argument that China's economy was 'in a healthier state than that in England, America and other countries of the capitalist world' was stupid. And the proposition that missionaries were agents of imperialism was more a personal catharsis than communist propaganda. The official line on Christians was more careful when China needed friends abroad. British cleric Hewlett Johnson was an honoured guest in 1952 at a time when former missionary James G. Endicott contributed a number of articles to *People's China*.[53] Burchett promised a second book to explain the 'how' of the revolution but, preoccupied with Korea, never delivered.

In one regard he wrote unvarnished truth: if her security could be guaranteed, China wanted peace and trade with the West.[54] Raja Hutheesing recalled that the Panmunjom negotiations were reported in the press 'with increased bitterness'. He never doubted that 'China's anxiety to end the war in Korea' was 'genuine'.[55] Although Burchett sometimes let his own enthusiasm get the better of him such as when he told his father that 'our chaps' were besting 'the enemy', the result forced the Americans back to the talks.[56] It was his style to film in black and white. 'I really believe,' he also wrote home, 'that despite all their efforts, they are going to miss out on their Third World War and the Korean and Chinese people can take credit for having stopped them.'[57] More neutral observers in Peking confirmed that the wall posters read:

'Fight a small war to avoid a big one',[58] words heard, alas, on American troopships. That was the tragedy of Korea.

Pannikar remembered how 'Burchett was a cocksure advocate of peace, who gave the impression that he felt convinced that he was saving the world by shouting the slogans of the peace congress.'[59] Peter Lum, a British diplomat, had a term for the other foreigners who flocked to the Asian-Pacific Peace Conference in November 1952: 'The Peace Duck'. He discovered that most of those he talked to were 'kindly people, deeply devoted to the cause of peace and the common man, conscious of the great sufferings of China' but they had come to a point of commitment, often before they reached Peking: 'If they accept certain premises, if they believe certain things they have been told are beyond doubt true, and that they are dealing with men of goodwill and sincerity, then the rest follows.'[60] This perfectly described Burchett but I could easily write the same about those outside, who saw only evil in the Chinese revolution.

Whether Burchett became a communist does not particularly concern me. He admitted that he had intended to join the party when he returned to Australia;[61] that will be enough for his enemies. Those who believe that he courageously reported the truth about the Cold War and America's expanding global influence seldom worry about the things he left out. With his knack for being at the right place at the right time, he might have won a journalistic prize. He need not have been neutral for that is too much to ask of both time and place. Members of the United States Department of State lost their desks long before Burchett was deprived of his passport for telling, in dispassionate detail, why the communists would come to power.

Journalists must be judged by what they write. Burchett's scoop was stillborn. Others living in China in the early 1950s left the lasting legacy: the diplomats, Trevelyan, Lum, Rooning and Pannikar; missionaries like the Lapwoods or Endicotts; and the growing stream of visitors.[62]

China: The Quality of Life, which he wrote with Rewi Alley, found a popular market twenty years later. But when the 'Gang of Four' fell and the wind from the West picked up strength, the work became an embarrassment. Talk of 'learning from Tachai', the famous commune, and one last effort to make the 'Great Leap Forward' a success would bring a laugh, even in the People's Republic. Only the biographical sketch of Alley is worth reading. Toward the end of his life, when confused by the schisms that so often destroy religious movements, Burchett described himself as an 'independent, non-aligned radical'.[63] Among other things this meant that he had turned his back on China.

Our world does not revolve because idealists turn crank nor can the winds of change be so easily predicted. The Italian communist, Maria Antonietta Macciocchi, who first visited China in October 1954 and returned during the Cultural Revolution, has written: 'None of us, arriving in China, are able to write *for the Chinese* – this is a common flaw which underlies "leftist gibberish"; we can write only for *us*, for ill-informed people living in a distant Western world.' 'Emotion,' as she

concluded, 'does not mean hagiography.'[64] Jacques Marcuse attacked
Han Suyin and Felix Greene for their one-sided reporting.[65] Yet today
when Rewi Alley holds an honorary doctorate from a New Zealand
university for what he did for Mao, and the Americans who sided with
the Chinese revolution have been forgiven, it seems silly to debate
Burchett's life and times in China. What he said of other lands is beyond
my brief but perhaps left and right might agree with Rosa Luxemburg,
another 'true believer': 'Freedom is only and always the right to think
differently.'

Wilfred Burchett need not be remembered, not even in infamy, for
what he wrote about China.

Notes

1. *At the Barricades*, Macmillan, Melbourne, 1981, p.153.
2. Letter from Peking, 16 April 1951, Burchett Papers, State Library of Victoria.
3. See *Barricades*, pp.62-84; *Passport: An Autobiography*, Nelson, Melbourne, 1969,
   pp.153–61; *Bombs Over Burma*, Melbourne, 1944, pp.23–35; and *Democracy with a
   Tommygun*, Melbourne, 1946. (Hereafter referred to as *Barricades; Passport;
   Bombs;* and *Tommygun.*)
4. *Barricades*, p.66.
5. *Tommygun*, p.54. The 'my first weeks' reference is from *Barricades*, p.326. *Bombs*,
   p.23, concedes: 'most members of the Press Hostel attended the conference'. Readers
   may want to compare the various accounts themselves to see if I have been fair. But
   here are two examples from *Tommygun*: p.46, 'One of the attracting reasons for my
   return to China had been a half promise from Assistant Information Minister, Dr
   Hollington K. Tong ("Holly" to the Press Corps), that he would arrange an interview
   with the Generalissimo'; and p.113, 'an excited Holly raced down to our rooms . . .
   waving an impressively be-sealed piece of parchment . . . our invitation to see the
   Generalissimo . . .'
6. J.K. Fairbank, *China Bound: A Fifty Year Memoir*, New York, 1982, 273–6; H.F.
   Snow, *My China Years*, New York, 1984, p.120.
7. *Tommygun*, pp.47–8,106. I am of the opinion that Willkie had a better grasp of the
   situation. Compare Burchett with W.L. Willkie, *One World*, New York, 1943,
   pp.117–48 which covers the period the two may have been together.
8. *Tommygun*, pp.80,88. Yang Gang was said to have overheard a merchant say: ' "That
   Chiang Ching Kuo. He ought to be shot for a Red, and he would be if he were not the
   Generalissimo's son." That last part of his observation, strangely enough, was true.'
   (p.85.)
9. Copy of Burchett cable enclosed with letter to Department of External Affairs,
   Canberra, from the Australian legation, Chungking, 19 October 1942.
10. *Tommygun*, p.68. In *Passport*, p.185, Burchett wrote that when he returned to China
    in 1951 he rediscovered 'The Chinese characteristics of hard work, self-sacrifice,
    dignity and pride in good work . . . but on an incomparably higher level'.
11. *A Learner in China: A Life of Rewi Alley*, Willis Airey, Christchurch, 1970, pp.
    260–3. On 1 June 1952 Alley wrote in the Wellington newspaper, *Dominion*: 'I have
    never "lent" myself to anything except the cause of the common man. . .' p.240. It is
    not certain when Burchett first met Alley but the opportunity could have come during
    the Willkie tour. Alley is one of the best known of the foreigners who 'stayed on' in
    the People's Republic. For more information, see: E. Grey Diamond, *Inside China
    Today: A Western View*, New York, 1983.
12. John Fraser, *The Chinese: Portrait of a People*, Glasgow, 1982, pp. 186–7. Burchett's
    version is in *Barricades*, pp.153–5.
13. J.W. Klein and A.B. Clark, *Biographical Dictionary of Chinese Communism
    1921–1965*, Cambridge, Mass., 1971, pp.99–101.

14. 16 March 1951, p.10.
15. Fairbank, op.cit., pp.267–73. As Felix Greene, *The Wall Has Two Sides: A Portrait of China Today*, London, 1962, p.33, commented: 'Madame Kung has become something of a legend among foreign writers who have visited China. I first heard of her from James Cameron of the *News Chronicle*. Sooner or later her name crops up in any conversation among journalists dealing with China.'
16. *Barricades*, pp.66–7. Fairbank, op.cit., p.273, noted that even Joseph Alsop who would later lead the China Lobby was 'outrageously' enthusiastic about her. She did take risks during the civil war. However, Jacques Marcuse remembered the way 'correspondents from the corrupt, rotten, imperialist press in Shanghai went to the greatest trouble to provide Madame Kung Peng with Hong Kong bought stencils and other stationery, duty free, to help her put out her propaganda handouts'. *The Peking Papers*, New York, 1967, p.81.
17. Snow, op.cit., p.158.
18. *Biographical Dictionary*, 179–82. Fairbank also described the couple as did Han Suyin who was a very close friend.
19. Ibid., pp.181–2.
20. *Barricades*, p.185. For more on Zhou's entourage, see Arthur Lall, *How Communist China Negotiates*, New York, 1968 or Kenneth Young, *Negotiating with the Chinese Communists*, New York, 1968.
21. Letter, 23 April 1955, Burchett Papers. J. Cameron, *Mandarin Red*, New York, 1955, pp.34, 324.
22. Humphrey Trevelyan, *Worlds Apart: China 1953–5, Soviet Union, 1962–5*, London, 1971, p.30. For other comments on the foreign community, see pp. 51–66.
23. *The Times*, London, 20 March 1954.
24. Trevelyan, op.cit., p.30. See note 22, above.
25. Fraser, op.cit., p.181. See 'The Foreign Experts', pp.176–95.
26. Ibid.
27. Diamond, op.cit., pp.42–7. For another view of Strong, see: David Caute, *The Fellow-Travellers: A Postscript to the Enlightenment*, London, 1973, p.379.
28. *Peking Papers*, chapter 18, pp. 115–26.
29. Sidney Shapiro, *An American in China: Thirty Years in the People's Republic*, New York, 1979. The original edition was published in Peking, 1979. Shapiro noted that when the new office building of the Foreign Language Press was opened in 1954, it was reserved for 'foreigners and invalids'.
30. For some of the others, see Diamond; Fraser; Marcuse; *passim*. The story of Epstein is also covered in Stuart and Roma Gelder, *Memories for a Chinese Grand-daughter*, London, 1967.
31. The case can be followed in the *New York Times* but is summarized by Stanley I. Kutler, *The American Inquisition: Justice and Injustice in the Cold War*, New York, 1982, pp.215–42.
32. K.M. Panikkar, *In Two Chinas: Memoirs of a Diplomat*, London, 1955, p.132. Hatem, who was with the communists in Yenan, is described in many works. He married a movie star. See Diamond, op.cit., for one of the most recent accounts.
33. Shapiro, op.cit., pp.44, 65–7.
34. Cameron, op.cit., p.34. In *Barricades*, p. 155, he tells of settling into a modest hotel, then ringing *Xinhua*. Tass had separate facilities.
35. Letter from Peking, 16 April 1951, Burchett Papers.
36. Jack Chen, *Inside the Cultural Revolution*, London, 1975, pp.53–54.
37. Norman MacSwan, *The Man Who Read the East Wind: A Biography of Richard Hughes*, Kenthurst, 1982, p.127.
38. George Gale, *No Flies in China*, New York, 1955, p.69.
39. *Barricades*, p.155. From photographs in *People's China*, the two looked something alike.
40. Esther Cheo Ying, *Black Country Girl in Red China*, London, 1980. The Russell story is from Gale, op.cit., p.67.
41. Ibid., pp.137–8.
42. Ibid., pp.117–18. As Marcuse continued: 'I cannot follow the Epsteins in their

philosophy – but I can also not disapprove of them. They are immensely genuine'.
43. Ibid., p.185.
44. Raja Hutheesing, *The Great Peace: An Asian's Candid Report on Red China*, New York, 1953, pp.212–25. Frank Moraes, who was in China from April to June 1952 with an official Indian government cultural delegation, was similarly sceptical. See *Report on Mao's China*, New York, 1953; He was particularly sensitive to questions of press freedom and concluded: 'Even the style of writing is stereotyped', p.154. At the time of the 'Great Leap Forward', even the noted apologist for the regime Han Suyin reportedly told Gong Peng that China's propaganda was 'appallingly childish and has no influence or impact', *My House Has Two Doors*, pp.126–7.
45. New York Times, 24 December 1951, which identified him as 'Communist correspondent for a Paris newspaper'.
46. Letters to father, 18 December 1951 and 24 December 1952, Burchett Papers.
47. World Unity Publications, 1952, apparently his father.
48. See, for example, A. Doak Barnett, *Communist China: the Early Years, 1949–55*, New York, 1956. Even the malevolent Richard L. Walker, *China Under Communism: The First Five Years*, New Haven, 1955, was able to use NCNA despatches and refugee reports to provide a more accurate picture.
49. Peter Lum, *Peking 1950–1953*, London, 1958, pp.50–74. Shapiro claims not to have been persecuted but he may have stayed put. Ralph and Nancy Lapwood, missionary-educators, were denied permission to visit the Huai River project although their friend Rewi Alley had made the trip. See Ralph and Nancy Lapwood, *Through the Chinese Revolution*, London, 1954, p.146. Esther Ying goes so far as to suggest that 'foreign friends' had armed escorts, pp.106–7.
50. Letter, 16 April 1951, Burchett Papers.
51. Ibid.
52. See Barnett, op.cit., pp.274–75 or Walker, op.cit., pp.11–12, on 'reform through labour': 'The most important of the latter was the vaunted Huai River flood control project, which has been the subject of praise in all the accounts of fellow travellers who have visited China.' Moraes, op.cit., pp.91–100, and Hutheesing, op.cit., pp.101–14, were not particularly impressed one way or the other. After the Lapwoods had left China, they explained with some fairness, I think, that the work on the Huai needed to be described as 'hard labour' rather than 'slave labour': 'This is not to say that there were no coerced workers. In many cases persons convicted of crimes and sentenced to "reform by labour" were employed on such projects.' For an objective discussion of the system based in part on the accounts of visitors, see Jerome Allan Cohen, *The Criminal Process in the People's Republic of China, 1949–1963: An Introduction*, Cambridge, Mass., 1968.
53. The book he wrote with his wife and published privately in Canada, while extremely favourable to the People's Republic, is non-polemical and far superior to *China's Feet Unbound*. The pair visited the Huai River project and have the obligatory chapters on workers, industries, etc. but also describe smaller points of human interest. They also visted Shanghai and have left one of the few descriptions of the foreign community in that city including the Powells. I recommend: Mary Austin Endicott, *Five Stars Over China*, Toronto, 1953.
54. *China's Feet Unbound*, p.292. Burchett was fairly consistent. Much of what was condemned as propaganda in 1951, from my quick reading of *The Times* and the *New York Times*, could be called peace feelers. For example, after the alleged straffing incident in September, the Australian was quoted as saying 'as far as this side is concerned, armistice talks can be resumed immediately', *NYT*, 21 September 1951.
55. Hutheesing, op.cit., p.70. Lum, op.cit., p.25, noted in his diary after witnessing anti-American demonstrations in Peking in December 1950: 'One of the things that strikes you most strongly is that this Chinese fear of America seems in large measure genuine.'
56. Letter, 26 October 1951, Burchett Papers.
57. Letter, 19 November 1952, Burchett Papers.
58. Lapwood, op.cit., p.157.
59. Pannikar, op.cit., p.132.

60. Lum, op.cit., pp.147–8.
61. *Barricades*, p.326.
62. I have not compiled a bibliography but readers should sift the notes above. The French communist Claude Roy, who was in Peking in May 1952, wrote of his experiences in early 1953. It was translated as *Into China*, London, 1955. See also Basil Davidson, *Day Break in China*, London, 1953. There are dozens of visitors after the Geneva Conference.
63. *Barricades*, p.327. *China: The Quality of Life* was published by Penguin in 1976.
64. *Daily Life in Revolutionary China*, Maria Antonietta Macciocchi, New York, 1972, pp.23–4.
65. Marcuse called them 'VIPs' – 'Vested Interest Persons' who dared not criticize China since their careers required access. Even in the 1980s journalists who hope to have their visas renewed are careful about what they say.

8

Korea: Wilfred Burchett's Thirty Years' War

Gavan McCormack

Wilfred Burchett's activities in the Korean War in the early 1950s are among the most controversial in his career. At the height of the Cold War he not only rejected anti-communism – that much was clear from his European writing in the late 1940s – but he was one of a handful in the West who also supported the struggle of the communist side in one of the great conflagrations of the age. He would have no truck with the idea that by his Australian nationality he was deprived of the right to challenge the official view of the war propounded by his country's government. Had the government spoken the truth at the time and conceded that its purpose in Korea was to curry favour with the United States – or 'primarily in the interests of Australian–American diplomacy' as the official historian of the war puts it[1] – dissent might have been much stronger. But Burchett's position in the 1950s was lonely and exposed. The price he paid for writing the Korean story as he saw it was prolonged and enforced exile from his country and intense vilification which persisted for the rest of his life. What actually did Burchett do in Korea? What is he alleged to have done, and with what justification?

Full-scale war began in Korea on 25 June 1950 and escalated almost immediately from a civil war between the rival regimes of north and south (Kim Il Sung's communist forces in the Democratic People's Republic of Korea or DPRK, and Syngman Rhee's US-supported Republic of Korea or ROK) into an international anti-communist crusade led by the United States under the banner of the United Nations. By far the majority of foreign troops committed were American, but France, Britain, Canada, Australia, Turkey, the Philippines and other countries, sixteen in all, sent contingents in response to UN resolutions.

For the first twelve months the war raged across the peninsula as fortunes shifted drastically from one side to the other and the front line fluctuated from the deep south-eastern UN perimeter of August 1950 to the Yalu River in October and back again after the commitment of the Chinese People's Volunteers in support of North Korea. By mid-1951 the battle line appeared to have more or less stabilized in a position very close to where it had been when the war began. Attempts by both sides to annihilate the other and impose a unified Korean regime had failed. The prospect of a ceasefire became attractive enough to draw both sides into negotiations, while the underlying political difficulties of the country's division were set aside.

Ceasefire negotiations began at Kaesong on 10 July 1951. Burchett, who had been in China preparing a book on the nature of immediate post-revolutionary society there and contributing to the French left-wing evening newspaper, *Ce Soir*, decided to cover the talks. He was given press accreditation to the Chinese delegation to the talks and headed for the neutral zone at Kaesong, expecting to be away for a few weeks. Kaesong, and later Panmunjom, was, however, to become his home through protracted and bitter negotiations that kept him in Korea for nearly two and a half years.

During that two and a half years conditions were often hard. Especially during the first year of the peace talks Burchett says that he lost 'a very great deal of weight'.[2] Communications with the outside world, via China, were poor and even the so-called 'neutral zone' in which he lived was liable to be bombed or strafed by US planes. The rest of the country, through which of course he had to travel from time to time, was pulverized.

He wrote a great deal, and his writings were not only published in French in *Ce Soir* or in the illustrated magazine *Regards* or (during the last few months of the war and after the close of *Ce Soir*) in *L'Humanité* (the French communist paper), but in English from time to time in the London *Daily Worker*, a communist daily paper, or broadcast over Chinese radio by the New China News Agency from Peking or released as part of Hsinhua (the Chinese news service) despatches.[3]

Burchett himself wrote about this in 1970 as follows: 'I was lodged and fed free of charge just as I was bombed and strafed free of charge; my journalistic services for two and a half years were also free of charge. I wrote this off at the time as my contribution to the world peace cause.'[4]

He had some income from books he had written, and although his standing in Fleet Street still seemed to be good he preferred the independence that went with freelancing: 'There is no one in the wide world that can tell me where to go and what to write, no editor or publisher, no political organization, no government.'[5]

Curiously, Burchett's insistence on independence, when combined with an apparent lack of concern as to how or by whom his writing was circulated, led to him being regarded as the mouthpiece of communist governments when often he seems not even to have known that his writing was being reproduced by them.[6]

Enormous effort has been devoted over the years to the task of proving that Wilfred Burchett was either a Soviet or North Korean agent but, as will be argued in what follows, there is nothing in the record of what he did, in Korea at least, to lend support to such a view or to cause one to doubt that what he wrote above was true. In 1974, when the anti-Burchett forces mobilized witnesses from all over the world to testify against him, the presiding Sydney judge, after listening to all they had to say, finally told them they had no case on the facts, advising them instead to take a stand on a technical point of law. This important case is discussed below.

Burchett's primary commitment was undoubtedly to the peace talks. He did not cover battles or the fighting fronts, and he therefore insisted that he was not a war correspondent but a 'peace correspondent'.[7] He did, however, write a good deal about some issues which were hotly contested at the peace talks – especially the treatment of prisoners of war (POWs). He also wrote on the question of germ warfare, and he wrote general accounts of the war and of Korean politics both pre- and post-war. So, while not attempting here to essay a comprehensive account of the origins and roots of the Korean War,[8] attention will be focused on the major areas he wrote about.

His Korean writings are contained in three books written at the time, *This Monstrous War* (Melbourne, 1952), *Koje Unscreened* (Peking, 1953, with Alan Winnington), *Plain Perfidy* (Peking, 1954, with Alan Winnington),[9] and in various subsequent or autobiographical writings, notably *Again Korea* (New York, 1968), 'The Struggle for Korea's National Rights', *Journal of Contemporary Asia*, 5, 2, 1975, and in *Passport* (Sydney, 1969) and *At the Barricades* (Melbourne, 1981). The first three books in particular are rare items. *This Monstrous War* was published independently in Melbourne by Mr Joe Waters in 1952. It is rare enough in Australia, but in the United States the entire consignment of the book (500 copies) was seized by US Customs and dumped in the sea on its arrival in that country late in the same year,[10] and as a result no major American library possesses a copy to this day. The other two were both privately published in Peking by the authors and, although later reissued in a separate edition by the Britain–China Friendship Association in London, were never widely circulated or commented upon in the West. Both academic and political writing in particular has tended to ignore them completely.

One of the richest sources of information about Wilfred Burchett is the archives of the Australian government. Substantial files on him were built up in at least six federal departments – Prime Minister, Attorney General, Defence, Immigration, External Affairs and Australian Security and Intelligence Organization (ASIO) – and the release during 1984–85 of much of this material has made it possible to draw a more definitive picture than ever before of what Wilfred Burchett did in Korea just over thirty years ago.

Peace Talks

When Burchett arrived at the talks site in Korea, late in July 1951, there were several major issues: determination of the demarcation line, exchange of prisoners, the disposition of the huge armies, including both UN and Chinese forces, and establishment of some post-war security arrangements. The 'UN' negotiating team, then and throughout the negotiations, was exclusively American.

The conventional Western view of the prolonged Korean negotiations is derived from the published accounts of the top US negotiators.

Burchett's reports precisely reverse the common stereotype. On a number of basic issues through the negotiations it is now clear that his reporting was more accurate and truthful than the self-serving and widely accepted accounts emanating from the UN Command. Deviousness and lying were an important part of the UN negotiating arsenal. We know now from the official American records that actually the UN negotiators were under instructions to be 'terse, blunt, forceful, and rude' and to employ 'such language and methods as these treacherous communists cannot fail to understand',[11] and Burchett demonstrated that they performed this commission faithfully. Furthermore the American negotiators, in the words of the recent study of the official US archives by Barton Bernstein, 'lacked diplomatic experience and mistrusted both diplomacy and compromise, did not want to bargain. They wanted to present a position as an immutable principle and then wait for communist compliance.'[12] Mass bombing raids, they believed, especially if carried out without publicity, were the best means to secure that compliance.[13]

General Matthew Ridgway, Commander-in-chief of the UN forces from April 1951 to May 1952, spoke of the negotiations as 'tedious, exasperating, dreary, repetitious and frustrating'.[14] Vice-Admiral C. Turner Joy, who headed the negotiating team for the UN side from July 1951 to May 1952, described the communist side as marked by 'vituperation, rage and insult . . . suspicion, greed, deviousness',[15] while General Mark Clark, who succeeded General Ridgway to the UN Command in May 1952, saw the enemy as a 'voracious beast' from whom the UN negotiators had to endure 'a daily fare of insult, arrogance, and vituperation'.[16] President Truman in similar vein described the negotiations as 'like an honest man trying to deal with the head of a dope ring'.[17] By contrast, in the common Western view, negotiators on the UN side were marked by what Admiral Joy described as 'our restraint, our constructive suggestions, our willingness to conciliate and compromise, and our patience'.[18] The record of the talks does not support these US claims.

Negotiation over the fixing of the Demilitarized Line was the occasion, according to Burchett, for 'one of the great hoaxes of history'.[19] The clear pre-talks position of US and UN spokesmen was that a reinstatement of the pre-war line, the Thirty-Eighth parallel, was the objective. That objective was also clear in the Soviet proposal for talks by Jacob Malik, Deputy Soviet Foreign Minister, on 23 July, in the Chinese endorsement of 25 July, and in the statement by Dean Acheson, Secretary of State, to a Congressional Committee on 26 July.[20] When discussions at Kaesong turned to this issue, however, the US negotiators shifted, in the words of Evan Luard's *A History of the United Nations*, to arguing 'that the line should be north of the parallel to create a defensible position'.[21] In the early weeks of negotiations, while the UN side was castigating the communists for refusal to discuss a Demilitarized Line along the Thirty-Eighth parallel, in fact the opposite was true; the *Americans* were refusing to discuss such a possibility.[22] For the next four months the 'UN' insistence that the other side should open the negotiations by ordering its armies to yield up a substantial slice of territory by withdrawing an average of over thirty-two miles in depth along the whole 150 miles of the battlefront[23] constituted a major stumbling block.[24] It was the role of Burchett and another 'renegade' Western newsman, Alan Winnington of the British *Daily Worker*, to expose the lies being fed to the Western press by the US military.[25] The first major deception of the negotiations was Western, not communist, and Burchett played a major role in exposing it. Later, US Secretary of State Dean Acheson agreed that the other side might have seen this as 'trickery' by the US.[26]

From the night of 22 August 1951 negotiations were suddenly suspended. According to Burchett's eyewitness account the Chinese and North Korean delegation headquarters in Kaesong were bombed and napalmed, and the residence of the Korean delegation chief, General Nam Il, only narrowly missed obliteration. Burchett saw it as 'a deliberate attempt to murder the Korean–Chinese delegates',[27] and to provoke a suspension of the talks. However improbable this may seem it is clear, as the *New York Times* noted on 12 August, that the communist side did *not* want a break in the talks and had three times made concessions to prevent any such break. In the angry altercations which followed the raid the US denied all knowledge of it and refused to make any investigation. When the Chinese–Korean side announced their decision to boycott the next day's session of the talks in protest this was presented as a unilateral, indefinite abrogation of the talks. As tension mounted, raids continued, which Burchett witnessed and reported. It was at this juncture that probably the first published criticisms of Burchett's role in Korea appeared in Australia. In the *News Weekly*, a right-wing Catholic paper in Melbourne, for 12 September 1951, he is attacked for supporting 'the phoney communist story' about a UN plane bombing the Kaesong talks area. Ironically, the first UN admission of such raids had been issued on 10 September, two days earlier.[28]

From 19 August, a major new UN offensive was secretly launched, which was publicly revealed on 4 September.[29] The Chinese–Korean side counter-attacked to try to recover the lost territory, and talks were not resumed till 25 October, this time at a new location, Panmunjom.

When the communist side accepted the new military line that General Van Fleet's autumn offensive had won as the basis for reopened negotiations the *New York Times* noted that, again, the communist side seemed to have accepted much of the UN side's demands.[30] According to Burchett's account, the UN–US side again sought to better its battlefield position by immediately demanding further negotiating-table concessions from the enemy, specifically its abandonment of the ancient city of Kaesong. Only when Burchett divulged the details of the true negotiating position of the two parties, showing the map in the UN press tent to be a fake, did the US negotiators reluctantly shift ground to accept the existing battlelines as the basis for negotiations.[31]

It is difficult to see in the record of these months any evidence of bad faith or 'lies and distortions' on the communist side. Burchett's reports, written from a position of personal danger as he himself experienced regular strafing and bombing, remain quite credible and even today essential to understanding the peace negotiations.

On 27 November 1951, agreement was reached on the line which was to separate the opposing forces, and on a two-mile demilitarized strip on either side of it. Tension eased along the front. On 1 December the US Eighth Army was actually reported to have issued an order that its soldiers should not engage the enemy except in defence and unless first fired on.[32] Yet the fighting was not to be stopped for another year and a half, and the Americans continued to insist that fighting must continue till all the issues were settled. The US air war in particular was intensified late in 1951 with the launching of 'Operation Strangler' to try to halt all movement of the enemy's men and supplies towards the front lines.

The US was determined to leave no stone unturned in the effort to inflict defeat on the enemy. Its worldwide power and prestige stood to be undermined if it was seen to be unable to impose its 'solution' in Korea. At the same time the image of peace-loving reasonableness was important, and to maintain it UN correspondents were fed a carefully concocted 'mixture of lies, half-truths, and serious distortions'.[33] When correspondents like Burchett punctured the image to expose the reality behind the US negotiating posture at Panmunjom it is scarcely surprising that they made many enemies as a result.

Prisoners of War

From November 1951 the land war was effectively stalemated. While on the one hand the UN side placed great stress on the air war – gradually pulverizing North Korea – on the other hand it sought means to achieve, if not an outright military victory, at least a *moral* one.

The quest for moral victory was pursued on two fronts, both of which relied heavily on the media to achieve their effect. At the very moment in November when Western battlefield reports spoke of a spreading conviction among the UN troops that 'the communists have made important concessions, while the United Nations Command, as they view it, continues to make more and more demands',[34] US military authorities suddenly launched a campaign to accuse the other side of mass atrocities.

It was a highly emotional issue. In the early stages of the war some American prisoners were murdered. The private estimate of the number by General Ridgway's Chief of Staff was several dozen, and the public estimate given by General Ridgway was 365. This was now massively inflated by the inclusion of those who were simply *missing* or unaccounted for, and on 14 November 1951 a completely fabricated figure of 5,500 American atrocity victims was published, changed two days later to 6,270. After enormous publicity around the world, the allegation was quietly buried.[35] The allegations implied that atrocities were continuing in POW camps in North Korea, and it seems clear they were lauched to help stiffen the allied resolve to persist with the war and to undermine talk of peace. It would be difficult to find anything, among all that is alleged against Wilfred Burchett, to match the official cynicism and mendacity shown in this episode.

Burchett's involvement in the POW issue began in the context of controversy over the atrocity allegations. Early in 1952, when the Chinese–Korean side at Panmunjom produced a list of names of prisoners held by them, including those of over 3,000 Americans, the American side denounced the list as fake, alleging that most Americans had either been massacred or starved to death.[36]

At this point Burchett began to visit the camps. Whether by coincidence or partly because of representations he made on behalf of the prisoners it is generally agreed that conditions in the camps began to show significant improvement from about the same time. Terrible privations had been suffered by prisoners in North Korea during the first year of the war, especially during the winter of 1950–51 as drastic shifts of the battlefront led to sudden, long, forced marches, and as supplies, for prisoner and captor alike, were drastically curtailed. Many prisoners died as a result of ill-treatment, and some were killed. However, William White's semi-official account of the treatment of US prisoners notes that in 1952 indoctrination ceased, food and medical facilities improved and reading matter and good music began to brighten camp life.[37] There was one notable exception to this change: the US pilots. They were subject to prolonged periods of solitary confinement and intensive interrogation, though apparently not direct physical violence. They were central to the 'germ warfare' issue which broke in 1952, and their case is therefore discussed separately below.

One of the first prisoners that Burchett met was Major-General William F. Dean, Commander of the Twenty-Fourth Division, the highest ranking of all captives held in the north and one for whom the North Koreans (not the Chinese) were exclusively responsible. Dean was one of those alleged by General Ridgway's staff to be dead. He was a former military governor of South Korea and terrible atrocities had either occurred during his time in that office or at least were believed in North Korea to have occurred.[38] His captors might be expected to have singled him out for exceptionally harsh treatment. When Burchett visited him, and took a series of photographs of Dean playing chess, exercising, walking in a forest, which were then given wide coverage in the US Army newspaper, *Stars and Stripes*, the effect was sensational. Dean himself later wrote a detailed account of his acquaintance with Burchett in his book *General Dean's Story* under the bold title 'My Friend Wilfred Burchett'.[39] Two things in particular are striking in Dean's account: first, that Burchett provided him with accurate information about the state of the war and the peace negotiations and made no attempt to 'brainwash' him – 'the only bias being in the method of telling, not in the facts'[40] – and second, not only did Burchett personally impress him as a decent and honourable man, but Dean also believed that Burchett's representations to his captors were responsible for a significant improvement in the conditions of his captivity: 'He is widely known, and opinions about him vary, but this man made nearly two years of my life livable, by treating me as a human being when I was out of the habit of being so treated, and by causing my North Korean captors to reverse their whole policy toward me.'[41]

Then Burchett turned his attention to the major camps in the far north of the country, on the Yalu River, in which most POWs were held. In May 1952 he wrote of one camp: 'This camp looks like a holiday resort in Switzerland. The atmosphere of the camp is also nearer that of a luxury resort than a prisoner-of-war camp.'[42] Recording his impressions a little later, he added:

The first day I visited Camp No. 5 where American, British and all the 'minority' prisoners are held, including Turks, Puerto Ricans, French and others from a dozen nations, music was being broadcast through the loudspeakers. I passed a group of shining Negroes playing basketball, Turks wrestling in a sand-pit, British troops exercising on the horizontal bars, Americans lounging about reading, some playing volley-ball, a group of Puerto Ricans cleaning a troughful of fish which they had caught themselves earlier in the day. Further along . . . the bulk of the prisoners were stretched sunbathing on the rocks, swimming in the crystal-clear water or tending their fishing lines. From a height overlooking the camp, with a dozen teams engaged in various sports and ball games, the camp resembled nothing but a summer camp for youth.[43]

It is an altogether roseate description, and one he later regretted having written.[44] A prison camp, after all, can by its nature bear only the most superficial resemblance to a 'luxury holiday resort', no matter how beautiful the physical surroundings may be. The comparison is both superficial and offensive to those who were incarcerated. Yet Burchett's description is confirmed in substance by a man who later became one of Burchett's most bitter critics: Colonel Walker Mahurin of the US Air Force. Colonel Mahurin, at the time a prisoner held in solitary confinement near this camp, wrote in his memoirs in 1962 of seeing 'Many of the prisoners . . . standing around in groups chatting. More were playing basketball, and still more pitched baseballs back and forth. Few Chinese guards were in evidence.'[45] From this there would seem to be no reason to doubt the truth of Burchett's factual description; it is the analogy with the holiday camp, inspired partly by the location itself, which is at issue.

Still, the contrast Burchett felt between the reality and the brutality-and-massacre stories emanating from American Army sources *was* significant. He was outraged by it, and concluded that the Americans were deliberately blocking progress in the peace talks. The contrast with conditions in South Korea, where hundreds of prisoners were being killed in violent clashes over the 'screening' process, and in North Korea *outside* the camps, where he saw people reduced to 'boiling bark in their pots', also struck him forcibly.[46]

Burchett made arrangements with the Chinese camp authorities, at the request of the Associated Press (AP), to have a camera sent in to another prisoner, the Pulitzer Prize-winning photographer, Frank Noel. In this way he was indirectly responsible for a series of photographs of POW camp life which thereafter appeared in US and other Western papers.[47] At a time when the official US position was that loss of life had been heavy among prisoners in Korean and Chinese camps and that brutality and ill-treatment were continuing, these pictures, showing apparently contented POWs playing cards or chess or soccer, fishing in the river, singing, even participating in an elaborate inter-camp 'POW Olympic Games' at Pyoktong in November 1952, were powerful counter-propaganda.[48] However much the element of misinformation may have been suspected, Noel was a photographer of high reputation and his pictures were irrefutable evidence that at least a significant number of POWs were in good health and under reasonable physical conditions at that time.

The Associated Press appreciated what Burchett did, and later confirmed to Australian intelligence that Burchett had acted for them in delivering the camera and that he had never 'tried to trick' Noel or in any way influence his work. Noel subsequently expressed his appreciation for Burchett's friendliness.[49]

The impact of Burchett's challenge to official US propaganda was such that in February 1952 General Ridgway issued a formal 'ban' on contacts between 'UN' and 'communist' correspondents'.[50] The editor of *Stars and Stripes* was dismissed and returned to the United States for having used Burchett's photographs of General Dean.[51] Charlie Barnard of AP wrote on 10 February 1952, 'The army doesn't like the newsworthy information and pictures the communists give out . . . But many's the time they have given out hot news stories on what is happening in the armistice tents to allied correspondents and the stories have turned out to be correct.' Dwight Martin of *Time* agreed: 'Communist newsmen whom they see every day at Panmunjom are often a better news source than the sparse briefings by the UN's own information officers.'[52] These tributes are so much the more remarkable in the circumstances of the time since Burchett clearly was *believed* to be a communist.

Finally, it should be noted that, although the 'Interim Historical Report' of the US Army's Korea War Crimes Division (29 October 1953) referred to twenty Australians among a 'probable' total of 29,815 atrocity victims, the Australians soon discovered that the figure of twenty Australians was made up of seventeen Australians, one New Zealander, one American, and one unidentified person, all of whom were confirmed battle deaths. Interrogation of Australian POWs after their release revealed 'NO [*sic*] evidence of torture or atrocities to AUST POW'. The Australian government was reluctant to publicize the matter, however, for fear of embarrassing the US government by the suggestion that atrocity evidence or statistics were being fabricated, and the Pentagon asked that publicity be minimized. The eventual statement by Mr Casey, Minister of External Affairs, made clear that there was 'no evidence that any Australian servicemen were victims of atrocities in Korea' (*Hansard*, 27 November 1953), but was couched in such a way as to suggest that the atrocities had occurred but had been mistakenly identified as Australian, rather than the truth, that twenty battle deaths were wrongly identified as victims of atrocities.[53]

In 1985 the official Australian history of the Korean War also confirmed that '[T]he treatment generally afforded Australian prisoners of war in Korea could be considered fair, especially if local conditions are taken into account.'[54]

B) PRISONERS IN SOUTH KOREA

While the peace talks remained stalled, and pictures by Frank Noel or the *Daily Worker*'s Alan Winnington of apparently happy POWs in North Korea were receiving wide circulation, attention also began to focus on the reverse story – the treatment of Chinese and North Korean POWs in the UN camps in South Korea, all of which were directly run by the Americans. Here, there certainly was no soccer or fishing. In clashes which began to occur with increasing frequency from late 1951 hundreds of prisoners were actually *killed* by their guards. Searching for a parallel in modern history for this, Burchett turned to the treatment of prisoners in the camps of Nazi Germany. This of course stirred bitter resentment and incredulity. The charges were given little serious consideration, either then or since.

The level of violence in these camps was undoubtedly very high, but the official US position rests on the allegation that the prisoners were themselves responsible for it. The POWs were said to have taken advantage of the 'softness' of US camp administration to try to wrest control of the camps from their captors; and they were said to have deliberately provoked their guards to violent and repressive assaults in order to discredit the US and build up pressure on it for concessions at the armistice talks.[55]

The second of these allegations is purely speculative, though of course it is possible. The first, however, is very misleading. Self-regulation is a crucial part of the administration of any prison camp, including for example those camps of the UN prisoners run by the Chinese and North Koreans in North Korea, and when 150,000 prisoners were confined, as they were in one case, to a single small island off the coast of South Korea, this was so much the more necessary. What happened was that the Americans decided not to tolerate the continuance of communist-controlled sections of the camps.

The major cause of friction in the camps from the latter part of 1951 was the intensive American campaign to subvert the loyalties of their prisoners, to convert 'communists' to 'democracy' (as represented by the regimes of Syngman Rhee and Chiang Kai-shek), an endeavour which, however positively one may wish to view it, is not easy to distinguish from the 'brainwashing' of which the enemy was being accused at the same time.

The Americans, in collaboration with their British allies, had undertaken a similar programme only four years earlier in Greece. Concentration camps were set up there during the struggle to defeat the Greek communist forces in the late 1940s. The head of AMAG (American Mission for Aid to Greece) approved of 're-education' in the case of those 'found to have affiliations which cast grave doubt upon their loyalty to the state', and the US attaché, Karl Rankin, defended *execution* of prisoners on the grounds that even in the case of those who were non-communist at the time of their arrest, it was 'unlikely that they would have been able to resist the influence of communist indoctrination organization existing within most prisons'.[56]

The Korean 'reindoctrination' effort was launched by the United States on a small scale after the Inchon landings of September 1950, in accordance with the recommendations of the US Army's Psychological Warfare Branch, and on a larger scale from late 1951.[57] As Sydney Bailey notes in his recent study: 'The United States had decided as early as 1950 that the POW issue could be exploited for propaganda purposes. Communist POWs were to be interned, and then indoctrinated for purposes of psychological warfare.'[58] Moral victory, it was thought, could be wrested in the midst of an intractably bogged-down military conflict if a sufficient number of the enemy could be persuaded to renounce communism and choose 'democracy'. The intensive effort to achieve this result was responsible for dragging out the peace negotiations for an extra twenty months and through two winters.

The intensive strategic (terror) bombing and napalming of villages and towns throughout North Korea during these years also forced upon the population the alternatives of grim survival, often living underground in caves, or attempting to flee to the south as refugees – a choice which could then be represented as a moral victory for the anti-communist cause. Flight induced by fear that the atom bomb might be used, fed by semi-open discussions in Washington of the pros and cons of its use, could fit the same category, while destruction of the economic infrastructure of North Korea had the added advantage that post-war reconstruction would very likely have to rely on draconian methods, further diminishing whatever appeal the 'communist' side might have. All of this helped to pluck elements of 'victory' from a war that could not be won.

Ideological fanaticism, or insistence that the enemy should lose face if he could not actually be made to lose the war, was therefore much stronger on the US than on the communist side. Burchett, in understanding and reporting this *at the time* demonstrated remarkable acumen and courage.

Article 128 of the Geneva Convention on Prisoners of War, which the US had played a leading role in getting adopted in 1949, was quite unambiguous: '[P]risoners of war should be released and repatriated without delay after the cessation of hostilities.'[59] The United States argued, however, that this was to be understood only in conjunction with other clauses concerning the welfare of prisoners, so that those who did not wish to be repatriated should not be compelled. In other words Article 128, even when read in conjunction with Article 7, which stated that in no circumstances could prisoners of war renounce the rights secured to them in the convention, did not mean what it said. When it was announced by the UN side in April 1952 that approximately 60,000 out of 130,000 communist prisoners did not wish to be repatriated,[60] (and this after the total figure for prisoners in allied hands had been reduced by 50,000 due to the reclassification of many prisoners of South Korean origin as non-combatants) the affront to the Chinese–Korean side was obvious. Deadlock ensued.

That no one should be forced to go anywhere, and that in particular released prisoners should not be forced to return to their country of origin, is obviously correct as a general principle. But in a war such as this, which was seen in the West as one between democracy or freedom and communism or tyranny, and in a situation where men are physically captives, and where, as Admiral Joy put it, 'the major objective of the Washington decision to insist on voluntary repatriation was to inflict upon the communists a propaganda defeat',[61] the conditions for the exercise of free choice simply did not exist.

Screening – the process of finding out which prisoners would accept repatriation and which not – became a bitter issue. Agents of the Rhee (South Korean) and Chiang (Taiwan) regimes were given facilities to organize within the camps, which split into two warring factions as a result. A US State Department official, Frank Stelle, described the camps as 'violently totalitarian [and run by] thugs'.[62] Thus the conditions were created for a series of violent incidents in which hundreds of prisoners lost their lives.

Burchett wrote extensively about the camp on Koje Island, about twenty miles off the southern coast of Korea where, as of mid-1951, about 150,000 Chinese and North Korean prisoners were held.[63] Of course neither he nor his co-author, Alan Winnington, was able to visit this or any other camp in the south, but their sources included prisoners who had escaped from it, others who became agents for the southern regime and were later captured after parachuting into North Korea on various missions, former Koje Island camp guards, among them several Canadians who were later captured, and Red Cross reports and other materials published in the West at the time of the Koje Island trouble in 1952. The 1953 Burchett and Winnington account, *Koje Unscreened*, can now conveniently be read in conjunction with two later official or semi-official accounts of the same incidents, William White's *The Captives of Korea: An Unofficial White Paper on the Treatment of War Prisoners* (1957)[64] and Hal Vetter's *Mutiny on Koje Island* (1965),[65] as well as even more recent accounts like that in Sydney Bailey's *How Wars End* (1982). It may be noted that none of these makes reference to the Burchett and Winnington study.

And yet there is a wide area of agreement in substance between all these books. The United States in late 1950, out of Psychological Warfare considerations, introduced political training into the camps under the name of 'Rehabilitation Project' or 'Educational and Vocational Training Scheme',[66] and later moved to intensive political 'screening' in which agents of the Syngman Rhee regime and the Chiang Kai-shek regime in Taiwan were given facilities to propagandize and organize the prisoners,[67] whereupon the prisoners in the late summer of 1951 became, in the words of the International Red Cross, 'excitable, unstable and restless'.[68]

A series of riots ensued in the camps. Casualties were astonishingly high. According to the official US figures only, they numbered over 300 dead and nearly a thousand wounded (see table on page 175, opposite).

Tear gas and concussion grenades were frequently used by the authorities, and guards opened fire directly on the prisoners on at least four occasions – 18 February, 13 March, 1 October, and 14 December 1952 – while tanks were mobilized against them in June 1952. The International Committee of the Red Cross was severely critical of the degree of violence employed by the camp authorities and of the political education programme followed by the Americans.[69]

CASUALTIES IN US-CONTROLLED POW-CAMP CLASHES IN SOUTH KOREA,
JUNE 1951 – DECEMBER 1953[a]

Date	POWs Killed	POWs Wounded	US/South Korean Casualties	Issue (according to US claims)
18.6.1951	7	4	—	'attempted mass escape'
15.8.1951	17	47	—	ditto (2 incidents)
9.1951	—	20	31	'faction fighting'
10.12.1951	—	3	—	Chinese-Korean fight, guard intervention
18.12.1951	24	27	—	—
18.2.1952	77	140	4	—
13.3.1952	12	26	2	POW-guards clash
10.4.1952	3[b]	60	11	'resistance to screening'
6–10.5.1952		capture by POWs of commandant[c]		General Francis T. Dodd, Koje camp
20.5.1952	1	85	—	'incident' at Pusan hospital
10.6.1952	31	139	15	resistance to attempted relocation
27.7.1952	1	7	—	assaults upon alleged 'agitators'
30.7.1952	—	24	—	assaults upon alleged 'agitators'
1.10.1952	56	80	9	US intervention to remove Chinese flags
25.11.1952	—	?	?	—
14.12.1952	85	200	4	'disturbances on Pongam Island'
2.1953	—	?	?	unauthorized removal of military insignia
TOTAL	334	873	45	

a. Compiled from data given in Bailey, *How Wars End: the United Nations and the Termination of Armed Conflict, 1946–1964*, Clarendon Press, Oxford, 1982, vol. 2, pp. 455–60. There are slight, but not significant discrepancies in figures given in other sources for some incidents. Incidents recorded by Burchett and Winnington alone are not included here.

b. Burchett and Winnington (*Koje Unscreened*, p.62) give 33 as the figure for deaths on this occasion.

c. General Dodd was seized by POWs on 7 May 1952 and released unharmed three days later after signing an agreement to end forced screening and ill-treatment of prisoners and to see that the camps were run in accord with the Geneva Conventions. Immediately after his release the agreement was rejected by the Americans because it was said to have been negotiated under duress.

In addition to the incidents listed here, one should probably include
the raids on POW camps by military police of the Syngman Rhee regime
in June 1953, on the eve of the armistice, in which some 27,000 North
Korean prisoners were seized and carried off for drafting into the South
Korean army. Sixty-one prisoners were killed and 116 injured in these
operations, whether shot 'by unknown persons' or 'trampled to death',
and the casualties almost certainly increased as 'unco-operative'
prisoners were dealt with after removal from the camps.[70]

Beyond this, though this much in itself is a damning record, accounts
differ radically. For White and Vetter, the democratic and liberal
sentiments of the camp authorities had led them to relax controls to such
an extent that, by means of intimidation and murder, fanatical
communists were able to wrest effective control over sections of the
camp, and the violence of the authorities was a justified attempt to
reassert control and to protect the right of free response by individual
prisoners to the 'screening' process. Bailey is more detached:

> In any large prison camp, a certain degree of self-administration is
> necessary. Soon the prisoners in the camps of the unified command
> had segregated themselves into pro- and anti-communist elements.
> Political commissars and bully boys began to take control, with
> kangaroo courts, intimidation, and even murder. South Korean
> guards were none too gentle with their charges, leading to angry
> reactions . . . and the forced screening of POWs caused great
> resentment.[71]

This brings us to the Burchett and Winnington account.[72] They stress
the political pressures to which prisoners were subjected by the
American authorities (including counter-intelligence) and the Chinese
Kuomintang and Korean Syngman Rhee forces. Their sources give an
account of 'education' that was blatant and provocative anti-communist
indoctrination. Organizations such as the 'Oppose Communism Resist
Russia Association' encouraged the tattooing of anti-communist slogans
on those under their control. In particular the determination of camp
authorities to *rescreen* compounds which had already pronounced
themselves communist provoked resistance and led to violent repression, especially in the case of the 18 February 1952 incident.[73] Incidents
of terrorism and murder by named Kuomintang and South Korean
officers are given in detail, as are cases where POWs were recruited for
various military operations on the UN–US side (also contrary to the
Geneva Convention). Perhaps the most damning account they give is of
the 14 December 1952 incident in which, according to a United Press
report by Fred Painton which quotes the camp commander, the
prisoners were shot down while singing, arms linked, in rows four
deep.[74] A Canadian guard, Corporal Jollymore, interviewed by
Burchett and Winnington, also gave details of the rape of women
prisoners.[75] In their later book, Burchett and Winnington describe
various tortures practised in the Koje Island camp, in particular on

those involved in attempting to resist the machinery of manipulation and ideological control.[76]

It is a grim and shocking picture they paint. They quote the words of Judge John J. Parker, US member of the Nuremberg tribunal on Nazi war crimes, sentencing three Nazis to death for, *inter alia*, issuing orders allowing the use of arms against POWs in cases of 'insubordination, active or passive resistance'.[77] Burchett and Winnington believed the camp authorities in South Korea were guilty of atrocities comparable with those of the Nazis. Had they known of the character of US involvement in Greece in the late 1940s they would certainly have quoted that too as a precedent. The book is written in anger, but is based on the kind of materials newsmen have always relied on and it presents a powerful and persuasive case. The 'Psywar' campaigns and the screening and rescreening which all sources admit could scarcely have been conducted without provoking resistance, and the scale of violence agreed by all sources is such that White and Vetter's justification becomes quite inadequate. At the very least Burchett and Winnington present a case which calls for fuller investigation.

In their subsequent volume, *Plain Perfidy*, published privately in Peking in 1954, Burchett and Winnington turn their attention to the last stages of the war, again focusing on the POW issue. They argue, in short, that the conduct of UN camps in South Korea was marked throughout this period by brutality, torture, forced tattooing, murder and abduction of prisoners (for press-ganging into the armies of Syngman Rhee and Chiang Kai-shek). This process persisted even after the armistice, during the six-month period under neutral nation supervision which was designed to ensure that no prisoners were forced to 'return' to their countries against their will, while the conduct of camps run by the Chinese and North Koreans in North Korea, according to Burchett and Winnington, was proper and even benevolent.

Here too the effect of the book (discussed in detail in the section which follows) is weakened by hyperbole and by the unrestrained and emotional commitment of the authors. A more detached and objective study might have been more persuasive. Still, they are dealing with shocking events and would have been less than human not to have experienced anger and outrage as they recorded them. Much of this book is very 'raw' material, evidently transcribed almost directly from their notebooks. There are, however, no known Chinese or Korean accounts of these matters and only very committed and polemical writing, from an opposite perspective, from American sources, none of which faces seriously the charges laid by Burchett and Winnington.

It was perhaps inevitable that the passions of two bitter civil wars, Chinese and Korean, would concentrate on the issue of treatment and repatriation of prisoners. The combination of the American pursuit of 'moral' victory in the global struggle against communism and the local passions of the Rhee and Chiang Kai-shek forces deriving from civil war created intolerable pressures in the camps. In these microcosms of

combined Cold War and Civil War there was little room for detachment
or impartiality. For the commentators, as for the prisoners, there was no
neutral ground upon which to stand and observe.

c) PRISONER EXCHANGE

In April 1953 there was an exchange of sick and wounded prisoners –
'Operation Little Switch'. Burchett and Winnington reported that the
Americans and South Koreans who were returned from the north
'stepped jauntily out, sunburned, ruddy, happy and laughing, shaking
hands with their Chinese escorts', while the Chinese and Koreans
released from camps in the south were 'harried wrecks of men and
women . . . with all the horrors of Belsen and Buchenwald stamped
unmistakably on their wan faces and dank skin'.[78] Burchett had
first-hand knowledge of the horrors of Nazi and Japanese prison camps

---

REPATRIATION OF POWS, APRIL 1953 – JANUARY 1954[a]

1. *April 1953* 'Operation Little Switch' (Exchange of Sick and Wounded)

   Returned to China/DPRK   5,800   to UN side   600

2. *August 1953* 'Operation Big Switch' (Major prisoner exchange)

   (a) Returned to DPRK   70,183   to South Korea   7,862
              China   5,640   to UN countries   4,911

   (b) Refused repatriation and entrusted to Neutral Nations Repatriation
       Commission (India, Czechoslovakia, Poland, Sweden, Switzerland):

   From UN side   7,900 Koreans   *From China/DPRK side*   333 Koreans
                    14,704 Chinese   23 US
                    ———   1 British
        Total   22,604   ———
                                              Total   357

3. *December 1953 – January 1954* Disposition of those listed in 2b above.

   (a) *UN side prisoners*
       To China   440   To Taiwan   14,235
       To North Korea   188   To South Korea   7,604
       Died, escaped, disappeared   51   ———
       To neutral countries   86   Total   21,839

                        Total   765

   (b) *China/Korea side prisoners*
       To China and North Korea   347
       To UN side   10
       To neutral countries   2
                                    ———
                        Total   359

[a]Compiled from figures in Burchett and Winnington, *Plain Perfidy*, p. 14 (April 1953
figures only) and Bailey, op. cit., vol. 2, 468–71 (all others).

and he would not have used these words lightly. The photographs reproduced in *Plain Perfidy* tend to reinforce his claims, while the bland counter-claim by the UN side that it returned '77,000 well-fed and healthy repatriates' who were 'fattened now to the pink of condition'[79] is simply absurd.

The record on repatriation of POWs is complex and best reproduced in a separate table (see page 178, opposite).

The upshot of this is that 21,839 men and women, ninety-six per cent of those entrusted to the final neutral nations-supervised screening process, were sent to Taiwan or remained in South Korea instead of being repatriated to China or North Korea. To this number should be added the 27,000 who were abducted by South Korea in June 1953 (see above). One recent study concludes from all this that 'about 50,000 (including 14,000 Chinese) *decided* not to return to their communist homelands' (italics added).[80] Were that the case, of course, it would represent a moral defeat for the communist side. But the matter is not so simple. The 27,000 in June were aducted by force; nor did the final group of 22,604 veterans in fact have any 'free' choice – they were organized in such a way as to ensure that as few as possible would ever actually be able to choose repatriation. The explanations upon which choice was supposed to be based were given to only 3,190 prisoners (of the 22,604 total) in ten out of the fifty compounds of the main camp.[81] The December 1953 report of the Neutral Nations Repatriation Commission (NNRC) was a damning indictment of the processes it had supposedly supervised: 'the prisoner-of-war organizations in the South [UN] camp, and the leadership which sustained them, negate all assumptions or assertions about freedom of choice . . . *any prisoner who desired repatriation had to do so clandestinely and in fear of his life*' (italics added).[82]

The report is replete with details of what can only be described as a reign of terror, which the Indian troops of the NNRC were simply too few to prevent. Casualties (prisoners murdered or severely injured) were high. One incident in a UN camp may be cited as an example: 'On 1 November, 1953, in the very presence of the commission's subordinate body, two prisoners of war were severely beaten because they expressed a desire for repatriation. It was with the greatest difficulty that the [Indian] Custodial Force was able to extricate these two Chinese prisoners from compound D.28 alive.'[83]

What *Plain Perfidy* does is to fill in a detailed picture of this reign of terror under the direction of South Korean and Taiwan agents, ultimately the responsibility of the US military authorities. They flesh out the full implications of the bare statement of the commission report italicized above. Intimidation, rape of women prisoners (pp. 86–7, 90), beatings, forced tattooings,[84] and murder, were part of the process. Pak Sang Hyon, the prisoner who led the group which seized General Dodd in May 1952, is said as a result to have suffered eleven months' unbroken torture in an attempt to extract a confession which would suit American propaganda purposes (pp. 89ff, photo opp. p. 92). 'Unnecessary and criminal amputation' of prisoners' limbs, or the use of prisoners as guinea pigs for medical or epidemic research (by deliberate non-treatment) (pp. 103ff) are also among the allegations laid and documented with a good deal of persuasive evidence in this book. The refusal by the anti-communist forces in control of most compounds to allow their members to participate in the 'explanations' process was testimony to the 'brutal coercion'[85] that prevailed in the camps under the supposed control of the neutral nations. White's account, prepared with the full support of the US military, defends this as 'discipline which the men felt was needed'.[86] Yet, according to evidence published by the commission, the Korean compounds were under the direct control of agents responsible to the provost Marshal of the Republic of Korea, i.e., the South Korean authorities.[87]

In short, *Plain Perfidy* is an appalling record of atrocities and contempt for the humanity and integrity of the UN prisoners in the name of 'freedom'. It has considerable plausibility, and the hyperbole of some of the value judgements it offers cannot be used to dismiss the evidence it documents.

D) THE BURCHETT 'EXFILTRATION' PLAN

Late in 1953, while Burchett was publishing the material contained in *Plain Perfidy* and was in regular contact with Western newsmen at Panmunjom, Australian and US authorities both concentrated their attention on him.

A prominent American journalist, Edward Hymoff, then bureau chief for International News Service in Seoul, was authorized by the American CIA to offer Burchett the huge sum of $100,000 if he would co-operate. The CIA plan called for Burchett to shout 'sanctuary' and run to a waiting helicopter which would whisk him out of the area. In Burchett's words: 'The only intelligence agency which ever tried to recruit me was the CIA, during the Korean Armistice Talks, some twenty-four years ago, for a down payment of $100,000. I refused the offer, of course.'[88] Hymoff confirmed this: 'Burchett just grinned and said nothing. He didn't take the bait.'[89]

Unfortunately, neither Burchett nor Hymoff is very precise as to when this exchange took place. Burchett put it at '1952 or 1953'; Hymoff mentioned that the money offer was in the form of a bid to buy Burchett's 'memoirs' in the same way that General Dean's had been bought (for $50,000) by the *Saturday Evening Post*, which means it must have come *after* Dean's repatriation on 4 September. Clear evidence of strong US interest around this time in getting Burchett's co-operation is contained in a despatch from the Australian embassy in Tokyo dated 7 September 1953, reporting an approach from General Mark Clark, the US commander in Korea, indicating that Burchett wanted to return to Australia. Clark proposed that the US should make arrangements for 'exfiltrating' him across the truce line, pay him for whatever information he then provided concerning his Chinese and North Korean contacts, and return him to Australia.[90] The matter was considered 'at highest level' in Canberra and a reply was cabled the following day indicating that the Australian government 'has not the least desire that Burchett should return, may have no legal power to stop him; but will do what it can'. It would in particular give no assurances of immunity from prosecution.[91] A two-man team from Australian Security Intelligence Organization (ASIO) was despatched to Japan and Korea late in October to investigate the case against Burchett.[92] It is unclear whether the $100,000 US offer came before or after the Australians were consulted; what is clear is that Burchett was not for sale.

The Australian determination to discredit Burchett, to which considerable resources and bureaucratic energies were devoted and in which huge files were accumulated over subsequent decades, is a matter deserving extended treatment in its own right. As early as 1953 this episode shows that Australia felt strongly enough about Burchett to reject outright a proposal concerning him *even when* that proposal emanated from the commander of UN forces in Korea. When an anonymous article about Burchett and the British *Daily Worker* correspondent, Alan Winnington, appeared in the weekly *US News and World Report* (2 October 1953) under the heading 'Strange Case of Two Traitors', noting that 'American diplomatic and military officials' viewed the two men as traitors who 'worked actively for the enemy', 'made a success of the germ warfare hoax', and 'processed "confessions" extracted from American aviators by torture', the substance of the attack was at once cabled from New York to Australia by Peter Hastings of the Australian Associated Press.[93] The Secretary of the Department of External Affairs, Alan Watt, sent a copy of the American journal article to the Attorney General's Department, drawing attention to 'the harm that could be done to Australia's standing in the United States . . . by an article of this nature'.[94] Copies were also sent to ASIO, the Attorney General and 'at his request' to Prime Minister Menzies.[95]

The question of Burchett's passport was raised in passing in the article, with the implication that he did not deserve to possess one. The anonymous New York author was here echoing a point made in 1951 by Burchett's former friend, Denis Warner, protesting over the apparent freedom of movement in communist countries Burchett enjoyed.[96] In April 1953 Burchett was placed on the 'Migration Warning List' at the request of ASIO; this time a full investigation was launched and on 27 April 1954 Immigration Minister Holt issued a specific order banning Burchett.[97] (See Chapter 4.)

E) WESTERN PRISONERS IN NORTH KOREA AND THE CASE AGAINST BURCHETT

Burchett's treatment of Western POWs in the Chinese and North Korean camps in North Korea is one of the most controversial matters in his entire journalistic career. The various allegations that he participated in attempts to 'brainwash' allied prisoners, or 'harangued' them in political lectures, or took part in interrogation sessions, or helped mould propaganda campaigns built around induced confessions which he knew to be false, are very serious and have been reiterated on many occasions. Such charges were evidently at the root of the Australian government's long and bitter feud with Burchett. Upon his death in 1983 the accusations burst forth again in Australia, where several prominent critics suggested Burchett should have been tried for treason.[98] During his life Burchett made vain attempts to secure an inquiry into the allegations in an effort to clear his name, at a London press conference in July 1968 (the *Age*, 29 July 1968) and through his solicitor, Mr Frank Galbally, to Prime Minister Gorton in February 1969 (the *Herald*, 17 February 1969). There was no response. Similarly, when the same request was put by a relative of Burchett, Sir Ronald East, in a 1969 approach to Mr B. Snedden, Minister for Immigration, there was no response.[99] Was Burchett's behaviour in this matter treasonable?

The most comprehensive public presentation of the case against Burchett occurred in October 1974. Burchett himself launched a defamation action in the Supreme Court of New South Wales against Senator Jack Kane, a member of the right-wing splinter party, the Democratic Labor Party, over an article published in that party's organ.[100]

The article by Kane was based on allegations made before a US Senate Internal Security Sub-Committee in 1969 by a defector from the Soviet KGB, Yuri Krotkov (also known as George Karlin). According to Krotkov, Burchett in the 1940s and 1950s was a paid agent of Soviet, Korean, Chinese and Vietnamese communist governments and/or parties.[101]

The courtroom saw an extraordinary procession of witnesses, most of whom were called by the defence in support of Krotkov's allegations. A considerable international organization was put together to back Senator Kane, who later boasted that he had enjoyed the co-operation of the reservists' associations of the American and Australian armies, a 'private research organization in the US' which had 'a big research library in Boston', and a legal staff which assembled materials from Los Angeles, Washington, New York, Arlington (Virginia), Montreal, Hong Kong, Saigon, Bangkok, Paris, Rome, Firenze, London, and throughout Australia.[102] Evidence was taken under oath from Krotkov himself by deposition in Washington. The major witnesses were the following:

i)   Derek Kinne, an Englishman who won the George Cross in Korea, spoke of an occasion in 1952 when he said Burchett came to his camp to address prisoners from a table set up in a football field. When Kinne objected to Burchett, and spoke of the sufferings of the camp prisoners, Burchett is said to have replied, 'I can have you shot.' When Kinne asked to see the grave of his brother who had been killed in action in Korea, Burchett is said to have 'crossed his arms and legs and said: "You want to see that grave – you beg."' Burchett's reception from the

POWs was said to be very hostile, in the face of which, according to Kinne, an angry Burchett shouted: ' "All right, you people – you think when the peace talks break down and the Americans come this way you will be liberated; but I have got news for you, you are going that-a-way." And he pointed to China.'[103]

ii) Former Australian prisoners, Robert Parker, Thomas Hollis and Ronald Buck, spoke of having been taken, with one other prisoner, to meet Burchett. A brief altercation occurred, in which Hollis claimed to have come to Korea to 'kill as many so-and-so communist bastards like you as possible'. According to Hollis, Burchett also urged the Australians to collaborate with their captors in order to receive better treatment. This altercation is basic to the charge of treason against Burchett as it is the only incident in which he is alleged to have mistreated or 'brainwashed' fellow Australians.

iii) A former American fighter pilot, Paul Kniss, spoke of meeting Burchett to discuss a confession which he (Kniss) had signed, admitting involvement in bacteriological warfare (BW) raids into China and North Korea. According to Kniss, Burchett admitted having 'edited' the confession and later served as an 'interrogator' when Kniss was called to give evidence before an International Scientific Commission investigating the BW allegations at Pyoktong in North Korea in August 1952.

iv) Another former US fighter pilot, Colonel Walker M. Mahurin, spoke of having *seen* Burchett once somewhere in the vicinity while he was imprisoned. Apparently no words were exchanged but Burchett 'stared at me like a snake staring at a mouse'. Later, after he too had made a BW confession and was about to be released in August 1953, he was taken to meet Burchett. On this occasion, Burchett asked him questions about the confession. Mahurin said he felt at the time that Burchett 'had control over my destiny', though he mentions nothing threatening or otherwise of interest that passed between them.

v) High-ranking Australian army witnesses spoke of Burchett's reputation in their circles. A former correspondent spoke of discussions with Burchett at Panmunjom in which Burchett had made allegations about ill-treatment of prisoners held by the US, and another former correspondent, Denis Warner, spoke of Burchett having used 'the wildest communist expressions' in denouncing the UN and US role in Korea. Warner said he also found Burchett's behaviour to POWs to have been 'abominable'.

In the end the most remarkable feature of the case is that all these allegations were *irrelevant* to the outcome. The judge himself, after listening to all the evidence, declared that there had been nothing to prove the main allegation against Burchett:

> You [speaking to counsel for Kane] show me where there is any evidence on which the jury could find that it is true to say that he applied to become a member of the KGB, and then he became one; that he was put on the payroll, that he was paid by the KGB, or that

he worked for the KGB . . . It seems to me that all these matters just cannot go.[104]

The judge suggested that the defence rely instead on the defence of 'fair report'; whereupon two questions were put to the jury. In response the jury agreed, first, that Burchett had indeed been defamed by the article in question but also, second, that the article was a 'fair report' of proceedings in the Australian Senate since the original Krotkov allegations had been read into the Senate record. Mr Justice Taylor therefore ruled the defamatory statements covered by 'absolute privilege'.[105] Costs were awarded against Burchett.

Before considering this evidence in more detail it is worth noting that the case went to appeal, and three judges of the New South Wales Court of Appeal on 20 May 1976 again decided against Burchett. In doing so, however, they accepted that there had been, in the words of Mr Justice Samuels, 'a substantial miscarriage of justice' since the article in question 'was not at all a report of proceedings in the Senate'. It was therefore not privileged and the crucial question should not have been put to the jury.[106] However, the judges declined to order a new trial for two reasons: Burchett's counsel in the 1974 proceedings had consented to the procedure adopted, so that the error was of the party rather than the tribunal, and because many of the defence witnesses had come from overseas and therefore 'one likely consequence of a new trial would be to deprive the defendant of substantial and important parts of his evidence' (i.e. if some or all of those witnesses could not, or would not, attend a retrial).[107]

So in the end all that was decided in court was that Burchett had been defamed, since the original decision that the defamation was covered by parliamentary privilege was rejected by the appeal court bench. Despite this very inconclusive outcome, the trial has commonly been cited as evidence that Burchett was guilty of the various matters alleged against him (and denied by him). It is of course nothing of the kind, because the jury was never called upon to pronounce on the truth or justifiability of the defamation, and the presiding judge himself opined that there was no case to put to the jury on the main allegations.

The evidence of Krotkov and the Korean War veterans was central. The former of these does not concern Korea, and consists primarily of the retraction under cross-examination in 1974 of the allegations launched against Burchett by ex-KGB man Krotkov in 1969.

Before turning to examine the Korean War evidence, one related matter, not brought up in court, should be mentioned. In a series of newspaper articles in 1953, just after his release from a POW camp, Private Keith 'Mo' Gwyther of Leongatha in Victoria spoke of Burchett having visited his camp and asked for an interview with the four Australians present in it. They rejected his offer to contact their families on their behalf and after a brief argument of 'a minute and a half' the interview ended.[108] The others present at the interview were Parker, Hollis and Buck. It was obviously the interview referred to above.

Given the publicity which surrounded the trial and the resources deployed by the defence in mobilizing against Burchett witnesses from all over Australia, as well as from the US, Hong Kong and Vietnam, and from the involvement in the case of two former chiefs of staff of the Australian Army, it can be assumed that evidence of Burchett's relations with Australian POWs at least is exhaustively covered in it. Yet this evidence amounts only to a 'one-minute-and-a-half' conversation in POW Camp Five in 1952. Burchett himself agreed that the meeting certainly took place and he also agreed that in the course of it he said that, although not a communist, 'I sympathize with North Korea and China in this war.'[109]

The circumstances within which this single contact with Australian POWs in the camps took place are important. Denis Warner, himself a journalist, told the court that he 'knew of no reputable war correspondent going to a prisoner of war camp. Correspondents were not allowed to interview war prisoners.' Warner was of course wrong about this, and correspondents certainly visited camps under UN/US control in the south, like Koje Island, on many occasions. Russell Spurr, a prominent journalist who represented the *Daily Express* in Korea from September–October 1952 till early 1954, gave evidence that he and other UN correspondents had recognized no such ban: 'The last part of the war was over prisoners. The war was extended because of a great argument as to whether prisoners should return or not and therefore it was very important that correspondents visit the camps and hear from the prisoners themselves.'[110]

What is particularly significant about this meeting between Burchett and the Australian prisoners is that Burchett had been pursuing enquiries on behalf of a major Melbourne newspaper, the *Herald*, whose editor, Mr Jack Waters, had *asked* him to make enquiries as to whether an Australian prisoner named Gwyther, reported missing, was alive or not. Burchett discovered that Gwyther was indeed alive and in Camp Five, corresponded with him, and only visited the camp after Gwyther had agreed to see him.[111] This important fact, along with the whole of Burchett's recollection of the meeting, was confirmed on 6 February 1969 by Mr Keith Gwyther himself in an interview with Sir Ronald East and Miss Myra Roper, taped and witnessed by an official of the local Returned Soldiers' organization sub-branch,[112] and early in 1985 ASIO released a substantial proportion of its Burchett files, including both the text of the letter from the *Herald* editor, Jack Waters, to Burchett (dated 9 January 1952) and Burchett's subsequent letter to Gwyther (dated 29 January 1952).[113]

An account of the 1952 encounter which had been specially prepared by Burchett was presented to Gwyther in written form and also read to him, in 1969; whereupon Gwyther confirmed that it was substantially a correct account of what had happened. The account, although somewhat long, deserves to be quoted in full:[114]

At some point in the Korean war, I received a letter from John

Waters, then editor or assistant editor of the Melbourne *Sun*. It referred to an Australian soldier (Keith Gwyther) who had been reported killed, but his name later appeared on a POW list from Peking. Waters asked me to check and find out if the chap was still alive, and, if so, what had happened. I wrote to the POW camp and, after some time, received a reply from him, giving details of how he had been left for dead, but had in fact been captured. He expressed gratitude that I had taken the trouble to find out about him and said he would be very glad to see me if ever I came to the POW camp.

Eventually I did get to the camp where this chap was held and asked to see him. The Korean Chinese [*sic*] in charge of the camp said there were a number of other Australians there and it would be better if I saw them all together. This I did, together with half a dozen French POWs. The Australians were dominated by one very big chap with a black beard who seemed to be their spokesman and dominated them. He was very aggressive.

I started by asking how were things? He snarled 'It's no fault of the Koreans and Chinese that we're alive today.' Then he asked 'Are you a communist?' I replied that in this war I supported the Korean–Chinese side. He snarled back: 'We came here to kill communists and we'd kill you too, if we could . . .' I asked what was their main grievance, to which 'Black-beard' replied that the food was only fit for animals to eat. I made my one break at that and said 'Next time you set out to kill communists, you'd better do it in a country where steak and bread is the staple diet.'

Then I asked if I could do anything about their mail, take letters . . . He snarled 'No.' I asked if that went for the others too; they nodded their heads. I asked if the man from Leongatha (Gwyther) was there and he raised his hand. I said that I had got his letter. Did he have anything to say? He shook his head. And that was that.

The whole thing took about ten minutes. I said it was no good continuing the conversation, and let them go.

Gwyther refused to testify against Burchett in the 1974 trial, and in 1980 Hollis ('Black-beard') advised a researcher not to interview Gwyther because 'he thinks Burchett helped him while he was a prisoner'.[115] When the original reports made for Australian security by Buck, Hollis and Parker (17 December 1953) and Gwyther (11 November 1953) were released early in 1985 they also confirmed Burchett's account.[116]

A contact described by one of the participants very shortly after it occurred as lasting 'a minute and a half' and by Burchett much later as 'about ten minutes', which took place at the suggestion of a prisoner after an Australian newspaper had asked Burchett to find out whether that prisoner was still alive, and in which all the prisoners agreed they had felt free to speak their minds, and had indeed insulted Burchett in very clear terms, is rather thin evidence upon which to hang allegations of 'brainwashing' Australian prisoners. Certainly they had a discussion, which soon stalled in bitter disagreement over the character of the war.

That seems neither surprising nor reprehensible.

Though the incident was trivial enough, it was upon this meeting alone that the Australian government (and others) pinned the accusation of improper contact between Burchett and Australian POWs. Two other contacts between Burchett and Australian POWs seem to have taken place. Flight Lieutenant Gordon Harvey told Australian security in October 1953 that he had met Burchett briefly during April 1952, and that Burchett had given him information about the progress of the peace talks and about current affairs generally, and he had given Burchett his mother's address to pass on to her the news that he was alive and well.[117] Much later, as the POWs were leaving North Korea via Panmunjom in 1953, another group of Australians also met Burchett. Nothing untoward happened on this occasion, save that one of the prisoners concerned gave evidence at the trial that he had not received the beer and fruit which Burchett once, in a television programme, claimed he had then distributed. Burchett in court thought this might have been because this particular witness had been ill or asleep at the time.[118] Affidavits collected by Australian security officials in 1953 and declassified in 1985 make it clear that Burchett's account was substantially correct, the only discrepancy being that while Burchett thought he had distributed beer and fruit, one of this group of POWs, John Frederick Davis of Maryborough in Queensland, claimed that Burchett had brought two bottles of whisky, while another, John Houston Mackay of Perth, could only recall one large bottle. Both agreed he brought whisky rather than beer and that the whisky was bourbon.[119]

The incidents are extremely trivial; yet trivial incidents can often have large consequences. In 1970 the Australian Prime Minister was asked several questions in the Senate and replied, via a spokesman, in the following terms:[120]

(1) Were any Australian soldiers who were prisoners of war during the United Nations' operations in Korea in 1950–1953 interrogated by Wilfred Burchett; if so, was such interrogation in any way requested or approved by the Australian government or any person acting under its authority.

(2) Was Wilfred Burchett, in interrogating Australian prisoners of war, assisting the North Korean and Chinese forces.

Senator ANDERSON – The Prime Minister has provided the following answer to the honourable senator's questions:

(1) A number of Australian soldiers who were prisoners of war during the United Nations' operations in Korea in 1950–1953 were interviewed by Wilfred Burchett and questioned by him; these interviews were not requested or approved by the Australian government or by anyone acting under its authority.

(2) It is the view of the Australian government that these interviews were calculated to assist the North Korean and Chinese forces in that, in conducting these interviews, Burchett was seeking either to disseminate propaganda inimical to the cause of the United Nations

forces or to obtain information to be used as propaganda to assist the
North Korean and Chinese cause.

With the release of much of the Australian government Burchett files,
especially the substantial security files, in 1984–85, it is now possible to
say that the two encounters described were the only occasions on which
Burchett met and talked with Australian POWs.

Apart from this Burchett in 1974 said that he had given talks in POW
camps in Korea on a total of three occasions, twice in Camp Five and
once in Camp One.[121] These talks, he said, were given by invitation
after Burchett had talked to the representative camp committees about
the state of the war and the peace negotiations, and they asked him to
provide a similar briefing for the benefit of the larger POW
community.[122] As noted, the most senior American officer held in
North Korea, General Dean, has recorded his gratitude to Burchett for
precisely such a briefing.

Burchett had displayed a sympathetic understanding of the POW
predicament, particularly the thirst for reliable information about the
world outside the camps, on one previous occasion, in early September
1945.

After scooping the world with his reports for the *Daily Express* on the
aftermath of the Hiroshima bomb he was en route back to Tokyo, still
with major details of his story to be filed. While passing through Kyoto
he learned that Australian POW camps in the area were still under
Japanese military control – US occupation forces were still very few and
confined to Tokyo – and men were 'dying every day'. He therefore went
out of his way to visit the Australian camps in that area as well as the
camps of British and American prisoners in the Kobe-Osaka area, to
speak to the assembled troops and tell them that the Allies had indeed
landed and that they would soon be on their way home. Part of his
description is as follows: 'In one camp there was a very bad situation;
the Japanese commander "the Pig" had brought troops down to
surround it, people were starving. I forced the deputy to bring me the
commander, and pistol on hip, I told him to remove his troops and
provide the POWs with some fresh meat immediately.'[123] The story was
well reported in the Australian media at the time. (See *Preface*.)

This leaves the question of Burchett's contacts with British and
American POWs in Korea. The allegation that Burchett took part in the
'interrogation' of prisoners was made at the 1974 trial by Kniss and
Mahurin but their evidence, outlined above, did not support such a
charge. (And of course by no stretch of the imagination could Burchett's
encounters with Australian POWs be seen as 'interrogation'.)

One point, however, is not disputed. Burchett's alleged 'interrogation' of these men did not occur till *after* they had made their
confessions, and amounted to asking whether the confessions were true
and for a repetition of the stories already given. In the major American
studies of the POW confessions matter, by White and Kinkead,[124] this is
all that is alleged, save that in one case, the confession of a pilot named

Enoch, a first draft of the confession had been given to Burchett who gave it 'literary form and style'.[125] The allegation that Burchett was actually involved in the interrogation process rests upon a single piece of evidence.[126] One day during Kniss's interrogation, a list of questions was inadvertently dropped in his cell. According to Kniss, these questions concerned exclusively military matters and at the bottom, both typed and signed, was the name Wilfred Burchett.[127]

The allegation also appears, very briefly, in the statement made by Kniss for US intelligence immediately after his release in 1953, yet in a very considerable volume of testimony collected by the security services of Australia, the US and Britain, it stands notably uncorroborated.[128]

There is also another problem with the evidence of the airmen. This is that they *did*, in fact, confess to involvement in BW raids. Once the war was over they had to cope with strong feelings of guilt, either the guilt they expressed in their confessions over participation in BW, or the guilt they felt at having made the confessions untruthfully. They were under strong pressure to justify themselves before their military peers and before US public opinion, pressure which included the explicit threat of court-martial for the capital crime of treason.[129] Under these pressures Colonel Mahurin, whose allegation against Burchett is referred to above, remarked that, in telling his story to US military authorities, he wanted 'to be sure I told it in a way that was satisfactory to my government'.[130] Kniss and the others who confessed were in the same boat. In all, thirty-eight US airmen made confessions of active involvement in BW raids[131] and seventy per cent of all US prisoners collaborated to some degree.[132] After release they were all subjected to intensive 'debriefing' by counter-intelligence, refused immediate access to their family or the press, and despatched to the US on a slow boat under close psychiatric supervision.[133]

The *San Francisco Chronicle* (11 August 1953) carried a very revealing report from Keyes Beech:

> This is a fear-ridden atmosphere in which Amerian POWs are being shipped back to the US . . . All interviews with repatriates are conducted in the presence of a censor and a Counter-Intelligence Corps agent. Unless the repatriate is an exceptional man, this is, to say the least, an inhibiting influence . . . Often during the course of the interviews, ex-prisoners have turned to the counter-intelligence men for consent before answering questions.[134]

Thus the threats and ill-treatment under which these men had confessed in Korea were compounded by the threats and intensive psychological pressures under which they later denied their confessions. It is impossible to say with absolute confidence that such men told the truth always in the latter case and untruth always in the former. Their confusion was evident in the 1974 Sydney trial when Kniss, shown Burchett's account of their 1952 discussions, began by denouncing it as 'a bunch of damn lies' but, under questioning, agreed that it was he himself who had told Burchett 'a bunch of lies', which Burchett had faithfully reproduced.[135] Under such circumstances, without independent evidence, it is impossible to settle the question of which were lies, which truth. Had the airmen published a detailed breakdown of where *precisely* their confessions had been false, instead of improbably rejecting them as total fabrications, their repudiations might have carried more weight.

As of 1985, all other 'evidence' having been cleared away, Paul Kniss's claims alone remain to support the allegation that Burchett interrogated any POW in Korea. It is impossible now to reconstruct much about the Burchett–Kniss relationship during the war, and there are no independent witnesses. They did have a correspondence, however, which Kniss told the Sydney court he himself initiated – an odd thing for him to have done if he really believed that Burchett had forced a false confession out of him.

Furthermore, the one fragment of that correspondence which survives today in the Archives is quite out of keeping with Kniss's later description of the relationship. In this surviving letter, dated 20 November 1952 from Kaesong, Burchett wrote to Kniss:

> I hope you are getting on alright and are comfortably installed for the approaching winter, also that you are getting plenty of reading material to fill in the time. Reading is the only way to overcome boredom in such circumstances. At present I am mightily bored myself since the US delegates walked out of the conference room at Panmunjom there has been little to do. And I am short of reading material – my wife is back in Peking – so I am able to imagine myself in your position quite well.[136]

He added that he had taken up the study of Chinese, and recommended that Kniss too take advantage of the opportunity of reading and studying, a 'unique opportunity' that constituted the 'one bright side' of the current situation. This Burchett does not sound much like the 'chronic alcoholic' and possible 'drug addict' that Kniss later denounced to US intelligence. (See *Appendix*.)

Finally, in his sworn testimony in 1974, Kniss claimed that the 'interrogation' piece of paper allegedly signed by Burchett was lost, 'when it was taken off me together with my diary, everything I had'. On 4 September 1953, Kniss claimed, 'the Chinese . . . the guards took everything away from me'.[137] We now know that this is false, since Burchett's letter to Kniss of November 1952 survived, and found its way into Burchett's ASIO file. If the alleged incriminating piece of paper ever existed, it certainly disappeared rather mysteriously, and not because Kniss lost 'everything he had'.

On two further occasions Burchett agrees that he acted as interpreter in meetings between the captive US airmen and other foreigners: on one occasion for two Frenchmen who spoke no English and on another for the International Scientific Commission which visited China and North

Korea in 1952 to investigate the BW allegations, when he helped Dr Joseph Needham of Cambridge University and Dr Andreen of Sweden in interpreting to and from French. Burchett himself observes of this,

But again this was not anything in the nature of an intelligence interrogation by the captors. They had already, long ago, extracted everything they wanted. I was acting in my capacity as a journalist to report on the work of these international investigation groups, helping out from time to time as an interpreter. At no time during these sessions was there any intervention by Korean or Chinese personnel.[138]

The asking of questions on this occasion can hardly be deemed interrogation. No such charge has ever been made against Dr Joseph Needham or other members of the commission.

Burchett faltered momentarily during the trial when confronted with a published report, under his name, of an interview apparently conducted with Colonel Mahurin, while Mahurin was on his way out of the country at Panmunjom in 1953. Burchett had denied any memory of such an interview.[139] However, his journalistic output over the previous thirty years was prodigious, and since he thereupon agreed with the court that he probably had written such an article, it is the content rather than the existence of the article which is important, and the substance of the published interview is the same as that discussed above between Burchett and Kniss.

Colonel Mahurin, released from captivity in September 1953, gave accounts of his experiences on at least four subsequent occasions: to an American journalist on the day he was released, in his memoirs published in 1962, in a letter to a US journal in 1972, and to the Sydney court in 1974. In the first account, to *Chicago Daily News* correspondent Keyes Beech (9 September 1953), Mahurin began by saying that Burchett and English *Daily Worker* correspondent Alan Winnington were 'editing our confessions'. Having spelt out detailed allegations of *Winnington*'s participation in interrogation sessions he was asked 'What about Burchett?', and replied that he had 'only met him [Burchett] last night and Burchett was very pleasant to me. Very pleasant. No military business at all.' Mahurin is not mentioned in a US army report for Major-General Ennis dated 30 October 1953 in response to an instruction to 'obtain all available information and leads on Wilfred Burchett, an Australian national, which might be utilized by the Australian government in developing a case against Burchett'.[140] In 1962 Mahurin wrote an autobiography in which he described his encounter with Burchett in this way: 'I felt that Burchett . . . was going to try to get something from me. *But he didn't*. I think, in retrospect, that he must have been lonely for someone to talk to' (italics added).[141]

But by 1972, at the height of the Vietnam War, when Mahurin was president of the American Fighter Pilots' Association and Burchett a most prominent opponent of the war, Mahurin suddenly remembered that Burchett had 'harangued and threatened' him in Korea,[142] and by 1974, his memory clarifying with the passage of years, he could recall *two* encounters, in the first of which (mentioned above) Burchett 'stared at me like a snake staring at a mouse', while on the second, on the eve of his release, Mahurin was literally 'shaking like a leaf', his fate in Burchett's hands.[143]

Burchett's initial failure to remember meeting Mahurin pales into insignificance beside Mahurin's progressive ability to remember more and more of the meeting and the fact that his recollection of it changed from 'very pleasant' to very threatening. Mahurin's professed desire to tell it all 'in a way that was satisfactory to my government' worked a subtle chemistry in his memory over the years.

Colonel Mahurin also told the court in 1974 that when he first saw Burchett (on the occasion he did not think to mention *until* 1974) Burchett had been wearing a Chinese military uniform with a star on it to denote officer rank. This point has been repeated by hostile commentators as very significant.[144] However, on turning to the transcript of what actually was said, one finds *both* Mahurin's statement in his presentation of evidence that he did not see whether there were any such insignia on Burchett's clothing *and* his statement under cross-examination that he did and the star was present. No other POW witness reported seeing Burchett in such a uniform. One Australian soldier, D.P. Buck, recalled him as being dressed in the sort of clothing worn by Chinese 'civilians a little above the rank of coolie';[145] another Australian, Keith Gwyther, speaking of the indentical occasion, described him simply as in 'civilian' clothes'.[146] A number of Western correspondents who were in contact with Burchett during the peace talks at Panmunjom were later asked by security officers about this point. Some were clear that they had 'never seen him in uniform'; [147] others thought they had seen him in a 'Sun Yat-sen uniform' or a 'Lenin-type uniform'[148] or 'dressed in communist style'.[149] All agreed that, as UN correspondents, they themselves had always been dressed in military uniform. One hesitates to draw from this anything more than that memory of such details is extremely fallible.

The US government made public its official view on these matters in 1977, when the State Department announced it had 'no evidence' that Burchett had ever been involved in torture or brainwashing of American POWs, and no 'independent information' on any KGB connection, thus implicitly dismissing both the Krotkov allegations and those of Kniss and Mahurin.[150]

Burchett also denied having met the British soldier, Derek Kinne. There is no independent evidence of such a meeting. In 1955 the British Ministry of Defence published a study entitled *Treatment of British Prisoners of War in Korea* which discusses the case of Kinne at length but does not mention any such meeting or report any allegation against Burchett.[151] However, another British journalist, Michael Shapiro of the *Daily Worker*, is quoted as having expostulated with British soldiers in an interview, telling a sergeant of the Royal Ulster Rifles, 'I'll have you shot'.[152] This is so close to the purported remark of Burchett to Kinne ('I could have you shot') as to make one wonder whether Kinne may have been mistaken in his courtroom recollections. All that the British government paper says of Burchett is that he 'collected prisoners' mail, chatted to suitable men, and gave lectures'.[153] None of this is at issue. Since the paper is quite detailed on other matters it is curious that Kinne's allegations against Burchett were not published until twenty years after they supposedly occurred.

There is further, even more powerful reason to doubt the reliability of Kinne's later memory of his war experiences. Although, under oath in 1974, he spoke of an angry Burchett having told a crowd of hostile POWs that when the war was over they would be going 'that-a-way', (pointing to China), in a book he published in 1955 called *The Wooden Boxes* (F. Muller, London) he wrote of an *American* prisoner who was co-operating with the Chinese and who concluded a camp lecture in almost exactly the same way: ' "A lotta you guys think that now the peace talks have broken down, the American aggressors will come up north to release you all. Well, you're wrong. Even if they did manage to get up here, you'd all go that way" – he jerked his thumb northwards to Manchuria, a few miles across the Yalu River' (p. 92). For Kinne in 1974 to tell this identical story under oath, substituting Burchett for the 'American sergeant' he wrote about in 1955, is sufficient to cast doubt on the accuracy of the rest of his recollection. (Although in truth, beyond the admitted fact that Burchett did on several occasions speak to groups of assembled prisoners, there is nothing very substantial to it, unless Burchett's very presence in the camps is deemed offensive or treasonous.)

There is one story which Kinne tells both in 1955 and 1974 in more or less identical terms. It concerns an occasion when Burchett arose to address a crowd of POWs and was confronted by men swinging makeshift nooses and shouting 'You'll hang, you bastard!' *This* story, however, is recounted in the British White Paper as a story about Alan Winnington. It is of course possible that various speakers were greeted by their audiences in this way – which would indicate that the atmosphere in such gatherings was far from intimidatory – but it is also possible, as in Kinne's stories about Shapiro and the 'American sergeant', that we are dealing with a case of mistaken identity. The official White Paper version, which makes no criticism of Burchett, has to be preferred. The comment by a journalist who interviewed a broad cross-section of prisoners immediately after their release and compared notes with other correspondents at the time is worth quoting: 'Burchett, it seemed, was considered fairly harmless. However, a number of POWs levelled serious charges against another person from a Western country who was operating behind the communist lines. Perhaps some confusion has arisen concerning the target of these charges.'[154]

Furthermore, Kinne's reference to wanting to visit his brother's grave is misleading. His brother, Raymond, was killed in action in October 1950. Derek had visited the grave as soon as he arrived in Korea the following year, and there is no reason to think it was located anywhere near Camp Five.[155] This part of his story is also not to be found in his book, although the general story of the altercation is recounted there.

The international campaign of vilification of Burchett, based very largely on these events, is a subject worthy of separate treatment in detail. A central role in it, however, has been played by Denis Warner, himself an Australian journalist contemporary and former friend of Burchett, who in court in 1974 spoke of having shared a cabin with Burchett in the Pacific during the Battle of the Philippine Sea, and of having welcomed him to his pre-wedding party in Melbourne in 1945.

When interviewed about Burchett by security officers in November 1953 Warner was full of praise for Burchett's courage and journalistic ability, but thought he had been a communist 'since at least 1944'. There in one hint of personal animus in this statement when Warner remarked:'He [Burchett] is very fond of women, and *for some reason not apparent* [italics added], is a great success with them.'[156] From 1951 to 1985 Warner has been the central figure in the anti-Burchett campaign, and this hint of sexual jealousy or rivalry recurs in the 1985 reference (attributed to Warner) to Burchett's 'Don Juan sexual adventures'.[157]

Denis Warner and the Anti-Burchett Campaign

1951–1955

Warner's 1951 article (the *Herald,* 5 October 1951), complaining of Burchett's apparent freedom of movement behind the 'iron curtain', prompted the investigation into Burchett's passport status, and a 'Burchett file' was thereupon opened in the Department of Immigration.

The next Warner article, entitled 'He Writes the Enemy's Story', appeared in the Melbourne *Herald* on 21 June 1952. It contained a brief biography of Burchett, together with a number of excerpts from articles written by him during the Korean War which were heavily critical of US policy and the actions in Korea, blaming the US for causing the war, prolonging it, and launching germ-warfare attacks on North Korea, while praising the treatment accorded to American and other allied prisoners in North Korean POW camps. That Burchett did do such things is not in question, although the possibility that any of these propositions might be true *or even arguable* is not considered by Warner, who concludes that Burchett is therefore the enemy of his countrymen, 'as surely as if he had had a rifle and bayonet, instead of a typewriter'.

In 1955, both Warner and Burchett covered the Bandung conference. Warner wrote in the *Herald* (19 April 1955) that Burchett's freedom to travel on his British passport was 'puzzling'. He followed this up by suggesting to Australian diplomat K.C.O. (later Sir Keith) Shann that Australia should do something 'about muzzling Burchett by having his passport withdrawn'.[158] By what must be presumed an extraordinary coincidence Burchett's passport did in fact disappear on the very day Shann penned his memo – Burchett was convinced it had been stolen – and for the next seventeen years, deprived of any passport by both Australian and British governments, he was forced to travel on temporary papers issued by friends such as Ho Chi Minh or Fidel Castro.

'*Who is Wilfred Burchett?*'

1967

Warner's next major attack was in 1967 in an article entitled 'Who is Wilfred Burchett?' published in both New York and Sydney.[159] This article also contained a brief biography, repeated the main points of his 1952 article, and launched the 'brainwashing' charge based on allegations supposedly contained in the British government document: 'In 1953, the British Ministry of Defence accused Burchett of having "actively engaged in brainwashing procedures" in prisoner-of-war camps.' Warner gives no precise location of this document, but if he is referring to the British Ministry of Defence report already cited (and there does not appear to be any other) he is wrong both as to the date of the study and its contents. The report was in 1955, and the word 'brainwashing' does not appear in it *at all*, much less as an accusation against Burchett.[160]

Neither, for that matter, does the American Army allege that any of *its* prisoners were brainwashed. In the major study prepared with the full co-operation of the US Army and approved by the Department of Defense, it is stated:

> The treatment American prisoners [in Korea] underwent at the hands of the communists cannot, the army believes, be called 'brainwashing'. 'Brainwashing', as defined by the army, is a process producing obvious alteration of character. However the alteration is accomplished – whether by hypnosis, drugs, physical torture, extreme psychological pressures, or some combination of these – the subject clearly ceases to be the person he was before. According to the repatriates' own accounts, the kind of severe measures required to effect a personality change were not employed at any time with army prisoners.[161]

So Warner is not only fabricating an allegation against Burchett; he is also repeating a canard long ago dismissed by the military authorities of both Britain and the United States. Lest there be any misunderstanding on this, it should be made clear that various forms of ill-treatment of prisoners did occur, including prolonged interrogation, beating and threatened execution, although of course Burchett was not alleged to be responsible for or involved in this.[162]

Denis Warner goes on to state that: 'A team of Australian investigators subsequently obtained affidavits from prisoners who had been interrogated by Burchett.'[163] This is false. Most of the affidavits merely record having sighted Burchett in the camps, and the only ones relevant to accusations of 'brainwashing' and intimidation are those that have already been discussed above. Warner's 1967 article was the first published reference to the affidavits, whose existence was not publicly revealed till 7 July 1970, when the Prime Minister made a statement to the Senate saying, however, that it would be 'not proper to make public' what they contained. Only a select group of right-wing journalists, including Warner and B.A. Santamaria,[164] appeared to be privy to the secret information, presumably leaked to them by the security agencies. In 1985 the affidavits were de-classified.

This 1967 article also contains a brief account of the post-armistice repatriation proceedings at Panmunjom, which Warner represents as a triumph of free choice since so few POWs from China and North Korea 'chose' repatriation. (The problems about this whole procedure, even the devastating admission of failure by the supervising body, the Neutral Nations Repatriation Commission, he does not mention.) He also makes a gratuitous slur on Burchett, alleging that he absented himself from all further repatriation proceedings after the first day, though on the evidence of Burchett's very detailed written accounts of those proceedings there is no reason to doubt that he was present throughout.

Warner's 1967 article also contained a brief discussion of Burchett's role in Indochina, and concluded by accusing him of being 'a clever, calculating communist'.

The article appeared during a time of escalation of the US (and Australian) war-effort in Vietnam, and it followed by some months a vitriolic *New York Times* attack on Burchett because of his 'diligence to initiate Vietnam peace negotiations on the communist pattern, again trying to expel the United States from the Far East'.[165] Burchett's offence was to have suggested that Hanoi would be willing to discuss peace terms with the United States if Washington would halt the bombing of North Vietnam.[166] Warner's article was nicely timed to serve the requirements of US policy and it was given wide distribution.

'The Germ-Warfare Campaign'

1969

Warner's third onslaught was launched in 1969 in an article in the Melbourne *Herald* (4 February). This was notable for one new allegation: according to information 'from a very high level', Burchett was said to have made overtures to the Australian government in 1955 (or thereabouts) in which he 'hinted' that he 'would tell all about the germ-warfare campaign' (i.e. expose its fabrication) if allowed to return to Australia with assurance of immunity from prosecution. Burchett, in an unpublished comment, totally denied this.[167] There is no reference to any such overtures in the files released by the various government departments for this period. Presumably it is a garbled reference to the 1953 occasion when Burchett actually refused the $100,000 offered him by the CIA.

'The Spy Who Came in for the Gold'

1974–75

Late in 1974 Warner gave evidence at the Sydney defamation hearings and produced a film based on the evidence presented there. Early in the following year he published articles in the Japanese and American media reporting on the trial. The article for Japan was apparently designed to discredit Burchett in a country where his reputation was high and his books and articles well-known. It was entitled 'The Spy Who Came in for the Gold' ('Ogon o tori ni kita supai', *Seiron*, March 1975, pp. 42–51). A slightly different version of the same article appeared in the United States under the title 'Australian Lord Haw-Haw' (*National Review*, 11 April 1975, pp. 395–7, 410). The thrust of the articles is clear from their titles, and the testimony of Krotkov and the POWs (Kniss, Mahurin and Kinne) makes up most of their content.

   These 1975 articles include a serious allegation about the American airman, Paul Kniss: that Burchett only agreed to post a letter to Kniss's wife in the United States in return for an agreement from Kniss to have his confession published and recorded, and to appear before the International Commission of Enquiry into bacteriological warfare. No such accusation is made either in Kniss's reports to security officers in 1953, or in the first published versions of his story in the United States in 1971,[168] or in his evidence in Sydney in 1974. On the latter occasion Kniss merely mentions a sequence of events. It is Warner who reads causal significance into them. Nor does Warner mention the wartime correspondence between Burchett and Kniss , initiated *by Kniss*.

'The Germ-Warfare Hoax'

1977

Warner's next attack was in a booklet published in Seoul in 1977 under the title *The Germ Warfare Hoax* (UN Korean War Allies Association, 1977). Here, reference to the claimed 'British' allegations was dropped.

   Apart from resuming the evidence given at the Sydney hearings of 1974, this 1977 publication concentrated on advancing the argument that Burchett was responsible for the deliberate fabrication and propagation of the germ-warfare story, and for aiding in the questioning and torture of US airmen to secure 'confessions'.

   Although the general question of germ warfare (bacteriological warfare) is discussed separately below, this question of the US airmen's 'confessions', already mentioned above, calls for further comment. The harshest treatment of all among the POWs, featuring 'isolation and extreme psychological pressures . . . often in the most confined and uncomfortable surroundings' and under almost ceaseless interrogation, was reserved for the US airmen.[169] It was treatment of a pattern familiar from the literature on 'confessions' under regimes such as that of Stalin in the Soviet Union, Mao in China, the Ayatollah Khomeini in Iran, or even in Japan, pre- and post-war.[170] Fifty-nine US Air Force prisoners were subjected to this treatment, of whom thirty-eight made confessions of germ-warfare involvement.[171]

The treatment they were subjected to is clearly indefensible, but the problem for the historian is that some confessions may also happen to be true. One example is the confessions of Japanese captives of the Soviet Union (at trials held at Khabarovsk in the late 1940s) to the prosecution of germ warfare against China and the Soviet Union. These were much later confirmed down to their most macabre and shocking details by spontaneous revelations coming from ageing Japanese veterans of the same unit, under no compulsion whatever.[172]

Burchett was aware that the US airmen were being kept in solitary confinement. He claims to have protested to the Chinese authorities and urged their relocation among ordinary POWs.[173] Even if this were the case, however, there is no indication that he showed any scepticism about the spontaneity or veracity of their confessions. For this Warner was right, in principle at least, to have taken Burchett to task, although his correctness on this principle is undermined by the demonstrable falsity of so much else in his case against Burchett.

Burchett seems to have been a straightforward man, and to have had such *faith*, in the Chinese in particular, as to have believed them incapable of serious evil.[174] This is not to imply that he played some overt intelligence or propaganda role on their behalf. He was, however, caught up in events of enormous moment and steered his course according to the faith he had developed – the *a priori* belief that there was an identifiable pattern to the flow of history and that the Soviet, Chinese, Korean (and later Vietnamese) revolutions were part of a general process of human liberation which deserved his full support.

The further he ventured away from reporting what he himself had actually seen or knew from his own experience to be true, the less reliable he became. Burchett's reporting on the East European political trials of the late 1940s is discussed elsewhere in this volume. In Korea, he was not only quite unsceptical about the confessions by US airmen but had no comment to make when a significant section of the North Korean leadership (actually *South* Korean in origin) was tried and executed in a well-publicized purge that began in 1953, while Burchett was in the country. The accused were sentenced on scarcely credible charges of having spied for *both* the Japanese in the 1930s *and* the Americans before and during the Korean War.[175] Furthermore, as the cult of the 'great leader', Kim Il Sung, grew increasingly feverish and his control of party and state was consolidated through a series of subsequent purges, Burchett continued to visit Pyongyang.[176] He gave no indication that he found anything untoward there and indeed praised Kim Il Sung's 'success in imposing his own style of work at all levels in party, government, factory, and farm management'.[177] His account of those events which he did not himself witness – and that includes the history of the Korean revolution and events preceding the outbreak of the war on the one hand, and the process of post-war reconstruction and the development of the institutions of the North Korean state on the other – tends to correspond precisely with the official line of the regime at that time, not surprisingly since he recounted what he was told. Though he finds much worthy of praise in the internal affairs of Korea (and other 'socialist' countries), he avoided any criticism, and his writing on such matters was of limited use as a result.[178] Perhaps this stems from the faith that constituted the well-springs of his life as a journalist and writer – faith in the essentially progressive orientation of history and in the basic correctness of *all* anti-fascist and anti-imperialist forces.

However, the reservations about how Burchett's work should finally be assessed in the scales of history do not touch the issues upon which he has been attacked by critics like Warner, particularly the allegations of 'brainwashing' and interrogation of prisoners, and ultimately the allegation of treason. Warner's allegations of 1967 in particular were extraordinarily influential. They were repeated in 1969 by the New South Wales branch of the Returned Servicemen's League (RSL), which called for Burchett to be tried for treason since he was 'in the same camp as Lord Haw Haw and Tokyo Rose',[179] and they were a staple in many of the attacks on Burchett's reputation launched right up until his death in 1983. With the release of the affidavits by the Australian government in 1984–85, it is clear that there is no more to the anti-Burchett case than was presented in court in Sydney in 1974; and that Burchett's integrity stands unimpugned.

Burchett in the Official War History

Even after his death in 1983, Burchett continued to excite outrage and hatred among influential quarters in Australia because of his Korean War activities. This was most conspicuous in the second volume of the official Australian history of the war, published in 1985 by the Australian War Memorial and the Australian Government Publishing Service.[180] Robert O'Neill, author of this study, enjoyed the full co-operation of all relevant government departments and archives in its preparation, and he describes the work as 'my major research project for nine years'.[181] Yet the most remarkable feature of the treatment of Burchett in O'Neill's study is that, while many of the accusations that had been launched against Burchett over the previous thirty years are repeated, not one shred of evidence is drawn from the government's files and archives to support them. This lack of concern for truth, or of interest in the quality of evidence, has long marked the anti-Burchett cause.

In neither volume of the study are Burchett's general writings on the war, the negotiations, the issue of bacteriological warfare, or the treatment of prisoners actually analysed. His work is dismissed with a brief contemptuous reference.[182] The discussion of Burchett's role is confined to Chapter 23 of the second volume of the book, 'The Australian Prisoners of War', which is written not by O'Neill himself but by Brigadier P.F. Greville. Greville's main contention is that Burchett functioned not as a journalist but as 'part of the Chinese Prisoner-of-War Administration Command' in North Korea.[183]

Greville writes that when Burchett met the Australian POWs Buck, Hollis, Parker and Gwyther, on the occasion already discussed at length, '[H]e was wearing, as he often did, the uniform of a Chinese army officer – without the badges of an officer but with the trappings of office.'[184] No source is given for this information, but since these are very close to the words used in the 1974 trial by Corporal Buck it seems he is relying on records of that trial. Why then does Greville not reveal that Buck is the only one of the four to make such a claim, and that, under questioning, he went on to explain that what he meant was the kind of clothing worn by 'civilians a little above the rank of coolie'?[185] And elsewhere in the government files he might have noted Private Gwyther's recollection, of the same occasion, that Burchett was in 'civilian clothes'. The evidence in 1974 was contradictory on this point, and the only other witness who made this allegation was the American, Colonel Mahurin, who is on record as making two statements, both that he did *not* see whether there were any insignia on Burchett's clothing and that he *did* and the star denoting (Chinese) officer rank was present.[186] The official history demonstrates scant concern for historical truth in the way it treats such an important point; the long Australian government denigration of Burchett continues.

Greville also repeats the 1974 Derek Kinne allegations, the 'I can have you shot' story,[187] apparently unaware of the discrepancies between Kinne's 1974 evidence and the account of his POW experiences which he published in 1955, and of the fact that the Burchett encounter is not mentioned at all in the detailed account of Kinne's POW experiences published by the British Ministry of Defence, also in 1955.[188] Kinne's 1974 evidence to the effect that Burchett's POW camp lecture in 1952 was greeted by prisoners shouting 'You'll hang, you bastard,' has a 1955 version in the British government paper, save that here it is alleged of a completely different man, the *Daily Worker* correspondent, Alan Winnington.[189]

On the bacteriological warfare issue, Greville writes that all four Americans (Quinn, Enoch, O'Neal and Kniss) who made 'confessions' to the International Scientific Commission in 1952, allege editing of their confessions by Burchett for purposes of making a propaganda film, and claims that 'as the four Americans testified', Burchett sat at the ISC table, where he read out the confessions and directed the questioning.[190] Actually only Kniss testified to this effect in court, although O'Neal and Enoch included the allegation in their 'debriefing' sessions in 1953. Two comments, however, are in order. Burchett believed that he was witnessing an escalation of warfare by methods comparable to those he had witnessed in Hiroshima. The scientific credentials of the members of the commission were impressive, and presumably Burchett would have felt no hesitation in offering it his assistance had it been asked for. Second, however, the most eminent member of the ISC, Dr Joseph Needham of Cambridge University, asked about this in 1984, could not recall Burchett having been present at the hearings at all, much less playing any central role in them,[191] although, as noted above, Burchett insists that he did occasionally interpret (from French) for the commission.[192]

Greville's claim that Burchett had the power to influence the Chinese and North Koreans so as to achieve an improvement in POW conditions, but chose to exercise it only if prisoners accepted Chinese demands,[193] is repudiated by a US general, no less, in a book which Greville and O'Neill must have known but decided to ignore, *General Dean's Story*. Greville's claim that Burchett 'exploited the mail services in the same way as the Chinese did, carrying mail for those prisoners who co-operated with their captors but not for others',[194] is contradicted by testimony from the Australian prisoners stating that he made the offer to post mail for them even after they had abused him and threatened to kill him, but the offer was refused.[195] And, although Greville alleges that Burchett fed deliberately misleading information to prisoners 'to shatter the faith of prisoners in their own Western leadership',[196] Paul Kniss, for one, told the court that he had initiated the correspondence with Burchett in order to find out what was happening in the world, and that from Burchett he learnt news of Eisenhower's election and of the course of the peace negotiations. As for Burchett's alleged role in 'concocting' confessions, we have already noted that Kniss told the court that what he meant by describing Burchett's account as 'a bunch of damned lies' was that he, Kniss, had told Burchett a 'bunch of lies' which Burchett had simply reported.

For Greville and O'Neill to make no mention of all of this is at best disingenuous. Their account would not be worth discussing were it not for the fact that it issues from such an 'authoritative' source and that it demonstrates so starkly the crudity and carelessness that has marked the powerfully orchestrated campaign to denigrate Burchett for over thirty years. What this official history, with the privilege of free access to the archives and nine years of government sponsorship, has given us is not scientific fact but vituperation of the character of a man who can no longer defend himself.

It is, as Brigadier Greville tells us in the context of US soldiers' confessions to bacteriological warfare, 'difficult for the average Australian to understand how someone would confess to doing something which he had not done';[197] it is, however, no less difficult for the average Australian to understand why a fellow citizen should be persistently accused of the gravest of crimes on the basis of a shoddy piece of argument like this, with the victim persistently denied the right to clear his name or have the evidence fairly scrutinized, even posthumously.

Whether the interests of Australian POWs, who undoubtedly suffered greatly in Korea, are somehow advanced (as Greville suggests) by squeezing from the record whatever may be thought appropriate to the cause of blackening Burchett's name may be doubted. One may even wonder whether the POWs, and the Australians who died in Korea, would have gone to fight in Korea at all had they been able to read Burchett's writings, and hear them honestly debated, *at the time*, instead of merely the official propaganda about Soviet communist plans for world conquest. Ironically, it was Burchett alone of Australians who, *during the war*, offered the kind of assessment at which official Australia arrived thirty years later: that it was a war to which Australian troops were committed in order to please the United States.[198]

Bacteriological Warfare (BW)

Burchett is also accused of having invented the whole bacteriological warfare (BW) or 'germ-warfare' story. According to Colonel Mahurin, it was Burchett who provided the Chinese with the idea of mobilizing their people and discrediting the enemy through allegations of BW on the basis of a 1903 Jack London story.[199] How Mahurin became party to such information he does not reveal. Warner too looks to a Jack London story for the origin of the campaign, though it is a '1914' story called 'The Unparalleled Invasion' which he identifies.[200] Burchett, he notes ominously, was 'a known admirer of Jack London'.

Denis Warner points to a reference to 'germ warfare' in the introduction to Burchett's book *China's Feet Unbound*, dated July 1951. This date, Warner believes, is significant because it is earlier than the main Korean War allegations, and because the book links the allegations against the United States in Korea to the earlier, Japanese germ warfare against China and the Soviet Union. Warner sees Burchett's writing as part of a process of planned 'communist propaganda penetration of the non-communist world'. In this, as in much of his pamphlet, he is simply rehashing (without acknowledging) a book by John Clews, *Communist Propaganda Techniques* (Methuen, London) published in 1964.[201]

In his evidence in 1974, Burchett was puzzled by the July 1951 date. He thought he could not have written the introduction before 1952, and that therefore the date in the book must have been wrong.[202] However, *even if* the July 1951 date is correct, the fact would not seem to be very significant.

Allegations of the use of BW were made *by both sides* in the Korean War from late 1950. From March 1951, communists specifically linked the US to Japanese BW work in China during World War Two, and the

North Korean Foreign Ministry made formal protest to the chairman of the United Nations Security Council in a letter dated 8 May 1951.[203]

The BW issue is contentious and has been discussed at length elsewhere.[204] Several general points can be made here. Japan *did* engage in BW against China in the late 1930s and early 1940s and some of the most extraordinary and shocking atrocities of the entire Second World War were committed at the principal Japanese BW station at Harbin in China. At the end of the war, the principals of the Japanese operation were given immunity from prosecution by US authorities in return for handing over all their secrets. For twenty-five years the US covered up this deal. It denounced as propaganda the trials, held in the Soviet Union in 1949, of other members of the Japanese unit. Warner, in his 1977 attack on Burchett, continued to cast doubt on the authenticity of the evidence produced in these trials.

In 1980, however, a fully documented study upholding the evidence in all major particulars was published in the US,[205] based on materials obtained from the US government under the Freedom of Information Act, and admissions of guilt by key members of the unit were published in Japan.[206] Early in 1983 it was revealed that the US had acquired not only the Japanese but also the Nazi germ-warfare-programme secrets. In a similar deal, the head of the German unit, Schreiber, was also given immunity and protection in the US.[207] That these things happened has been part of the North Korean case since the Korean War.[208] Yet its charges were ignored or ridiculed in the West. Warner is but one of the most recent of a line of writers who rejected it all as absurd and as merely a part of 'communist propaganda'. His attempts to represent Burchett as the initiator of a false propaganda campaign by the communist world collapses: the allegations of bacteriological warfare pre-date anything written by Burchett about them, and the Soviet trials have been proved true in every detail – if anything, the revelations published in Japan and the United States in recent years are even *more* shocking than those which emerged from the Soviet trials. On the Japanese crimes and the US purchase and cover-up of the entire Japanese programme, both crimes and criminals, Burchett and the North Koreans and Chinese were right; Warner and Clews were wrong.

That the US government lied to cover up its acquisition of these Nazi and Japanese secrets does not necessarily mean it also lied in denying its own use of BW in Korea; but it does mean that the allegations deserve very careful scrutiny and it is not enough simply to throw scorn on them. BW research began in the US as early as 1941, and the military possibilities it presented were enthusiastically and publicly proclaimed by senior officers of the US Army both before and during the Korean War. Supplies of nerve gas, subject to similar international constraints as BW, were *prepared* for use in Korea and that option was seriously considered in 1950–51; germ-warfare tests were carried out, with some casualties, in the US itself later in 1950.[209] The United States refused until 1975 to become party to the Geneva Convention which banned both bacteriological and chemical weapons.

The headquarters of the US programme for BW, whether or not one believes it was merely a research programme, were at Fort Detrick in Maryland. Both in his prison confession in Korea *and later*, upon his return to the US, Colonel Mahurin (one of the main witnesses against Burchett) admitted his connection with the Fort Detrick establishment.[210]

This should be sufficient to indicate that the BW case is one worthy of careful examination on its merits and is far from inherently implausible. Burchett's conviction that BW was being waged was based initially on reports he heard from China and Korea, and corroborated by the US confessions. It was then reinforced by his own direct observation of what he was convinced was a direct BW raid, on the Yalu River on 6 June 1952,[211] and by the experience of interviewing a black US soldier who, 'expressing his patriotic disbelief in "germ warfare"' picked up and swallowed a fly which dropped over his POW camp and the following day collapsed with high fever and the general symptoms of pulmonary anthrax.[212] Expert scientific opinion seemed also to support the charges and Burchett conferred at length with the members of the International Scientific Commission on the question.

Unpopularity with the US military authorities in Japan in 1945 did not deter Burchett from issuing his famous 'Warning to the World' on nuclear weapons after his unique personal observation of Hiroshima. It was quite in character for Burchett, while covering the peace.talks in Korea, to have recognized the importance of the BW story and to have devoted himself to pursuing all journalistic leads which came to him – from on-the-spot investigation and discussion with witnesses and experts to interviews with those who had confessed to being perpetrators. Throughout, there is no satisfactory evidence to indicate that his integrity or his status as an independent investigative journalist was in any way compromised. Whether in the end he was correct or not in the conclusion he drew from the evidence that came to him – and the question remains unresolved – he had to report it.

Conclusion

That Burchett interrogated, brainwashed, or tortured Australian, American or British prisoners of war, or that he fabricated and then disseminated propaganda on behalf of China, North Korea or, for that matter, the Soviet Union, is completely unproven and highly improbable, though such charges lay at the heart of official Australia's long feud with him and are still widely believed in other Western countries too. Burchett's real 'crime', it seems, was that he chose to report the peace talks and POW issue *from the other side*, as a journalist whose accreditation came from the Press Department of the Chinese Ministry of Foreign Affairs, and that the substance of what he reported was diametrically opposed to the way the political and military leadership of the West saw the war and tried, falsely, to present it.

Perhaps the most persuasive opinion is that of General William Dean, the most senior of all US (and UN) prisoners in North Korea, and a man who saw a great deal of Wilfred Burchett during the war. Dean's assessment is that Burchett was a decent man whom, despite deep differences of opinion, he later proclaimed publicly as 'my friend'.

Burchett was a journalist inspired by an uncommon moral passion. When all the false, garbled and malicious stories of his activities in Korea are discounted, what remains is the portrait of an honest man who tried to tell the truth, who was almost alone in seeing the war primarily from the viewpoint of the suffering Korean people rather than that of the 'Great Powers' or his own or any other government, and who, by helping to crack the censorship and lies which other journalists propagated whenever they were told to do so by 'responsible military headquarters',[213] may well have helped shorten the war.

In spite of the contradictions, unsupported allegations, and proven falsities of so much of the case against Burchett, two years after his death, and one year after the publication of a brief digest of some of the points in this chapter, the accusation that he was a traitor and a KGB agent was renewed amid massive publicity. It is the phenomenon of which Sir Robert Menzies once wrote: 'But, as so often happens in life, the picturesque slander outlives the sober answer.'[214]

Acknowledgements

Many people have helped me, in particular ways, in preparing this article. The contribution by Jon Halliday, however, in directing my attention to obscure sources or in commenting critically on my manuscript, has been of exceptional importance. The chapter could not have been written without his help, for which I am extremely grateful. Officials in various Australian government departments, especially in the Department of Foreign Affairs and the Australian Archives, have also been extremely generous in helping me locate and gain access to official records. Mr Roy F. Turner, of Turner Freeman, Solicitors, Sydney, allowed me to peruse his copy of the transcript of the 1974 New South Wales case of Burchett *vs* Kane. Mr Winston Burchett provided access to family papers. I am grateful to all. For inadvertent errors, however, whether in materials or their interpretation, I am alone responsible.

Notes

1. Robert O'Neill, *Australia in the Korean War 1950–53, vol 1. Strategy and Diplomacy*, the Australian War Memorial and Australian Government Publishing Service, Canberra, 1981, p. 76.
2. *Burchett vs Kane*, Supreme Court of New South Wales, Common Law Division, No. 193 of 1973, 21 October – 2 November 1974, p. 212. This case, which is discussed in detail below, was not entered in the official law reports and is therefore available in full only in transcript form. For preparation of this article I am indebted to Mr Roy F. Turner, of Turner Freeman Solicitors, Sydney, solicitors for Mr Burchett in 1974, for the opportunity to refer to his copy of the transcript (cited hereafter as Transcript). The case was extensively, but far from exhaustively, reported in the Australian press at the time. Probably the best published coverage is to be found in *Sydney Morning Herald*, 23 October – 2 November 1974. The judgement of the Court of Appeal (20 May 1976) was eventually reported in *New South Wales Law Reports*, 1980, vol. 2, pp. 266–80.

  3. Ibid., p. 199.
  4. Wilfred Burchett, letter to Melbourne *Age*, 16 March 1970; also Transcript, p. 197.
  5. Ibid.
  6. Transcript, pp. 210, 220ff.
  7. Ibid., p. 220.
  8. See Bruce Cumings, *The Origins of the Korean War: Liberation and the Emergence of Separate Regimes, 1945–1947*, Princeton University Press, 1981; and Gavan McCormack, *Cold War Hot War: An Australian Perspective on the Korean War*, Hale and Iremonger, Sydney, 1983, and references there.
  9. *Koje Unscreened* is by Burchett and Winnington; *Plain Perfidy* is by Winnington and Burchett.
 10. Information from Mr Joe Waters, private communication, 1 January 1984.
 11. Quoted in Sydney D. Bailey, *How Wars End: the United Nations and the Termination of Armed Conflict, 1946–1964*, Clarendon Press, Oxford, 1982, 2 vols, vol. 2, p. 434.
 12. Barton J. Bernstein, 'The Struggle over the Korean Armistice: Prisoners of Repatriation?', in Bruce Cumings, ed., *Child of Conflict: the Korean-American Relationship 1945–1953*, University of Washington Press, Seattle and London, 1983, p. 268.
 13. Ibid., pp. 269, 296.
 14. Matthew Ridgway, *The Korean War*, Doubleday, Garden City, New York, 1967, pp. 201, 204.
 15. Allen E. Goodman, *Negotiating While Fighting: the Diary of Admiral C. Turner Joy*, Hoover Institution, Stanford, 1978, pp. 5, 436.
 16. General Mark Clark, *From the Danube to the Yalu*, Harrap, London, 1954, pp. 14, 104.
 17. Truman, 27 January 1952, quoted in Bernstein, op. cit., p. 290.
 18. Goodman, op. cit., p. 437.
 19. Burchett, *Again Korea*, New York, 1968, p. 33.
 20. Bernstein, op. cit., pp. 265, 296.
 21. Evan Luard, *A History of the United Nations, vol. 1, The Years of Western Domination*, 1945–1955, Macmillan, London, 1982, p. 263. See also Goodman, op. cit., pp. 16 ff.
 22. See, for example, *New York Times*, 2 August 1951.
 23. *Again Korea*, p. 34.
 24. Bailey, op. cit., vol. 2, p. 439; Luard, op. cit., p. 263.
 25. *Again Korea*, p. 35.
 26. Dean Acheson, *The Korean War*, New York, 1969, p. 125.
 27. *Again Korea*, p. 43.
 28. Ibid.; also Bailey, op. cit., pp. 436–7, Goodman, op. cit., pp. 41–2.
 29. I.F. Stone, *The Hidden History of the Korean War*, New York, 1952, pp. 293–4.
 30. *New York Times*, 8 November 1951.
 31. Phillip Knightley, *The First Casualty: the War Correspondent as Hero, Propagandist, and Myth Maker, from the Crimea to Vietnam*, Deutsch, London, 1975, p. 353; also *Again Korea*, p. 54. And see despatch by Sidney Brooks, Reuter's Tokyo bureau chief, in *Again Korea*, p. 61.
 32. According to an Associated Press despatch of 2 December, quoted in David Conde, *Chosen Gendaishi* (Contemporary History of Korea), Tokyo, 1971, 3 vols, vol.2, p. 385.
 33. Knightley, op. cit., p. 353.
 34. *New York Times*, 12 November 1951.
 35. For the evidence, see McCormack, op. cit., pp. 142–6.
 36. Burchett, *Passport, An Autobiography*, Nelson, Melbourne, 1969, p. 194; *Again Korea* pp. 62–3.
 37. William L. White, *The Captives of Korea: An Unofficial White Paper on the Treatment of War Prisoners*, Charles Scribner's Sons, New York, 1957, pp. 218ff.
 38. *Passport*, p. 203.
 40. Ibid., p. 191.
 41. Ibid., p. 194.

42. Peking Radio of 24, 25, 26 May, quoted in Denis Warner, *The Germ Warfare Hoax*, Seoul, 1977, p. 21. See also BBC *Summary of World Broadcasts*, Part 5 (Far East), No. 162, 27 May 1952, p. 29.
43. Burchett, *This Monstrous War*, 1953, pp. 300–1. The text of the broadcasts, recorded by US intelligence in Japan, is preserved in Australian Archives, CRS A6119, attachment to item 13.
44. Letter of 2 February 1969, Burchett Papers, in the La Trobe Collection, State Library of Victoria, Melbourne, (hereafter 'Burchett Papers').
45. *Honest John: The Autobiography of Walker M. Mahurin*, G.L. Putnam's Sons, New York, 1962, p. 244.
46. Transcript, p. 212.
47. Knightley, op. cit., p. 354; *Again Korea*, pp. 62 ff.
48. For a brief description of camp life written by Noel, see Chinese People's Committee for World Peace, *United Nations' POWs in Korea*, Peking, 1953, pp. 6 ff. Many of Noel's photographs are also collected in this book. The 'Inter-Camp Olympic Games' of November 1952 is given extensive coverage.
49. Robert Eunson, Chief of Tokyo bureau of Associated Press, to ASIO, n.d. (November 1953). AA A6119, XR1, 14.
50. *Again Korea*, pp. 62–3; *Koje Unscreened*, pp. 142–3.
51. Knightley, op. cit., p. 354.
52. *Time*, 28 February 1952; see also Knightley, op. cit., p. 355.
53. Material in this paragraph from Australian Archives Vic, MP 729/8, Dept of the Army, Classified Correspondence files, 1945–1957 File No. 66/431/25. (My thanks to Richard Glenister for drawing my attention to this file.)
54. R.J. O'Neill, *Australia in the Korean War 1950–53, vol. II, Combat Operations*, Canberra, 1985, p. 533 (Hereafter 'O'Neill II'.)
55. White, op. cit., passim; Hal Vetter, *Mutiny on Koje Island*, Charles Tuttle, Rutland, Vermont, and Tokyo, 1965, pp. 43–4, 83ff, 137, 201–2.
56. Lawrence S. Wittner, 'The Truman Doctrine and the Defence of Freedom', *Diplomatic History*, 4, Spring 1980, quoted in Noam Chomsky, *Towards a New Cold War*, Pantheon, New York, 1981, p. 198.
57. Demaree Bess, *Saturday Evening Post*, 1 November 1952, quoted in *Koje Unscreened*, p. 2.
58. Bailey, op. cit., vol. 2, p. 446; see also vol. 1, p. 311.
59. Geneva Convention, 1949, Article 128, see Bailey, op. cit., vol 2, p. 443.
60. Luard, op. cit., p. 264.
61. Quoted in McCormack, op. cit., p. 123.
62. Quoted in Bernstein, op. cit., p. 285.
63. *Koje Unscreened*, Peking, April 1953.
64. See note 37, above.
65. See note 55, above.
66. White, op. cit., p. 111.
67. On this point, see also General Mark Clark, op. cit., p. 57.
68. International Red Cross report, August 1951, quoted Vetter, op. cit., p. 64.
69. International Committee of Red Cross reports, Vetter, op. cit., pp. 77, 176–7; see also Alan Winnington, *Daily Worker*, 17 May 1952.
70. This episode is commonly referred to as the 'release' of prisoners. (See, for example General Mark Clark, op. cit., p. 263, or Bailey, op. cit., vol. 2, pp. 463–4.) However no explanation is offered for how sixty-one people, the official figure, could have been killed resisting 'release'. Alan Winnington's account is in *Daily Worker*, 19–22 June 1953.
71. Bailey, op. cit., p. 455.
72. References below are to *Koje Unscreened* unless otherwise indicated.
73. Ibid., p. 39.
74. Ibid., p. 134.
75. Ibid., p. 140.
76. *Plain Perfidy*, Peking, 1954, pp. 88–98.
77. *Koje Unscreened*, p. 129.
78. *Plain Perfidy*, p. 15.

79. White, op. cit., pp. 234, 217.

80. Bernstein, op. cit., p. 307.

81. *The Korean Question – Reports of the Neutral Nations Repatriation Commission*, covering the period 9 September 1953 to 21 February 1954, General Assembly Official Records, Supplement No. 18, A/2641, New York, 1954 (hereafter *NNRC*), p. 108; also at White, op. cit., p. 317.

82. Ibid., p. 5; also at Bailey, op. cit., p. 471, White, op. cit., p. 325, *Koje Unscreened*, p. 236.

83. *NNRC*, p. 15.

84. The fate of some of these forcibly tattooed prisoners who got through the net and were able to escape back to China was doubly tragic: they were imprisoned in China as Nationalist agents. See Bao Ruo-wang (Jean Pasqualini) and Jean Chelminski, *Prisoner of Mao*, Penguin, 1976, pp. 161–4.

85. Bailey, op. cit., p. 469.

86. White, op. cit., p. 269.

87. *NNRC*, pp. 15, 90–1.

88. The *Guardian* (New York), 16 November 1977. (See also ibid. for 30 November.)

89. John Hamilton, reporting from Washington in the *Herald* (Melbourne), 27 and 28 December 1977.

90. Cablegram, Top Secret, 7 September 1953. Declassified January 1985. Australian Archives (AA), CRS A1838, item 131/6.

91. Department of External Affairs (Alan Watt), Top Secret cable to Embassy in Tokyo, 10 September 1953, ibid.

92. These officers arrived in Tokyo on 3 November. Ibid., passim.

93. Ronald Monson, of the *Daily Telegraph*, Sydney, gave a resumé of the Hastings article to an ASIO officer in an interview dated 25 October 1953. Though the wording of the *US News and World Report* article is slightly different, the substance is identical. For the Monson interview, see AA, CRS A6119/XR1, item 13.

94. Watt, memo of 16 October 1953, declassified 27 March 1985 by Ministry of Foreign Affairs.

95. File memo from Solicitor General, 23 October 1953, AA, CRS 1838, item 131/6.

96. *The Herald*, 5 October 1951.

97. AA CRS 1984, 460 XR1 (Department of Immigration file).

98. Bruce Ruxton, *The Australian*, 4 October 1983; Frank Knopfelmacher, 'Traitor Burchett', *Quadrant*, November 1983; Anthony McAdam, Melbourne *Herald*, 7 October 1983; Brigadier P. J. Greville, *Pacific Defence Reporter*, November 1983.

99. Sir Ronald East, *A South Australian Colonist and his Descendants: the East Family*, Melbourne, 1976, p. 285.

100. Transcript.

101. As Burchett pointed out (the *Guardian*, New York, 16 November 1977) Krotkov's evidence attracted little attention in Washington, partly because of the improbability of some of the accusations. Not only Burchett, but also a number of French, Indian, and Canadian diplomats, the philosopher Jean-Paul Sartre and even John Kenneth Galbraith, the economist, were all named as KGB agents. On these matters see my article 'An Australian Dreyfus?', *Australian Society*, August 1984, and *Appendix*.

102. Interview with Kane, the *Australian*, 2 November 1974.

103. Transcript, p. 32.

104. Ibid., p. 239.

105. 'Summing-up', Transcript, p. 56.

106. New South Wales Court of Appeal, 30 May 1976, decision of Samuels, J.A., Mahoney, J.A., and Moffit, P. (Transcript).

107. Ibid.

108. The *Argus*, Weekender, 19 September 1953. (The five-part series of articles was published on 22 and 29 August, 5, 12 and 19 September 1953.)

109. Wilfred Burchett, letter to Winston Burchett (his brother), 26 December 1968.

110. Transcript, p. 147.

111. Burchett, *Passport*, pp. 200–1, also letter to Winston Burchett (his brother), 26 December 1968, Burchett Papers.

112. Sir Ronald East, *More Australian Pioneers: the Burchetts, and related families,*

Australian Family Who's Who, vol. 3, Melbourne, 1976, pp. 167–8.
113. AA, CRS A6119, XR1, item 13.
114. East, op. cit., p. 168.
115. David Gourlay, 'The Burchett Affair 1955–1972', BA Honours thesis, University of New South Wales, 1980, p. 30. Despite the complaints of the POW spokesman, Hollis, about camp food and conditions, he himself was healthy and strong enough to have been a member of the winning tug-of-war team at the POW Inter-Camp Olympics of November 1952. See photograph in Chinese People's Committee for World Peace, *United Nations' POWs in Korea*, Peking, 1953, p. 87.
116. AA, CRS A6119, item 13 and 14.
117. Ibid.
118. Transcript, pp. 38, 214.
119. AA, CRS A6119, item 14.
120. Hansard, Senate, 7 May 1970, p. 1201.
121. Transcript, p. 172.
122. Ibid., p. 215.
123. This description from letter cited in note 109 above. Published accounts of the incident in Burchett's *Democracy with a Tommygun*, 1946, pp. 278–80, and report by Brisbane *Courier-Mail* correspondent, Jim Vine, on 11 September 1945, reproduced in Harry Gordon, ed., *An Eye-Witness History of Australia*, Rigby, 1976, p. 364.
124. White, op. cit.; Eugene Kinkead, *Why they Collaborated*, Longmans, London, 1960 (in US under title *In Every War But One*, Norton, New York, 1959).
125. White, op. cit., p. 168. Another study, Albert D. Biderman's *March to Calumny: the story of American POW's in the Korean War,* Macmillan, New York and London, 1963, makes no reference to Burchett save as author.
126. The fact that Burchett possessed a transcript of Kniss's confession, to which Kniss in 1974 attributed significance, seems neither here nor there since any journalist would surely type up his copy of such an important document as soon as shown it.
127. Transcript, p. 72; also Denis Warner, *The Germ Warfare Hoax*, UN Korean War Allies Association, Seoul, December 1977, p. 40.
128. 'Communist Intelligence and Propaganda Activities of Wilfred C. Burchett and Allan (sic) Winnington', US Army Intelligence Report undated (1954?), contained in the ASIO file, AA CRS 6119, XR1, item 15.
129. Attorney-General Herbert Brownell, quoted in *New York Times*, 15 August 1953.
130. Quoted in Stephen L. Endicott, 'Germ Warfare and "Plausible Denial": the Korean War 1950–1953', *Modern China*, vol. 5, No. 1 January 1979, p. 100.
131. Kinkead, op. cit., p. 161.
132. Knightley, op. cit., p. 351.
133. Robert J. Lifton, *Thought Reform and the Psychology of Totalism*, Norton, New York, 1961, p. 6.
134. Cited in James Aronson, *The Press and the Cold War*, Beacon, Boston, 1970, p.124.
135. Transcript, pp. 85–91.
136. AA, CRS A6119, item 15.
137. Transcript, p. 172.
138. Letter to Winston Burchett, 16 February 1969. Burchett Papers.
139. *Daily Worker*, 7 September 1953.
140. Report by Joseph S. Carusi. AA, CRS A6119, item 13.
141. *Honest John* (see note 45, above).
142. Mahurin, letter in *Aviation Week and Space Technology*, 4 September 1972.
143. Court evidence. Transcript, 1974.
144. Anthony McAdam, the *Herald* (Melbourne), 7 October 1983.
145. Transcript, pp. 93, 102, 19. An even more blatant example of misrepresentation of the Transcript record is the article by Stephen Morris 'Debunking the Burchett Legend', published in New York in *Commentary* and reproduced in Sydney in the *Bulletin*, 17 November 1981. According to Morris, three Australian POWs and Mahurin had all testified that Burchett wore Chinese officer uniform in Korea. He is totally wrong about the Australians and only half right, ignoring the accompanying statement to the opposite effect, about Mahurin.
146. Statement dated 11 November 1953. AA CRS A6119, XR1, item 14.

147. James Lloyd Greenfield of *Time-Life*, who covered the talks continuously save for the period March to November 1952.
148. Keyes Beech of *Chicago Daily News*. Ibid.
149. Eric Britter of *The Times*. Ibid.
150. State Department briefing by Mr Hodding Carter III, 21 November 1977, and letter from Mr Kenneth Brown, Deputy Director, Office of Press Relations, Department of State, to Mr Abe Weisburd of the *Guardian* newspaper in New York, 29 November 1977.
151. London, HMSO, 1955.
152. Ibid., p. 27.
153. Ibid., p. 26.
154. Ian Stewart (then of AAP-Reuter), *Sydney Morning Herald*, 6 August 1985.
155. See story on Kinne family in *Daily Worker*, 14 June 1952.
156. Statement of 2 November 1953. AA, CRS A6119, item 13.
157. Quoted in Robert Manne, 'The Fortunes of Wilfred Burchett', *Quadrant*, August 1985, p. 28.
158. Shann memo dated 9 May 1955, Ministry of Foreign Affairs, file number 131/6, released in May 1984.
159. The *Reporter*, New York, 1 June 1967; *Quadrant*, July–August 1967.
160. The words 're-education' and 'indoctrination' are used.
161. Kinkead, op. cit., p. 125.
162. For various details of ill-treatment, see the British Ministry of Defence paper cited above, or Kinkead or White. The only place in which Burchett is positively accused of having 'systematically . . . tortured captive American airmen' is the introduction to Warner's 1977 Seoul text, cited above.
163. Warner, *Quadrant*, 1967, p. 73.
164. See his article in *Sunday Telegraph* (Sydney), 1 March 1970.
165. Tom Lambert, *New York Times*, 26 February 1967.
166. Cedric Belfrage and James Aronson, *Something to Guard: The Stormy Life of the National Guardian 1948–1967*, Columbia University Press, 1978, p. 193.
167. Burchett to Reverend J. Lloyd, letter, 8 February 1969. Burchett Papers.
168. 'Burchett's brazen court maneuver', *Tactics* (Arlington, Virginia), vol. 8, no. 2, February 1971, p. 12.
169. Kinkead, op. cit., pp. 160–1.
170. See Solzhenitsyn, Bao Ruo-wang (on Mao's China), Andrew Veitch ('Rebels who Repent in the Ayatollah's dungeons', *Guardian Weekly*, 11 Decmeber 1983) on Iran and, more surprisingly, on contemporary Japan, Igarashi Futaba, 'Koshite "jihaku" saserareta' (Forced to Confess), *Sekai* (Toyko), February 1984, pp. 220–32. (For my translation of the latter, see *Law in Context* La Trobe University, No. 2, 1984.)
171. Kinkead, op. cit., p. 161. .
172. See discussion below.
173. Transcript, p. 168 (and for Burchett's representations on behalf of ordinary POWs, p. 211).
174. This is partly a general impression from an extensive reading of Burchett's writing, but it also appears impossible to account for some of his statements except by such a faith. See for example the following statement, from a letter to his father, from Peking, 16 April 1951 (in the Burchett Papers): 'There is such humanity and beauty in life here, such tolerance and understanding that I feel very small and conscious of my inability to express what is going on. I would do anything at all for these people and their government because they represent the fullest flowering of all the finest instincts of humanity.' See Chapter 7.
175. For discussion of this episode see, for example, Koon Woo Nam, *The North Korean Communist Leadership*, University of Alabama Press, 1974, pp. 92ff.
176. Burchett visited North Korea in 1967, 1973, 1975 and 1980.
177. *Again Korea*, p. 105.
178. *In private*, Burchett's dismay at the trend of developments was clear. After a visit to North Korea in 1980 he wrote to his brother: 'Korea was exasperating. They have done such remarkable things on the economic, social fronts – and in the arts – but the ever-growing cult of the personality is nauseating, if not frightening' (Letter, 23

October 1980, Burchett Papers).
179. *Age*, Melbourne, 10 February 1969.
180. O'Neill II (see note 54, above).
181. Ibid., I, p. xvii.
182. 'Utterly biased and thoroughly unreliable'. O'Neill II, p. 567.
183. Ibid., p. 564.
184. Ibid., p. 566.
185. See discussion of this point above.
186. See above.
187. See above.
188. See discussion above.
189. See my article 'An Australian Dreyfus; A Re-examination of the Strange Case against Wilfred Burchett, Journalist', *Australian Society*, 1 August 1984, pp. 8–9.
190. O'Neill II, p. 564.
191. Interview with Jon Halliday, Cambridge, 8 May 1984.
192. See above.
193. O'Neill II, p. 566.
194. Ibid., p. 566.
195. Transcript, passim.
196. O'Neill II, p. 567.
197. Ibid., p. 564.
198. Ibid, vol. I, p. 76 ('primarily in the interests of Australian–American diplomacy').
199. White, for example, accepts this. See pp. 218ff.
200. Warner, 1977, pp. 52–3. London's story 'The Unparalleled Invasion' seems actually to have been published in 1910 (*McClure's*, vol. 35, May–October 1910, pp. 308–14).
201. Ibid, p. 13, also pp. 46, 52. Here, as in so much of what he has written, Warner displays a shockingly cavalier attitude to accuracy. In what he borrows from Clews he mixes up the Soviet and Polish navies; he gets the title of a book of Burchett's wrong in several places, misquotes from one book and actually makes up a quote in another. On page 48 he includes a passage described as a quotation from Burchett's *This Monstrous War* which begins: 'Obviously after the war was over . . .' and goes on to describe how the US airmen who confessed to bacteriological warfare crimes later blamed Burchett and Alan Winnington of the London *Daily Worker* for inventing the story. Yet *This Monstrous War* not only does not contain any such quotation; it could not, since it was published before the war had ended and before the POWs were exchanged.
    However tedious it may be to recount the errors, carelessness and fabrications in Warner's writing, the exercise is nevertheless important, for it is upon precisely such foundations that the international campaign to destroy the reputation and the credibility of Wilfred Burchett was built.
202. Transcript, p. 201.
203. See, for example, Albert E. Cowdrey, '"Germ Warfare" and Public Health in the Korean Conflict', *Asian Perspective*, vol. 7, no. 2, Fall–Winter 1983, p. 213–17.
204. McCormack, 1983, pp. 147–58, and references there.
205. John W. Powell, 'Japan's Biological Weapons: 1930–1945', *The Bulletin of Atomic Scientists*, October 1981, and 'Japan's Germ Warfare: The U.S. Cover-up of a Crime', *Bulletin of Concerned Asian Scholars*, 12, 4, 1980, pp. 2–17.
206. Especially Morimura Seiichi, *Akuma no hoshoku*, Tokyo, 1981.
207. *International Herald Tribune*, 21 February 1983.
208. See Jaap Van Ginneken, 'Bacteriological Warfare', *Journal of Contemporary Asia*, vol. 7, No. 2, 1977, p. 135.
209. Leonard Cole, 'The Army's Secret Germ-War Testing', *The Nation* (New York), 23 October 1982, p. 397.
210. Endicott, pp. 93–4.
211. *Passport*, p. 221.
212. Ibid., p. 222.
213. See speech by Robert C. Miller of UPI in the spring of 1952, quoted in Aronson, op. cit., pp. 122–3.
214. Sir Robert Menzies, *The Measure of the Years*, Cassell, London, 1970, p. 154.

9

Burchett on Vietnam

David G. Marr

Burchett came to Vietnam for the first time in March 1954, almost directly from the Panmunjom ceasefire talks. Having decided to cover the forthcoming Geneva Conference, and being aware that Indochina as well as Korea was on the agenda, he wanted at least a glimpse of the Viet Minh liberated area, and perhaps some briefings from Vietnam People's Army (VPA) officers, before returning to Peking and travelling to Switzerland. As it turned out, he arrived just at the time the VPA was unleashing its surprise artillery barrage against the French bastion at Dien Bien Phu, and his most perceptive briefing came from President Ho Chi Minh.

Burchett used that interview to set the scene for his first book about Vietnam, *North of the Seventeenth Parallel*. Ho Chi Minh, never lacking in dramatic flair, described the battle unfolding 300 kilometres away as follows:

'This is Dien Bien Phu,' he said and tipped his sun-helmet upside down on the table. 'Here are mountains,' and his slim, strong fingers traced the outside rim of the helmet, 'and that's where we are too. Down here,' and his fist plunged to the bottom of the helmet, 'is the valley of Dien Bien Phu. There – are the French. They can't get out. It may take a long time, but they can't get out,' he repeated.[1]

212

Both men would have been amused to know that ordinary French soldiers and pilots had already evoked a similar metaphor – the pisspot – to describe military reality at Dien Bien Phu. Less than two months later the French garrison surrendered.

During the next two decades Burchett wrote a great deal about Vietnam. In fact from 1963 to 1973 almost all his journalistic attention focused on the war. As he explained in 1969:

> I saw it not only in terms of what I considered to be the final and most heroic phase of the millennia-long struggle of the Vietnamese people for complete independence of foreign rule, but historically as perhaps the last of the old-type colonial wars. [. . .] If [the Americans] lost, as I was convinced they would after my first visit, then it would most probably be the last such war. The United States would be too frustrated to engage in further such adventures.[2]

Although this assessment has a quaintly idealistic ring, Burchett should indeed be credited with grasping the epic implications of the Vietnam conflict before any other Western writer. From the time he wrote about John Foster Dulles's obstructionism at the Geneva Conference, to his 1964 fireside conversations with guerrillas who had just blown up an American cinema in Saigon, to his witnessing 1966 US air attacks over North Vietnam, Burchett successfully conveyed to readers a sense of the vast historical stakes involved. Tragically, the majority of Americans did not begin to grasp the depth and sophistication of Vietnamese opposition until the 1968 Tet Offensive, and even then they allowed Nixon and Kissinger to protract the death and destruction for another seven years.

In the history of twentieth-century journalism, Burchett will be remembered as one of those who got to important places first. Obviously he loved to travel, had a nose for news, enjoyed scooping his peers, and proved extremely resourceful when it came to obtaining clearances and gaining interviews. Those traits could have combined to make him a top-flight establishment journalist, perhaps the best on Fleet Street. Two things ruled that out. First, during the 1940s Burchett assiduously avoided coming back from tours as a foreign correspondent to work in an editorial office, which rendered his institutional position inherently vulnerable. More importantly, Burchett not only strengthened his personal convictions about socialist good and capitalist evil throughout the world, but insisted on writing that way – a patent impossibility on Fleet Street during the Cold War.

North Korea was Burchett's Rubicon. Although quite prepared to try to survive as a freelancer, he probably had no inkling of how his scope for travel would be limited subsequently by British, Australian and American governmental harassment. In addition, whether he liked it or not, most establishment editors had come to regard him as a simple communist apologist, to be printed only if there was no alternative. Forced to work within those limits, Burchett turned them to advantage to some degree, cultivating confidential sources of information in the socialist countries, obtaining exclusive interviews with international luminaries like Chou En-lai, Ho Chi Minh, Pham Van Dong and Norodom Sihanouk. Meanwhile, besides landing the occasional article in an establishment periodical, Burchett developed a more sustained, dedicated readership via small progressive journals in western Europe, Australia and the United States.

At regular intervals Burchett used his published articles and voluminous notes to put together a book-length manuscript. Altogether he published six books about Vietnam, and it is those, rather than his articles, that deserve general scrutiny today. Obviously a book gave him more scope to describe, explain and analyse events. Also, we can assume the author expected his books to be read long after his articles had disappeared into newspaper morgues and library microfilm drawers. On the other hand, Burchett's books shared with his articles an immediate, sometimes overwhelming desire to proselytize. Quite simply, he wanted to convince readers to join with him and with the Vietnamese revolutionaries to defeat the American imperialists. When assessing Burchett's books, therefore, it is necessary both to recall the highly charged context in which they were written, and to stand back and ask what remains of value now that times have changed.

North of the Seventeenth Parallel is one book that ought to be read decades hence. For about ten years after release in 1956 it received very little attention, partly because it was published in India, partly because whatever Western interest existed tended to focus narrowly on South Vietnam. A great deal of the information conveyed by Burchett in this book would have been extemely valuable in comprehending what happened subsequently. For example, his flashback descriptions of the 1945–54 Resistance War, based mainly on interviews, proved to be remarkable harbingers of what took place in the South again from 1959, complete with hit-and-run guerrilla tactics, booby traps, sophisticated tunnel systems and clandestine political operations. Accounts of French population resettlement and food-denial tactics also offer grim previews of much larger American projects, such as strategic hamlets, forced urbanization and herbicide spraying programmes in the 1960s.

I can still remember how surprised I was in early 1965 to read Burchett's brief description of systematic French efforts in the early 1950s to kill water buffaloes.[3] Two years before, I had witnessed US Marine Corps helicopter pilots pursuing terror-stricken buffaloes across fields as a source of amusement and target practice. I now wondered if that 'sport' had subsequently been promoted to an American counter-insurgency tactic. In 1967, making enquiries around South Vietnam, my worst fears were confirmed. By the early 1970s, in the central part of the country at least, an estimated two-thirds of all water buffaloes had been killed, the same proportion Burchett had reported in the Red River delta of northern Vietnam twenty years earlier.

As far as I can tell, only one other Western journalist had preceded Burchett to Ho Chi Minh's mountain headquarters. That was Joseph

Starobin, foreign correspondent for the US Communist Party's *Daily Worker* newspaper, who spent five weeks in Viet Minh-liberated areas in February–March 1953. In his book, *Eyewitness in Indo-China*, Starobin provided a more vivid account of jungle travel conditions than Burchett in *North of the Seventeenth Parallel*, and introduced readers to a wider range of Vietnamese personalities.[4] However, perhaps because he lacked Burchett's extensive wartime experience, Starobin failed to take full advantage of numerous encounters with Vietnamese combatants, from General Vo Nguyen Giap to local guerrillas and road-repair teams. Burchett's grasp of strategy and tactics, his ability to convey military reality to untutored readers, stand out all the more sharply when these two books are compared. On the other hand, Starobin was somewhat more forthcoming than Burchett about Chinese assistance to the VPA, and less prone to turn individual Vietnamese revolutionaries into stereotypical paragons.

Burchett was in a Vietnam People's Army convoy when it re-entered Hanoi peacefully in October 1954. Block by block the French were relinquishing control to the same Vietnamese fighters who had been forced out of the city almost eight years before. It is a moving account, all the more poignant because we know something the author did not: Vietnam was destined to be at war for another twenty-one years. During a brief halt in the convoy's advance, Burchett observed his interpreter go pale upon hearing a cry from someone in the crowd. It was the interpreter's niece, who had also brought along his two daughters, not seen since 1946:

> The girls smiled, then wept softly. He had only a moment to clasp them in his arms. Then the convoy began moving again and he leaped into the vehicle, shouting something to the elder girl, noting an address on the back of his hand as she called back and the convoy moved out of earshot, his eyes and those of everyone else in the vehicle filled with tears.[5]

Precisely the same sort of scenes would reoccur in Saigon in 1975.

During Burchett's stay in North Vietnam in 1955 and 1956 a great deal of reconstruction work was being accomplished. One of his best interviews was with a peasant woman named Nguyen Thi Luong, found hammering holes in a rockface to insert gelignite sticks, part of a massive push to reopen the railway line between Hanoi and Nanning, China. Active in the Viet Minh from late 1945, Nguyen Thi Luong had been forced into a life of clandestine organizing and sabotage when the French occupied her district in 1949. In early 1954 she left to carry ammunition at the battle of Dien Bien Phu, and after the armistice volunteered for the railroad-construction brigade. When Burchett first met her she was in charge of 150 women workers. In March 1955, Burchett, an honoured guest aboard the first scheduled train to run between the DRV and PRC,* was surprised to meet Nguyen Thi Luong

---

* DRV = Democratic Republic of Vietnam; PRC = People's Republic of China

again. Now a labour heroine, she was thrilled to be able for the first time
to ride a train, to visit China and to attend a sumptuous celebration
banquet. Soon she would be attending a conference to analyse the
railway-construction experience and plan future projects, 'because
there are other big jobs to be done before we can sit back and take
things easy'.[6] It was clear that Nguyen Thi Luong had no intention of
returning meekly to previous roles as housewife and mother in her home
village.

North of the Seventeenth Parallel contains the first eyewitness Western
account of land-reform campaigns in the DRV.[7] Burchett witnessed a
March 1954 meeting in Thai Nguyen province where a Communist Party
official enumerated the results of early redistribution efforts, and
villagers eagerly threw old property titles and contracts into a roaring
fire. He recorded the story of Nguyen Thi Dam, an elderly agricultural
labourer who had been kicked around by a series of landlords for more
than forty years. Her narrative, even though coming to Burchett via an
interpreter, was remarkably similar to the highly charged grievance
speeches which constituted an important part of landlord-denunciation
agendas in each village. Indeed she was probably re-enacting her own
grievance speech for Burchett's benefit.

By mid-1955, the campaign had advanced beyond a few pilot villages,
and Burchett was present at the public trial of a 'big, brutish landlord
who, being taller than most Vietnamese, was forced to stand in a small
hole so that his head would not be higher than any of the many witnesses
about to confront him. While this trial demonstrates Burchett's acute
powers of observation, it also reveals his readiness to leave out
uncomfortable details and to repeat official explanations uncritically.
Thus, Burchett focuses the reader's attention effectively on the hated
landlord and the newly confident peasants, but he says nothing of the
landlord's children, for example, who almost surely would have been
compelled to witness the trial, to endure ostracism and worse penalties
because of the action and status of their father. One wonders if Burchett
in his own youth, having endured brutish treatment from 'the Boss', a
New South Wales landlord, ever contemplated punishing the entire
family. If so, there is no hint in his autobiography.[8]

In North Vietnam during 1955 and 1956, thousands of individuals
were unjustly classified as landlords and punished. Heroic VPA officers
and dedicated party cadres were humiliated, imprisoned, in a few cases
executed, simply because they had been born into landlord families. On
the other hand, some peasants were listed as landlords because they had
collaborated, or were alleged to have collaborated with the French.
Neither of these practices was Communist Party policy, but on the basis
of what had happened previously in the Soviet Union, China and North
Korea, they could have been predicted. Eventually the party had to
concede serious errors, demote several Politburo members, reverse a
host of local decisions, and try to soothe the feelings of those who had
been unfairly treated.

None of this side of the land-reform drama appeared in *North of the*

Seventeenth Parallel. Admittedly, the book went to press before the party's public confession, but it is hard to imagine that Burchett had never heard talk or seen evidence of problems developing. As far as I can tell, Burchett never again discussed the North Vietnam land-reform campaign, except for a brief reference in 1963 to 'mistakes'.[9]

Burchett had already lived in China and North Korea, where such violent class confrontations and old political scores had earlier produced exactly the 'excesses' and 'mistakes' the Lao Dong Party confessed to openly in 1956. He must have known that most DRV land-reform techniques had been borrowed from the Chinese, yet that fact was never mentioned.

Indeed, for someone who admired international socialist solidarity, Burchett had very little to say in *North of the Seventeenth Parallel* about Chinese and Soviet contributions to Vietnamese revolutionary success. He did credit both countries with assisting North Vietnam's industrial reconstruction and planned development. However, he completely ignored large-scale Chinese military support to the DRV in the 1950–54 period. He went so far as to claim that the VPA relied almost exclusively on weapons captured from the French, whereas he must have known, for example, that most of the artillery weapons and trucks in VPA hands had been captured by the Chinese from the Americans in Korea. Nor is there any hint in his account that some of the anti-aircraft guns at Dien Bien Phu were manned by Chinese crews.

It is hard to explain this down-grading of internationalism except in terms of Burchett's growing identification with Vietnam's fierce small-country pride, combined with an almost Maoist faith in man over machines. Being Australian, Burchett was probably quicker than foreigners from more populous countries to appreciate Vietnamese self-esteem and professed self-reliance. There also was a deep populist streak in Burchett which had little or nothing to do with Marxism-Leninism. It was thus not artillery and anti-aircraft guns, but the 'superb morale of troops fighting for a just cause', which had proved decisive at Dien Bien Phu.[10] Viewing tens of thousands of peasants constructing a dam and canal with only the simplest of tools, and allegedly minus any engineers, Burchett extolled the virtues of working with one's hands. Perhaps most telling, he quoted a veteran of the meticulously planned, superbly executed sapper attack on Cat Bi airfield (March 1954), explaining the mission's success: 'President Ho and the party would never set us a task unless it could be carried out.'[11] It does not seem to have occurred to Burchett that millions of men had gone to their deaths in two world wars holding similar absolute faith in the Generalissimo, Czar, Kaiser, Emperor, King, Führer or Republic.

Of course, Burchett was witnessing something real, the desire of people engaged in a great movement to merge themselves totally with a supreme, all-knowing leader or institution. It was an important aspect of life in North Vietnam until perhaps the mid-1960s, when people began to take a more measured view of reality. Across the border in China the process reached its logical extreme in the Great Proletarian Cultural

Revolution, which shocked most Lao Dong Party leaders in North Vietnam, among other things making them aware of the dangers as well as the potentialities of mass zeal. Before that happened, however, Burchett had carried his populism below the seventeenth parallel to encounters with members of the National Front for the Liberation of South Vietnam (NFL).

In 1963, Burchett published *The Furtive War: the United States in Vietnam and Laos*. At that point, not yet able to enter the liberated areas of South Vietnam, he was forced to rely on interviews with individuals who had crossed into Cambodia or North Vietnam. One of his most moving encounters was with a dignified Khmer bonze who had fled Saigon terror squads moving through villages in the lower Mekong delta. The bonze described not only a series of arrests, extortions and burnings of villages, but efforts of the Ngo Dinh Diem regime to repress Khmer minority culture and language. Another in this group of Khmer Krom refugees, a peasant now crippled by Diemist torture, concluded his sad story by emphasizing how the younger men of his village had fled not to Cambodia, but to the forest inside Vietnam to make weapons and fight back. 'If they [the Saigon authorities] want "Viet Cong",' he remarked ominously, 'they've got them now from our village.'[12]

The main theme of the Vietnam portion of this book was the utter futility and barbarity of US–Diem efforts to separate peasants from guerrillas by putting the former into 'strategic hamlets', thus forcing the latter to come out into the open to be cut down by modern artillery, tanks and aircraft. In reality, Burchett argued, this strategy had exactly the reverse effect, leading ordinarily peaceful farmers to try to defend home and family with any primitive weapons at hand (hoes, bamboo spears, sickles) and, failing that, to make contact with veterans of the anti-French Resistance who knew how to fabricate mines, capture enemy firearms, and mount an ambush with limited risk. Burchett's scenario proved far more accurate than that of scores of counter-insurgency specialists in Saigon and Washington.

Already, however, Burchett had sensed how much additional death and destruction would result if the American government persisted in its strategy. He used the words of Prince Sihanouk to particular effect: 'What do the Americans think they can do? They can massacre the population. They can destroy the villages and cause terrible suffering. They can ruin the forests. Yes, monsieur, [. . .] they even make war against the trees now.'[13] Subsequently, Burchett made a point of asking refugees from Vietnam about that 'war against trees', and was horrified to learn details of herbicide sprayings in numerous locations from January 1962. In some cases the US purpose clearly went beyond stripping vegetation from hiding places, instead involving the killing of food crops to try to force peasants into Saigon-controlled zones. Refugees also described a variety of harmful physical effects of the spray on human beings – an issue that twenty-two years later continues to haunt not only exposed Vietnamese but Americans and Australians as well.

In *The Furtive War* there exists an underlying faith in the capacity of ordinary Americans to alter existing policies if only they can learn the truth. Burchett wonders rhetorically, for example, what all his 'good decent American friends' would think if they could sit down like him and talk with people at the violent receiving end of US 'freedom' and 'justice'.[14] It is an interesting question, and one cannot help but wonder if Burchett was as confident of a favourable answer ten years later. As in many such situations, it is one thing for people to glean reliable information and form an opinion, quite another to take resolute, persistent action.

Burchett often railed against US government news blackouts and disinformation campaigns relating to Vietnam, of which there were certainly plenty in the 1960s and 1970s. However, in *The Furtive War* he relied heavily on 1962 reportage in American newspapers to support his own case. To put it gently, his quotations were selective. Anyone bothering to read the original articles in the *New York Times*, for example, would have quickly realized that the journalists and editors responsible continued to uphold the basic US commitment to the Saigon regime, while entertaining growing doubts about the efficacy of particular policies. This continued to be true throughout the war, except that after the 1968 Tet offensive most establishment papers argued for removing US ground troops somehow from the overall commitment.

Burchett devoted considerable space in *The Furtive War* to refuting a December 1961 booklet issued by the US Department of State, entitled 'A Threat to Peace – North Vietnam's Effort to Conquer South Vietnam'. Today, the whole argument seems very distant, the language on both sides strident and overblown. However, at the time, and throughout the remainder of the war, allegations of a specifically North Vietnamese attempt to eliminate the Republic of Vietnam (RVN) by force constituted the linchpin of American interventionism. A great deal of ink was spilled debating this issue, with Burchett in the thick of it. Significantly, he never denied the right of Vietnamese coming from anywhere to struggle for reunification of their country. At the same time, he took the lead in the West in professing the autonomous southern origins and development of the National Front for the Liberation of South Vietnam (NFL), which he insisted on calling the 'South Vietnam Front of National Liberation' to emphasize his point.[15] Either way, considerable evidence could be put forward suggesting that the NFL was seen as legitimate by the majority of peasants in South Vietnam.

The book that made Burchett famous was *Vietnam: Inside Story of the Guerilla War*. Based on an intrepid odyssey through liberated and contested regions of South Vietnam from late 1963 to early 1964, it appeared on bookshelves in the West just as American ground troops were pouring into the country in 1965. Here was Burchett at his best, going somewhere unprecedented, meeting people high and low, describing their past as well as present achievements. It also proved to be Burchett's most literary work, with events of the trip keeping us

involved, the author's personality shining through, even occasional
subtle revelations about the human condition surfacing amidst the
single-minded anti-imperialism.

Burchett was then fifty-two years old, and perhaps he sensed that this
might be the last full-fledged test of his physical strength, dexterity and
endurance. He trained rigorously in advance, then marched for months
over some of the most tortuous terrain in the world, eating and drinking
from the same supplies as his NFL hosts, yet only becoming ill and
feverish once. On that occasion he was revived by an ice-cold bottle of
Saigon beer which somehow materialized in the midst of the jungle.
Although his armed escort always stood ready to improvise a palanquin
to carry him, Burchett was immensely proud to have avoided that
indignity throughout. His one real fear was being forced by US attacks
to enter tunnels not constructed for individuals of his size. As it
happened, several times he had no choice. Once tunnel claustrophobia
and nearby shooting led him to request to send a cable to his wife in
Moscow, possibly the last she would ever receive. Amazingly it reached
her only three days later.

When he wished, Burchett was very good at re-creating a particular
environment, complete with appropriate sights, sounds and smells.
Already in *The Furtive War* he had painted a vivid picture of the
terraced ricefields, forests and mountains around Dien Bien Phu in
1962. That was: 'Nature tamed and embellished, set in the compelling
drama of nature in the raw – calm and powerful.'[16]

In *Inside Story*, Burchett shares with readers the innocent sounds of
the jungle, the simple routine of life around a campfire, the silent
movement of canoes. Then suddenly he introduces us to the rude clatter
of helicopters, the rush to hide, the feeling of being stalked and perhaps
attacked with rockets and machine guns. A pattern develops: resourceful man versus evil, intruding machine. However, the pattern is not
total. Advancing into a village not far from Saigon, he hears a 'rare,
friendly mechanical noise – electric-powered irrigation pumps for the
local market gardens'.[17] Immediately following an enemy artillery
barrage against an NFL fortified hamlet, Burchett hears the sound of a
Lambretta taxi starting up, 'probably delivering ice from Saigon'.[18] The
pattern is finally shattered when Burchett, visiting an NFL jungle
arsenal producing mines and grenades, records that, 'It was pleasant
again to hear the humming of machinery; to hear mechanical noises
which were not from the adversary's planes or gunboats.'[19]

With or without machines, Burchett is always eager to point out the
ingenuity of the little man. In *Inside Story* we are introduced to the
'Dien Bien Phu Kitchen', a covered fireplace employing a number of
small tunnels to distribute the smoke widely and thus make detection
difficult. We meet the omnipresent little lamp made from a French
perfume bottle fitted with a cartridge case and tiny spring, which causes
the wick to pop up when the cap is unscrewed. In the mountains we view
booby traps constructed of rough vines and boulders, but triggered by
delicate, nearly invisible nylon fishing line. We hear of large monkeys

that are captured, dressed up, affixed with anti-American slogans and then let loose in the marketplace, both to provoke mocking laughter and to divert government police away from clandestine meetings. Even bees are allegedly trained to attack enemy patrols. As Burchett remarks, no central military staff could invent and plan deployment of such weapons and techniques. They originate locally and, if successful, spread quickly.

During his 1963–64 travels inside South Vietnam, Burchett observed a considerable amount of American equipment in the hands of the guerrillas. Much of it still bore the US Agency for International Development stamp. Even the famous Ho Chi Minh rubber sandals were now fabricated from US Goodyear rather than French Michelin truck tyres. Local cadres often told Burchett about their 'mother carbine', the first firearm to be acquired from the enemy, which was then employed skilfully to create many 'babies'. Later, in *Vietnam Will Win!*, Burchett provided more detail on NFL operations prior to 1965. While there is no doubt that some stories became embellished with time, I can confirm from personal experience that the guerrillas in 1962–63 relied almost entirely on a combination of local fabrication and material captured, pilfered or purchased from Saigon government sources.

Burchett probably brings us closer to understanding the overall symbiotic relationship between the NFL and the Republic of Vietnam (RVN) in those days than any Western author. Whereas in *The Furtive War* the Saigon apparatus seems to be composed entirely of murderers, rapists and torturers, *Inside Story* suggests a more complicated story. For example, at one point Burchett's party encounters a group of peasant women going to an RVN district seat, among other things to demand higher pay for their relatives in the Saigon army. Burchett is incredulous, so his interpreter patiently explains how such slogans are designed to gain the sympathy of puppet troops, perhaps even convince them to make demands on their officers. It is part of a much broader military-political strategy which recognizes that most Saigon soldiers are peasant conscripts, who, if they cannot necessarily be won over to the NFL side, will at least enter into tacit live-and-let-live arrangements at the local level.

However, the symbiosis went further than that. Not only ordinary soldiers but RVN officers commanding local garrisons often made tacit arrangements with the NFL, a practice they had to try to hide from American 'advisors', however, who demanded their recall and punishment if sufficient evidence was uncovered. In turn, Burchett learned, the NFL deliberately avoided cutting certain roads because it depended on supplies from the city almost as much as did government garrisons. When organizing public demonstrations aimed at Saigon troops and officials, NFL cadres encouraged participants to carry their RVN identification cards and to affirm loyalty to the government, not only as a tactic to avoid instant repression, but also to challenge the sense of decency and sincerity of RVN personnel in responding to grievances. One of the most common grievances, of course, was loss of life and property due to Saigon-initiated assaults. As US 'advisors' pushed ever harder for offensive action, and especially as air attacks proliferated, RVN province and district officials found the theory of government response to popular needs and desires being transformed into a perverse joke, at their expense.

There was yet another level of interaction in 1964 that Burchett probably knew about, but avoided raising in *Inside Story*. Sufficient contact existed between NFL and RVN leaders at various levels to make it possible to consider bilateral negotiations aimed at a ceasefire and formation of a 'neutralist' coalition government. Interestingly enough, Burchett had floated this idea in his 1963 book, *The Furtive War*, but at that time no Vietnamese really believed Ngo Dinh Diem would be party to such discussions. However, the triumvirate of generals who overthrew Diem in November 1963 *did* countenance such an option, which was one of the main reasons why the US government, or at least the US military commander in Saigon, encouraged their overthrow in turn only three months later. From then on, every Saigon military officer knew that contacts with the NFL, or even internal discussion of negotiation options, risked vigorous American counter-action. Some officers were still prepared to take that risk, but with the arrival of US combat troops in early 1965 the historical opportunity vanished. Henceforth the US government had the means both to ensure that no 'neutralist'-inclined RVN officer came close to power, and to control the content of any future negotiations with the NFL or the DRV.

Inside Story contains some valuable retrospective interviews with NFL cadres, particularly on the period 1955–59, when former Viet Minh adherents were hounded, jailed and often killed by Diem police and terror squads. Some of the comments represent rebukes to the Lao Dong Party leadership in Hanoi, although the party is never named. Thus, 'Quyet Thang' describes painfully to Burchett how adherence to top-level instructions not to go beyond the bounds of legal struggle had 'cost us the lives of the finest of our comrades'.[20] Another activist explains how a series of village-level refusals to endure further losses at the hands of RVN security units eventually forced provincial-level cadres to violate 'the line as we had last known it', by organizing armed resistance. Even then, the fact that cadres in adjacent provinces continued to obey the non-violent line enabled Diem to concentrate his forces against those who did not.[21]

Burchett's main purpose in publishing such revelations in 1965 was not to chide the Lao Dong Party Politburo in Hanoi, but to support his argument that the North had not intervened in the South. The NFL had emerged spontaneously in response to intolerable pressures from the RVN, he insisted. There is much truth to that, as subsequent research has demonstrated. However, Burchett neglected to mention that the Lao Dong Party line regarding the South did eventually change, before the NFL came into existence, and that this resulted in many Viet Minh personnel regrouped to the North in 1954 being returned to the South to take part in the armed liberation struggle. Ngo Dinh Diem suddenly found himself trying to deal with small-scale attacks in almost every province. By 1961 his forces were entirely on the defensive, in danger of falling apart. This led President Kennedy to introduce a variety of American combat support units, most notably helicopter and heavy air transport squadrons, which greatly increased ARVN* mobility. Burchett's NFL informants admitted that 1962 was a grim year, particularly in the Mekong delta, where consideration was given to withdrawing regular battalions entirely. However, the battle of Ap Bac in January 1963 demonstrated that a properly trained, carefully positioned Liberation Army battalion could hold its ground in the delta in daylight and cause heavy enemy casualties, before slipping through the cordon and escaping at night. Henceforth the RVN came under pressure once again.

Writing *Inside Story* in late 1964, Burchett still insisted that the NFL did not need the North for inspiration, leadership, technical expertise or weapons. What may have been largely true in 1963 was already changing in 1964, however. More fundamentally, it was clear from the context that a number of the men Burchett interviewed owed their allegiance to a nation-wide (South and North) organization. They might criticize its policies, but they did not question its legitimacy or its ultimate success. That organization was the Lao Dong Party, although in the South a variety of cover names were employed.

As mentioned earlier, Burchett never denied the legitimacy of co-ordinated nation-wide struggle. In late 1964 he warned that a major US escalation would mean fighting North Vietnam as well, 'at the very least' – presumably a veiled reference to possible Chinese or Soviet involvement.[22] If the US pushed the war to the North, using aircraft based in Laos, it might find to its dismay that it had created a 'single war front in Indochina'.[23] Given Burchett's sources, and his own increasing comprehension of events, these warnings ought to have been taken seriously. But of course they were not, and the terrible logic of armed action and counter-action persisted for another decade.

Burchett's next book was *Vietnam North*, based on two visits to the DRV in February and April–May 1966. The theme was simple, and stated in the first line: 'Prepare for the worst.'[24] Everyone he met in North Vietnam, although confident of ultimate victory, was busy planning and implementing ways to absorb the worst that the US imperialists could throw at them. Hanoi University classes were being shifted to the hills, even though Washington said it did not intend to bomb the capital. Surgeons performed a stomach operation under the feeble light of a peddle-driven dynamo, despite the availability of power lines a kilometre away, because they needed the practice in case US aircraft destroyed the power plants. Requests to the Soviet Union and China for equipment and training were revised on the assumption that the war might last another ten or twenty years. Attempts were made to compartmentalize the flood plain of the Red River delta in the event of

*Army of the Republic of Vietnam (Saigon regime)

American attacks on the dyke system. Local militia units trained for the possibility that the US might launch an amphibious invasion of the North.

Of course, Burchett's purpose in detailing Vietnamese contingency efforts was to convince readers in the West to oppose President Johnson's escalation policies, either because they were immoral or because they could not succeed. Burchett's emphasis was on inefficacy, perhaps because he imagined that individuals responsive to moral argument had already turned against the war, but I think mainly because descriptions of suffering might have given comfort to US strategists convinced that the Vietnamese will to fight could be broken. As a result, he made almost flippant assessments of the results of US air attacks to date, suggesting that American taxpayers were not getting their money's worth, since the trains were still running, trucks were still using the roads. Burchett also cited his earlier experience in North Korea, when persistent US Air Force bombing and strafing had failed to prevent him from travelling at least twenty times between Panmunjom and the Chinese frontier. However, he neglected to recall what he had seen of human suffering due to air power in Japan and Germany.

It seems evident from Burchett's tone that he did not expect 'the worst' to happen in Vietnam. Yet, when he came back in later years the power plants had been pulverized, Hanoi and the Red River dykes had been bombed (albeit not thoroughly), the war had dragged on another nine years. Only the US landings never occurred. The North Vietnamese had indeed refused to be cowed, but the price was very high, and it is still being paid today in psychological as well as material terms.

In *Vietnam North* Burchett began to explore possible grounds for a negotiated settlement of the war. Almost two years would elapse before US and DRV representations even sat down for preliminary discussions, and more than six years before an agreement could be signed in Paris, but Burchett had already sketched the essentials of a settlement. These included: cessation of American bombing; a ceasefire in place in the South; withdrawal of US troops; acceptance that Vietnam is one nation; and formation of a coalition government in Saigon. As Burchett ascertained from General Nguyen Van Vinh in 1966, the DRV steadfastly refused to link withdrawal of US troops to any regroupment of Vietnamese troops to the North as had occurred following the 1954 Geneva Accords. Only the last point, formation of a coalition government, was watered down substantially in 1972. Ironically, failure to implement any political accommodation meant that the ceasefire would be jeopardized the moment American troops departed. Because Liberation Army units remained intact in the South, they could defend substantial areas against renewed RVN assault in 1973–74. When the time was ripe, in early 1975, they launched the final victorious offensive.

Starting with *Vietnam North*, Burchett's writings about Vietnam took on didactic stridency. He seemed to see himself locked in direct rhetorical combat with the White House, the Pentagon and the commander of US forces in Saigon. Burchett's books and articles were indeed being used increasingly as ammunition by American, European, Australian and Japanese anti-war activists. He could not let them down. In the process, however, Burchett's feel for the 'little man' in Vietnam appeared to diminish. New insights became less frequent, and it was not unusual to see the same material being repeated in several works. Above all, his appreciation of the dynamic character of the conflict waned.

None the less, Burchett remained a proficient, hard-working writer, able to gain access to important people and to report from unique locations. From the late 1960s DRV leaders permitted an increasing number of Western writers to visit and ask questions, but none of them possessed Burchett's depth of experience. More importantly, Burchett always put the Vietnamese at the centre of his analysis, unlike most Western writers, above all the Americans. Ultimately American troops and aircraft would have to be withdrawn because of intractable realities inside Vietnam, not because of attitudes in Washington, Moscow or Peking.

By 1968, Burchett seemed to be spending most of his time on the polemical barricades, leaving little time for reflection or in-depth reporting. *Vietnam Will Win!*, first published late in that year, was perhaps his least satisfactory book from the point of view of new information or analysis. His rhetoric was more passionate than ever:

> Never in the history of any nation had so many with so much been arrayed against so few with so little. In comparison with the US versus the Vietnamese people, the story of David and Goliath seems like a combat between two equals. But miracle of miracles, despite all the laws of averages and statistics, it is the Vietnamese people who are winning on all fronts.[25]

Of course, Burchett was writing those words in the wake of the massive Tet offensive launched in late January 1968. Many less committed journalists in the West had suddenly come to the same conclusion after Liberation Army units slipped into scores of cities and towns around South Vietnam, forcing US and ARVN forces to root them out. None the less, given his excellent sources, Burchett must have been aware of the heavy losses suffered by the Liberation Army, especially during its May 1968 attempt to mount a second offensive. Of that he said nothing.

In the second edition of *Vietnam Will Win!*, published in mid-1970, Burchett added a two-page introduction emphasizing how the US government, having lost its opportunity in late 1968 to negotiate a withdrawal 'without too much loss of face', now was busily expanding the war to Cambodia and Laos. In response, the peoples of Indochina were reforging ties of solidarity that had existed during the previous struggle against the French. Thailand might become embroiled as well. Much more blood would flow because of President Nixon's obduracy, yet victory would still go to the liberation forces. In an epilogue, Burchett admitted the Vietnamese 'could perhaps be annihilated if the ultimate madness comes over Nixon and he orders the use of nuclear weapons, but they will never be defeated'.[26]

Much of *Vietnam Will Win!* is composed of further exposition on the years 1955–65 in the South. We hear of the formation in 1957 of two armed resistance units in the U Minh forest area, the furthest southern tip of Vietnam. We learn more about destruction of Saigon's strategic hamlet system in 1963–64. We receive a more detailed account of the important battle of Binh Gia in December 1964. Perhaps most revealing, we observe a Liberation Army regiment undergoing meticulous training for assaulting a fortified camp in Binh Duong province. Either because he was unable to travel again in South Vietnam, or because he found the revolutionary spirit of that period more to his tastes, Burchett repeatedly took his reader's attention away from the present.

Vietnam Will Win! contains an uncharacteristic venture by Burchett into the realm of political theory. His aim is to demonstrate the existence of a 'Repression-Resistance Principle', whereby:

> . . .There is a continuing upward spiral from police repression of political struggle to the highest stage with a foreign expeditionary force trying to protect a satellite government from people's war. In the light of South Vietnamese experience the repression and resistance principle must be qualified by the further principle that once the struggle is resolutely engaged there is a developing modification of the relation of forces in favour of the resistance.[27]

Presumably Burchett was not aware that Ho Chi Minh had upstaged him forty-two years previously, asserting flatly that 'the more a person is oppressed, the more lasting is his revolutionary spirit, and the more determined his revolutionary intent'.[28] Put somewhat differently, the revolutionary firmness of a social class was determined more by the degree of oppression it suffered than by the actual mode of production involved. Thus, because Vietnamese workers and peasants were *both* suffering extreme oppression at the hands of the French colonialists and Vietnamese landlords, they would tend to unite their struggles rather than divide them.

While there are a number of interesting aspects to both Ho Chi Minh's and Burchett's formulations, no detailed discussion is possible here. Suffice to say that each in his own way was trying to turn Social Darwinism on its head. Weak, backward, exploited nations could turn the tables on strong, clever imperialists. Effort was determined by its challenge, so that the greater the opposition the harder people would struggle to overcome it.[29]

From the point of view of history as opposed to millenarian faith, however, neither Ho Chi Minh nor Burchett bothered to ask how many popular uprisings against oppressive governments had failed for each one that succeeded. Admittedly the global ratio seemed to improve in the first half of the twentieth century, but by the 1950s one can argue that oppression again had the upper hand, partly as the result of a series of technological innovations that favoured ruling elites against incipient mass movements. If this is true, then ironically the success of Vietnamese revolutionaries against both the French and the Americans becomes all the more remarkable.

In contrast to Burchett's 1968 rhetoric, NFL cadres involved in day-to-day struggle treated the enemy with respect bred of bitter experience. They knew there was such a thing as counter-revolution, and that it possessed a logic and perverse vitality of its own. Tran Nam Trung touched on this when he credited Ngo Dinh Diem with having been a formidable opponent, succeeding in establishing an army, a police apparatus, a civil administration and a nascent political machine.[30]

No subsequent Saigon leader measured up to Diem, yet the NFL suffered such heavy casualties over time that the character of the conflict changed, from a contest for the allegiance or control of southern villagers, to pitched battles between well-equipped military units. Liberation Army regiments were increasingly composed of northern recruits, while ARVN resorted to seizing young men off the streets and dragooning them into front-line service. Meanwhile, from 1970, President Nixon moved to limit American combat losses. The climax to this trend – indeed the military turning point of the war – came in southern Laos in early 1971, when ARVN units panicked in the face of Liberation Army tanks and heavy artillery barrages, fleeing back across the border in total disorder.[31] It was a harbinger of what would happen in Quang Tri in 1972, and throughout South Vietnam in 1975.

Burchett's last book on Vietnam was *Grasshoppers and Elephants: Why Viet Nam Fell*, published in 1977. The title came from a pithy 1951 comment by Ho Chi Minh addressed to waverers and pessimists: 'Today, yes, it's the grasshoppers that dare stand up to the elephants. Tomorrow, it's the elephant that leaves its skin behind.'[32] This book was Burchett's way of sharing in Vietnamese victory, and of reminding Western readers that he had been right all along.

Above all, Burchett wanted to reaffirm the decisive role of the masses in the Vietnamese revolution. Almost one half of *Grasshoppers and Elephants* is devoted to arguing that a 'people's uprising' occurred in South Vietnam in March–April 1975. At times Burchett almost seems to be donning the cloak of recently deceased Mao Tse-tung, for example claiming that, 'Unendurable repression had made the South Vietnamese people as ripe for generalized uprising as a long dry summer prepares grass and undergrowth for hurricane-force brush fires.'[33] Elsewhere he speaks of a powerful people's army being built up in the countryside, then encircling the cities 'to bring about that final fruition of the workers-peasants alliance'.[34] The individuals he interviews in 1975 never make such sweeping claims, however. Instead, they describe a sophisticated military offensive supported by classic fifth-column operations, particularly rumour campaigns and sabotaging of ARVN communications. Peasants observe concealed Liberation Army units and do not betray them. On the last day of battle, crowds surge around some ARVN tanks and convince gunners to cease firing. While all of this paramilitary and civilian effort proves very useful to final victory, it is not decisive, and it is certainly not a mass seizure of power.

Aside from possessing an unbendingly romantic vision of revolution, Burchett was in this case impelled by pugnaciousness: he wanted to refute those many Western writers who pictured the 1975 communist campaign as a North Vietnamese blitzkrieg against an outclassed, outgunned ARVN. It is quite true that most Western accounts grossly over-emphasized the role of military technology in producing a communist victory. Ironically, they were assisted in this distortion by the widely publicized memoirs of General Van Tien Dung, North Vietnamese campaign commander, who exulted in the force of his conventional military juggernaut.[35]

Both Burchett and Van Tien Dung largely ignored the most important factor in defeat of the Saigon regime, which was the progressive loss of confidence among the ARVN officers corps before March 1975, brought about by American troop withdrawals, US congressional limitations on aid, rampant inflation, growing urban unrest, and an inability to make any headway in local confrontations with Liberation Army units. After well-equipped ARVN divisions in the central highlands were dealt several sharp blows in March, the entire RVN system began to fall apart like a house of cards. So fast did panic seize the minds of officers, soldiers, policemen and functionaries, that Liberation Army divisions could not keep up with the fleeing enemy. As Liberation Army tanks began to converge on Saigon from the east and north in mid-April, lightly equipped regional units cut off the possible routes of further ARVN retreat south into the Mekong delta. No ARVN units attempted to break out of the cordon. Instead, most top commanders fled overseas, leaving it to a retired general, Duong Van Minh, to arrange capitulation.

Grasshoppers and Elephants also contains Burchett's most detailed description of the Paris peace negotiations. It is a very personal account, based almost entirely on what Burchett saw and heard, with only seven references to other sources. He provides new background to his important interview in January 1967 with DRV Foreign Minister Nguyen Duy Trinh, wherein Hanoi for the first time signalled that talks could begin with the US if bombing raids over the North were halted. He describes his May 1968 four-hour lunch with Averell Harriman, then head of the American delegation, and his October 1971 breakfast with Henry Kissinger.[36] There is a brief, rather veiled reference to the Nixon-Kissinger strategy of wooing China away from support of the DRV and PRG.* Only after Peking and Hanoi denounced each other publicly, in 1978, does Burchett feel free to join the polemic openly on the side of Vietnam.

Some of Burchett's capacity to convey reality from the 'little man's'

* Provisional Revolutionary Government of South Vietnam

point of view is again evident in his brief account of Lunar New Year celebrations in Hanoi in late January 1973, immediately following cessation of B-52 bombings and signing of the Paris Peace Agreement. In a few well-chosen words he etches in our minds the terrible destruction and first pathetic attempts to clean up the debris. He then contrasts all this with the proud determination of citizens to celebrate Tet properly, complete with family reunions, flowers, goldfish, paper lanterns, firecrackers and glutinous rice cakes. At the Hanoi Zoo, Burchett finds himself staring at the carcass of a B-52 with a peasant from the city outskirts, who proceeds to give him a cogent summary of recent history and a prediction: 'The Geneva Agreement gave us half the country "red". The Paris Agreement gives us half the South "red". That took twenty years. It will take much less to make the other half of the South "red".'[37]

Standing back and surveying all of Burchett's six books on Vietnam, we see him at his best as a war correspondent in the classic tradition, trying to be where the military action is, or, failing that, interviewing people on his side of the line who have taken part. Shifting his attention to diplomacy after 1967, he retains the same outlook, but now ventures across the lines to attend press conferences and to eat, drink and talk *tête-à-tête* with 'enemy' leaders. In this new role Burchett sees himself as a 'drop of oil', sometimes making the clogged machinery of diplomacy move again.[38] However, it seems he could not avoid wielding the screwdriver at certain junctures, as when he told Harriman that Hanoi would evacuate its troops from the South if a good agreement was in sight.[39] To the degree that Harriman took this to be a signal from Hanoi, Burchett misled.

Burchett never tried to present a comprehensive picture of life inside Vietnam. His descriptions of conditions in RVN-held regions of South Vietnam often descended to moralistic caricature, partly because he had only been able to visit there once, briefly, in 1954, but also because he felt uncomfortable with human paradox, or at least refused to clutter the minds of his readers with ambiguity. The partial exception was *Inside Story of the Guerilla War*, one reason why it remains his best book on Vietnam. Burchett had even more opportunity to examine life in the DRV, and his first effort, *North of the Seventeenth Parallel*, showed great promise. Unfortunately, his later portrayals of the North lacked depth and authorial control. Burchett never developed much interest in economics, a crucial part of the overall Vietnam story, and he probably realized that he lacked the background to dwell at length on Vietnamese history, literature, language or popular culture.

Two aspects of life in Vietnam did attract Burchett's attention persistently, and, in the process, change his own outlook. First, he became fascinated by the ethnic minorities. In *North of the Seventeenth Parallel* he devoted an entire chapter to the Thai-Meo Autonomous Zone, noting the lifestyles of different groups, interviewing local spokesmen, and marvelling at the rugged environment. This was an important time for the zone, with the colonial triumvirate of Thai seigneurial families, Vietnamese mandarins and French military officers having only recently disappeared, and the new Party system just getting under way. Ethnic Vietnamese cadres received so much praise from highland interviewees that even Burchett must have smiled. Thus, one Thai hamlet leader mixed metaphors as follows: '[Vietnamese cadres] were like the sun. When the sun shines you are sure to find shade under the banyan tree. Before they came we were like fish on a platter, not knowing what to do, how to defend ourselves.'[40] Allegedly the most popular poem of the region compared President Ho Chi Minh to 'a bright star in a dark night, the sun which shines into the darkest corner'.[41]

Burchett made subsequent visits to minority areas in North Vietnam, detailing his findings in *The Furtive War*.[42] He was convinced that Hanoi had the best interests of these 'backward' peoples at heart, selling them salt at special low prices, encouraging them to enrol in government schools, employing them on road construction projects, urging them to discontinue 'superstitious' customs. The government had also forbidden minorities to continue slash-and-burn agriculture in certain regions, while trying elsewhere to control their rate of plot rotation. It was assumed that all mountain peoples would eventually settle down on state farms or co-operatives, at which time the age-old practice of migratory farming would 'die a natural death'.[43] It did not seem to bother Burchett that an entire way of life was being called into question, that highland minorities were being asked in large part to assimilate to Kinh majority ways, despite the creation of 'autonomous zones' for them.

Burchett had recently interviewed a number of minority people escaping from South Vietnam, who presented a dark, indeed terrifying contrast to the relatively non-coercive policies of the North. The government of Ngo Dinh Diem was systematically settling Kinh majority farmers on time-honoured minority land, forcing isolated minority villagers to concentrate in barbed-wire-enclosed 'strategic hamlets', torturing or killing those who objected. ARVN soldiers routinely stole pigs and chickens, raped women and forcibly conscripted young men.[44] If compelled to choose between treatment in North or South, there is no doubt ethnic minorities would have opted for the former.

In 1963–64, Burchett had an opportunity to live for many weeks amidst minority groups in the central highlands of South Vietnam. Clearly it was a moving experience. In a letter to his father Burchett admitted, 'I have entirely revised my opinion about savages.' Although naked except for tattoo marks and loincloths, these people practised all of the virtues 'which we learn at school and church'. Indeed, the real savages were those Westerners who received formal moral instruction, yet came with 'medieval cruelty and twentieth century techniques to torture and slay, wiping out whole villages'.[45]

Among the Jeh people of Kontum province, Burchett reflected further: 'They were faces one never tired of studying because essential truths were engraved there; human qualities which we prize in theory in the West, but which have been preserved by tribespeople in purer, elemental form.'[46] It is tempting to speculate that behind Burchett's impressions of the Jeh lay a Christian sense of Paradise Lost, as had surely been true during his blissful interlude in Tahiti twenty-seven years earlier. Also, behind his outrage at American attacks on the Jeh may have lain guilt at white Australian treatment of Aboriginals. None the less, what impressed Burchett most about the Jeh and other central highlanders was their readiness to fight for their beliefs, to organize and employ primitive weapons with surprising effectiveness. He himself was dependent on these people for survival. As a result, Burchett to some degree came to appreciate them as individuals, understanding them on their own terms, not simply as virtuous archetypes, passive victims, or uncivilized tribals needing to learn modern ways.

In September 1964, several thousand highland minority conscripts to ARVN revolted at Ban Me Thuot, killing their Vietnamese instructors and taking hostage six American instructors. Eventually the hostages were released in exchange for a pledge that henceforth *montagnard* units would deal directly with American officers, ignoring the ARVN structure entirely. The American objective, of course, was to direct anti-Vietnamese feelings towards the NFL. Some French nationals who retained nostalgic memories of the simple *Moi* (savages) also made contact with the trainees, urging them to be anti-American as well as anti-Vietnamese. When the movement spilled over into Cambodia, Prince Sihanouk took an interest as well. By this time it was known as FULRO (Front Uni pour la Libération de la Race Opprimée), and Burchett, living in Phnom Penh, followed events intently.

Here was the sort of complex, ambiguous development which a person of Burchett's knowledge and contacts might have tried to unravel for a puzzled Western readership. To have done so, however, could well have jeopardized his relationships with Hanoi and the NFL. His solution was to include a meagre three-page account in *Vietnam Will Win!*, admitting that 'elements' of FULRO accepted US support in their struggle against the NFL, but emphasizing the foolishness of this position and claiming a later American double cross.[47] It is my impression, however, that FULRO split under pressure from *all* sides, some leaders continuing to co-operate with the US Special Forces until 1973, others linking up with either Saigon or the NFL, still others retreating into Cambodia and eventually being liquidated by Pol Pot. Remnants of FULRO are said to have fought on until 1985 in Vietnam's central highlands in opposition to the SRV.*

Besides ethnic minorities, Burchett developed an abiding interest in public health and medicine in Vietnam. In 1955, he was deeply impressed by DRV efforts to inoculate millions of citizens, to disseminate basic hygiene principles, and to make modern medical services available to ordinary villagers. He discovered that hygiene

---

* Socialist Republic of Vietnam, proclaimed in 1976

campaigns had begun in 1945 and continued in Viet Minh liberated zones throughout the Resistance period. Moving from village to village, health cadres explained the importance of digging simple privies, boiling drinking water, protecting food against flies, and sterilizing instruments for minor operations (above all, when cutting the umbilical cord at childbirth). By the early 1950s, DRV pharmacists had pieced together several laboratories in the hills to produce injections against typhoid, cholera and bacillary dysentery. Simultaneously the Faculty of Medicine of the former University of Hanoi was successfully re-established in the forest to train surgeons, general practitioners, dentists and nurses.

Burchett was predictably caustic in his criticism of French colonial rulers for neglecting to improve the health of their Vietnamese subjects before 1945. At best, he said, they alleviated conditions in the cities and towns wherein resided most of the French population. Although French performance was indeed deficient, Burchett once again oversimplified, in this case not bothering to cross-check his interviews with available historical sources. For example, by the 1920s French scientists, epidemiologists and medical inspectors had managed to reduce considerably the number of deaths due to plague, cholera and smallpox. French professors trained the 147 Vietnamese physicians available in 1945, admittedly a paltry number given total needs, yet undeniably the pool from which came all of the DRV's first generation of medical specialists. Perhaps most importantly, Vietnamese teachers in colonial primary schools had already begun disseminating basic concepts of hygiene. As a result, Viet Minh cadres did not need to invent a vocabulary or search very far for a villager willing to take responsibility for local health training.

In 1955, however, Burchett reserved his most stinging comments for those Vietnamese 'charlatans and sorcerers' who continued to employ mumbo jumbo to dupe ignorant peasants into wasting scarce family resources to ward off illness. Although he excused herbalists from that blanket charge of wilful deception, it was clear Burchett did not believe concoctions of leaves and roots did much good for patients. He was also shocked to hear that Vietnamese mothers often gave birth in a sitting position, labelling it a 'ritual' which jeopardized the life of both mother and infant. In Burchett's opinion, all these 'feudalist and colonialist' attitudes towards disease and health could only be overcome by provision of modern medical services at the village level. He seemed unaware that the Viet Minh had relied extensively on traditional practitioners during the anti-French Resistance, or that President Ho Chi Minh in 1955 was urging all medical cadres to study means of 'harmonizing' Eastern and Western remedies.

By 1964, Burchett's attitude had changed. He had nothing more to say about charlatans, and he reported favourably on the NFL's use of 'oriental medicines' produced from local ingredients. Although some were only regarded as substitutes for extremely scarce Western medicines, others were considered superior or unique. For example, when sleeping in the jungle, Burchett himself always had a particular

NFL-produced snake-bite antidote 'in a handy position for immediate application'.[48] A French-trained pharmaceutical chemist astonished Burchett by saying that the NFL produced seventy per cent of its own medicine, mainly thanks to a careful inventory of local vegetable, animal and mineral ingredients. Allegedly, the chemist's research team had invented a technique based on forest products for dealing with gangrenous wounds, which, however, needed to remain a secret as a 'source of national wealth for the future'.[49] On the other hand, Burchett also was able to report effective NFL use of Western X-ray machines, surgical equipment, penicillin and streptomycin – all either captured from RVN clinics or purchased in Saigon and smuggled through enemy lines.

One of Burchett's earliest friends in Hanoi seems to have been Dr Pham Ngoc Thach, a prominent Western-trained lung specialist and former political activist in Saigon. By 1966, Dr Thach, now DRV Health Minister, was devoting attention to local forest products, for example ordering analysis of particular plants which seemed to be effective against arteriosclerosis, malaria and intestinal diseases. He escorted Burchett to a laboratory where a liquid plant extract similar to indigo was being tested on female rabbits to produce miscarriages. Dr Thach was especially enthusiastic about another set of plants which highland tribespeople allegedly used to produce sterility or fertility, depending on need. None the less, he retained a firm scientific perspective: potential clinical benefits had to be tested first on animals; and laboratory analysts aimed to understand any favourable results in chemical and biological terms.

This was not the attitude of 'Eastern medicine' practitioners, who still approached problems of illness and healing from a very different perspective, yet were also encouraged by the government to continue working. Burchett did notice traditional medicinal plants growing in a hamlet garden, and hear the local health officer assure him that eighty-five per cent of all patients were cured by traditional means, but unfortunately he chose not to pursue the matter further. In fact, at least two distinct medical ideologies continued to function in the DRV. While the government talked of 'harmonizing' them, and practitioners gave lip-service to the idea, important theoretical and institutional differences persisted.

In 1975, not long after liberation of South Vietnam, Burchett talked at length with Dr Nguyen Van Thu, who was working desperately to prevent epidemics in the sprawling, chaotic metropolis of Saigon. Prior to May, only 120 garbage trucks had serviced a population of four and a half million. Rats were everywhere, large shanty-town sections of the city had no sewerage system, and some people drew water directly from the fetid canals. Dr Thu's public-health cadres had organized regular garbage pick-ups, mass inoculations against plague and typhoid, and reopening of local health clinics. None the less, huge problems remained. No funds existed to improve the sewers or extend water pipes. Many Saigon doctors, nurses and laboratory technicians had fled overseas; it would take years to train replacements. Dr Thu's cadres had brought stocks of traditional and Western medicines from the liberated zones, but the latter quickly ran out and could not easily be replaced. Some valuable pharmaceutical equipment left behind by the Americans had been inadvertently damaged, due to the inexperience of Liberation Army personnel trying to put them into production. 'Carrying on the war was difficult, but trying to run a state even more so,' Dr Thu mused to Burchett.[50]

How should we evaluate Burchett on Vietnam? Obviously it would be unfair to criticize him for things he did not attempt. Thus, Burchett did not wish to write for an academic audience, nor did he try to be objective in any scholarly sense. He was a practising journalist who believed passionately that liberation forces should win and imperialist forces lose. He would not publish anything which undermined that faith.

Burchett's particular upbringing in Australia and early political experiences led him to see the world in opposing primary colours. He sided with those who worked with their hands, or who organized the poor to defend themselves, and developed an abiding hatred for bullies, landlords and moneylenders. Already in 1941 he identified himself so totally with the anti-fascist cause that he deliberately withheld information if he thought it might disillusion progressive friends at home.[51] When the anti-fascist alliance came to an abrupt end in 1945, Burchett decided that the Soviet Union continued to represent the forces of goodness, peace and productivity, while the US government was bent on promoting conflict and exploitation. Henceforth, whatever the topic, Burchett could be relied on to disagree completely with the official American view.

When covering the 1954 Geneva Conference, Burchett seemed to develop a personal abhorrence for the American Secretary of State, for example asserting that John Foster Dulles's 'very appearance, bullying, cynical, crafty and predatory, fits him for his role of chief representative of a class and system condemned by humanity on the march to die, a system and class already moribund and putrifying'.[52] Dulles was said to epitomize war, slavery and death, whereas the DRV's chief negotiator, Pham Van Dong, represented peace, freedom and life. Admittedly such chiliastic language – so reminiscent of the 1930s – became much less common in Burchett's later writings. Compared to Dulles, his treatment of Henry Kissinger was almost gentle, yet history may well put the latter in a special purgatory reserved for totally immoral and deceitful diplomats. Late in life, Burchett argued that a journalist of integrity could 'enjoy the trust of heads of state, prime ministers and diplomats while giving his readers the most truthful possible account of what is really going on'.[53] Significantly, no distinction was made here between socialist and capitalist leaders.

Did Burchett tell the truth about Vietnam? The record is mixed. He certainly worked hard to dig out the facts, organize them and present them forcefully to readers. On the other hand, he sometimes deliberately left out important evidence, and he wilfully distorted evidence presented by the 'other side'. In that sense he was more like a lawyer or solicitor than a reporter. However, pursuing that metaphor a step further, I have yet to pinpoint a place where Burchett risked perjury by deliberately lying to enhance his client's case. He may have published favourable testimony from others which he knew to be inaccurate, but generally without embellishment, leaving it to readers to discern a degree of authorial disassociation. Burchett's most common failing was to repeat information given to him that was inherently controversial, without flagging it for readers, much less subjecting the data to careful cross-checking.[54] Over time he came to believe in his own near infallibility as a judge of character and truthfulness among people he interviewed.

Of course, Burchett rejected the model of 'detached' reporter as taught in Western schools of journalism. He refused to accept that contradiction existed between trying to write the truth and urging events in a desired direction. As he once affirmed: 'To ensure an honorable place in future records, one has to be convinced not only that one is writing an historic record and informing the public, but also that one is helping to shape history and public opinion in the best interests of humanity.'[55] Burchett also quoted approvingly an NFL journalist who argued that the best sort of propaganda was based on the truth.[56] What did one do, however, when facts emerged which were contrary to propaganda aimed at 'the best interests of humanity'? For example, Burchett never wrote about NFL atrocities or use of torture, although he must have heard stories, and he knew enough about war to surmise that no army could remain entirely blameless. In such cases Burchett presumably felt that because evil on the imperialist side vastly outweighed evil on the liberation side, and because the imperialists had far greater resources to propagandize their illegitimate interests, it was not his responsibility to give them free help.

We know, however, that Burchett kept some record or at least memory of unpalatable facts. Thus, after Peking and Hanoi became overtly antagonistic in 1978, Burchett pulled out and used old material critical of the Chinese.[57] Only a check of his original notes would reveal whether Burchett recorded such things at the time as a conscientious journalist, or merely reconstructed a few anecdotes once the political context had changed dramatically.

In the Introduction to *At the Barricades*, Harrison Salisbury calls Burchett 'the iconoclast of contemporary radicalism'.[58] To me, that is rather wide of the mark. An iconoclast goes after untruth, obfuscation, deception, pomposity, manipulation and mindless orthodoxy *wherever* he finds them, not just one side of the barricades. A more apt candidate for Salisbury's accolade would be someone like I.F. Stone, who wrote and published his own weekly newsletter in Washington, DC from 1953 to 1971, sifting immense amounts of written evidence, taking nothing for granted, combining radical analysis with a passionate concern for accuracy. I.F. Stone seldom travelled or interviewed people directly, depending instead almost entirely on data generated by others. Burchett had different intellectual priorities, and he used secondary data only when there was no other choice.

A better comparison with Burchett might be Harold Isaacs, an American correspondent of almost the same age who spent most of the 1930s in China, returned home briefly, then reported from China, India and South East Asia during and after World War II. His *No Peace for Asia*, published in 1947, conveyed to readers a mixture of sharp disenchantment with US post-war policies and plaintive hopes that people everywhere would continue to struggle for freedom, democracy and socialism.[59] From 1951, however, Isaacs edged his way out of journalism and into academia, eventually becoming professor of political science at the Massachusetts Institute of Technology. His interests shifted to ethnicity and acculturation. As the United States became increasingly embroiled in Vietnam, Isaacs had surprisingly little to say. His introduction to the 1967 edition of *No Peace for Asia* condemned America's 'monumental myopia' and provided a master- fully sensitive re-examination of his own past judgements, yet deliber- ately avoided taking a stand on current US policy in Vietnam. Twenty years, Isaacs said, had made him 'still angry but unsure and filled with an awareness of diversity, elusiveness and tentativeness of meanings'.[60]

If Burchett had been offered an academic post he probably would have turned it down or spent several uncomfortable years there and then moved on. He had to be where the action was, reporting it in his own inimitable way. He had no patience for people like Isaacs whose long experience seemed to limit rather than enhance their skills as public advocates. Burchett may have become a bit cynical in old age, but never passive, never avoiding a fight.

Burchett's commitments sometimes led him astray. Nowhere is this more evident than in his dealings with American prisoners of war in Korea and Vietnam. It should have been apparent to Burchett that prisoners anywhere, no matter what their prior actions or current beliefs, are the ultimate underdogs, almost totally dependent on the whims of their jailors. To come into prison with permission of the authorities, ask probing questions, expect answers, offer assistance, make suggestions, is automatically to become enmeshed in a system of institutionalized violence and covert resistance. Whatever Burchett's intentions, which I personally think were muddled but not malign, they were bound to be misconstrued. He seems to have sensed this when meeting four American POWs in 1964.[61] Yet Burchett could still be surprised and mildly offended when three other POWs being released via Phnom Penh never returned an overcoat and some long underwear he lent them for the cold trip home to America.[62]

Burchett's books on Vietnam lack the element of human tragedy in the Greek dramatic sense. One way or another he had to be in the play, battling, not standing outside the events being described. In December 1978, as Vietnam, Kampuchea and China moved towards war, Burchett came closest to understanding his dilemma: 'Now my Asian friends were at each other's throats – each waving the banner of socialism and revolution – and I was again in the thick of it. It was a shattering blow to a vision of things acquired during the previous four decades, including my certainty as to the superior wisdom and morality of Asian revolutionaries.'[63] None the less, Burchett quickly picked himself up, decided who to support, and pushed on.

Ironically, if Burchett had been a more tentative, introspective person he probably would never have generated so much information of value from so many unlikely locations. Although his books on Vietnam will not stand as the final word on anything (how many books do?), and should each be read in conjunction with books representing contrasting opinions, they possess an immediacy based on persistent interviewing and sharp observation which cannot be equalled by any other author. Future students of the period 1954-75 in Vietnam will thus remain in his debt.

Burchett should also be read by anyone thinking of becoming a journalist, especially a foreign correspondent. Besides reporting from places where history is being made, perhaps even making an occasional impact oneself, there is a price to be paid. If one remains within the establishment system of big city papers, glossy weeklies and TV networks, it is the editors who will decide not only which stories reach the public, but what the moral and political punchlines will be. On the other hand, if one freelances, as Burchett did for thirty-five years, material existence can be tenuous, professional accolades few and far between. Then, too, only a handful of freelancers ever manage like Burchett to develop their own loyal reader constituencies, thus being able to finesse editors to some degree and project individual convictions consistently.

In short, Burchett will be remembered because he was different. Anyone trying to follow his example may find that the mould was broken after they created 'Wilf'.

Notes

1. Wilfred Burchett, *North of the Seventeenth Parallel*, People's Publishing House, Delhi, 1956, p.2. Apparently first published in Hanoi in 1955.
2. Wilfred Burchett, *Passport: An Autobiography*, Nelson, Melbourne, 1969, p.271.
3. *North of the Seventeenth Parallel*, pp.149–50.
4. Joseph R. Starobin, *Eyewitness in Indo-China*, Cameron and Kahn, New York, 1954.
5. *North of the Seventeenth Parallel*, p.82.
6. Ibid., p.101.
7. Starobin, in *Eyewitness*, pp.92–5, provides an earlier description of a landlord denunciation meeting, but it is second-hand.
8. *Passport*, pp.62–76.
9. Wilfred Burchett, *The Furtive War: The United States in Vietnam and Laos*, International Publishers, New York, 1963, p.129. (According to Bernard Fall, however, the 1958 edition of *North of the Seventeenth Parallel* carries 'a self-criticism for the errors of 1956–57'. *Le Viet-Minh*, Paris, 1960, p.362 [ed.]).
10. *North of the Seventeenth Parallel*, p.51.
11. Ibid., p.36.
12. *The Furtive War*, p.16.
13. Ibid., p.60.

14. Ibid., p.16.
15. The Vietnamese name is Mặt Trân Dân Tôe Giai Phóng Miên Nam Viêt Nam. Admittedly the French Language translation used from the beginning by adherents, 'Front National de Liberation du Sud Viet-Nam', favours Burchett's version.
16. *The Furtive War*, p.132.
17. *Vietnam: Inside Story of the Guerilla War*, International Publishers, New York, 1965, p.31.
18. Ibid., p.41.
19. Ibid., pp.74–5.
20. Ibid., p.113.
21. Ibid., pp.143–5.
22. Ibid., p.226.
23. Ibid., p.232
24. *Vietnam North*, International Publishers, London, 1966, p.7.
25. *Vietnam Will Win!*, Guardian, New York, 1968, p.xix.
26. Ibid., p.213.
27. Ibid., p.115.
28. *Duong Kach Menh* (1926), as quoted in Dang Cong San Viet Nam, *Cac To Chuc Tien Than cua Dang* (Hanoi, 1977), p.24.
29. Other Vietnamese writers of the late 1920s and 1930s often invoked the image of river water pushing harder against dykes the higher they are raised. At some point a break was inevitable. Mao Tse-tung used the metaphor of the strength of a river increasing as mountains push in and constrict its flow.
30. *Inside Story*, pp.217–19.
31. Burchett eventually did discuss the importance of the 1971 Laos battle, in *Grasshoppers and Elephants: Why Viet Nam Fell*, Urizen Books, New York, 1977, pp.143–7.
32. Ibid., p.15.
33. Ibid., p.72.
34. Ibid., p.202.
35. Van Tien Dung, *Our Great Spring Victory*, Monthly Review Press, New York, 1977. Translated by John Spragens, Jr. In retrospect, this memoir probably had as much to do with internal Workers' Party politics in mid-1975 as with historical veracity.
36. Each of these encounters is further discussed in Burchett's second autobiography, *At the Barricades*, Macmillan, Melbourne, 1981, pp.255–7, 272–81.
37. *Grasshoppers and Elephants*, pp.176–7.
38. Ibid., p.127.
39. Ibid., p.136.
40. *North of the Seventeenth Parallel*, p.161.
41. Ibid., p.172.
42. *The Furtive War*, pp.120–31.
43. Ibid., p.126.
44. Ibid., pp.21–2, 113–20.
45. Undated letter from Wilfred Burchett to his father, George Burchett. I'd like to thank Ben Kiernan for bringing this to my attention. Burchett Papers, State library of Victoria.
46. *Inside Story*, p.171.
47. *Vietnam Will Win!*, pp.132–4.
48. *Inside Story*, p.77.
49. Ibid., p.79.
50. *Grasshoppers and Elephants*, p.217.
51. *Passport*, p.157.
52. *North of the Seventeenth Parallel*, pp.56–7.
53. *Guardian* (New York), 14 December 1977, p.9.
54. See, for example, Burchett's reporting of Vietnamese assertions that the famous Saigon singer, Thanh Nga, had been assassinated at Chinese instigation. *Nation Review*, 15 March 1979, p.392.
55. *Passport*, p.137.

56. *Inside Story*, p.202.
57. See, for example, *At the Barricades*, pp.241–3.
58. *At the Barricades*, p.viii.
59. Harold R. Isaacs, *No Peace for Asia*, Macmillan, New York, 1947.
60. *No Peace for Asia*, 2nd edition, MIT Press, Cambridge, 1967, pp.xxviii–xxix.
61. I draw this inference from a prisoner's account of that meeting: George E. Smith, *P.O.W.: Two Years with the Vietcong*, Ramparts Press, Berkeley, 1971, pp.157–61. It is not apparent from Burchett's own account, in *Inside Story*, pp.101–106.
62. Wilfred Burchett, letter to David D. Gourlay, 22 September 1980.
63. *At the Barricades*, p.12.

10

The West Wind Blows Back

Joseph T. Miller

In April 1965, Wilfred Burchett travelled to Indonesia for the tenth anniversary of the Bandung Conference. There he met with China's Premier Zhou Enlai, their first meeting since 1941. From the subsequent filmed interview with Zhou, it seems that Zhou considered Burchett to have become an exceptionally knowledgeable person regarding *Vietnamese* affairs. But perhaps not Chinese ones.

Zhou claimed that China was 'ready to send out men to fight shoulder to shoulder with the South Vietnamese people when they so require'.[1] Burchett speculated in 1981 (with the help of new documentation released by Vietnam) that this expression of potential military support for the Vietnamese revolution was merely Zhou's view, that it was in contradiction to Mao, who had sent a message in 1964 to Ho Chi Minh (through Deng Xiaoping) 'offering all necessary military and other aid – on condition that Vietnam refuse any aid at all from the Soviet Union . . . this was rejected'.[2] Zhou's public commitment contained no such conditions.

As had happened once before, in 1954 at Geneva, the closed nature of China's domestic and foreign politicking prevented Burchett, even with his inside sources, from clearly measuring China's real support for the Vietnamese. Burchett, as well as other journalists and scholars, would only learn this through trial and error over the space of some twenty years.[3] For now, in 1965, China was to many a 'revolutionary power' on the edge of a shooting war with the United States over Vietnam.

It is in this context that Burchett's later relationship with China should be viewed.

The years 1966–81 saw great changes in Wilfred Burchett's relationship with, and attitude towards, the People's Republic of China. On the one hand, there was very high regard for China's domestic accomplishments on Burchett's part, an attitude which apparently never changed (at least as far as available materials suggest) and which he shared with a wide range of China observers, journalists and scholars. On the other hand, Burchett experienced gradual disillusion with China's foreign policy, reaching total estrangement by the late 1970s during his on-the-spot investigation of the China-Kampuchea-Vietnam events from 1978 to 1980.

Burchett's major concern, and the subject of most of his writing throughout the 1960s and early 1970s, was the Vietnam war. He did manage to stay in touch with events in China, however. An early (and private) comment from Burchett, for example, on Mao's 'Great Proletarian Cultural Revolution' is found in a letter to his father dated 14 November 1966. He remarked that China's efforts in this campaign were directed toward 'what may well be its greatest threat since the CP [Communist Party] came to power'. He recalled that Stalin had also faced a 'great new threat' (though 'from abroad') and had engaged in 'a crude and wrongly conceived attempt to put his house in order'. Mao Ze-dong, however, was 'cleaning up the sclerotics in the CP . . . in a way that has a great deal of grassroots democracy in it'. This, at least, was the view of a friend of Burchett's. Further, the letter points out that his long experience with communist parties had caused Burchett to be sympathetic to Mao's efforts:

> The CPs in all the countries I have visited, where they are in power, except perhaps Vietnam, tend to become a closed-society where those who have joined to have the good jobs, the social-material benefits, far outnumber the old veterans who joined in the days when CP membership meant just the opposite, social and material sacrifices, sacrifice of life and family happiness, etc.[4]

Even with this relatively positive view of the Cultural Revolution, Burchett admitted: 'There are some aspects of it all that I don't like very much, but then I am not Chinese, not Asiatic and cannot sit in judgement on what is good for them; on their way of handling things.' He expressed happiness, though, that his 'good friends' still had their jobs in China, while 'a few that I didn't admire very much are out of their jobs'.[5]

By April–May 1967, Burchett was in Beijing once again, experiencing at first-hand this Cultural Revolution. As he described the scene in *At the Barricades*, China was in 'convulsions', with rival factions in the streets fighting for pre-eminence as 'the only true champion' of the Cultural Revolution.[6] While making this visit, Burchett called upon some old friends, such as Dr George Hatem (known to the Chinese as Dr Ma Hai-teh) and Anna Louise Strong, both American advocates for the Chinese revolution. In his discussion with Strong concerning the Cultural Revolution, Burchett was told that '"Mao has let the genie out of the bottle, and I'm not sure he's going to be able to get it back in."'[7] She also made it quite clear that Mao's status was not as great as the outside world was led to believe. In what Burchett described as 'what for her was probably the greatest heresy of her life', Strong then said '"At this stage of affairs, it's more important that Chou [Zhou Enlai] survives than Mao."'[8] These comments were not revealed by Burchett at the time, possibly out of concern for Strong's safety, given the overall situation.

Another incident during this 1967 China visit linked Burchett's Vietnam interest with the *realpolitik* of China. Anna Louise Strong invited Burchett to address a group of 'progressives in the foreign community' in Beijing on the topic of Vietnam. Just four months earlier, Burchett had made international news when he interviewed the Foreign Minister of the Democratic Republic of Vietnam (DRV), Nguyen Duy Trinh, who stated that peace talks with the United States could begin 'after the unconditional cessation of bombing and all other acts of war against the DRV. . .'[9] This was generally seen as a major DRV concession in response to the statements by Rusk and Johnson about US willingness to 'go anywhere, anytime' to engage in negotiations. The DRV was calling the US bluff.[10] As Burchett learned after his talk, these foreign 'progressives' who lived in Beijing viewed this move by the DRV as a 'betrayal' of the Vietnamese revolution. According to Burchett, such attitudes reflected an assumption that there were two separate forces conduct the struggle in Vietnam, when, in reality, 'there was one single revolutionary strategy for the military, political, and diplomatic fronts of Vietnam and one united leadership of that strategy, but that was still secret', so he could not reveal this to these critics.

Burchett heard attacks on Vietnamese strategy by staunch 'Maoists' at this meeting, such as Sidney Rittenberg, an American who worked as an advisor at Beijing Radio. Of Rittenberg Burchett had this to say: 'His brown shirt and Red Guard armband took me back to Berlin in 1939. Wagging his finger at me, he shouted, "You don't negotiate with imperialism – you destroy it!"'[12]

Finally Burchett asked, 'Where does it come from? Is this official Chinese policy?' He learned, through further discussions with some of his old friends, like Qiao Guanhua, that this was the case, and it was further confirmed by talks with Vietnamese officials later. And, in 1968, when the negotiations began in Paris, Burchett was told at the Chinese Embassy 'that the talks were indeed regarded as a "betrayal"'.[13] Was this simply another example of the 'excesses' of Mao's Cultural Revolution? Burchett was not saying, and, as far as I can determine, he produced no open criticism of the Chinese policies at this time.

Early 1971 saw the beginning of so-called 'ping-pong diplomacy' and of a new period of closer relations between the United States and China. This period also produced some of Wilfred Burchett's most extensive reporting on Chinese affairs. His primary interest concerned the theory and practice of Chinese foreign policy, especially as it related to the continuing Indochina War. In a *Guardian* piece on 20 March 1971, Burchett warned the then US President Richard Nixon of the danger inherent in ignoring China while trying to secure an 'acceptable' resolution of the war in Indochina (by then extended into Laos and Kampuchea). It was his strong impression that China was 'extremely serious' in its support for the 'Indochinese peoples'.[14] This report was written just prior to the invitation to the US Ping Pong Team to visit China, an event which drastically shifted the attentions and perceptions of many observers of world politics. All of a sudden, China had appeared on the international scene, newly stable after years of isolation and internal convulsion, visible in its desire to reach out – even to a major foe: the United States.

In the face of this, Burchett argued that Chinese foreign policy perspectives and goals had not really changed: 'Any illusion that the olive branch offered the American people betokens the slightest modification in China's attitude toward US imperialism and aggression must be immediately dismissed.'[15] He referred to this new initiative as a 'two-edged foreign policy', that is, a combination of 'diplomacy . . . based on the five principles of peaceful coexistence, and avowed Chinese support for revolutionary forces abroad'. China's more outward approach, according to Burchett, reflected the re-emergence of his old friend, Zhou Enlai, who seemed to be asserting himself much more after relative quietude during the Cultural Revolution. In this June 1971 article Burchett rather confidently predicted that China might gain its rightful place in the United Nations, 'perhaps by the coming autumn'.[16] But there would be no serious questioning of the China-Vietnam relationship on the part of Burchett and some others over the next few years, though some sectors of the left voiced suspicion.[17]

We will now turn to Burchett's last writing on China's internal developments during the early 1970s. He made three working trips to China over 1971–73, including his assignment with the Nixon press entourage in 1972. What seems to have been his final trip, in the summer of 1973, was made with a book contract under his arm. He was to produce a manuscript with Rewi Alley on China's domestic affairs, a topic of great interest in those early days of China's new 'opening' to the world. As he remarked about this work in 1981: 'We were lucky enough to have caught China in a period of relative calm after the storms of the Cultural Revolution and before the convulsions which occurred after the deaths of Chou En-lai and Mao Tse-tung and the denunciation of the Gang of Four.'[18]

Prior to this, Burchett wrote a series of articles on various Chinese

domestic issues for papers like the *Guardian*. In essence, the 1973 tour
and the benefit of long-time China resident, Rewi Alley, as co-author,
allowed Burchett to expand on this earlier work. This would be the
second major work on China, as he had promised his father back in
1951. In the introductory remarks to the new book, *China: The Quality
of Life*, he stressed the real difficulty facing anyone who tried to
'generalize' about China on the basis of limited knowledge. He hoped to
produce a work, based on extensive travels across China and Alley's
forty-six years of China experience, which would 'remain valid for a
whole period . . . ' He wrote that a 'central interest' of the authors was
to 'measure the changes that have occurred in recent years . . . and to
set them in perspective against what we know of old China'. This would
all be done from the perspective of the 'ordinary Chinese' citizen.[19]

First of all, a look at Burchett's discussion of the communes, a topic of
central concern to all visitors during this period. He refers to this project
as 'most controversial' and 'most audacious' in its departure from the
Soviet model, having been instituted about the time of the downturn in
Sino-Soviet relations. To Burchett, in 1973, the 'setting-up of the
communes . . . marked a point of no return in the social, economic and
administrative organization of China', and this gave 'more power than
ever before' to the Chinese peasantry.[20] In his investigation of this
continuing process, having visited a series of communes over many
years, Burchett (and Alley, for they speak in one voice) generally allow
leading figures in the various units (or *danwei*) to speak for the group
and tell its story. This format produces page after page of extensive
quotations, but it does give one the impression that China and its people
are telling the story.

Even prior to the Cultural Revolution, the commune system had
been, out of necessity, drawn back from the ambitious 1958 programme
which had resulted in large-scale dislocation and disruption of China's
agricultural production and great suffering for the peasantry. This
background is not mentioned by Burchett; rather the system he viewed
in 1973 as one fundamentally unchanged from 1958 onwards, is highly
praised for having been accomplished 'without any interruption of
production'.[21] In large part, this portrait of what Burchett calls 'fifty
thousand policeless states' is an official one, even though it is the result
of direct observation.

Of course, much that was written on China and its commune system
was as positive and generally uncritical as the picture given by Burchett.
For example, the first delegation of the US Committee of Concerned
Asian Scholars to visit China in mid-1971, as well as the economists Joan
Robinson and Dwight Perkins, also made favourable reports of life in
the communes.[22] The data Burchett and Alley collected and the
attitudes expressed to them in interviews must be seen as part of a
widely accepted, 'official' reality of China in that period.[23]

The same goes for the Burchett-Alley material on women in China in
1973. Chinese women are presented here as fully involved in all sectors

of China's production effort. They are housewives who banded together to form the Chongqing Motor Vehicle Lights Workshop in 1966, responding to 'Chairman Mao's call during the Great Proletarian Cultural Revolution to go into production in a big way'.[24] They are representatives on local revolutionary committees (administrative organs set up at all levels of Chinese society during the Cultural Revolution), such as Chu Li and Feng Tze-niu in the Nanjing Radio Elements Factory.[25] As Burchett reports, the older women are 'integrated into the ever-expanding social and economic life of their street committees'.[26] After visiting a wide range of units all over China, which contained large contingents of housewives and other women in the workforce, Burchett commented: 'By releasing the potential energies and talents of that half of the adult population which had previously been "supporting half of heaven" by household drudgery, the housewives' factories play a major role in women's real liberation.'[27]

Further evidence of the basic integration of women into all levels of the Chinese workforce is found in Burchett's notes on the Daqing oilfields in Heilongjiang Province. There he visited what were called 'Women's Wells', since they were supervised by teams of young women, apparently not housewives, as with the other units described above.[28] In discussions with these and other women in the Daqing Municipality, the 'real essence of Women's Lib [*sic*] in China' was presented by Li Chang-yung, a vice-chairwoman of the revolutionary committee:

> Before, we women had only our menfolk, kids and household chores to think about. Now we think about the whole country – the whole world – starting with the oilfield and ending with Tien An Men. There has been a revolution in family relations . . . Now there is real respect for each other . . . We've acquired really equal status. When our husbands come home they help with the cooking and washing-up. They help look after the kids. We're really emancipated, socially, politically, economically.[29]

Finally, a look at the question of education and the role of intellectuals as recorded by Burchett and Alley. This was possibly *the* central issue of the Cultural Revolution, other than the top-level power struggle. In Burchett's report, Chinese who were directly involved speak for themselves and provide a vivid portrait of the new role for intellectuals and the changed process of education in the early 1970s.

The focus is on Qinghua (Tsinghua) University, scene of some of the most violent clashes between various Red Guard factions at the height of the Cultural Revolution. Burchett talked with Ma Wen-tsung, who explained the 'fundamentally new attitude' regarding education. Ma referred to Mao Ze-dong's idea 'that education should serve proletarian politics and be combined with productive labour' as propagated during the 'Great Leap Forward', but knocked off course through the efforts of Liu Shaoqi. Liu, according to Ma, 'insisted on reverting to the classical bourgeois yardsticks for measuring the results and methods of teaching'.[30] This caused rising discontent at universities like Qinghua, and it all exploded with Mao's 7 May 1966 directive cutting short the school period and proclaiming 'There should be a revolution in education and the leadership of education by bourgeois intellectuals should no longer be tolerated.'[31]

With the establishment of the revolutionary committees in 1969, new methods and new standards were put into effect. The idea was to produce 'graduates to serve a proletarian and not a bourgeois state'. Some of these new methods included: sending teaching faculty and administrators into communes and factories to develop hands-on knowledge; bringing in 'veteran workers' to serve as full-time teachers; setting up workshops and laboratories within the university which would serve factory production; and recruiting new students directly from among workers, peasants and soldiers.[32]

As for the intellectuals, the professors who were expected to function under these new, 'experimental' conditions, Burchett recorded the story of Professor Chien Wei-ch'ang, a graduate of the California Institute of Technology, who had come to Qinghua in 1946. Professor Chien felt that the Cultural Revolution was of 'paramount importance' in his life, 'a real turning-point'. He had now decided that he had 'overlooked . . . that what I was teaching and the way I was teaching it were way out of line with the needs of the new society. . .' He held fast to his 'totally bourgeois outlook', infecting his students with the same views. Professor Chien was 'one of the chief targets of criticism' at Qinghua, and he became very much concerned about the possible loss of his job.[33]

As the violence settled down and the workers' propaganda teams moved on to the campus, Professor Chien recognized the need to engage in 'self-criticism' about his 'bourgeois' attitudes and practices. Since that time, Professor Chien had done some work in various factories in order to go beyond his mere theoretical knowledge regarding steel and to learn the practical side of steel-making from the workers themselves.[34]

Professor Chien's story is presented by Burchett as one example of the phenomenon to be found all over China in those days. There are no critical comments; selected Chinese are left to describe in their own terms one important aspect of their new 'quality of life' following the Cultural Revolution.[35]

Richard M. Pfeffer, writing in 1973, agreed that 'one of the main purposes of the CR [Cultural Revolution] was to transform China's educational system'. His review of the goals of this effort was almost exactly the same as that found in Burchett's report. Pfeffer saw this new set of policies in a quite positive light, pointing to the importance of this 'practical service orientation' over the previously-held élite views of education.[36] He pointed to this new orientation as directly linked to the revolutionary ideals embraced by the Chinese people, thus not easily transferable to any society uncommitted to similar revolutionary values and lifestyles.[37]

Thus, in three major areas out of many covered by *China: The Quality of Life*, the authors were really quite representative of much of the writing on these issues in the early 1970s. In fact, if one were to review the whole of the book in greater detail, this would be true across the board. What we cannot do is say very much at all about Burchett's later views, concerning the post-Mao era in China's internal development, for the book he wrote with Rewi Alley is really his last word on the topic.[38]

In the end, it would be Indochina and the *foreign policy* of China towards that region (and Africa) which caused a final parting of the ways between Wilfred Burchett and the People's Republic.[39] His real horror at Chinese complicity in the attacks on Vietnam by the Pol Pot regime in Kampuchea (not to mention China's own invasion of Vietnam in 1979) is supported with extensive documentation in his 1981 book, *The China–Cambodia–Vietnam Triangle*. Here he admits his own ignorance about China's behind-the-scenes role at Geneva in 1954 (when it pressured the Vietnamese to accept division of their country), about China's role in hindering aid to Vietnam during the war with the United States, and about China's role in attempting to fight the Vietnamese down 'to the last Kampuchean' into the 1980s.[40]

With the full realization of China's negative role in the region of Indochina and elsewhere, Burchett went very public with his criticisms, quite a departure from the early days of his relations with China. He had learned the hard way just what China's policies meant in the cost of human lives under Pol Pot. It is one thing to be a friend of the Chinese people, but quite another to be 'friendly' toward a government which sponsors such horrors in the pursuit of its own 'national interest', just like any other superpower. Burchett's account of Kampuchea contains a strong sense of remorse mixed with the horror, almost as if to say, 'Why didn't I speak out sooner?' This is apparently something that those who offered undiscriminating support for the struggles of the Indochinese against the United States must now also share.[41]

Wilfred Burchett's writings on China cover a vast expanse in space and time and emotion, and it is clear from this writing that he remained what he started out to be: a working journalist who was fully part of the human stories covered day after day. Many may quarrel with this or that story on China, its focus and interpretation, but we can see in its unfolding, through Burchett's craft, the flesh-and-blood existence of a whole people struggling to overcome many serious obstacles.

Questions may be raised about the choices Burchett made about some stories. There are the glowing reports about 'New China' in the early 1950s, with no apparent coverage of the other side, the 'underside', of the story, the social and political suppression of those days of early revolutionary reconstruction. Of course, that side of the story has been told over and over by other journalists and scholars, indeed it has been presented as the whole story of China in revolution. Readers of Burchett's reports can at least be thankful that he was interested in looking at the other picture and that he focused upon the real hopes and ideals of any revolutionary process. Stories of the larger human struggle and its small successes against all odds presented by Burchett and others must be seen as welcome correctives, even necessary ones.

Burchett's lack of public comment on the 'underside' of the Cultural Revolution can be criticized. He certainly found fault with, and reported on, some of the extremes of violence and vandalism, but he didn't 'see' the true extent of social, political and economic disruption that many now take for granted as part and parcel of that period. He was not alone in this, surely, and from accounts we now have from those immediately involved, such as Ruth Earnshaw Lo, we might understand why many visitors, knowledgeable or not, 'friend' or not, came away with little in-depth understanding of the whole story.

Burchett's main emphasis in the 1960s and 1970s was coverage of the Indochina Wars, and reports on China during that period were about China as 'partner' in the revolutionary struggle. It may be difficult to see how one as close to the leaderships of Vietnam, Kampuchea, and China as was Burchett could not know the full background of these struggles, could not pick up on the strains and tensions in this triangular relationship. But such a person might not seek, or expect to find, the divisiveness and conflict which has been at the base of so much of China's relationship with Indochina. The real tragedy of this belated understanding is expressed best by Wilfred Burchett himself, in the closing pages of his last work on this topic:

> It is a sad, sad story not only in terms of the immeasurable human sufferings in the countries involved but also in terms of the blasted hopes of hundreds of millions of people throughout the world who believed in a new order of international, socialist solidarity in which peace would reign supreme.[42]

Thus we have a sometimes sad, sometimes joyful and always human story in the relationship between Wilfred Burchett and China. It seems clear from his last writings that he derived many personal and professional lessons from that relationship, and one hopes that those are taken up by others, learned well, and passed on.

Notes

1. Wilfred Burchett, *At the Barricades*, Quartet, London, 1980, p.225; in Burchett's 1976 obituary on Zhou Enlai, this line is rendered: 'We are ready to send our troops to fight side by side with the people of South Vietnam whenever they need them.' See 'Comrade Chou En-lai is dead', *Guardian*, 21 January 1976.
2. *At the Barricades*, p.226; also, Hemen Ray, *China's Vietnam War*, Radiant Publishers, New Delhi, 1983, pp.25, 30–2; and Donald S. Zagoria, *Vietnam Triangle: Moscow, Peking, Hanoi*, Pegasus, New York, 1967, pp.48–51.
3. See Edward Friedman, 'The Original Chinese Revolution Remains in Power', *Bulletin of Concerned Asian Scholars*, vol. 13, no.3 (July–September 1981), and Mark Selden, 'The Logic – and Limits – of Chinese Socialist Development', in Neville

Maxwell and Bruce McFarlane (eds), *China's Changed Road to Development*, Pergamon Press, Oxford, New York, Sydney, 1984, pp.1–7

4. Letter of 14 November 1966; notes supplied by Ben Kiernan. Burchett Papers, State library of Victoria.

5. Ibid. Commenting on his 1951 trip to China thirty years later, Burchett wrote: 'The passion and conviction with which engineer Chien expressed herself symbolized the ardour with which, I was later to find, many intellectuals from well-to-do families identified themselves with the Chinese Revolution (but were poorly repaid in what was termed the Great Proletarian Cultural Revolution).' *At the Barricades*, p.161. As to the cultural relativism in Burchett's remark about not being Chinese and, therefore, being unwilling to judge the practices of the Cultural Revolution, this has been a common reaction by many, whether journalist or scholar, sympathetic to the Chinese revolution, who are fearful that their own ethnocentrism might cause them to criticize Chinese practices unfairly. This was especially true during the late 1960s and early 1970s, when there was a great deal of Western guilt in the air (justifiable though it might have been) over mistreatment of 'third world' peoples. Of course, the horror of the war in Vietnam helped fuel this reaction and caused many scholarly efforts and travel records about post-revolutionary societies like China to gloss over anything that might make those societies look bad. More recently, there has been a greater willingness to maintain a critical perspective, even toward those societies with which we sympathize in their efforts to break away from the stranglehold of international capital. See Claudie Broyelle, Jacques Broyelle, Evelyne Tschirhart, *China: A Second Look*, Harvester Press, Sussex, 1980, esp. Chapters I and VII.

6. *At the Barricades*, p.241.

7. Ibid., p.242.

8. Ibid.

9. Ibid., p.237; also, George C. Herring, (ed.), *The Secret Diplomacy of the Vietnam War: The Negotiating Volumes of the Pentagon Papers*, University of Texas Press, Austin, 1983, pp.422–4, 549–50, 613–17, 769–70.

10. Zagoria, op.cit., pp.60–61, 121, 157–8.

11. *At the Barricades*, p.242.

12. Ibid.; see Burchett's 'Mao's Problems with "Maoists" ', *Guardian*, 12 May 1971, and John Fraser, *The Chinese: Portrait of a People*, Summit Books, New York, 1980, pp.183–95. In 1981, Burchett referred to the 'thesis that China was prepared to fight the United States "to the last Vietnamese" ' as having been 'indignantly refuted by myself and other pro-Chinese "Vietnam watchers", but it has been subsequently proven to be only too correct'. *The China–Cambodia–Vietnam Triangle*, Vanguard Books, Chicago, 1981, p.224.

13. *At the Barricades*, p.243; *The China–Cambodia–Vietnam Triangle*, p.171.

14. Wilfred Burchett, 'Nixon Ignores China at His Peril', *Guardian*, 20 March 1971.

15. Wilfred Burchett, 'No Changes in Basic Chinese Foreign Policy', *Guardian*, 24 April 1971.

16. Wilfred Burchett, 'China's Two-edged Foreign Policy', *Guardian*, 2 June 1971. Burchett might have expected a much more 'revolutionary' foreign policy from China with this 'return' of Zhou Enlai, recalling Zhou's willingness, in 1965, to offer Chinese troops to Vietnam to assist in the war. At the very least, Vietnam would not be undercut in its attempts to resolve the war in its *own* way – negotiations would no longer be seen as 'betrayal'. Much later, Burchett learned that Chinese collusion with the United States in opposition to Vietnamese interests began almost immediately upon the PRC's entrance into the United Nations in October 1971. See references to secret meetings between Henry Kissinger and Qiao Guanhua, then Chairman of the PRC's UN delegation, in *At the Barricades*, p.287, and *The China–Cambodia–Vietnam Triangle*, p.171.

17. Though not dealt with in detail here, Burchett's forceful and informative *Guardian* articles on China and the United Nations (see issues of 6, 13, 27 October; 3, 10, 17, 24 November 1971) are very useful for anyone doing particular research in this area. Burchett was especially critical of any attempts to promote the so-called 'two-China' policy, or 'One China, One Taiwan'. Articles relating to Vietnam or broader

questions concerning US-China relations are: 'Nixon Can't End War in Peking', 20 October 1971 (see his reconstruction of his secret meeting with Kissinger in the White House on 11 October 1971, in *At the Barricades*, pp.274–81); 'What's Nixon Looking for in China?', 16 February 1972; and 'China Pledges Solidarity with Vietnam', 22 March 1972. One example of the most vehement responses from the 'pro-China' sectors of the US left can be found in *Progressive Labor*, vol. 8, no.3 (November 1971). Other, more solidly researched and cogently argued, leftist critiques were written by Les Evans and Dick Roberts in the journal *International Socialist Review* (see issues June 1971; March and December 1972; January and November 1973; June 1974), as well as by David Horowitz, then editor of *Ramparts* magazine, for that journal's July and August issues in 1972. Each of these pieces is important in trying to understand just how the US left responded to changing US-China relations in this early period.

18. *At the Barricades*, p.292.
19. Wilfred Burchett and Rewi Alley, *China: The Quality of Life*, Penguin, London, 1976, pp.10–11. It was during this 1973 trip to China that Burchett contributed the cover story on Lin Piao for the *Far Eastern Economic Review (FEER)*. See 'Lin Piao's Plot – The Full Story', *FEER*, 20 August 1973.
20. Ibid., p.15.
21. Ibid.; also, see Andrew Watson, *Living in China*, Rowman and Littlefield, Totowa, New Jersey, 1975, pp.65–70; Dwight H. Perkins, 'Development of Agriculture', in Michel Oksenberg (ed.), *China's Developmental Experience*, Praeger, New York, Washington, London, 1973, pp.66–7; for an early oppositional Chinese critique of the communes, see P'eng Shu-tse, 'A Criticism of the Various Views Supporting the Rural People's Communes', in his *The Chinese Communist Party in Power*, Monad Press, New York, 1980, pp.171–223.
22. Burchett and Alley, op.cit., p.33, from *Economic Management: China 1972*, Anglo-Chinese Educational Institute, London, March 1973; also, Joan Robinson, *The Cultural Revolution in China*, Penguin, Baltimore, Maryland, 1969, pp.34–9. In 1982, Robinson wrote: 'I have not written anything about China since the death of Mao. I have been accused of being starry-eyed about the revolution and I have to admit some truth in the accusation . . . [I] was always fighting off disillusionment until I could no longer accept the obscurantism, the violence and the downright silliness of the last stages of the Cultural Revolution.' *China Now*, no.100 (January–February 1982), p.2. See Committee of Concerned Asian Scholars, *China! Inside the People's Republic*, Bantam Books, New York, 1972, Chapter 5.
23. See these Burchett pieces for the *Guardian*: 'Mao's Daring Experiment is Succeeding', 19 May 1971; 'Peasants Shape Future', 10 May 1972; 'Self-reliance in Communes', 17 May 1972. Also, Tillman Durdin, James Reston, Seymour Topping, *The New York Times Report from Red China*, edited by Frank Ching, Quadrangle Books, New York and Chicago, 1971, Chapters 2 and 3. Even the *Wall Street Journal* had positive things to say about the communes; see 'Commune Living – Chinese Style', in Warren H. Phillips and Robert Keatley, *China: Behind the Mask*, Dow Jones Books, Princeton, New Jersey, 1973, pp.102–10.
24. Burchett and Alley, op.cit., p.84.
25. Ibid., p.91.
26. Ibid.
27. Ibid., p.100.
28. Ibid., pp.107–8.
29. Ibid., p.117; for a review and critique of women's liberation in China, see Phyllis Andors, *The Unfinished Liberation of Chinese Women, 1949–1980* Indiana University Press, Bloomington, 1983, esp. Chapter 6.
30. Burchett and Alley, op.cit., pp.181–2.
31. Ibid.,
32. Ibid., p.183; see p.184 for selection criteria.
33. Ibid., p.186.
34. Ibid., pp.188–9.
35. See Tillman Durdin on Professor Chien, in Durdin, Reston, Topping, op.cit.,

pp.283–285. For a recent insider's view of just what this period was like for intellectuals in China, see Ruth Earnshaw Lo and Katherine S. Kinderman, *In the Eye of the Typhoon*, Harcourt Brace Jovanovich, New York and London,1980.

36. Richard M. Pfeffer, 'Leaders and Masses', in Oksenberg (ed.), op.cit., pp.166–7.
37. Ibid., p.172; also, Committee of Concerned Asian Scholars, op.cit., Chapter 7.
38. As for Rewi Alley, there are some revealing remarks by and about him in E. Grey Dimond, MD, *Inside China Today: A Western View*, Norton, New York and London, 1983. For example, in a quotation from Geoff Chapple's biography of Alley, Dimond reports Alley as saying: 'The trouble is . . . you are limited in not being able to say anything without getting others implicated who don't want to be implicated.' (p.50). Further, in July, 1977, Dimond noted: 'The return of Deng Xiaoping to power was the best possible thing that could happen as far as George [Hatem] and Rewi were concerned . . . Rewi said that he and George had "breathed a sigh of relief when Deng took over".' (p.93)
39. Wilfred Burchett, 'China's Foreign Policy: A Friend of China Raises Some Questions', *Guardian*, 5 May 1976. William Hinton presented a defence of Chinese foreign policy in the same issue. It is interesting to note that China's foreign minister during this period was Burchett's 'old friend' from wartime China, Qiao Guanhua. We should also note that Burchett's critique has attained some prominence in a 'mainstream' text on the topic. See Robert C. North, *The Foreign Relations of China*, Third Edition. Duxbury Press, North Scituate, Massachusetts, 1978, pp.192–3, 215.
40. *The China–Cambodia–Vietnam Triangle*, pp.40–42, 171–2, 224; Hemen Ray, op.cit., Chapters 1, 4, 7; also, Grant Evans and Kelvin Rowley, *Red Brotherhood at War: Indochina Since the Fall of Saigon*, Verso Editions, London, 1984, esp. Chapter 5.
41. *At the Barricades*, pp.12–13; Wilfred Burchett, 'China *vs* Vietnam', *New York Times*, Op-Ed page, 23 January 1979; see his series concerning China and Indochina for *In These Times*, a leftist newspaper published in Chicago, written from February through October, 1979. Concerning Burchett's relationship with the *Guardian*, see: Cedric Belfrage and James Aronson, *Something to Guard: The Stormy Life of the National Guardian, 1948–1967*, Columbia University Press, New York, 1978, pp.112–13, 292–4, 303–304, and, Abe Weisburd, 'A Life Committed to the People's Cause', *Guardian*, 12 October 1983, a two-page obituary about Burchett, recounting his history with the *Guardian*.
42. *The China–Cambodia–Vietnam Triangle*, p.227.

11

Put Not Thy Trust in Princes: Burchett on Kampuchea

Ben Kiernan

A Buddhist monk, representing a group of 400 Khmer refugees who had just fled to safety across the border, sadly told Burchett what had been happening on the other side: 'Our schools have all been closed . . . With the slaughter of our people, the destruction of our villages, the repression of our culture and language, it seems our people are to be exterminated.' These Khmer refugees were not fleeing Pol Pot, who held power in Kampuchea from 1975 to 1979. This was early 1962, and the refugees were members of the Khmer minority in South Vietnam, or Khmer Krom. The atrocities, which they described in detail, and which were in many respects similar to those of Pol Pot, they laid at the door of the pro-American Diem regime in Saigon.[1] And the safety they found was under the protection of the neutralist Kampuchean regime of Prince Norodom Sihanouk, who ruled the country from 1954 to 1970.

There are several points of interest in this account. One is that Burchett's reporting was unique at the time. Only later was it substantiated, and even then only in passing, by other English-speaking journalists and writers.[2] The sufferings of these Khmer refugees, as they reported them after crossing the border from South Vietnam, went largely unnoticed in the West despite Prince Sihanouk's efforts to draw attention to them as early as 1961, when he claimed that 'a systematic racial policy' was being implemented by the Saigon government. The numbers of refugees increased greatly after US ground troops landed in Vietnam in 1965. From then until March 1968, over 17,000 Khmer Krom fled to Kampuchea, including over 2,300 Buddhist monks.[3] In September 1967 Burchett returned to the same spot, Phnom Den in Takeo province. He interviewed a Khmer Krom defector from the US Special Forces who detailed 'the destruction of Khmer villages and massacres of the Khmer population in our mopping-up operations'.[4] By then, however, Sihanouk had severed diplomatic relations with the USA, and few other Western journalists were allowed into Kampuchea.

In the Pol Pot period (1975–79), Khmer refugees who fled from Kampuchea to Thailand received much greater Western sympathy. Pol Pot's was an avowedly communist government, and Thailand an ally of the USA. But for the same reasons, Burchett declined to take up the refugees' cause. To the extent that he kept informed of what was happening in Kampuchea – Burchett's major interest in the mid–1970s was southern Africa – he was disinclined to believe the refugees' accounts of terror, starvation and cultural destruction. (To a large extent I also misjudged the Pol Pot regime's responsibility for this.) I believe this was the greatest reporting failure of Burchett's career, given his knowledge of Kampuchea (he had lived there for four years), his previous record of sympathy for Khmer refugees, and the enormity of Pol Pot's crimes (over a million Khmers died under his rule). The refugee issue is in fact a model of Burchett's reporting on Kampuchea in general – some of it was very good, some very bad.

There is another interesting point arising from Burchett's 1962 interviews at Phnom Den. His guide on that occasion was the governor of Takeo province, In Tam, then a rising star in Sihanouk's administration. But in 1970, Tam led the National Assembly in overthrowing Sihanouk in favour of General Lon Nol. Sihanouk took up exile in Beijing, and of course remained on good terms with Burchett, who helped him to write *My War with the CIA* in 1973. Lon Nol was defeated by Pol Pot's forces in 1975, and In Tam fled to Thailand. Sihanouk returned home, but was soon placed under house arrest. Like nearly all other journalists, Burchett was excluded from the country.

Then, with Pol Pot's overthrow by the Vietnamese army in early 1979, Sihanouk and In Tam resumed a relationship broken in 1970. While Sihanouk toured the world's capitals seeking support, Tam now became the Prince's man in Thailand, and eventually Commander-in-Chief of the Armée Nationale Sihanoukiste, a small force on the Thai-Kampuchean frontier. Burchett must have welcolmed this *rapprochement*, for in 1980 he was still praising Sihanouk as a 'dynamic, intelligent, highly articulate and courageous patriot'[5] – despite Sihanouk's opposition to the Vietnamese occupation which Burchett defended.

International politics being what it is, however, Sihanouk and In Tam were pressured (by China, ASEAN* and the USA) back into an alliance with the remnant forces of Pol Pot, with the aim of overthrowing the Vietnamese-backed government of Heng Samrin.

This was too much for Burchett. He had been wrong about Pol Pot's role once before, and had supported Sihanouk in an earlier alliance with Pol Pot, which ended in disaster for the Kampuchean people. But Burchett had also supported Sihanouk for the fourteen years before that, and the wrench, when it came, must have hurt. (Perhaps feeling betrayed, Burchett pointed out that Sihanouk was taking 'a step which he repeatedly swore he would never take'. Nevertheless, when Sihanouk consented in July 1982 to join in coalition with the Pol Pot forces, he became, in Burchett's mind, 'a relic of the past'.[6] Finally, in 1985 In Tam again broke with Sihanouk.

This *pas de trois* of Sihanouk, In Tam and Wilfred Burchett, which lasted for twenty years and through four regimes, is in many ways a lesson in modern Kampuchean politics. But there were other wrenches involved in Burchett's Kampuchean footwork. As he passed Washington, which was beginning to favour Pol Pot just as Burchett began to oppose him, the radical New York *Guardian* stood its ground, declining to take his anti-Pol Pot stance and even ignoring his on-the-spot despatches from the Vietnamese border in late 1978. Burchett resigned in protest, ending his only regular source of income and a close relationship that had begun in 1956 – the same year that he had first visited Kampuchea and met Sihanouk.

Mekong Upstream, which Burchett first published in Hanoi in 1957, was the first book about twentieth-century Kampuchean politics in any language.[7] It begins with a description of Phnom Penh's life and colour. To be sure, there is a slight tinge of socialist realism ('an endless stream of porters, carrying on their polished bronze and copper backs . . .'), as well as socialist imagination ('Cambodians, Vietnamese and Chinese fought side by side in the national liberation movement'). But it is a good description of one of the beautiful cities of Asia, then almost unknown outside the Frênch-speaking domains.

Burchett is master of the verbal snapshot, picturing, for instance, a sweet-toothed elephant flicking a load of sugar cane from one of those bronzed backs. But his camera also pans the Phnom Penh backdrop, capturing the mundane with the exotic:

> The most typical scene in any street . . . is the housewife returning from market with a few green vegetables stuffed on top of a basket of rice and a fish or two with their tails still flapping, dangling from a sliver of bamboo. Various exotic creatures are usually on display in the market to tempt the appetite of the gourmets; within a space of half a dozen paces, I saw one morning a civet cat, vampire bats, their embryo wings stretched out on boards showing a good yard between

* Association of South East Asian Nations

wing tips, a tortoise, a strange beast like an armadillo encased in armoured mail . . .

The focus is on street life, the waterfront, the different sessions of the day, the customs of the three ethnic communities; it is a unique account of Phnom Penh in the 1950s in that it ignores the opium dens and nightclubs so favoured in contemporary Western writings.[8] Nevertheless it manages to convey 'an exciting blend of colours and odours' and enthusiasm for 'the lovely soft, liquid national music of Cambodia which enchants all who hear it'.

After reading seven pages of this I suddenly wondered how Burchett could have kept his silence twenty years later when the entire capital was evacuated by Pol Pot. Burchett's politics (like the 1970–75 war) had obviously helped to dispel memory of the city sights, sounds and smells that he had once so vividly recorded.

Like many other Western observers, Burchett romanticized the Khmers. Perhaps unaware of the ruthlessness with which the anti-colonial war (as well as brutal internecine struggles within the resistance) had just been fought, Burchett praised the 'racial tolerance' of this people 'to whom violence of any kind is repugnant'. His enthusiasm for Khmer Buddhism, evident throughout the book, prepared him poorly for the terrible violence and racism of the Pol Pot regime.

In Chapters 2 and 3, however, Burchett is more sober. These are a celebration of the return of peace, of the landscape ('In no other part of the world have I ever had the sensation of being surrounded by fish in whatever direction I turned,') and of what Sihanouk proudly called the *joie de vivre* of the Khmer people. But Burchett still manages to portray their low living standards and occasionally fierce exploitation at the hands of powerful members of the elite.

Elephants fished from the water, fishes trapped in trees of the mock forest, are equally victims of the vagaries of the advance and retreat of the waters, which play such a vital role in the rhythm of Cambodian life.

I travelled for thousands of miles in Cambodia, but the theme in the countryside was always the same; rice and fish and man's efforts to exploit them for his livelihood. But work in the jungle or rice fields, methods of catching fish and preserving them suffered enormously from backward techniques . . . Only a rational scientific exploitation of the earth and the waters and a proper apportioning of the profits therefrom can cure these ills.

A new chapter then begins with a detailed description of a state farm where modern machinery was in use. After that the narrative moves in quick succession to the tropical jungle, to an account of life on the mountain gem diggings, to the exploitation of the diggers and of a pair of twin girl slaves by gem dealers, and finally to a tiger hunt which stampeded a herd of wild elephants. ('Normally they charge straight over the top of anything they dislike, and with their experiences and proverbial memory it is natural that they dislike humans.')

In two chapters Burchett provides a good introduction to the famous Angkor monuments and their history. He sees them in part as a terrible beauty. Although 'nothing prepares the emotions for that first glimpse' of Angkor Wat, the reader is not permitted to miss the conclusion of the French scholar Coedès: 'The Cambodian people sank under the crushing burden of the glory of their kings.' Not an assessment that Prince Sihanouk, putative descendant of the most crushing and glorious Khmer king, Jayavarman VII (r. 1181–1220), would have appreciated.

Nor would the Prince have savoured the chapter on the nineteenth-century French colonization of Kampuchea. The heroes here are those of a 1952 Khmer communist booklet – anti-French Buddhist monks and princes who opposed Sihanouk's great-grandfather King Norodom, and whose memory was honoured in the 1970s, incidentally, by the republican regimes of both Lon Nol and Heng Samrin.[9] Sihanouk scorned the part these figures had played in the independence movement, and only in 1969 did even a Khmer-language account of their role appear. Burchett made use of French materials on these and other issues, such as the exchanges between French officials and King Norodom and his son. A second English-language history of this period did not appear until 1969 either.[10]

The chapter on Buddhism in *Mekong Upstream* is informative and sympathetic, partly because of the role monks played in the independence and even communist movements. But Burchett went to the trouble of interviewing leading monks from both Khmer Buddhist sects, and the result is a rare glimpse of the thinking of two of the most influential men in the country at a critical point in its history. Burchett concludes: 'Despite many obscurantist ideas and beliefs that will not stand up to modern knowledge, Cambodian Buddhism is a genuine nationalist, patriotic force with a humanist and democratic content.'

It was the arrest of two Buddhist monks by the French authorities in 1942 that started modern Khmer politics. The French repression of the resulting demonstration sent a small number of participants off into the jungle, and they eventually founded the modern Khmer left and right. Burchett's account of this event is full of errors of detail, taken straight from the 1952 Khmer communist booklet; but he was the first foreign writer to take the demonstration seriously. And again, a detailed account did not appear, even in Khmer, until 1971, when it corrected 'the myth that Sihanouk alone was responsible for Cambodia's independence'.[11]

Burchett made a similar contribution on the foreign-language front. He acknowledges, perhaps even overstates, Sihanouk's role in negotiating and pressuring for French withdrawal, yet does not dismiss the Khmer revolutionaries and others who actually took up arms against the colonialists. He was the first, and for twenty years, the only Western writer to analyse the early history of communism in Kampuchea, so important as it is for understanding the shattering developments of the 1970s and 1980s. (Veterans of the struggle against the French came to form the major internal opposition to the Pol Pot regime, and their remnants now rule in Phnom Penh with the aid of Hanoi.)

Even ignoring the interest provoked by hindsight, *Mekong Upstream* was for sixteen years the only relatively balanced English-language account of Kampuchea's progress towards independence.[12]

One reason for the lack of balance in other Western sources was the French unwillingness to concede that their position was in any jeopardy at the time they withdrew in 1954. (Another reason, as noted, was Sihanouk's subsequent monopolization of nationalist prestige and the media. As late as 1980 he claimed on French television: 'I liberated Cambodia in 1953 . . .') For instance, even a secret 1952 French intelligence report admits only that 'massive repression' had been used in 1950 against striking rubber-plantation workers in Kampuchea, resulting in 'bloody incidents'; no details are given. Similarly, the English writer Norman Lewis wrote of the same affair: 'There are a few uneasily conducted plantations in Cambodia, and while I was there, in fact, there was a serious revolt in one of them.'[13] Massive repression and serious revolt notwithstanding, it was left to Burchett five years later to chase up and interview workers who participated in the events, and to provide their account: the strike began after twenty-six people were killed and fifty wounded in an attack on a village by a company of Foreign Legionnaires. The French intelligence report (released only in 1979) refers to subsequent 'massive desertions' of workers (Burchett says 1,500 of the labour force of 12,000 escaped to join the rebels), which necessitated the establishment of barbed-wire fortifications and guard towers in the plantations themselves. Burchett devotes a whole chapter, 'The People's Fight', to the conditions on the plantations and the resistance, active and passive, of the workers. His account is corroborated in its essentials by the French intelligence report.

True, the rubber-plantation workers were mostly of Vietnamese origin, but Burchett also interviewed some of the 'fair sprinkling of Cambodians' who worked alongside them. Such Khmer rubber-plantation workers were undoubtedly key personnel in the spread of communist-led resistance among the Khmer peasantry in many sur-rounding villages, a phenomenon noted with alarm by French intelli-gence in 1952. At least two local Issarak officials in this period survived French gaols and three succeeding regimes to take up senior positions in the Heng Samrin government in 1979.

But Burchett does not exaggerate the strength of the Khmer left at this point: 'the maximum ever claimed by the Khmer Issarak movement . . . was one third of their territory liberated'. Again in the light of declassified French intelligence, this appears quite accurate. (A further half of the country saw Issarak activity, if only by night.)[14]

Burchett seems to have been unaware that about 1,000 Khmers quietly went to Hanoi for sanctuary and training after the Geneva Conference in 1954. (Their silence over the next sixteen years – for fear

of upsetting Sihanouk's neutrality – was another reason for the lack of
attention given to their movement by Western observers.) But he did
give an account of the communist movement's development before 1954
and of its leader Son Ngoc Minh, an ex-monk who participated in the
1942 demonstration and died in Hanoi in 1972. Burchett's information
about Minh was more reliable than that of Bernard Fall, for example,
who wondered whether Minh ever 'existed' and confused him with
another figure, while as late as 1967 Minh was described in what was
then the major academic English text on Kampuchea as 'a possibly
fictitious character'.[15]

The Issaraks who remained behind formed the Pracheachon, or
People's party, a front for the Communist Party, and began to publish
their own newspapers. They were only just tolerated by Sihanouk, and
Burchett gave them a wide berth, apart from recounting their role in the
independence struggle. (Only in 1970 did he reveal that 'some of their
leading cadres' had told him in 1956 that 'Sihanouk would be forced to
align himself' with the domestic right wing, 'or be eliminated' by it. But
Burchett had backed his own judgement on the issue.)[16]

Burchett's aim, in his account of the independence issue, was
probably to credit *both* Sihanouk and the Issaraks for their efforts, while
regretting their lack of co-ordination and playing down their enmity
(pp.126–7). He perhaps takes this too far on the vexed issue of the *date*
of Kampuchea's accession to independence. Sihanouk dates it from 9
November 1953, when he achieved a 'successful conclusion of negotiations on subjects to which he had committed himself'.[17] The Issaraks,
communist and non-communist, date it from the July 1954 Geneva
Accords, as a result of which French forces withdrew from the country.
Burchett plumps for somewhere in between (perhaps slightly 'left of
centre'), noting the 'transfer of all essential powers, including the
transfer of military authority' on 10 March 1954. He does appear to
exaggerate Sihanouk's achievement, however, since the French military
retained operational command east of the Mekong until Geneva.

Obviously this compromise served a political purpose for Burchett –
as a backdrop for neutrality. (But the role of the Khmer left *was* one
reason for the foreign policy Sihanouk adopted.) It was to the story of
Kampuchea's drift towards neutrality that Burchett now turned his
attention. His two chapters on this are based on his interviews with
Sihanouk and his valuable eyewitness accounts of the Third and Fourth
Congresses of Sihanouk's party, the Sangkum, which sealed the issue in
1956 and 1957. He described US Ambassador McClintock's disastrous
walk-out from the Third Congress before Sihanouk rose to speak.
Burchett also gave the details of US pressure on Sihanouk to join
SEATO. He concluded: 'And the irony was that if there were one single
reason for the "slide to the left", it was the outrageous behaviour of the
US State Department and its representatives in Phnom Penh.'[18]
Burchett's final analysis of Sihanouk is equally unobjectionable,
certainly in hindsight. Referring to claims that Sihanouk wanted to
'communize' Kampuchea, Burchett retorted:

This is nonsense. Sihanouk stems from a feudal family and is an ardent defender of the monarchy. But his dominant characteristic is that he is a patriot and an anti-colonialist. Probably because of his own instincts and background he would have preferred in foreign policy a neutralist, independent Cambodia attached to the West and in internal affairs, the maintenance of a coalition directed against the left. (The progressive Pracheachon party is still virtually illegal in Cambodia except in the capital.)

Western governments might have saved themselves (and the Khmer people) a great deal of trouble had they heeded this early warning.[19] But then, *Mekong Upstream* was not published in any Western country.

The left, too, was at this stage unwilling to see much that was positive in Sihanouk's policies. Burchett reiterated his view when Sihanouk joined forces with the left in 1970, proud of what he had written 'in 1956, at a time when there was considerable suspicion in progressive circles and in the socialist camp about Sihanouk and the genuineness of his neutrality'.[20]

And this was the very issue that dominated Burchett's thinking and consumed his energies at the time. In May 1956 he wrote to his father:

Just before I left Hanoi, I had an interview with the Prime Minister, Pham Van Dong, on the question of relations between (North) Vietnam and Cambodia now that the latter had taken a firm stand on neutralism. The replies were excellent and I sent a copy to Cambodia. Sihanouk was delighted with the interview and gave instructions that it must be published in every Cambodian newspaper and used in all radio broadcasts. It was just what was needed to clinch Cambodia's position for peace, neutrality and coexistence. One more country slipped out of the American grasp . . .[21]

Burchett's contribution to the development of Kampuchean neutralism also included a very different three-cornered exchange – between Burchett, John Foster Dulles, and Sihanouk. In April 1956,

I wrote a series of articles describing the situation in Cambodia as ominously reminiscent of that on the eve of the CIA-sponsored action in Guatemala (in June 1954). Some were picked up and extracts were rebroadcast over Peking and Hanoi radio. John Foster Dulles took it upon himself to deny one of these in a letter to the Cambodian foreign ministry . . .

That was one of the moments when a journalist has a sinking feeling in his stomach, starts checking again the facts . . . But Sihanouk immediately published a declaration (saying in part): 'It so happens that I have in my hands overwhelming proof of a plot in Manila against Cambodian neutrality.'

Burchett had played a role he valued most – to 'help [history] along a little'. He wrote to his father: 'I am feeling extremely happy at having helped put another spoke in America's world-domination machine' through exposure of 'the intolerable bullying pressures being applied to this little country – just because she wanted to stay neutral . . .'[22]

Burchett may have felt he had something in common with Kampuchea's struggle for its own independent foreign policy. Indeed, in a separate chapter entitled 'Some Personal History', he tells of the problems he had without a passport in Indochina, despite the assistance he received from Sihanouk. But there were some amusing moments, too. Burchett was twice mistaken for Sir James Plimsoll, the Australian Under-Secretary of State for External Affairs, 'the man who had instructed the British consulate not to replace my passport'. On one occasion Burchett was handed Plimsoll's passport at an airport counter. 'A rather angry-looking figure behind me snatched it up. We travelled in the same plane to Phnom Penh with vacant seats between us.'[23] He added in a letter to his father: 'And I suppose we were both travelling on the same business. SEATO!! He trying to make it work and myself trying to wreck it. And I think my work is the more successful . . . in Cambodia, I can assure you that I had by far the warmer welcome.'[24] Later Burchett was even welcomed at Vientiane airport by British and Australian diplomats: Plimsoll was on a later plane. On another occasion the governor of Siemreap province in Kampuchea suggested that Burchett and his wife share a car, on a trip to a temple ruin, with Malcolm MacDonald, 'the most notorious British anti-communist in the Far East'. Burchett diplomatically declined, reckoning that MacDonald 'may have considered the Cambodian government was stretching coexistence too far'.[25]

There are a number of flaws in *Mekong Upstream* that reflect Burchett's political predilections. His description of the unpopularity of US citizens in Kampuchea in 1956–57 is probably greatly overdrawn;[26] certainly it was not the case by 1960, and there is no reason to believe that attitudes improved. (Similarly, he refers to the FBI as the 'US Gestapo'.)

Second, Burchett's crediting of 'great Indian scholars' alone for their translations of the Angkorian inscriptions is unusual, unless he could not find it in himself to give 'colonialist' French scholars their due. He does acknowledge, and quote at length, the historical and archaeological research of French *savants* – from 'the relentless anti-colonialist' Henri Marchal, to Georges Coedès (the actual translator of most of the inscriptions). But at two points he credits only Indians and Chinese travellers for their contributions to our knowledge of Angkor. This pro-Asian bias is just as unwarranted as the widely-held myth that French explorers 'discovered Angkor'.

Third, Burchett gives cursory treatment to the Vietnamese expansion into Kampuchea (prior to that of the French) in the nineteenth century. This expansion is put down to 'Annamites', an obsolete term for Vietnamese (as he recognized) which he uses in only one other context: the Vietnamese 'annihilation' of the Champa Empire (in modern central

Vietnam) in earlier centuries.[27]

However, he also uses the obsolescent term 'Siamese' in the context of Thai expansion into Kampuchea in this same period, while the modern word 'Thailand' crops up in other contexts.[28] Perhaps he saw these Asiatic imperialisms as a thing of the past, irrespective of whether the country concerned had since become communist or not; in any case he underplays them.

This is perhaps surprising given Burchett's antagonism to the Japanese militarists, an idea that had dominated his thinking since 1940 and was unaffected by his sympathy for the victims at Hiroshima. There is a detailed account of an alleged Japanese plot to reconquer Kampuchea after the war; an account based on thin evidence – namely the participation of several former Japanese officers in small, pro-French guerrilla movements after the war.[29] These commanders did exist, but a grand strategy 'to prepare bases for landing on the beaches' of Kampuchea is undoubtedly fantasy.

The same wartime attitudes coloured Burchett's view of Son Ngoc Thanh, the first modern Khmer nationalist and a longtime opponent of the French and later of Sihanouk. Thanh's close collaboration with the Japanese (he spent 1942–45 in Tokyo) was enough for Burchett to dismiss him totally. But Thanh was an inspiration to many Khmers, at least until he was taken under the wing of the American CIA in 1954. (Burchett's statement that 'according to all available evidence, the Americans are using Son Ngoc Thanh' was of course correct.)

Burchett nevertheless touches on a key issue in modern Khmer history when he says, no doubt with Thanh in mind:

> The national liberation struggle there has its own specific and often surprising features . . . When the decisive question was that of an attitude towards imperialism, feudal and religious forces played a more positive role than certain anti-feudal elements which collaborated with the invaders when they came and later sunk their roots deep into the mud of imperialism . . .[30]

In a letter to his father while writing *Mekong Upsteam*, Burchett referred to the apparent anomaly of 'kings and suchlike performing progressive roles and the bourgeoisie – or rising middle class – performing reactionary roles', adding that: 'According to many theories this is impossible.' He also wrote: 'I am very enthusiastic about this book . . . It provides the proof of just how important it is to study every problem and every country separately and not to apply some blind formulae or dogmas and believe they fit every situation.'[31]

Burchett attempts to come to grips with these contradictions in a chapter entitled 'Cross-Currents', in which he notes, among other things, that when Sihanouk founded the Sangkum Party in 1965 'reactionary forces . . . swarmed into leading positions'. This was largely true, but there were implications which Burchett missed. Despite Sihanouk's successful prosecution of his foreign policy, the corruption of these 'feudal forces' was a target of much of the right-wing opposition to Sihanouk as well as that from the left – contrary to his description of the December 1956 cabinet crisis. There were honest republican businessmen in Kampuchea, and they tended to be the 'modernizing' kind of capitalists rather than the 'compradors' who admittedly dominated the economy.[32] The cross-currents of internal Khmer politics were more turbulent than Burchett allowed.

After moving his base to Moscow in mid-1957, Burchett did not return to Indochina until 1962, when he again began reporting on Vietnam. In early September 1965 he took his family permanently to Phnom Penh, where he lived for the next four years. His main interest remained Vietnam, but his admiration for Sihanouk extended to the Prince's domestic as well as foreign policies. As he wrote to his father in November 1965:

> 'Put not thy trust in Princes,' said the Bible, and I always took that to mean: 'Put not thy faith in established orders.' As far as Cambodia is concerned, I put my faith very much in a Prince who has shown himself to be far more forward-looking and progressive than many so-called democrats and even representatives of the 'revolution'.[33]

Burchett almost certainly did not know it at the time (if he did, the significance is much greater), but Pol Pot and his colleagues of the 'revolution' had now decided to launch an armed revolt against the progressive Prince. Pol Pot was just then in China, securing qualified approval for his plans. The old grassroots leftists, ex-Issaraks, were in gaol, back on their farms, or underground. But Sihanouk, who had severed diplomatic relations with the US in May 1965, was allowing a modicum of left-wing participation, mainly by intellectuals, in national politics. This was a situation unique in non-communist South East Asia – at least after the bloody suppression of the Indonesian left from October 1965. And as the war raged on in Vietnam, Burchett was even more attracted to Sihanouk's 'oasis of peace'. Even when the 'Khmer Rouge' rebellions did break out in Kampuchea in 1967–68, the contrast with Vietnam was still uppermost in Burchett's mind. He wrote to his father from Phnom Penh: 'Despite the tremendous, historic battles being waged across the frontiers, only about fifty miles from Phnom Penh, life continues quiet and peaceful here.'[34] He concentrated on reporting Vietnam. At the time of the 1966 election campaign in Kampuchea, for instance, Burchett was on his fourth visit to the NLF zones across the border. And during the eventful year 1967, he made a visit to Cuba, spending at least five months out of the country. He did not get to know Kampuchea as well as he later claimed.

Burchett never met Pol Pot, or his deputy Nuon Chea,[35] and he also seems to have gone out of his way to avoid contact with any others on the Khmer left between 1957 and 1970. In mid-1968 he was approached by a left-wing Khmer intellectual requesting support for the anti-Sihanouk rebellion. This was a matter of 'great consternation' to

Burchett, who pointed out that there were no foreign occupiers against whom a 'national-liberation' struggle could be launched in Kampuchea, whose future at any rate 'would be decisively affected by the outcome of the struggle in Vietnam'. ' "There are no avenues of legal struggle left to us, so we have to take to arms," were the final words of Pok Deuskomar. He had the courage of his convictions and disappeared on the day following our conversation.'[36] The Khmer Rouge rebellion was also a major worry to the Vietnamese communists, who were increasingly dependent on Sihanouk's benign neutrality, which protected their rear and allowed them to ship in supplies. Burchett did not report the dissension between the two communist parties at the time; but when he did, retrospectively, in *The Second Indochina War* in 1970, he was still the first to do so. He also noted with prescience that although the parties were now allied, 'there is no mention of setting up a joint military command, which might have been expected . . .'[37] He did not hammer this theme, of course. But he was known to have excellent sources on such issues, and had people like Henry Kissinger read his work carefully the débâcle of US Cambodia policy may have been avoided.

Even as late as 1979 Kissinger maintained that 'Hanoi . . . organized the Khmer Rouge long before *any* American bombs fell on Cambodia soil.'[38] Kissinger's belief that the Khmer Rouge were puppets of Hanoi (now revealed as a ludicrous proposition) was part of the construction of politics which led him to demand that Hanoi deliver the Khmer Rouge to the negotiating table in 1972, and to carpet-bomb both Hanoi and the Kampuchean countryside when it could not. Kissinger's ignorance led to policies which fed the fanatically chauvinist elements of Khmer nationalism.

Burchett was taken by surprise when rightists led by Lon Nol overthrew Sihanouk in March 1970. He had been planning a book on Laos, and as he admitted in a letter to his brother about *The Second Indochina War*, the sixty pages on Kampuchea were 'somewhat hastily done, really tacked on'.[39] But the book was out by the end of the year, and managed to contain a number of minor scoops. Burchett was the first Western reporter to refer to Pol Pot (then known only by his real name, Saloth Sar). He gave a brief but accurate account of Sar's background,[40] although Burchett could have had little idea of the role Sar played: General-Secretary of the Communist Party of Kampuchea. He and his followers were described as 'progressive intellectuals . . . among the first to start organizing resistance bases'. Fulsome praise was reserved for three other Khmers, known as Marxists, two of whom were later executed by Pol Pot.[41] Sar's group had disappeared from the capital in 1963 (the others in 1967) and all were still believed to be dead in Phnom Penh government circles. Only in 1972 was this proved incorrect, and Burchett's view vindicated, when photographs of them became available. But even then Sar was named only as 'Vice-Chairman of the Supreme Military Command' of the Kampuchean insurgency. The confusion was compounded in 1976 when he emerged into the open as 'Pol Pot'. The next year the Third Indochina War began.

Burchett attributed the 1970 overthrow of Sihanouk to the American CIA, although he did acknowledge 'antagonisms within the ruling class'. These, he said, were 'symbolized by' differences between Lon Nol and Sihanouk, and by 'right-wing reaction against Sihanouk's modest attempts at Buddhist socialism'.[42] This is simplistic. Sihanouk and his Defence Minister Lon Nol were close until at least 1967, and even after that Sihanouk took a rightward turn in domestic policy. To an extent, also, Lon Nol was drawn reluctantly into the coup by others behind the scenes, notably Sirik Matak and Son Ngoc Thanh. Burchett did report accurately the mysterious 'defections' of hundreds of Thanh's Khmer Serei followers in 1969; they were integrated into the army by Lon Nol and were in a good position to support the coup when it came, which they did. As for 'CIA' involvement in the 1970 events, there is in fact no evidence of it whatsoever. But in 1983 a good deal of evidence did surface pointing to a role played by other US agencies in Sihanouk's demise, particularly naval intelligence and the Army Special Forces.[43]

From 1970 to 1973, Burchett, now living in Paris, devoted most of his time to Indochina, covering the Vietnam peace talks and helping Sihanouk write *My War with the CIA* (1973). This book should however be seen as Sihanouk's own, and will not be discussed here, except to note the very close relationship that had now developed between the two men. In his Preface, Sihanouk described Burchett as having 'consistently shown sympathy, comprehension and respect .for our national dignity, for the aspirations of my people, and for my own part in defending those aspirations'. He was probably closer than any other politician had ever been to Burchett, who was now at the height of his career. (The Introduction to the book is by Andreas Papandreou, now Prime Minister of Greece.)

The book is of course self-serving and unreliable in parts, and a poor predictor of Kampuchea's future after victory, but there is a good deal of truth in the history it sketches. And it is worth reading as the best case yet made for a man who has left his mark on South East Asia over a thirty-year period. Sihanouk concludes: 'My highest reward will be the moral compensation for having led my people to victory in the greatest trial Cambodia has known.'[44] In fact, that trial was yet to come.

Three days after the Khmer Rouge took Phnom Penh on 17 April 1975, Burchett set out for Beijing in the expectation of a visa to Kampuchea. He was unsuccessful, and all journalists who had remained in the capital to cover the communist victory were expelled. The city was cleared of its two million people, in the first phase of an enormous tragedy in which over a million Khmers died. Burchett did get to Vietnam and Laos, however, and covered the relatively peaceful transitions to communist rule there. He wrote to his brother from Vientiane: 'Each one of the countries of the former Indochina has its own very special ways of doing things . . .'[45] But there is no suggestion that he was aware of the implications of this; rather, probably, he saw it as a good sign, reflecting flexible, 'national' communisms. He later wrote:

> I was certain that there were three more problems, with which I had been intimately linked, solved for the foreseeable future . . . Never had I made a greater mistake, but it was how things looked at the time . . . It was natural that my thoughts should turn towards southern Africa, where the people of several countries were struggling for independence.[46]

In January 1976, Burchett assessed from afar the new constitution of 'Democratic Kampuchea'; it was 'one of the most democratic and revolutionary constitutions in existence anywhere'.[47] This may have been true, but it said little about the actual situation in Kampuchea, to which the constitution proved irrelevant. A week later Burchett was still expecting to be the first Western journalist into the country, 'especially with Sihanouk confirmed as President'.[48] But he was just as ignorant of the regime's real leadership as most Western observers. When Sihanouk stood down on 4 April 1976 (and was secretly put under house arrest), Burchett named the new Prime Minister as 'Tol Sat', the garble for Pol Pot that was picked up by Western monitors of Phnom Penh Radio. From Sihanouk's reference, in his resignation speech, to the revolutionary 'organization' or *angkar* (later identified as the Pol Pot-led Communist Party), Burchett read this as 'Angkor' and assumed that the ruling party had taken 'the name of the great Cambodian kingdom which flourished for a thousand years'. He was certainly correct to say that 'we know little in detail what goes on in Cambodia'.[49]

But his greatest error was to ignore his own rule of thumb: 'Usually, I refrain from writing about matters I have not investigated on the spot. However, having lived in Cambodia for four years and having visited regularly for fifteen, a careful study of reports and photographs of areas I knew quite well has convinced me . . . I feel compelled to respond to the current wave of US-inspired slanders.' His main sources for this were Khmer leftists in Paris, who were apparently equally ignorant about the regime. (At the time, even the Director of the Asia Department of the Kampuchean Foreign Ministry, Thiounn Prasith, seemed not to know who Pol Pot was when he gave Khmers in Paris a very incorrect description of him.) Despite this, Burchett was never trusted by the Pol Pot regime, and never got his visa.

Burchett remained quite silent about Kampuchea for the next two years or so, while more and more evidence of executions and starvation filtered out with refugees. In December 1977, when asked if he supported the Khmer Rouge, he paused and said only that he 'supported them during their initial struggle'. And although he 'would have to discount refugee reports', he was 'distressed that [the country's leaders] have cut themselves off from the rest of the world . . . I mean to go to Cambodia . . . that's a first priority . . . as soon as possible . . . [to] find out.'[50]

Two weeks later, Burchett's former classmate from Ballarat High School, E.F. Hill, Chairman of the Communist Party of Australia (Marxist–Leninist) flew to Phnom Penh while on a visit to Beijing. On 31 December Kampuchea broke off diplomatic relations with Vietnam, and over the next year a number of Western Maoists and sympathizers were invited to visit Kampuchea, but not Burchett.

By November 1978, if not before, he was convinced that the Vietnamese allegations of genocide against Pol Pot were largely true. In early December he visited the crowded Khmer refugee camps in Vietnam and saw evidence of Pol Pot's attacks across the border. (He narrowly escaped an artillery barrage.) According to his detailed notes, one of the five refugees he interviewed on 7 December, an ethnic Chinese woman, told him in part: ' "My husband was killed because he accused of having contact with Vietnamese . . . He was a peasant . . . I left four children behind, three daughters twenty-five, twenty-two, twenty – and son of fifteen. I since learned they all been killed because I fled." (At this point started weeping, my interpreter weeping and broke off interview.)'[51] The others told similar stories. Burchett had caught up with the Western press on the issue. One can understand his fury when the leftist New York *Guardian* shelved his despatches.

Three weeks later the Vietnamese army swept into Kampuchea and drove Pol Pot's forces to the Thai border. By May 1979 Burchett was in Phnom Penh, now filing reports for the London *Guardian*; he was the first Westerner to report the nerve centre of Pol Pot's regime, the Tuol Sleng political prison/extermination camp. There he found prison records on over 10,000 victims and lists of many of their names. 'Among those names were almost all the Cambodians I had known during four years' residence in Phnom Penh and many years of contact with Cambodian leaders, and diplomats abroad who had accepted Pol Pot's blandishments to return.'[52] Only five people are known to have survived imprisonment at Tuol Sleng.

Burchett also filed a report about a document he had found and photographed, which detailed the execution of the British leftist academic Malcolm Caldwell by Pol Pot security forces during his visit to Phnom Penh in December 1978. This despatch was not published in the *Guardian*,[53] although it was confirmed in 1982 by the discovery of further documents.[54]

Over the next two years Burchett made four more visits to Heng Samrin's People's Republic of Kampuchea. His book *The China–Cambodia–Vietnam Triangle* reveals a strong sympathy for Heng Samrin and the Vietnamese. But it also gives a detailed account of the Pol Pot period and Chinese and Vietnamese policies towards it (as well as Western diplomatic support for Pol Pot after his overthrow). Some of the interpretations contained in the book are much overdrawn, even misleading, but it is a good compilation of evidence about the Pol Pot regime – at least in its worst phases – from sources previously inaccessible to the English reader. One theme taken up by Burchett which is largely ignored by other sources is the fact that Hanoi invaded

Kampuchea only after suffering a long series of border attacks by the Pol Pot regime, and after the refusal of the latter to negotiate or accept international supervision of the border. But he is largely uncritical on the internal policies of Heng Samrin and the Vietnamese occupiers. What naturally impressed him and other observers was the encouraging revival of the Kampuchean people and culture under Vietnamese protection, and Burchett emphasized this theme at length.

One reason, perhaps, was his own experience of the Khmers' need for a guarantee against Pol Pot's return to power. In May 1980, Burchett narrowly survived a Khmer Rouge ambush. His Vietnamese driver was hit, but put his foot flat to the floor: 'he never faltered until he had driven us out of the field of fire . . . The attackers failed by only a few millimetres. Had the bullet which went through Muon's cheek been a trifle higher, it would have blown his head apart and then nothing would have saved us from the bazooka attacks.' The commander of the Khmer Rouge squad was captured soon after, and stated that his aim had been to 'get Burchett'.[55] The next month Khmer Rouge guerrillas ambushed the Phnom Penh–Battambang train, and massacred 180 Khmer civilians. A few months later the conservative Australian government voted with the UN majority to recognize Pol Pot's Khmer Rouge as Kampuchea's legitimate 'government'.[56] They remain ensconced in the world forum even today.

Notes

1. Wilfred Burchett, *The Furtive War: The United States in Vietnam and Laos*, International Publishers, New York, 1963, pp.11–16.
2. Michael Leifer wrote, in *Cambodia: The Search for Security*, 1967, pp.94–5, that by the mid-1960s 'a small but steady stream of refugees across the frontier substantiated Cambodian charges' which were that 'a systematic racial policy is being implemented with the obvious intention of eventually eliminating all traces likely to testify to the Cambodian character of the Cochinchina territory' (the Mekong delta). In an earlier account, Denis Warner (*The Last Confucian*, 1964, pp.151–3) described the effects of a Saigon army sweep of a Khmer area in the delta in July 1961, which created 'thousands of unhappy peasants'. But Warner does not use the word 'Khmer' and he appears unaware of the ethnic dimension of this incident.
3. See Ben Kiernan and Chanthou Boua, *Peasants and Politics in Kampuchea, 1942–81*, Zed Books, London and M.E. Sharpe, New York, 1982, p.199.
4. Wilfred Burchett, *Vietnam Will Win!* Second Edition, 1970, p.111–13.
5. *The Nation* (USA), 9 February 1980.
6. *Guardian*, New York, 22 September 1982.
7. A multi-authored American academic study, *Cambodia: Its People, Its Society, Its Culture*, by David J. Steinberg and seven others, was first published in New Haven in the same year, and is more substantial.
8. See for instance, Norman Lewis, *A Dragon Apparent*, 1951, pp.198–203.
9. In *Mekong Upsteam*, Red River, Hanoi, 1957, pp.83, 87, Burchett corrects dating errors in the 1952 booklet. But he repeats other errors of detail and adds some of his own. See *Khmer Armed Resistance*, published by the Khmer Peace Committee, October 1952, 23pp. at p.6.
10. This was also written by an Australian; see Milton E. Osborne, *The French Presence in Cochinchina and Cambodia: Rule and Response (1859–1905)*, Cornell University Press, 1969, pp.175–258.

11. David P. Chandler, review of Bunchhan Mul, *Kuk Niyobay* (Political Prison), *Journal of the Siam Society*, January 1972, p.440.

12. The only other account before David P. Chandler's *A History of Cambodia*, Boulder, 1983, was V.M. Reddi's *A History of the Cambodian Independence Movement, 1863–1953*, Sri Venkatesvara University, 1973, which is more detailed but lacks any serious treatment of the largest, left-wing, Khmer Issarak group.

13. Lewis, op.cit.,, p.194.

14. See Ben Kiernan, *How Pol Pot Came to Power*, Verso, London, 1985, Chapter 3.

15. Bernard Fall, *Le Viet-Minh*, Paris, 1960, p.129, and Michael Leifer, *Cambodia: The Search for Security*, 1967, p.42. Despite his superior information, Burchett never cracked the Anglo-Saxon academic market. In his authoritative French study, *Essai sur la democratie au Cambodge*, Paris, 1961, Philippe Preschez refers more widely and frequently to Burchett's *Mekong Upstream* than to any other source in French or English (with the exception of the newspaper *Réalités Cambodgiennes*). Preschez cites Burchett, for instance, as the source of his account of the 1942 demonstration; and his last paragraph on page 114 is taken almost word-for-word from *Mekong Upstream* (p.103, paragraph one), without acknowledgement in this case. But Leifer, who cites no source for his account of the 1942 demonstration (p.26), manages to refer (p.194) to Preschez's work as 'valuable' without ever mentioning *Mekong Upstream*.

16. Wilfred Burchett, *The Second Indochina War: Cambodia and Laos Today*, Lorrimer, London, 1970, p.40.

17. Leifer, op. cit., p.49.

18. *Mekong Upstream*, p.185. Other reasons were, as noted, the Khmer left, Sihanouk's fear of both Vietnam and Thailand, and Chinese aid.

19. Ibid., p.207. For a revealing account of the US Embassy's off-the-record view of Sihanouk in 1963, see Richard West, *Victory in Vietnam*, p.141.

20. *The Second Indochina War*, p.22.

21. Letter to his father from Vientiane, 6 May 1956. Original in the Wilfred Burchett Papers, State Library of Victoria.

22. Letters to his father from Hanoi, 30 January 1957, and Phnom Penh, undated.

23. *Mekong Upstream*, p.217.

24. Letter to his father from Hanoi, 31 March 1956.

25. *Mekong Upstream*, p.218.

26. Ibid., pp.13–16. (See, however, Christopher Pym, *Mistapim in Cambodia*, London, 1960, pp.150–3.) I am grateful to Michael Vickery for his comments.

27. Ibid., pp.80–1. Burchett did not use the word 'Annamites' for those Vietnamese who fought for the French in the First Indochina War (p.126).

28. Ibid., pp.80, 48.

29. Ibid., pp.119–21.

30. Ibid., pp.166, 92.

31. Letter from Hanoi dated 14 February 1957, p.1.

32. *Mekong Upstream*, pp.196–7, 92.

33. Letter to his father from Phnom Penh, 2 November 1965.

34. Letter to his father from Phnom Penh, 26 February 1968.

35. In 1976 he did describe Pol Pot's no.3, Ieng Sary, as 'an old friend', apparently from the years 1971–72 when they would have met in Beijing. Letter to his brother from Paris, 16 January 1976.

36. Preface to *Peasants and Politics in Kampuchea, 1942–81*, London, 1982, edited by Ben Kiernan and Chanthou Boua, p.iii.

37. *The Second Indochina War*, pp. 54, 58. The first passage reads in part: 'Once the "Khmers Rouges" had gone over to armed resistance in 1967 they were in fact something of an embarrassment to the NFL ("Vietcong") . . . it became a very difficult problem to handle . . . To the best of my knowledge the only help given the Cambodian resistance fighters was occasionally when a group was hard-pressed by Lon Nol's troops in the frontier areas and they would be allowed to slip through NFL positions to be passed back onto Cambodian territory as soon as possible – perhaps in some other sector.'

38. Henry Kissinger, *The White House Years*, p.518.

39. Letter to Winston Burchett from Paris, 20 December 1970.
40. *The Second Indochina War*, p.41.
41. Ibid., p.53.
42. Ibid., p.40, and *Sunday Observer*, Melbourne, 22 March 1970.
43. Seymour M. Hersh, *Kissinger: The Price of Power*, 1983, pp.177–83.
44. Norodom Sihanouk, *My War with the CIA*, Penguin, 1973, p.262.
45. Letter to his brother Winston from Vientiane, 2 July 1975.
46. Wilfred Burchett, *At the Barricades* (Macmillan, 1981), p.293.
47. *Guardian*, New York, 14 January 1976.
48. Letter to his brother Winston from Paris, 16 January 1976.
49. *Guardian*, New York, 21 April 1976.
50. *Sun*, Melbourne, 16 December 1977.
51. Burchett's notes of his interview with Mrs Yap Mor, 49, at Tay Ninh on 7 December 1978. Burchett kindly provided the author with a copy in 1979.
52. *Guardian*, London, 11 May 1979.
53. The text of the document, with Burchett's comments were published as a letter in the Australian *Nation Review*, 2 August 1979.
54. *Far Eastern Economic Review*, 16 April 1982, pp.20–1, and 7 May 1982, p.3.
55. Wilfred Burchett, *The China–Cambodia–Vietnam Triangle*. Vanguard Books, Chicago, pp.214–15.
56. One of Burchett's old enemies, the Australian conservative Frank Knopfelmacher, was an ardent advocate of this position of diplomatically assisting Pol Pot's 'Democratic Kampuchea' government-in-exile, because of what he saw as 'the need to help to get Peking off the hook in Kampuchea'. (Letter to the Melbourne *Age*, 30 April 1981.)

12

A Half-way House for the Half-brothers: Burchett on Laos

Geoffrey C. Gunn

Although he wrote many despatches from Laos, Burchett never combined them into an entire book about that country. Instead he dealt with Laos and Cambodia together, or with Laos and Vietnam.[1] He was never given to apologia – academic or otherwise – for the separateness of US efforts in the different countries of Indochina: the ground war in South Vietnam, the air wars in North Vietnam and Cambodia, and the 'secret war' in Laos, which he identified quite early in his 1963 book, *The Furtive War*.[2]

Burchett constantly underscored the links, not only between the three national struggles of the Indochinese, but also between popular struggles across a span of generations: the anti-colonial uprisings against French rule, the war against US imperialism, and the more recent Vietnamese campaign against Pol Pot and his threatened restoration in Kampuchea. (It is not widely known that Laos, as well as Vietnam and Thailand, was subjected to border attacks by the Pol Pot regime, particularly in 1977.)[3]

On his first visit to Laos in May 1956, Burchett was amazed to find that there were no diplomatic relations or even air services between Vientiane and Phnom Penh, just as there were none with Hanoi or between Hanoi and Saigon. Perhaps seeing a parallel with the recent loss of his passport at the hands of the Australian government, he put this down to the 'imperialist concept' of divide and rule,[4] which he always regarded as a major threat to human emancipation.

How then did Laos fall, not only into the political scheme of things, but also into Burchett's political imagination?

Essentially Burchett's life and times in Laos, and his involvement with the Laos independence question, cover the period from 1954 to 1979. His geopolitical viewpoint did not diminish his sense of place, or of history, or his feel for local colour. That much shows up in the record of his earlier World War Two travels in the Shan State of Burma (the Shans are in fact ethnically very close to the Lao), and in south-west China.[5] These contacts with the minority peoples inhabiting the underbelly of China, it seems, fuelled Burchett's enthusiasm throughout his Laos days.

But his first direct contact with the Laos problem was in early March 1954. Just prior to the Geneva Conference on Indochina, he paid a visit to the Viet Minh headquarters in the jungle of North Vietnam. Here, besides meeting President Ho Chi Minh and other prominent Vietnamese communist leaders, Burchett met the titular head of the Pathet Lao, Prince Souphanouvong. (The Pathet Lao – the name means 'the Lao Country' – consisted of those members of the Lao Issara nationalist movement who had declined to side with the French in the late 1940s.)

Only during this visit, Burchett revealed, did he realize that 'Indochina' was not a single state but was made up of the three separate entities of Vietnam, Cambodia and Laos, each with its distinctive language, customs and culture, each in difference stages of social and economic development. Souphanouvong, who was duly interviewed and profiled by Burchett, had come to Ho Chi Minh's headquarters for the purpose of co-ordinating policies for the forthcoming Geneva Conference, where Laos was on the agenda.[6]

At this point, it should be recalled, the Pathet Lao were all but ignored by international news agencies, and were even regarded by the French at Geneva as 'phantoms', which brings home the temerity of Burchett in striking out virtually alone into the enemy camp. He was of course the first Western journalist to interview Souphanouvong, who became President of Laos in 1975.

The book *Mekong Upstream* is a classic of the Burchett genre. It was here that he introduced his readers to the Laos independence question. Rising above the cloying, part-nostalgia/part-deprecatory orientalism exhibited by contemporary observers of the 'Indianized' states of Laos and Cambodia, Burchett produced a work rich in historical, cultural and ethnic nuance, and vibrant with rage at what he perceived as imperialist perfidy subverting the cause of independence for the two states.[7]

For the first time, Burchett lifted the veil on the origins of rebellion in Laos, the little-known country of a little-known people, whose destiny came to be the object of the most banal international horsetrading over the next two decades. It is ironic that this country, subjected by the

USA to the most intensive conventional bombing in history – and one of the most destructive in human and ecological terms – was one of the least understood or studied of the so-called front-line states. Indeed Laos never attracted anything but derisory attention – in terms of diplomatic protocol – from US policymakers.

By contrast, Burchett actually played a role in assisting the formation of the first coalition agreement between Souphanouvong and his sometime neutralist, sometime rightist half-brother, Prince Souvanna Phouma. Burchett carried secret messages between the two princes in 1956.

It is interesting to trace Burchett's actions and the thinking behind them in his letters to his father during this period. In late 1955 he travelled 'for three weeks on horseback or foot every day' through the mountains of eastern Laos, 'following tiny mountain trails with mountain ponies climbing like cats'. 'I was . . . the first correspondent to enter those parts, to look the situation over. What an incredible country. People were so ground down under the French . . .'[8] Five months later he was in the capital, Vientiane,

> Trying to do my little to help Laos . . . swing solidly into the neutralist camp . . .
>
> American influence is still strong here. I am trying to see the Prime Minister, Prince Souvanna Phouma, and have an off-the-record talk as well as an official interview. If he can be persuaded to announce rejection of SEATO, then this would pave the way for a settlement of internal problems and for a normalization of relations with China and Democratic Vietnam. If he makes a good statement, then I'll return to Hanoi and get another interview with Pham Van Dong on perspectives for normal relations . . . Thus you see, even journalists can play a role sometimes.[9]

Indeed. Within six months he was triumphant:

> The US ambassador told an American journalist that 'Burchett was responsible for all the trouble here'. The trouble for them is that the two brother Princes, Souphanouvong of the Pathet Lao resistance forces and Souvanna Phouma, Prime Minister, got together after over a year of US-inspired and financed civil war and made a very good agreement. It is expected any day that a new government will be formed with Souphanouvong being included in the cabinet. I wish it were true that it was 'all my work', but I am very pleased that I did help it along a little.[10]

It is to be regretted that *Mekong Upstream*, which covers this period, was published in English only in Hanoi and East Berlin. Its strength lies in the way in which Burchett drew upon oral history to bring new light on social processes – revolutionary ones, as it happened. These processes were simply not on the agenda of establishment scholarship, or even on that of local royalist history. This is not to say that Burchett's work is flawless in its detail. (Given the veils of secrecy drawn over Laos by all protagonists in the conflict, its flaws are not surprising.)

By tracing the roots of left-wing resistance in Laos to French rule and the French reoccupation of the country in the wake of the capitulation of the Japanese Imperial Army in 1945, Burchett definitely came to grips with the *national* dimension of the struggle of the polyethnic peoples of Laos, first under the Lao Issara banner and then under that of the Pathet Lao.

What distinguishes *Mekong Upstream* as exceptional committed journalism is its eyewitness, on-the-spot quality. Memorable in this context are Burchett's interviews: for instance with Khamphan, son of the renowned Lao Theung rebel leader Kommadan, who fought the French in the hills from 1910 to 1937; and with Faydang, the Hmong chief whose own version of the alienation of that heroic tribal group from French tax collectors and their agents contrasts with the often contrived and specious half-truths about this people's place in history. As Faydang recounted to Burchett: 'It was in our area where the repression was most severe. When the Japanese came we had hope of something better, but they were just the same. Villages were destroyed, crops burnt to the ground, our people massacred. The French came back and carried on in the same way.'[11] Both Faydang and Khamphan took up senior positions in the Lao government when the struggle was finally won in 1975.

While Burchett's writings on Laos were indubitably the stuff of political advocacy, and betrayed a cosy working relationship with his communist tutors (and publishers), there is no question that for all his imperfections, errors and omissions, Burchett pioneered the Western study of contemporary Lao political history. This is all the more striking in that the well-placed French *savants* of the Ecole Française d'Extreme-Orient eschewed the task. One would have to return to 1930 for the no less ideological study of Laos by the French administrator, de Boulanger,[12] who wrote about French colonialism there. And it was not until the mid-1960s that American scholarship began to produce detailed studies of Laos and its politics.[13]

My own research in the French colonial archives, only recently opened to historians, has led me to confirm much of what Burchett wrote in 1957 about the origins of modern Laos. His account of Kommadan's movement, for instance, was the first to appear in print, and is quite accurate.

More significantly, perhaps, Burchett's political arguments in *Mekong Upstream* were largely vindicated one year later by the results of the May 1958 partial elections for one third of the seats in the Lao National Assembly. The Pathet Lao won nine of the twenty-one seats, and its ally, the Peace and Neutrality Party, won another four. (These are the only relatively free elections to have taken place in post-1945 Indochina.)

As an insider in the communist camp, it was not surprising that

Burchett had the distinction of being one of the first Westerners to travel behind the lines. But the nature of politics in Laos (the Pathet Lao joined their adversaries in the Royal Lao Government in three coalitions between 1956 and 1975, in line with international guarantees) meant that Burchett in fact reported from both sides. In doing so he received some salutary lessons in politics at the hands of the so-called 'Vientiane side' and its US patrons, who targeted Burchett as an unreconstituted enemy.

In *The Furtive War*, Burchett told of his first visit to Vientiane in 1956, at the height of the US campaign to 'subvert' the coalition agreement. Within twenty-four hours he was expelled by US advisors to the police force of Prime Minister Katay Don Sasorith. As Burchett pointed out, though, certain of Katay's domestic critics had received less benign treatment. (For instance Kou Voravong, Defence Minister and head of the Democratic Party, was assassinated in 1954.)[14]

And in *The Second Indochina War*, Burchett recounts an incident in Vientiane in mid-January 1957, and his explanation for it may well not have been the figment of a paranoid mind. Sipping an aperitif in a bar with his wife, Burchett was tipped off by a barman, who said he was a French intelligence agent, that a rogue CIA operative driving a specially fitted jeep was out to get him. Soon after, thanks to the tip-off, Burchett just managed to avoid being crushed by the jeep in an apparent murder attempt. As Burchett explained, the French had a more sanguine view of his role in the discreet attempt to bring together the two main political tendencies of Laos. By contrast, Burchett's express endorsement of Lao-style neutrality was anathema to the US State Department.[15] He wrote to his father at the time:

'The Americans are afraid of you,' a leading Indian official at the International [Control] Commission told me. The British ambassador told the same official: 'It is scandalous that Burchett can travel on the Commission planes.' Ha! Ha! They have tried hard to stop me travelling at all, but have not yet succeeded. A really good agreement has been made in Laos despite the most atrocious threats and pressures on the royal government. It remains now to be seen whether it can be applied. I fear even attempts at an American-organized coup d'etat. They hate to see that tiny country go neutralist . . .[16]

The CIA-sponsored coup took place in 1958, temporarily wrecking the coalition.[17]

Burchett's sentiments should have been understandable to those statesmen who had lived through the era of the national independence struggles of the Indian, Indonesian and Burmese peoples. He firmly believed that the struggle for complete independence and an end to foreign domination in Indochina was not only in line with the anti-colonial ideals of former US administrations, but was the moral high ground from which all debate over the Laos question should be conducted.

In *The Furtive War*, Burchett describes two more visits to Laos. One was at the end of February 1962, to study at first hand how a new ceasefire and the prospects for a new coalition were working out. The second was in April 1963. By this time the US was supporting another Laos rightist 'strongman', Phoumi Nosavan.

A riveting chapter of *The Furtive War* is 'Stranger Than Fiction'. This concerns Prince Souphanouvong's heroic escape from Vientiane on 23 May 1960, after his internment at the hands of Phoumi Nosavan. In the Red Prince's own words, as recorded by Burchett, '. . . for the next five months we tramped through the jungle, over three hundred miles back to our old bases, handed back from one guerilla unit to another, Nosavan's troops scanning the countryside after us'.[18] Burchett's sense of the hero in history was also apparent in his interview with Kong Le, whose short-lived military coup against Nosavan in August 1960 set the scene for the emergence of a progressive neutralist faction in Lao politics. Kong Le told Burchett: 'I carried out the coup to end the war and end foreign interference in Laos.'[19]

But one should not ignore Burchett's feel for mass involvement either:

Everyone I met in Laos, from Prince Souphanouvong to the minority people in the marketplace, from Kong Le's troops in their red berets and camouflage uniforms to the Pathet Lao partisans, from fishermen with their throwing nets to young students who had stopped their studies in France to take up a rifle with Kong Le – all of them wanted the war to end. But they were not prepared to accept continued foreign domination of their country.[20]

As he wrote in *The Furtive War*, the fruits of his research in Indochina over the previous few years led him to the following conclusions: 'From the moment the coalition government was formed and actually started functioning in Vientiane [in June 1962], US–Nosavan policy, backed by swarms of CIA agents, was to win the neutralists away from the Pathet Lao, isolating the latter as a prelude to destroying them.'[21] Other events, such as the assassination of Quinim Pholsena, head of a neutralist party and Foreign Minister, in April 1963, showed, according to Burchett, that the CIA had no intention of accepting defeat for their policies in Laos, which included the destabilization of a neutral government.

Burchett interviewed Quinim's widow, who was badly wounded in both legs by the assassins, and she told him that they had acted at CIA instigation. He wrote to his father: 'My fingers are fairly burning to write up the inside story of all this. It is another one of absolutely shocking perfidy. The US deliberately creating a situation by treachery, bribery and murder and then blaming the other side.'[22] Souphanouvong once again fled Vientiane for the hills, with five other ministers.

In essence the corpus of Burchett's writing on Laos carried this message: what the US could not achieve by legal means, it sought to achieve by stealth and subversion. The fact of the matter was that – as Burchett tirelessly pointed out – neutrality as a Lao political option was not entertained by the US and its various agencies.

Given this, Burchett devoted considerable time and energy to unravelling the inner dynamic of the byzantine inter-service rivalries that afflicted US agencies in Laos, as well as laying open the festering wounds of patronage politics.

The Second Indochina War was the locus of this incisive analysis. It was a timely publication, for, as Burchett indicates, the US role in Laos gradually started emerging from the shadows of official secrecy only towards the end of 1969. This book, published in 1970, is different from his earlier ones in that Burchett frequently alludes to Western secondary sources (for instance, Roger Hilsman's *To Move A Nation*),[23] and also to wire agency reports. As Burchett noted in the chapter entitled 'Laos in the Seventies': 'Newspapers began to show an interest in the extent of US involvement, prodding Congress to show an interest also.'[24] Thus the preliminary results of on-the-spot investigations by mainstream journalists produced what Burchett, with concealed amusement, described as 'scandalized' astonishment at what had been going on without the knowledge of the American people. By using the technique of citing the works of others, Burchett modestly shifted the political credit away from himself and on to the wire agencies, and thus placed the burden of proof more directly on to the US government. This was not his usual on-the-spot reporting, but he did point out that he had drawn attention to the beginnings of the 'secret war' in Laos in *The Furtive War* six years earlier,[25] and went on: 'I have been a witness on the receiving end "from the other side" to part of what has been happening, on and off for the past fifteen years. Professionally, I am pleased that other Western journalists, especially American journalists, by late 1969 were finally on the scent of what has been going on [in Laos].'[26]

His explanation was official fear of the reproduction of 'more Vietnams', most notably in Laos. And there is no doubt a good deal of truth in that, which strengthens his point about the links between the three Indochinese conflicts.

Almost as a footnote, Burchett points out that the 1969 US Senate hearings on Laos 'confirmed much of the skullduggery documented in this book'.[27] As one former US ambassador to Laos had already admitted: 'I struggled for sixteen months to prevent a coalition.'[28] It is a pity that the lessons of all this were ignored in the field, both in Laos and Cambodia, under the Nixon administration.

Later Burchett would have felt redeemed to some degree by the information that became available with the publication of the secret Pentagon Papers in 1971. For instance, US National Security Action Memorandum No. 162 of 19 June 1962 talked of the 'exploitation of minorities' as part of Washington's policy in Laos.[29] And General Edward Lansdale wrote of the Hmong as early as 1961: 'About 9,000

Meo [Hmong] tribesmen have been equipped for guerrilla operations, which they are now conducting with considerable effectiveness in communist-dominated territory in Laos . . . Command control of Meo operations is exercised by the Chief CIA Vientiane . . .'[30] For its part, the US Military Assistance Command Vietnam (MACV) noted in 1964 that US Special Forces teams in Laos had 'the purpose and effect of establishing US control over foreign forces'.[31]

The final end to the Lao conflict, with the 1973 coalition agreement, and Souvanna Phouma's decision to accept a Pathet Lao offer to stay on as an 'advisor' when the communist government was formed in 1975, must have made Burchett feel that twenty years of commitment had been worthwhile. He covered the relatively peaceful transition to communist rule during his last visit to Laos in mid-1975.

One of the last newspaper articles Burchett wrote was a favourable review of Grant Evans's *The Yellow Rainmakers*, a debunking of US charges that the Lao communists were using Soviet-supplied chemical weapons against remnants of the CIA-trained Hmong 'secret army'.[32] At the time of writing the issue is still being hotly debated, but scientific opinion seems to be shifting towards the scepticism shown by Evans and Burchett.[33]

Notes

1. *Mekong Upstream*, Red River, Hanoi, 1957; *The Second Indochina War*, Lorrimer, London, 1970; and *The Furtive War: The United States in Vietnam and Laos*, International Publishers, New York, 1963.
2. It was only around 1969 that the term 'secret war' became adopted by significant numbers of other journalists, to describe US activities in Laos since the 1950s.
3. *Far Eastern Economic Review*, 12 December 1978.
4. *Mekong Upstream*, pp.218–19.
5. *Bombs Over Burma*, 1944; and *Wingate's Phantom Army*, 1946.
6. *The Second Indochina War*, p.87. This book provides the most complete summation of Burchett's writings on Laos.
7. Of direct relevance are Parts 4 and 5, pp.213-305.
8. Letter to his father from Hanoi, 29 December 1955. Original in the Wilfred Burchett Papers, State Library of Victoria, Melbourne. I am grateful to Ben Kiernan for bringing this and other letters in the collection to my attention.
9. Letter to his father from Vientiane, 6 May 1956.
10. Letter to his father from Hanoi, 30 January 1957.
11. *Mekong Upstream*, p.264.
12. *Histoire du Laos*, 1930.
13. The first was probably Arthur J. Dommen's *Conflict in Laos*, 1964.
14. *The Furtive War*, pp.161–8.
15. *The Second Indochina War*, p.101.
16. Letter to his father from Hanoi, 30 January 1957.
17. Donald Kirk, *Wider War*, New York 1971, p.204.
18. *The Furtive War*, p.186.
19. Ibid., p.188.
20. Ibid., p.206.
21. Ibid., p.211.
22. Letter to his father from Peking, 24 April 1963.
23. Roger Hilsman, *To Move a Nation*, Dell Publishing Company, New York, 1968.

24. *The Second Indochina War*, p.81.
25. Ibid., p.91.
26. Ibid., p.136.
27. Ibid., p.156.
28. Ibid., p.99 Burchett cites a quotation in Hilsman, op.cit., p.118.
29. Len Ackland, *Credibility Gap: A Digest of the Pentagon Papers*, Philadelphia, n.d., p.62.
30. Ibid., p.63.
31. Ibid.
32. *Guardian*, London, 5 June 1983.
33. The science editor of the *New York Times*, for instance, described the White House case as 'a trove of erroneous scientific reasoning', *New York Times*, 14 February 1984. See also *Scientific American*, September 1985.

13

Carnations, Captains and Communists: Burchett on Portugal

Michael N. Pearson

Wilfred Burchett got off a plane from Paris at the just-reopened Lisbon airport on 28 April 1974, just three days after the overthrow of the half-century-old Portuguese dictatorship. Later he explained what he was doing there, an unusual place for a journalist who had made a reputation covering Asia, and especially Indochina. It was, he wrote ingenuously, instinctive: he was reacting as does an old war horse when it smells gunpowder.[1]

He was one of the first foreign journalists to see the famous Carnation Revolution in Portugal, so-called from the way young girls stuck carnations in the barrels of rifles held by grinning, and sympathetic, young soldiers. For Burchett this symbolized the nature of the revolution, and the hope for its future, for he found here a sign of the unity (which, as we shall see, he regarded as crucial) of the people and the army, led by the Armed Forces Movement (AFM), which had engineered the remarkably quick, bloodless and successful coup of three days before. Heady days indeed! Graffiti and posters appeared on the once compulsorily pristine walls of Lisbon. There was dancing in the streets; huge processions chanted the two key slogans of the Portuguese

Communist Party (PCP): 'The people are with the AFM,' and, less originally, 'The people, united, will never be defeated.'

Burchett's work on Portugal consists essentially of two books, *Portugal depois da revolucao dos capitaes* (referred to as *Revolution)* and *Portugal antes e depois 25 de Novembro* (referred to as *November*). He seems to have incorporated in these most of the despatches he wrote for the New York *Guardian*. Despite some useful eyewitness reporting, in comparison with his publications in other areas his contribution to an understanding of Portuguese affairs has to be regarded as minor; it is possibly for this reason that his two books were never published in English (see bibliographical note at the end). Nor have his books on Portugal been very widely appreciated. They are difficult to obtain today, and are seldom mentioned even in standard bibliographies of basic readings on the Portuguese revolution. This being the case, the following note will be comparatively brief.

Burchett had never been to Portugal before, and knew very little about the country, its past history, the leaders of the coup, or the struggles against Portuguese colonialism in their three African colonies of Angola, Mozambique and Guinea-Bissau. Not that one can blame him for this: he had had other preoccupations, and in any case a writer with his reputation would never have been allowed into Portugal or its colonies while the Salazar–Caetano dictatorship lasted. (Salazar in effect ruled Portugal from 1926 until he resigned due to ill health in September 1968 and was replaced by Caetano.)

Burchett must also have been handicapped by the fact that he spoke no Portuguese, though he could read newspapers and books, and speak Spanish as well as French. Fluent English is comparatively rare in Portugal, especially outside the cities. Sometimes Burchett met a French or Spanish speaker, even in the countryside,[2] but mostly he had to rely on interpreters.[3]

What Burchett did have, of course, was a frame of reference, a highly developed sense of right and wrong, of how things should be organized. Hence the frequent comparisons in his books. He saw the Portuguese revolution as a 'Long March', beginning in December 1961 when Salazar was humiliated by the Indian 'liberation' of Goa, and culminating in the April 1974 coup.[4] Northern Portugal, with its tiny private agricultural plots, is like Bulgaria before land reform, southern Portugal, with its large estates, like Hungary.[5] Activity in the countryside in 1974 reminded him of land reform in North Vietnam in 1954.[6] The role of the multinationals brought to mind ITT and Chile.[7] Thus his description, at the end of his autobiography, of his general frame of mind applies also to him on his arrival in Portugal. He was a person free of built-in loyalties to any government, party or organiza-tion, he claimed. 'The point of departure is a great faith in ordinary human beings and the sane and decent way they behave when they have the true facts of the case.'[8]

This is not the place to write in detail on the Salazar–Caetano period (1926–74) in Portugal. Nevertheless, a few comments may help to describe the Portugal Burchett arrived in on 28 April 1974.

Portugal has few natural advantages or resources. Most of its inhabitants were, and are, a deprived and numerous peasantry. For centuries the country's main source of wealth has come from exploitation of overseas areas. In the sixteenth century, after the famous 'Discoveries', a quasi-monopoly of the spice trade to Europe and other forcibly acquired trade advantages created quite large profits for Portugal. In the next two centuries sugar, produced by slave labour, had the same effect. Finally, in the first half of the nineteenth century, as other European nations withdrew from the slave trade Portuguese captains and financiers moved in, and the flow of profits back to Portugal continued. It was only from the late nineteenth century that Portugal finally had to live off its own meagre resources (for the remaining colonies, in Africa, were very little developed or exploited). The result was that, in comparison with the rest of Europe, Portugal's relative poverty increased.

Nor were the large profits of the earlier centuries in any way evenly distributed. This was essentially mercantile and royal wealth, and was used for display, for the purchase of titles, and for religious endowment, but not to generate production. Industry failed to develop. The countryside remained impoverished, except for some (usually absentee) latifundia owners in the south. Beggars sat, and still sit, in the shadows of ostentatious palaces and churches.

Portugal's relative poverty increased during the forty-eight years of the dictatorship. As a recent observer put it, 'Among other things, Salazar was a confirmed opponent of consumerism, urbanization, secularism, women's rights, trade unionism and dynamic capitalism. Portugal experienced a long political and social ice-age between 1926 and 1974. . .'[9] In 1960 Portugal's rate of infant mortality and the incidence of tuberculosis were the highest in Europe, while its per capita income was the lowest. To escape appalling poverty huge emigration took place. Between 1961 and 1974 one and a half million Portuguese left for overseas jobs, this representing one third of the country's total labour force.[10] In October 1983 a Lisbon newspaper reported on an area in Alentejo, near the coast. In 1977 seventy per cent of houses had no electric light, forty per cent of the rural population was illiterate, and in 1983 children still had to walk fourteen kilometres to get to a primary school.[11]

Finally, the contrast between north and south must be noted. In the south agricultural land is divided into large estates. In the Evora region at the time of the revolution ninety-four per cent of agricultural workers owned no land. In the north peasant farms are scattered, small and unproductive plots for a bare subsistence. Even religion varies greatly between north and south. In 1972 ninety per cent attended church in the north on Sundays, in the centre about twenty per cent, and in the south between five and ten per cent. Indeed parts of the south were officially classified by the church as mission fields.[12] The responsibility for all this lies mostly with Dr Antonio Salazar's benighted regime. (Not, however, that his was strictly a fascist rule: he was too Catholic, and not ruthless enough, to follow completely the Italian or German models.) It was thus not surprising that the prospect of wide-ranging social revolution genuinely attracted many Portuguese in 1974.

Burchett appears to have known little of this when he arrived in Lisbon, but his travelling and questioning soon filled in many gaps. He also had a series of questions in mind. He was convinced that the leftish AFM programme, and their success in overthrowing Caetano's 'fascist dictatorship', would create waves far beyond Portugal: in Europe all along the northern shores of the Mediterranean, and outside Europe in the Portuguese colonies in southern Africa and so in South Africa itself. (He was wrong in the first prediction, and partly right in the second.) But as a veteran observer of revolutions he had more general questions in mind also. Portugal's revolution was of interest because it was led by army captains. Could they really be anti-colonial? More specifically, could they end Portuguese colonialism in Africa? And how had these junior officers been able to overthrow such a long-lived and, even in early 1974, still apparently unchallenged dictatorship?

Burchett's books are more valuable on the first two of these questions than on the third. I see two major contributions. He does particularly well in capturing the brio, the excitement, the high hopes of the early days, in all of which he shared and with which he sympathized. Something of this is seen in his account of events at the dreaded prison of Caxias on the morning of the coup. Many of the freed political prisoners wanted to retaliate against their former jailers and torturers, and especially against the notorious International and State Police (PIDE: in fact since 1969 the Directorate-General of Security, DGS). However, the more experienced and aware prisoners tried to oppose this, saying that the whole point was to show that the revolutionaries were better than the old regime. How could Burchett, with his trust in the 'common man', not approve of this? (Here, as elsewhere later, pragmatics outweighed ideals: the PIDE agents spent some time in prison.)

Burchett's second major contribution came about rather fortuitously, or perhaps as an example of virtue rewarded. He was able to secure long interviews with all the major leaders of the coup. This was because he was already well-known to them. Most of them had read his books on Vietnam. Indeed, his *Vietnam: Inside Story of the Guerilla War*, although banned to the Portuguese public, had been required reading at the Military Academy, where it was prescribed as a text book on guerrilla war. The authorities of course hoped that their young officers would learn from Burchett how to win Portugal's own guerrilla war in southern Africa. Ironically, or perhaps predictably, many of them, especially those who later led the coup, got a very different message: if the mighty USA could not defeat the Vietnamese guerrillas, how could little Portugal hope to win in Angola and Mozambique? Thus his books made him well-known, and also contributed to a questioning of the attempt by Salazar and Caetano to hold on to southern Africa.[13] Hence his long interviews, reprinted in his books, with most of the leadership of the coup, and with an Angolan leader in 1976: all were devoted readers of his Vietnam books.[14]

Nevertheless, Burchett was far from unique in his access to the leaders. The whole AFM leadership was more than ready to talk endlessly to any progressive, whether Portuguese or foreign. Reporters of the calibre of Harry Debelius for *The Times*, and James MacManus and Antonio de Figueiredo for the *Manchester Guardian*, got to Lisbon as quickly as Burchett. Much of their reportage was based on interviews. Many of the main participants in the coup published their own accounts in 1974–75, thus decreasing the value of Burchett's interviews. Two early accounts of the revolution (Insight Team of the Sunday Times, *Insight on Portugal*, London, 1975; Rona M. Fields, *The Portuguese Revolution and the Armed Forces Movement*, New York, 1975) claimed to be based largely on interviews with the main participants, and being in English were much more widely circulated than Burchett's first book.

Burchett did interview many other people. He visited Portugal seven times between April 1974 and April 1975, and travelled extensively in the countryside. His first book, *Revolution*, provides not only a good description of events in Portugal during the year after the revolution (the book is dated Lisbon, 28 April 1975) but also much interesting analysis of the aims of the AFM, such as political liberation, nationalization, and ending the role of the multinationals. There are good chapters on the clandestine PCP during the dictatorship, on the role of Portuguese monopolies and their multinational backers, on agrarian society, on fishermen, and on decolonization. What lingers most in the mind of the reader is his long interviews not with the AFM elite and Lisbon intellectuals, valuable though these are, but with often illiterate yet politically conscious peasants and workers. Many of these had been imprisoned and tortured by the PIDE: their moving and dignified accounts of their experiences are a highlight of the book. It was these people, rather than the army, who kept alive opposition to the dictatorship in the long years before 1974.

Burchett's political sympathies are clear enough. In the first book his main theme is that if 'the people' and the AFM can stay together, then all will be well with the revolution. (He did at least see, and take seriously, the possibility of failure.) As we noted, this was also the policy or strategy of the PCP; indeed the two heroes of the book are probably Alvaro Cunhal, the leader of the PCP (who had been either in prison or exile since 1949), and Otelo Saraiva de Carvalho, the main strategist of the coup and subsequently the military leader most sympathetic to the PCP. Burchett ignores completely Cunhal's deserved reputation as an unreconstructed Stalinist, a man who saw the then fashionable Eurocommunism as more or less a betrayal. As for Otelo, the charismatic and erratic star of the revolution, Burchett was obviously captivated by him. True, this is preferable to the hostility or contempt with which the Western press treated him, including for example even the self-proclaimed liberal UK *Guardian*. Otelo had some excellent ideas buried within a rather ill-digested neo-Marxism, yet by his cavalier failure to assess correctly the strength of the opposition to the left in Portugal he must bear some responsibility for the failure of the revolution after 1975.

Otelo and Burchett through conviction, and Cunhal through calculation, believed that if the people and the AFM stuck together the revolution would succeed. Yet this rather mystical belief does little to explain either the success of the coup of April 1974 or the subsequent failure to carry through its aims. This is in fact a major weakness of Burchett's first book, *Revolution*. We really get little sense of how the coup succeeded. The first meeting of dissident officers took place as late as September 1973, and concerned conditions of service only. Yet within seven months the movement had spread and in a virtually bloodless coup displaced Europe's oldest dictatorship. Burchett points to the fact that the captains who led it had been radicalized by their experiences in Angola and Mozambique. They were the field commanders who did the actual fighting in these dirty guerrilla wars, which to them seemed designed to protect the interests of the Portuguese oligarchy and the racist white settlers. Yet this is nowhere near enough to explain their success. Where did they get the ideas for their programme? Why did Caetano, who was quite well informed of their pre-coup meetings, not intervene decisively? What role did the PCP play in the AFM before and after the coup? Burchett tells us little on these vital matters. A belief in the power of the 'people' and the sagelike and enlightened AFM leaders is not sufficient explanation.

This is the theme on which Burchett closes *Revolution*. In the first year of the revolution it may indeed have appeared that all was well. In September 1974 a half-hearted attempt at a counter-coup failed. General Spinola, a moderate whose book *Portugal and the Future* (February 1974) had done much to stimulate debate in Portugal, was implicated and forced to resign as President. In March 1975 he attempted an armed coup, and was forced to flee to Spain. In elections next month the Socialist Party (PS) did best, securing 37.8 per cent of the total vote, while the PCP gained only 12.5 per cent. Despite this, Burchett considered that the elections showed that the people–AFM alliance was still strong, and would conquer all attempts at a return to reaction. Here he was really having his cake and eating it, for the PS leader, Mario Soares, at least by now was a far from radical figure, despite his many years in jail or exile before the coup. Burchett had rightly criticized him for his lack of enthusiasm for decolonization; now he counted a vote for the PS as a vote for progressive forces.[15]

The story of 1975 in Portugal, as told in *November*, Burchett's second book on Portugal, is the story of the collapse of this very alliance. Burchett's tone is gloomy and depressed. In August 1975 the AFM split publicly, and in November, after a feeble attempt at a left coup, possibly a deliberate provocation by reactionary forces, the AFM lost all effective power. Hence the title of Burchett's second book, for 25

November did mark a real watershed. The AFM, thanks in part to internal division, passed into virtual oblivion with almost no protest from either the people or the mass of the armed forces. The way was then clear for the most radical measures of the revolution – nationalizations, and expropriation of latifundia – to be reversed.

Burchett seems seldom to have attempted to predict the future. Thus in *Revolution* he said, carefully, that the Portuguese revolution was an explosion 'whose historical importance is still difficult to determine'.[16] Yet at the end of *November* he did predict that during 1976 the right would try to undo all the gains of the revolution, but that this would be forcibly opposed by the organized working class, both urban and rural, at least in the south.[17] Here especially his faith in the people let him down, for the story of Portugal since *November* was finished in early 1976 is virtually one of unrelieved success for the right. President Eanes, elected in July 1976 and re-elected in December 1980, is a cautious moderate. The PCP vote has never reached twenty per cent, and Portugal has been governed by the PS, a centre-left party led by Soares, and by centre-right governments under Sa Carneiro and Balsemao. Since his reappointment as Prime Minister in June 1983 Soares has followed an economic policy imposed by the IMF, with consequent high unemployment, a twelve per cent devaluation of the escudo, and a general decline in living standards. The heady days of April 1974 are long gone. Burchett, like many others, must have followed events in Portugal after 1975 with increasing gloom and despair.

It seems to me that Burchett's major theme – the alliance of the people and the AFM – is flawed by wishful thinking. There are other problems also with his coverage. He is good on the multinationals and Portuguese monopolies, and on rural problems. His section on decolonization in *Revolution* is valuable for events in 1974 and early 1975 (the version in *Southern Africa Stands Up* is discussed in the next Chapter). Among the gaps in his coverage is his failure to describe many of the social effects of the revolution. I spent eight months in Portugal in 1969–70, before the revolution, and have since made two short visits, in 1980 and 1983. The whole atmosphere has changed. In 1970 one had a sense of a people controlled, disciplined, repressed. Now all the advantages and problems of freedom are evident. Literature of all opinions is sold. Many girls in Lisbon have abandoned sober dresses for jeans. The walls are covered in graffiti and slogans. Pornographic movies and magazines do well. Political demonstrations and strikes, once totally banned, are now commonplace. Little of this, at least after the 'Carnation' period, comes through in Burchett's books.

The second major gap is his total failure to assess the role of the church in Portugal. Perhaps progressives find it difficult to take the influence of religion seriously, yet in northern Portugal especially the church is immensely powerful. Its role under the dictatorship, and since, has been complex and important; to ignore it is to write only a partial account of revolutionary Portugal.

There are some more particular problems also. Burchett's lack of

Portuguese is obviously a disadvantage. One has to be worried by some errors in translation. Thus the PIDE is not the 'International Police for State Security', or for that matter quite the 'Portuguese Gestapo',[18] but instead it is the 'International and State Police'. Its successor, the DGS, is the Directorate-General of Security, not the 'Directorate of General Security'.[19] Nor is the Avenida Infante Santo really 'in the very heart of Lisbon'.[20]

These sorts of problems presumably explain why Burchett's books on Portugal are so little known, and have never been published in English. One can guess that the first book did not sell well (even though I was unable to obtain a copy in Lisbon in 1983). The publisher produced an ambitious 20,200 print-run, but only 5,200 of the second book, *November*. Nor are his books widely quoted today. The two Portuguese editions are listed in Lomax's detailed and specialized bibliography,[21] but two recent and important books on modern Portugal[22] which provide extensive bibliographies, do not list Burchett. Nor is this because of any political bias, for they do list a bewildering variety of 'left-wing' accounts. Of these, the best is probably Phil Mailer's *Portugal: The Impossible Revolution?* (Solidarity, London, 1977), which is much better informed, and ideologically much more rigorous, than Burchett's books. This is in fact probably the main reason why Burchett's books on Portugal cannot be considered as major contributions to the field, or as important parts of his own corpus. The revolution of 1974 and its aftermath has been described in detail by numerous writers of various political viewpoints (as Lomax's bibliography shows); most of them were better informed, and had better credentials for the task, than Burchett.

Bibliographical Note

Sorting out the bibliography for this note turned out to be a greater task than I had expected. Burchett's two books on Portugal are: *Portugal depois da revolucao dos capitaes*, trans. Luiz Sttau Monteiro, 'Coleccao de Leste e Oeste, 16', Lisbon, Seara Nova, 1975, pp. 317; and *Portugal antes e depois do 25 de Novembro*, trans. Ana Clara Soares, 'Coleccao de Leste e Oeste, 17', Lisbon, Seara Nova, 1976, pp. 61. Burchett listed the first of these on the inside page of several of his later books, but under the English title of *Portugal after the Captains' Coup*. The second book he did not list in his later publications. An extensive search has failed, despite even the resources of the British Library, to produce any English-language publication of either. However, the first was translated into Spanish (Ediciones Era, Mexico City, 1976) and Japanese (trans. by Masao Tajima, Jiji Tsgushinsha, Tokyo, 1976). Suprisingly, there is apparently no French or German edition. There was an Italian translation. This was published as *Una Democrazia confezionata? il caso del Portogallo*, Jaca Books, Milano, 1975, pp.277. ('Confezionata' can be translated as 'made-up', or 'ready to wear'.) In this book, pp.1–196 are essentially a translation of Burchett's *Revolution*, with some minor changes in the text and the omission of Chapters 8, 16 and 17 of the Portuguese version. The book is completed by two useful additional chapters. Hosea Jaffe writes well on the Portuguese colonies and decolonization (pp.197–232) and Eduardo Umberto (pp.233–77) gives an excellent account of the past and present role of the church in Portugal. This very helpfully makes good Burchett's failure to cover this topic. Burchett in *Southern Africa Stands Up* also provides a chapter (pp.57–74) on Portuguese internal affairs, as he also does in *At the Barricades*: neither of these adds to his account in *Revolution*. There is also an interesting nuance of terminology. In his Portuguese version the events of 1974 are described as a 'revolution', and this seems to be correct, even if it turned out to be a truncated one. Indeed, a major point of the book is that this was not just another military coup, but rather a genuine and major dislocation in Portuguese political life. Nevertheless, he lists the book in English translation as entitled the 'Coup', while the Italian version is titled 'Portugal after the Captains' Coup d'Etat'.

Notes

1. Wilfred Burchett, *Revolution*, p.11.
2. Wilfred Burchett, *November*, p.30.
3. *Revolution*, pp.67, 149.
4. Ibid., p.67.
5. Ibid., p.227.
6. Ibid., p.147.
7. Ibid., pp.195–208.
8. Wilfred Burchett, *At the Barricades*, Macmillan, Melbourne, 1981, p.328.
9. Tom Gallagher, *Portugal: A Twentieth-century Interpretation*, Manchester University Press, Manchester, 1983, p.vii.
10. Ibid., pp.143, 157.
11. *Expresso*, Lisbon, 22 October 1983.
12. Gallagher, op.cit., p.127.
13. *Revolution*, pp.12–13, 15.
14. Wilfred Burchett, *Southern Africa Stands Up*, Urizen Books, New York, 1978, pp.48–9.
15. *Revolution*, pp.298, 310–13.
16. Ibid., p.38.
17. *November*, p.61.
18. *Southern Africa Stand Up*, pp.4, 58; *At the Barricades*, p.300.
19. *Southern Africa Stands Up*, p.58.
20. Ibid., p.71; *Revolution*, p.178.
21. William Lomax, *Revolution in Portugal: 1974–76. A Bibliography*, University of New Hampshire, typescript, pp.37.
22. Gallagher, op.cit., p.260; Richard Robinson, *Contemporary Portugal*, George Allen and Unwin, London, 1979, pp.280–1.

14

Burchett on Southern Africa

Helen Hill

Wilfred Burchett's contributions to the literature on the liberation struggles in Africa, in particular the former Portuguese colonies of Angola and Mozambique, differ markedly from his earlier works in several respects. For one thing he was by no means the first writer to visit the areas of struggle, second, his visits to the by-then liberated countries were preceded by a visit to the colonial metropolis in April 1974; and third, he was already so well known as a writer on guerrilla warfare and liberation struggles that his reputation would have influenced, to some extent, the sort of answers he got from people he interviewed.

Burchett's own view of his African writings was probably that they formed but a small postscript to his other work, as seen by the limited attention paid to them in his autobiography, *At the Barricades*. Nevertheless, his contribution to debate on the liberation of the Portuguese colonies in Africa can be seen as a useful one, mainly due to those two factors which have been identified by other contributors to this book as his chief characteristics; namely his general frame of reference in favour of the liberation of peoples from oppressive structures, e.g. colonialism, and imperialism; and second, his freedom from built-in loyalties to any government, party or organization. This characteristic was vitally important to the independent role played by

Burchett in the debate over US policy in Angola during 1975 and 1976.

It was in the US *Guardian*, a weekly left-wing newspaper, published in New York but distributed nationally and internationally, that Burchett's most influential writing on Africa appeared. True, the same articles often appeared in translation in the other weekly publication to which he was a regular contributor, the Paris-based *Afrique-Asie*. But, to the Francophone readers of that magazine, Burchett was more or less confirming already firmly held convictions as to which of three movements were the real anti-colonial revolutionaries in Angola, whereas among American and other readers of the *Guardian* a debate with wide-ranging implications was in process. Burchett persuaded many to support the eventual winners, the Marxist MPLA, against the pro-Western FNLA and UNITA.

Burchett's only book on Africa, *Southern Africa Stands Up* (Urizen Books, New York 1978) seems to be aimed at an American audience, and includes a good deal of the material from the *Guardian* articles. Another book, *The Whores of War* (Penguin Books, UK, 1977), written with Derek Roebuck, at that time Professor of Law at the University of Tasmania (now at the University of Papua New Guinea), is mainly about the FNLA's use of mercenaries in Angola, and arose out of both authors' presence at the trial, in Luanda in June 1976, of thirteen British and American mercenaries.

Burchett's first visit to sub-Saharan Africa was in May 1973, accompanying Prince Norodom Sihanouk on a tour of several African countries. On that trip he met Presidents Kenneth Kaunda of Zambia, Marien Ngouabi of Congo-Brazzaville and Sekou Touré of Guinea-Conakry, and he recalled many years later that his main impression of those meetings had been the mistrust and fear which these leaders had had of South Africa.[1]

One of his colleagues on *Afrique-Asie* was the Goan scientist and journalist Aquino de Braganza, who covered the wars in the Portuguese African colonies, and whom he recalls giving him his first briefing on that part of the world, in Algiers in mid-1963.[2] But Burchett's serious interest in Africa did not develop until after the downfall of the fascist regime of Marcello Caetano in Portugal and the victory of the Armed Forces Movement there in 1974.

Initially it seems to have been Portugal, rather than its African colonies, which attracted Burchett's attention. As Michael Pearson has described in the previous chapter, Burchett was in Lisbon within three days of the overthrow of the Caetano dictatorship. He was also one of the first journalists to interview the leaders of the Armed Forces Movement, many of whom had gained their inspiration from the guerrillas they were fighting against, in the jungles of Angola, Mozambique and Guinea-Bissau. This first year after the revolution was a particularly exciting, if confusing, time to visit Portugal, and it was on that country's southern coast that Burchett first made contact with leaders of the three rival independence movements of Angola, attending the Alvor Conference with the Portuguese in January 1975.

In his autobiography Burchett recalls: 'It was natural that my thoughts should turn toward Southern Africa, where the peoples of three countries were struggling for independence. There was an Angola, Mozambique and Guinea-Bissau to match a Vietnam, Cambodia and Laos – all struggling against a common enemy: Portuguese colonialism.'[3] As with his writing on Indochina, Burchett turned to Africa because he saw that there were fast changes there, and a job which needed doing. With a readership who trusted his judgement and his independence he was in a good position to move into the next significant region of revolutionary activity.

The year 1975 was momentous for liberation movements around the world, particularly in Burchett's initial stamping-ground Indochina, which kept him busy as a reporter. Thus it was not surprising that his first visit to Angola came only in February 1976, over a year after the Alvor Conference. He visited Angola at the invitation of Dr Agostinho Neto of the MPLA, whom he had met at Alvor. Neto had since become the first President of the People's Republic of Angola.

During the year before his first visit to Angola, Burchett would no doubt have acquainted himself with the considerable literature on the Portuguese African colonies. A number of the liberation movement leaders had written detailed descriptive and theoretical accounts of Portuguese colonialism in their respective countries and had proposed strategies of opposition to it.[4]

In addition, a number of Western observers, including Canadian political scientist John Saul,[5] and Tony Gifford of the British House of Lords, had visited the liberated areas of Mozambique in the early 1970s and published their accounts. In 1973 a United Nations Mission had, unknown to the Portuguese, visited the liberated areas of Guinea-Bissau,[6] and their reports had led nearly ninety countries to recognize it as an independent state even before the 1974 'captains' coup' in Portugal.

But in many ways the 'Wilfred Burchett' of Portuguese-occupied Africa was the British historian and writer Basil Davidson. From the mid-1950s it was he who had travelled through the bush in Angola, Mozambique and Guinea-Bissau, listening to people's grievances against the Portuguese rulers and soldiers and interviewing the leaders of nascent liberation movements. His two books, *The Liberation of Guiné* (Penguin Books, 1969) and *In the Eye of the Storm: Angola's People* (Longman, 1972) have a similar flavour to Burchett's early books on Indochina; Burchett refers to him as 'the best informed' of the specialists on the Angolan liberation struggle.[7]

When Burchett arrived in Angola for the first time in February 1976 a civil war was raging between the three movements to whom the Portuguese had handed over power. The Movimiento Popular de Libertacao de Angola (Popular Movement for the Liberation of Angola, MPLA), held most of the country but was battling on two fronts against the Frente Nacional de Libertacao de Angola (National Front for the Liberation of Angola, FNLA), and the Uniao para la

Independencia Total de Angola (Union for the Total Independence of Angola, UNITA).

Burchett refers to his early trips to Africa as representing 'a watershed in my relations with Peking.' As a well-known 'Friend of China', he mixed in political circles in Europe which included a number of pro-Chinese left-wing supporters of Jonas Savimbi and the UNITA movement. These people, many of whom were Africans, argued that Savimbi's was the only movement genuinely fighting for independence in Angola, and that while shunning international conferences and contacts it used Mao's techniques of surrounding the cities with the countryside. I remember these arguments very well from time spent in London working with Zimbabwean exiles in the early 1970s. It was a common view taken by third world left-wingers that China was *the* true friend of movements for national liberation. When China later came to regard the Soviet Union as a more dangerous superpower than the United States this view developed further into regarding the Soviet Union, and, by implication, movements which were supported by it, as a danger to liberation and independence. In the case of Angola, these people would argue, all movements other than UNITA were compromised by their dependence on the CIA (in the case of the FNLA), or the Soviet Union (in the case of the MPLA), and as a result the Chinese, 'who should know about these things', had given their support to UNITA.

In the United States there was by no means such an ideological appraisal of the rival movements in Angola. Nevertheless as a result of certain quasi-Maoist rhetoric used by UNITA there did appear to be a modicum of support for it on the left, including readers and staff of the weekly, the *Guardian.*

Burchett has nowhere stated whether or not he ever held this view himself. As he had not written on Africa before 1976 he had not been put in the position of specifying which movement he would support. He was, however, a well-known, respected and loyal correspondent of the New York *Guardian,* which was published by a somewhat older generation of American left-wingers, several of whom had split from the pro-Soviet Communist Party of the USA. It followed a generally pro-Chinese line on foreign affairs. Burchett, as a visitor to China when most Americans could not get visas, was much in demand as a correspondent, and felt highly committed to the paper.

There is no doubt that Burchett's writings were influential on the readership and editorial staff of the *Guardian* in encouraging them to question Chinese foreign policy. The turning point was a series of despatches from Angola in May 1976 during which Burchett first made explicit his criticisms of Chinese foreign policy – in relation to Angola. On 5 May 1976 the *Guardian* opened its pages to both Wilfred Burchett and William Hinton of the US–China People's Friendship Association to argue their respective cases. Burchett charged that the Chinese had received top-level delegations from the MPLA in 1971 and 1975, which had provided documentary evidence of atrocities against them by FNLA and UNITA. By the time of the 1975 visit it was common knowledge that FNLA's Holden Roberto was a creature of the CIA and that Jonas Savimbi of UNITA had been a confidant of top Portuguese commanders during the fascist period. Yet China's reaction to these facts was that the MPLA should collaborate with these two movements in the interest of national unity. Although this had been the intention of the MPLA at the signing of the Alvor agreement, Burchett argues, it subsequently became impossible: 'such an unnatural alliance can never work for long, and the blunt truth is that Chinese arms in FNLA hands were not used against the Portuguese but against the MPLA'. Burchett was particularly critical of such an error on the part of the Chinese whose 'own experience with the Kuomintang and over the borders in Korea and in the countries of Indochina should have been sufficient for the leadership to know that agreement between patriots and traitors is impossible'.[8] The Chinese were also accused of 'partly letting racist South Africa off the hook', when, along with the US, China argued that the 1975 South African invasion of Angola was a reaction to Soviet–Cuban aggression, a statement which, as Burchett pointed out, 'turns facts upside down' with its reversed chronology. William Hinton, for his part, laid the blame for disrupting the coalition in Angola with the MPLA, using Russian arms and Cuban troops.[9]

Burchett's conclusions were quite unpalatable for a long-time 'Friend of China'. Two years later he claimed that 'it was no "switch of position", to have praised China for her support of the liberation struggles in Vietnam, Laos and Cambodia and to have criticized China for supporting the wrong side in Angola, Chile and elsewhere'.[10]

One insight which Burchett was able to contribute as a result of his personal acquaintance with many third world leaders is an explanation of the attitude of African countries towards Cuba. As he recalls, at the Non-aligned Summit in Algiers in 1973 the heads of government had been somewhat cool about Castro's suggestion that member states should lean more towards their 'natural allies' in the socialist world. Yet by the time of the fifth summit in Sri Lanka in 1976 the Cubans' stocks had risen enormously: Havana was chosen as the venue for the next summit and Castro as the chairman of the Non-aligned movement for the next three years. Why had this happened? Burchett's analysis is that in the intervening years Cuba had 'taken on the bogeymen', the South Africans, and beaten them in Angola, which counts for more than anything else in Africa.[11]

Another interesting reflection on this question comes in Chapter 8 of *Southern Africa Stands Up*, where Burchett muses on the question 'What are Cubans?' He is intrigued by Fidel Castro's characterization of Cuba as a 'Latin African' rather than a Latin American country, and a Cuban poet's description of Cubans as 'almost exclusively a mixture of Spaniards and Africans, descendants of the original conquerers and their African slaves'.[12]

The Cuban's presence in Africa is then claimed to be a response to a request from one of their ancestral homelands, rather than as agents of the Soviet Union. This interesting interpretation seems rather odd coming from a correspondent of a weekly newspaper which had the reputation of being 'Maoist'. It is, however, typical of Wilfred Burchett's approach, starting with the political movement itself to search for motivations for actions, rather than immediately turning to global political contentions for explanations of such actions. Nevertheless this approach may not be quite as applicable to the case of the Cubans as Burchett would have us believe, and it could lead to a severe *under*-estimation of the role of superpower contention in Africa.

Notwithstanding, in his identification of African governmental attitudes to the Cubans Burchett put his finger on one of the obstacles to the US government's attempts to seek a solution in Namibia (South-West Africa), still under South African rule. As long as Cuba is seen as the enemy of South Africa and the US as its friend, African governments will reject the attempts of the US government to tie a settlement in Namibia to the removal of Cuban troops from Angola. While superpower realities are important in Africa as elsewhere, a reading of Burchett's work on Africa shows that they are not the only motivation of people seeking their freedom, and on the African continent, perhaps more than Asia, they should not be seen as the sole explanation.

Wilfred Burchett's interest in Africa came about as a result of his involvement with the Non-aligned movement and his reputation as a writer on guerrilla warfare. These two factors led him to approach Africa through a consideration of the Portuguese-speaking territories, and not, as is usual for an English-speaking journalist, by way of an interest in South Africa or other former British colonies. In general the chapters in *Southern Africa Stands Up* on Rhodesia (Zimbabwe), Namibia and South Africa are less satisfactory than the ones on Angola and Mozambique. Nevertheless the book serves as a good introduction to some of the African leaders and their thinking, based as always on Burchett's personal interviews, which usually include personal histories of how the interviewees became involved in movements of national liberation.

The books, *Southern Africa Stands Up* and *The Whores of War* are regarded very differently by academic Africanists, the first being scarcely noticed by academic African Studies publications. The general view of African specialists is that, while well written and interesting, the book suffers from Burchett's general unfamiliarity with the continent and from being too hastily written. *The Whores of War*, however, was reviewed favourably by Sylvester Cohen in the *Journal of Modern African Studies*,[13] along with John Stockwell's *In Search of Enemies* (Norton, New York, 1978). Stockwell is a former CIA agent who was personally involved in the destabilization attempts in Angola, using UNITA forces and elaborate public relations techniques. Together the two books make interesting and complementary reading. Like Stockwell's book, Burchett and Roebuck's book is regarded as a piece of political reportage, an insider's story, although of course Burchett and

Roebuck were insiders on the Angolan side while Stockwell was on the CIA side. But *The Whores of War* is as much a book about Europe as it is about Africa. Its specific purpose, and the reason that the Angolan government opened its files to Burchett and Roebuck, was to expose the recruitment channels and organization of mercenaries in North America and western Europe. At the time of the book's publication the participation of such mercenaries was critical in the then Rhodesia and threatened the success of the Zimbabwean liberation struggle.[14]

How then are we to sum up this African postscript to Burchett's life, lived mainly in Asia and Europe? There is no doubt that Southern Africa excited him, at a time when Sino–Soviet rivalry and war between the Indochinese nations distressed him considerably. As Michael Wolfers, co-author of *Angola on the Frontline*, points out

> . . . it is worth mentioning that Wilfred by the mid to late 1970s (being over the usual 'retirement' age of working journalists and a distinguished personality) was in that equivocal position of an honoured guest who is not expected to do any 'work'. Wilfred, however, could not stop himself from working and he conducted himself modestly without a trace of grandeur. He did not push himself forward but kept busy observing and interviewing and collecting his impressions. Possibly the 'unprofessional' side was his enormous enthusiasm for and excitement about what he was seeing, and this was endearing to the Angolans and Mozambicans he met. His background on the former Portuguese colonies seemed to me less profound than his knowledge of the Asian countries, and Wilfred responded subjectively, and sometimes ahistorically, so he would readily find evidence to back his own preconceptions but was saved from serious errors by his own personal political instinct.[15]

One of Burchett's last journalistic trips was to Maputo, Mozambique in March 1983, during the Fourth Congress of the ruling party, FRELIMO. It was after he had suffered a serious illness and moved his home from Paris to Sofia, Bulgaria. During that Congress he told Australian observer Jim Gale that his main regret was not being able to visit Australia: 'Nobody lives a life that unfolds like an unending summer's day. I regret I'm still not free to visit Australia. I'd like to visit my family in Australia, to sit and talk with my brother in Melbourne. I wish I wasn't shut out by the result of that terrible court case.'[16] In Southern Africa Wilfred Burchett, 'exiled' from his homeland in his final years, was able to enjoy wide-open spaces, sunshine and a friendly informality which he had loved in Australia. He found it an exciting region, challenged with the tremendous problem of dislodging white racism from the continent, but one in which his political insights and achievements were praised rather than denigrated.

Notes

1. Wilfred Burchett, *At the Barricades*, Melbourne, Macmillan, 1981, p.321.
2. Wilfred Burchett, *Southern Africa Stands Up*, Urizen Books, New York; Outback Press, Melbourne, 1978, p.26.
3. *At the Barricades*, p.293.
4. Eduardo Mondlane, *The Struggle for Mozambique*, Penguin African Library, 1970; Amilcar Cabral, *Return to the Source: Selected Speeches*, Monthly Review Press, New York, 1973; Americo Boavida, *Angola: Five Centuries of Portuguese Exploitation*, Liberation Support Movement, Canada, 1972.
5. 'Portugal and the Mozambican Revolution', *Monthly Review*, September 1974.
6. 'UN Special Mission to Guinea (Bissau); Three-Member Mission of Special Committee on Decolonization visits Liberated Areas of West African Territory', *Objective Justice*, 4(3), 1972 pp.4–15.
7. *Southern Africa Stands Up*, p.23.
8. Wilfred Burchett, 'China's Foreign Policy: A Friend of China Raises some Questions', *Guardian*, New York, 5 May 1976 p.15.
9. William Hinton, 'China's World View', the *Guardian*, 5 May 1976, p.15.
10. *Guardian*, 1 November 1978, p.16.
11. *At the Barricades*, p.321.
12. *Southern Africa Stands Up*, p.88.
13. *Journal of Modern African Studies*, 17 (2), 1979, pp.342–4.
14. This is the only part of Burchett's African work which has attracted the criticism of the right in Australia. In the Melbourne *Herald* of 7 October 1983, Anthony McAdam made the extraordinary claim that 'the book's primary source for its thesis that Western perfidy is solely responsible for the horrors of Africa and Angola in particular was in fact the private diary of one of my best friends, Doug Newby, a Canadian photojournalist whom I had travelled with over much of Africa and with whom I had later shared a flat in London'. If the individual identified in the book as 'Canada' is indeed Newby, then the entries from his diaries quoted by Burchett and Roebuck indicate that Newby was involved in mercenary activity. McAdam's description of his death as 'both honorable and courageous' undermines his claimed 'distaste for mercenaries' when he reviewed the book in the *New Statesman* (25 November 1977). Furthermore McAdam charges that Burchett's 'reconstruction' was a 'fantastic fabrication of what actually happened'. What McAdam ignores is that the major part of the book is a report of a public trial of a number of European mercenaries at which Angolans gave extensive evidence; neither Burchett nor anyone else could have got away with a 'fantastic fabrication' of such a public event. The diary, whose authenticity McAdam appears to confirm, was still by no means Burchett and Roebuck's 'primary source'.
15. Michael Wolfers, personal communication.
16. 'Wilfred Burchett: A Memorial', the *Herald* (Australian Labor Party, South Australian Branch), October 1983.

Appendix

The Making of a Myth: Wilfred Burchett and the KGB

Ben Kiernan

The recent accusations that Wilfred Burchett was a 'KGB agent' and 'traitor' are nothing new. Such allegations have been circulating for two decades; no new evidence has been presented to substantiate them since the controversial 1974 Sydney court case, in which Burchett sued his main accusers.

What might be new to readers of Australian newspapers is the fact that the judge in the 1974 court case pronounced the evidence to be completely lacking in substance. (See pp. 180–190.)

The judge's view is not surprising. The confused claims about Burchett by the self-confessed former part-time KGB informer and pimp, the writer Yuri Krotkov, were dismissed by British intelligence as early as 1963. Apart from Burchett, Krotkov had also absurdly accused Jean-Paul Sartre, John Kenneth Galbraith and others of 'KGB' activity.

But according to Mr Robert Manne in the August 1985 issue of *Quadrant* magazine, Krotkov seemed a 'truthful' witness, 'potentially at least, the most important source of information concerning the establishment of Burchett's relations with the KGB'. Mr Manne cites no other source at all on the whole KGB issue, but concludes with respect to Krotkov: 'There is every reason to accept his story of how he helped recruit Burchett in 1956–7 for the KGB.'

There might have been *some* reason, if only Krotkov had not virtually abandoned the story himself, in sworn testimony given in 1974. There, Krotkov did claim that in 1956 the KGB 'arranged' a private dinner for Burchett, attended only by Krotkov and two alleged KGB Colonels. But Burchett's plan to work in Moscow was not mentioned. According to Krotkov: 'Oh no. These two [KGB] men didn't know about that. It was only between him and me.'

So what *was* discussed between the two of them? Krotkov further admitted that in all his dealings with Burchett, 'I never mentioned any word of KGB, and he never.' Krotkov reiterated this point on two occasions.

The transcript of his sworn testimony for the 1974 court case makes it clear that Krotkov harboured several presumptions, but (as the judge perceived) he had no knowledge of anything that showed Burchett to be a KGB agent.

It seems that no one else did either. On 21 November 1977, the US State Department spokesperson, Hodding Carter III, said: 'Insofar as the allegations about the KGB activity [of Burchett] are concerned, to be perfectly candid, we do not have independent information on this subject.' This was after Krotkov's claims had been 'taken into consideration', and Washington had consulted Australian authorities on the matter.

Mr Manne claims that in Berlin in 1946–47, 'Burchett intimated' to Krotkov 'that he was a communist' – an affiliation Burchett always publicly denied. Now in 1974, Krotkov was asked whether at that time he had had with Burchett, 'any discussions at all about the Communist Party . . . about communists?' Krotkov replied: 'Well, yes, it could be some, but not in such a way that "I am a communist; I prefer communism; I don't like capitalists" – nothing like that. He [Burchett] *was generally liberal*, there was no question about that.'

This 1974 testimony by Krotkov was referred to in a published article by Dr Gavan McCormack (*Australian Society*, August 1984) of which Mr Manne was aware. Mr Manne also claims to have read the transcript of the 1974 case, but he seems incapable of informing his readers of these important sections of Krotkov's 1974 account, or of the conclusion the judge drew from them.

Neither does Mr Manne tell us that when Krotkov had first publicized his original allegations in the USA in 1969, he had been brought there, as he confessed in 1974, by the 'CIA . . . high top officials'. Krotkov also admitted that he had arrived from London 'on parole'; only after he had made his allegations to the US Senate was he granted the right to stay in the United States. Apparently Mr Manne would have us believe what Krotkov said under such conditions, rather than what he said in sworn testimony for an Australian court.

Mr Manne also quotes liberally from Burchett's personal correspondence, but not on all relevant issues. For instance, Mr Manne claims that in Moscow, 'The KGB provided Burchett with a handsome flat.' Krotkov is the implied source, but he is not quoted. Nor is the following passage from Burchett's letter to his father in Australia, on 4 June 1957, which puts quite a different light on how Burchett found his accommodation:

> We are settling into Moscow now after three weeks. Still living in two hotel rooms but with prospects for a nice apartment before long. Housing is very short here, but I got my name on the list as far back as last September and something fairly nice and modern will soon be available . . . Rent will be between two pounds and two pounds ten a week.

Mr Manne *does* quote Burchett's description of the flat, from the middle of this same letter. But he avoids any mention of Burchett's side of the story as to how he obtained the flat, and as to whether it was a 'perquisite' provided by the KGB (Mr Manne's term) or if he paid for it himself. Of such use of evidence are myths made.

Another relevant passage from Burchett's correspondence ignored by Mr Manne, is in a second letter to his father from Moscow, dated 14 March 1960, after a visit to India. It is unlikely that a Soviet agent would have written this:

> A most appetising idea for me is to see the Cold War being expressed in terms of *East-West competition in giving economic aid to under-developed countries* . . . An interesting form of competition much better to observe and write about than the 'hot areas' of the 'cold war' which I have been covering for so long.

It is also remarkable that a journalist allegedly recruited into the KGB 'in 1956-57' (and, according to Edwin Morrisby's 'gut feeling' – expressed in *Quadrant* in October 1985 – still a member in the late 1960s), could have supported China against India in 1960, in direct contradiction to Soviet policy, and again supported China as 'not just 80–90 per cent right but 100 per cent right' in its 1963 *conflict with the Soviet Union*. Burchett then added to his letter to his father at that time (28 March 1963): 'In my position I have to be extremely careful as you can imagine and you should show this letter only to a few really good friends. And those should not gossip about it.' The irony is that Burchett apparently wanted to prevent ASIO and others from discovering that he was *not* a Soviet agent!

But he had other preoccupations too, as he wrote to his brother on 12 October 1969:

> Thank goodness I have been able to maintain my independence throughout all these years, awfully difficult from all viewpoints though it was. To be able to speak to Russians, Chinese, Vietnamese, Koreans, Cambodians as a friend but completely independent,

enables me to do and say things others may not. But now and again this yields positive results.

His unwillingness to take a *public* position on the Sino-Soviet split confirms that Wilfred Burchett was a committed left-winger. But objections to his political stance ought never be confused with allegations that he was a 'traitor'. Australian conservative governments' refusals for seventeen years to grant him the passport to which he should have had an automatic right as a citizen, and their fifteen-year denial of passports even to his children, constitute a scandal unique in Australian history.

The treatment accorded Burchett was usually justified on the grounds that he allegedly interrogated Australian prisoners of war in Korea in the early 1950s. It is significant indeed that Robert Manne has now conceded, in a letter to the Melbourne *Herald* on 17 September 1985, that 'there is no evidence' to support such an allegation.

Mr Manne went on to claim that in Korea Burchett *had* interrogated four Americans, who testified to this 'in their debriefings after release'. However, three of these pilots' debriefing statements have been declassified by the Australian government, and *they do not even mention Burchett*. The fourth pilot, Paul Kniss, did accuse Burchett, but his testimony is riddled with self-contradiction and falsity, as Gavan McCormack shows in Chapter 8.

It is worth stressing that the allegation that Burchett interrogated any POW in Korea relies entirely on the credibility of the man who swore to his US debriefers after his release in 1953: 'Burchett was drunk every time I saw him. He always sat and drank glass after glass of straight cognac, vodka and wine. He could have been a drug addict because the pupils of his eyes dilated and looked like pinpoints.'

In Korea in 1952, both the American Kniss and an Australian POW whom Burchett also met there, *wrote to him themselves* asking for information or aid. The treatment Burchett later received for having obliged them will undoubtedly deter others from helping Australian POWs in future wars. Nevertheless, years later Burchett still went out of his way to assist an Australian prisoner held by the Vietnamese NLF. As the Melbourne *Age* acknowledged on 29 November 1968: 'There seems little doubt that Wilfred Burchett's good offices helped secure the release of Mr Hyland.'

Wilfred Burchett was persecuted in life and is still being defamed after his death, because he reported *the other side* of Australia's military interventions abroad, in Korea and Vietnam. Some kind of amends should definitely be made to his family. At the very least, never again should Australian children be made to suffer official prejudice for the sins of their father.

Notes on Contributors

John Pilger is a journalist, war correspondent, film-maker and playwright. He is author of *The Last Day* (Mirror Books and Vintage Press, 1975) and, with Anthony Barnett, of *Aftermath: the Struggle of Cambodia and Vietnam* (New Statesman, 1982). A recent book, co-written by Michael Coren, is *The Outsiders* (Quartet Books, 1985). His latest book, *Heroes*, about journalism, was published in 1986 by Cape.

Phillip Knightley is a journalist and author of *The First Casualty* (Quartet, 1982). He is currently completing a history of intelligence agencies, *The Second Oldest Profession*, to be published in 1986 by André Deutsch (UK) and Norton (USA).

Richard Tanter MA is a PhD candidate at Monash University. He has written widely on problems of peace and militarization in East and South East Asia. In 1983 he was a Visiting Fellow at the Center for International Studies at Princeton University.

Kelvin Rowley is Lecturer in Social and Political Studies at the Swinburne Institute of Technology. He is co-author of *The Red Brotherhood at War: Cambodia, Laos and Vietnam since the Fall of Saigon* (Verso, 1984).

Alex Carey is Senior Lecturer in Psychology at the University of New South Wales. He has written widely on political influences in social science research and on corporate propaganda.

Beverley Smith MA is a visiting Research Fellow at the Center for Asian Studies, University of Adelaide. In addition to her work on contemporary Asian history, she has published articles on Australian history.

Dorothy Shineberg PhD is Reader in History at the Australian National University. She has written numerous articles on Pacific history, and is author of *They Came for Sandalwood* (1967) and *The Trading Voyages of Andrew Cheyne* (1971).

Michael R. Godley PhD is a Lecturer in Chinese History at Monash University. He is author of *The Mandarin Capitalists from Nanyang* and other writings on China and South East Asia.

Gavan McCormack PhD is Senior Lecturer in History at Latrobe University, Australia. He is co-author of *Japanese Imperialism Today* (Penguin, 1973) and author of *Chang Tso-lin in Northeast China, 1911–28* (Stanford, 1977) and *Cold War Hot War: An Australian Perspective on the Korean War* (Melbourne, 1983).

David G. Marr PhD is a Fellow in South East Asian History at the Australian National University. He is author of *Vietnamese Anti-Colonialism, 1885–1925* (University of California Press, 1971) and *Vietnamese Tradition on Trial, 1920–1945* (University of California Press, 1981).

Joseph T. Miller PhD has lectured in Chinese Politics and Political Theory at Melbourne University and the University of Illinois at Urbana-Champaign, where he is currently a Visiting Assistant Professor.

Ben Kiernan PhD is author of *How Pol Pot Came to Power* (Verso, London, 1985).

Geoffrey C. Gunn recently completed a PhD dissertation on the history of Laos from 1900 to 1953. He is co-author of *Revolution in Laos* (James Cook University of North Queensland, 1981).

Michael N. Pearson PhD is Associate Professor in History at the University of New South Wales. He is author of *Merchants and Rulers in Gujerat*, which won the annual Indian History Prize of the American Association for Asian Studies.

Helen Hill MA works at the Center for Continuing Education at the Australian National University. She is author of *The Timor Story* (1976) and *Fretilin* (1978). She is currently completing a PhD dissertation on non-formal education in the South Pacific.

Index

Solomon Islands, 143
Souphanouvong, Prince, 271–2, 275
South Africa, 282, 289, 292, 293
South Korea, America and, 119–20, 121; *see also* Korean War
South Vietnam, xx; boat people, xxii; French occupation, 109; Khmer refugees, 252–3; *see also* Vietnam War
Southern Africa Stands Up, 285, 289, 292–4
Souvanna Phouma, Prince, 272
Soviet Union: and African Liberation movements, 291, 292; Burchett in, xx–xxi; Burchett's alleged membership of KGB, 296–9; Cold War, 44–8, 55; de-Nazification of Germany, 47; Hasluck's visit to, 90; Hungarian uprising, xxi; invasion of Afghanistan, xxii; Khabarovsk trials, 198; and the Korean War, 79, 166; non-aggression pact with Hitler, xvii–xix, 43; Prague spring, xxii; Sino-Soviet split, xxii; space effort, xx, 53; and the Vietnam War, 123, 223; and the Vietnamese revolution, 217; World War II, xx, 43; and Yugoslavia, 50–1
Spain, 109, 284
Spanish Civil War, 41
Spender, 81
Spinola, General, 284
Spurr, Russell, 185
Sri Lanka, 292
Stalin, Joseph, xix, xxii, 43, 48, 50–1, 55, 56, 151, 198, 241
Stalinism, xx, 52
Starobin, Joseph, 214–15
Stars and Stripes, 169, 171
State Department (US), 79–80, 157, 174, 192, 219, 258, 274, 297
Stelle, Frank, 174
Stockholm, 28

Stockwell, John, 293–4
Stone, I.F., 123, 235
Stowe, Leland, 4, 149, 150
Strong, Anna Louise, 151, 153, 154, 242
Sunday Times, 283
Supreme Court of New South Wales, 182–5, 191
Swan River Mechanics' Institute, 111
Sydney, 72, 113
Sydney *Bulletin*, 108, 109, 119, 144
Sydney *Daily Telegraph*, 118
Sydney Morning Herald, 96, 138
Sydney *Sun Herald*, 96
Syndey *Sunday Telegraph*, 3–4, 5, 42–3, 116

Ta Kung Pao, 150
Tahiti, 138, 231
Taiwan, 75, 109, 121, 150, 174, 179
Takeo province, 253
Tam, In, 253–4
Tannebaum, Gerald, 153, 154
Tasmania, 125, 126
Taylor, Mr Justice, 184
Tet offensive, 213, 219, 225
Thach, Dr Pham Ngoe, 233
Thai–Meo Autonomous Zone, 229–30
Thai Nguyen province, 216
Thailand, 225, 253, 261, 270
Thanh, Son Ngoc, 261, 264
This Monstrous War, 164
Thomas, Julian (Stanley James), 139
Thu, Dr Nguyen Van, 233–4
Thurmond, Strom, xiv
Tiebaghi, 144
Time, 171
The Times, 48, 74, 283
Timor activists, 125, 126
Tinian, 33
Tito, 50–1
Titov, Gherman, 53
Tokyo, xii, 9, 10, 15, 21–3, 24, 27, 34–5